PSYCHOLOGY FOR MEDICINE

Edited by

Trevor W Robbins PhD

University Lecturer in Psychology, Department of Experimental Psychology, University of Cambridge; Director of Studies in Psychology, Downing College, Cambridge

and

Peter J Cooper DPhil

University Lecturer in Psychopathology, Departments of Experimental Psychology and Psychiatry, University of Cambridge

Edward Arnold

A division of Hodder & Stoughton

LONDON   NEW YORK   MELBOURNE   AUCKLAND

© 1988 Edward Arnold (Publishers) Ltd

First published in Great Britain 1988

British Library Cataloguing in Publication Data

Robbins, Trevor W.
  Psychology for medicine
  1. Psychology – For medicine
  I. Title   II. Cooper, Peter J.
  150′.2461

  ISBN 0–7131–4543–9

Whilst the advice and information in this book is believed to be true
and accurate at the date of going to press, neither the authors nor
the publisher can accept any legal responsibility or liability for any
error or omissions made.

Typeset in 10/11 Baskerville by Wearside Tradespools, Fulwell,
Sunderland. Printed and bound in Great Britain for Edward
Arnold, the educational, academic and medical publishing division
of Hodder and Stoughton Limited, 41 Bedford Square, London
WC1B 3DQ by Richard Clay Ltd, Suffolk.

Contributors

J Atkinson PhD   MRC Research Scientist, Department of Experimental Psychology, University of Cambridge

PJ Cooper DPhil   University Lecturer in Psychopathology, Departments of Experimental Psychology and Psychiatry, University of Cambridge

DA Frye PhD   Research Scientist at Departments of Psychology and Computer Science, Yale University; formerly University Lecturer, Department of Experimental Psychology, University of Cambridge

NJ Mackintosh DPhil   Professor and Head of Department of Experimental Psychology, University of Cambridge

R McCarthy PhD   University Lecturer, Department of Experimental Psychology, University of Cambridge

S Monsell DPhil   Assistant Director of Research, Department of Experimental Psychology, University of Cambridge

BCJ Moore PhD   University Lecturer, Department of Experimental Psychology, University of Cambridge

MPM Richards PhD   University Lecturer, Child Care and Development Group, University of Cambridge

TW Robbins PhD   University Lecturer, Department of Experimental Psychology, University of Cambridge

FN Watts MA, MSc, PhD   Research Clinical Psychologist, MRC Applied Psychology Unit, Cambridge

JMG Williams MSc, DPhil   Research Clinical Psychologist, MRC Applied Psychology Unit, Cambridge

Foreword

Over the last twenty years psychology has come into its own in the pre-clinical medical curriculum with the clear recognition of its place as one of the sciences basic to the study of human health and illness. As with other such subjects which are independent fields of study, when imported into medicine it may serve at least two purposes. It can stand as a paradigm for a particular kind of scientific approach. At the same time, understanding of the processes of thought, feeling and behaviour which are its fields of study is very important for good clinical practice.

The Cambridge pre-clinical course is factual and scientific, bringing together biological, experimental and, to a growing extent, social approaches. Drs Robbins and Cooper, who organize this course, have at their disposal as contributors a group of practiced lecturers and distinguished authors whose contributions cover a range of topics, from perception, intelligence, memory and conditioning, traditional concerns of the academic psychologist, to social development in childhood, psychopathology, psychological aspects of physical illnesses and of medical treatment, of high ultimate relevance to the aspiring clinician. The approach is clear, sophisticated and critical.

Psychology is basic not only to medicine, and the material should be useful to undergraduates in wider areas of the biomedical sciences and to postgraduates in psychiatry, as well as to clinical students. I am pleased to recommend this volume warmly to readership in these fields.

1988

ES Paykel MA, MD, FRCP, FRCPsych
Professor of Psychiatry,
University of Cambridge,
School of Clinical Medicine

Preface

Psychology is now a recognized part of a medical student's curriculum. There are two principal reasons why this has come about. First, many medical problems are most successfully understood and treated in the context of some understanding of the social circumstances in which they have arisen and of the psychological functioning of the patient. Second, there are several areas of medicine (e.g. neurology and psychiatry) where a thorough grounding in the scientific basis of psychology is essential.

This textbook is based on the Cambridge University psychology course for medical students. As the medical student's curriculum is inevitably crowded—the course at Cambridge University being no exception—it is the aim of the Cambridge psychology course to cover the main areas in psychology in a concise yet interesting way, focusing on those areas which are most relevant to medicine. Particular emphasis is placed on those aspects about which most is established. This is an important bias, given that medical psychology is still a young subject in which it is easier to talk about unsubstantiated theory than about fact. Psychology is taught both as a biological and as a social science in Cambridge, and the course for medical students reflects both of these approaches.

Individual lecturers have each contributed chapters. Psychology is a diverse subject and there is therefore a special advantage in drawing upon the experience of acknowledged experts in the different fields. This practice guards against both error, and obsolescent coverage. While striving to maintain the individual style of each chapter, we have also attempted to make the text integrated and cohesive, with appropriate cross-referencing. Each chapter is followed by a list of references, together with suggestions for further reading. To make the text more readable, each point made in the text has not invariably been supported by a specific reference. Such references can be found in the review articles mentioned under Suggested Reading.

An introductory chapter explains, to possibly sceptical medical students, how psychology can contribute to medical studies, and provides a conceptual framework for understanding the nature of that contribution (e.g. by distinguishing between psychological and neurophysiological accounts of brain function). The following chapters cover traditional aspects of psychology, for example perception and psychophysics, memory and attention, emotion, intelligence and child development. Finally, the more clinical chapters cover neuropsychology, psychopathology, and psychological principles applied to medicine.

The chapters covering experimental psychology are written from a medical perspective. It is, for example, important for physicians to understand aspects of perception and psychophysics in order to be able to evaluate effectively sensory function in the hearing impaired; this application is made clear in Chapter 2. It is also important for physicians to understand the constraints which our fallible cognitive systems place on medical decisions, and the influence of stress (Chapters 3 and 6). Conditioning (Chapter 8) is explained using examples from the fields of drug addiction and anxiety. In Chapter 4 the significance of social factors to health and well-being is illustrated and a child's reaction to parental divorce is described. Chapter 5 gives an understanding of the process of intellectual development in children which is essential if their perspective on the world is to be appreciated. The final chapters discuss the practical application of psychological principles to medicine which depend on the principles and material presented in earlier chapters.

It is apparent from the Contents that certain areas of psychology are not covered in separate chapters (e.g. there is not a specific chapter on Personality or on Ageing). Both these topics are, however, included in other chapters as specific examples of general principles—the association between personality factors in coronary heart disease in Chapter 10, and the effects of age on intellectual function in Chapter 6. Other chapters similarly incorporate a range of traditional psychological concepts.

The text is suitable for medical students in the UK and overseas, and for those in allied disciplines. Much of the material can therefore be used as an introduction for trainee psychiatrists. We have tried not to assume too much prior knowledge; an understanding of the chapter on perception does not require A-level physics, though this is a commonly required entrance qualification for medical courses. We have assumed that students will be doing courses in neuroanatomy and neurophysiology, so that reference to the neural substrates of the psychological processes has been included throughout, particularly in the special chapter on clinical neuropsychology (Chapter 7). For students not well versed in neurophysiology or neuroanatomy, we recommend reference to RHS Carpenter's text *Neurophysiology* (Edward Arnold, London, 1984).

We would like to thank several people who have helped in the preparation of the book. Ms J Hullyer provided many of the illustrations and several departmental secretaries helped by typing drafts of the manuscript. Drs A Dickinson and BJ Everitt read and commented most constructively on Chapter 8. Finally, several Cambridge medical students read and commented on draft versions of some of the chapters.

Cambridge 1988   TWR
                                                                 PJC

Contents

1

Psychology as a Basic Science for Medicine

S Monsell · TW Robbins · PJ Cooper

Psychology is the science of mind, brain and behaviour. It is fundamental to medicine and essential study for medical students for at least three reasons:

1. One studies psychology for the same reasons one studies the basic science relevant to any organ or physiological system i.e. (a) To acquire a basic repertoire of knowledge against which the concepts of normal and abnormal functioning have their meaning. (b) To be in a position to interpret and make use of measures and concepts developed in basic science and directly used in medical practice. Some examples are:

   - Psychophysical measures of sensory performance (as used for example in testing the capacities of visually handicapped or hearing-impaired people).
   - Neuropsychological tests of cognitive function (used in the diagnosis of brain damage and in designing rehabilitation programmes).
   - Psychometric tests of intelligence and personality.
   - Psychopharmacology (the objective assessment of the behavioural and psychological effects of drugs, and their associated neuropharmacological effects).
   - Assessment of, and conditions for, the social and intellectual development of young children.

2. The brain, although a marvellous product of evolutionary adaptation, has intrinsic limitations as a processor and recorder of information. We are all—including doctors and patients—victims of these limitations, and there are many domains in which medical practitioners should make careful allowance for them. For example:

   - To what extent is performance impaired by prolonged periods of sleeplessness (e.g. during clinical training) and by other stressors?

- How rational are people in making use of statistical information about risk factors, especially where low probabilities are involved? What kind of errors do people make in such reasoning?
- To what extent might a diagnosis be biased towards recent cases a physician has encountered?

3. The intelligent and sensitive physician will constantly be reminded in his or her practice of what may seem large and intractable philosophical problems. Psychology may not supply complete or uncontroversial solutions to those problems, but at least it offers a scientific perspective on some of them. For example:

- What may be regarded as normal behaviour? This is a central concern for psychiatric practice.
- What is the relation between the mind and brain states or brain activity?
- What is the private mental experience of others like—their pains, their sensations? This question is central to a humanistic perspective on the practice of medicine.
- What is the relation between psychological states and/or personality traits and somatic illness? This issue is central to the treatment of both organic and psychological disorders.

All these issues, and others, will be touched upon at points in the following chapters. The organization of the chapters to some extent derives from the organization of the lecture course we give to second year medical students at Cambridge. But we believe that the chapters provide a representative survey of aspects of contemporary psychology of especial relevance to medicine. Each chapter concludes with some suggestions for further reading.

Explanation and methodology in psychology

Some psychology is purely descriptive. As, in any natural science, the first step towards understanding is a systematic description of the phenomena. Thus, much effort has gone into describing stages of cognitive and social development in children, classifying forms of 'mental disturbance', devising measures of 'intelligence', discovering perceptual illusions. As will become clear, such descriptions are not theory-free, but their aim is initially classification.

Most psychologists want to do more than merely describe people's behaviour and experience: they want to explain it. But there is never going to be just one kind or level of explanation. The nervous system, for example, is complex and, as with all other complex systems, a full account requires multiple levels of explanation. (Compare, for example, the task of giving an account of the biology and chemistry of the living cell.) By the same token, there will be a range of different research strategies. Some psychologists try to make inferences about what goes on inside the head from measurements of the behaviour of the whole organism. Others use more invasive physiological techniques, recording from, or altering, component parts of the nervous system of animals. (This raises obvious questions about the degree to which particular animal preparations are adequate models of the analogous processes in humans.)

In addition to different levels of explanations in psychology, there are also different methodological strategies for collecting psychological data. Some forms of psychology depend upon measuring the behaviour of a whole population of individuals as, for example, in questionnaire-based surveys or intelligence tests. At the other extreme, Piaget built his cognitive theory of development largely on observations made on his own children. Similarly, neuropsychology has relied heavily on single-case studies (see Chapter 7). Between these extremes lie many studies in which a representative group of subjects is tested and statistical measures of variability within the group are used as a basis for determining the confidence with which the group results can be taken as representative of the population. Another important dimension of psychological study is the degree of intervention and systematic manipulation of the variables controlling behaviour in a particular situation. For example, conditioning theory has depended upon specifying very precise circumstances under which behaviour is acquired or learned (Chapter 8). On the other hand, much has been discovered about the acquisition of language (Chapter 5) and social development (Chapter 4) by minimal interference with the situation and careful observation and recording of behavioural change. All of these strategies are used in the collection of psychological data, often in a complementary way. We consider now three types of explanation that result, and the relation between them.

Introspective accounts

Every day we give each other, and ourselves, accounts of the behaviour of our fellow humans. For example, one might *explain* the action of a motorist who has knocked a cyclist off his bike in terms such as: "He did not *see* the cyclist", "He was *distracted* by the bus moving up on his right", "He was not *paying attention*", or "He *believed* that the cyclist was his wife's lover and *wanted* to injure him." The italicised words describe mental states of which we have direct introspective knowledge: sensations, beliefs, interpretations, desires, intentions. Philosophers refer to such accounts with the patronizing term 'folk psychology'. But such explanations are causal and predictive, and they have served us very well for millennia, even if they are not necessarily complete or fully reliable. To use this kind of explanation requires no special scientific technique or training other than normal social and linguistic development, although people undoubtedly vary in their ability to empathize with others or to describe articulately their own mental processes, and these abilities might be improved by training.

In our own century, faith in the adequacy of folk psychology has been undermined by the Freudian revolution. It is now widely accepted, in popular culture as well as in psychoanalytical circles, that a person's behaviour may be driven by *unconscious* desires, beliefs, wishes and habits: states which, though indubitably 'mental', may be inaccessible to deliberate introspection. It is also accepted that the ability to infer the content of these desires, beliefs, etc. from what another person does or says is a skill requiring years of training and a substantial body of theory. A certain scepticism about the details of such theories may be prudent, in view of the fundamental conflicts between rival psychoanalytic schools (Freudian, Jungian, Kleinian, etc.). Nevertheless, there can surely be no doubt that a sensitive and skilled therapist, of whatever theoretical persuasion, can indeed help a person bring to the surface, and perhaps modify emotions, beliefs, habits of thought, etc. of which he or she was hitherto literally unaware.

However, it might be said that unconscious beliefs or wishes of the sort proposed by Freud are really not fundamentally different in kind from conscious mental states, except inasmuch as they are, whether temporarily or permanently, denied access to awareness. One might also suppose that the implications of Freud's 'discovery' of the unconscious were restricted to access to emotionally laden mental activity. Since Freud, a less dramatic, but more fundamental revolution has taken place in the status attributed to introspective knowledge in psychology. It has become clear that, even if one considers only 'emotionally neutral' intellectual activities like reading, understanding speech, and reasoning, we really have very little conscious access to the underlying processes involved, no matter how diligently we introspect. This point is important enough for some concrete illustrations.

Consider first the process of reading a single, reasonably familiar word, like 'chair'. It is easy to demonstrate that within about half a second of such a word being presented to the centre of his visual field, a literate person can pronounce the word or make a response dependent on its meaning. What are some of the processing steps needed to perform this skill? The brain must form a representation of the letter forms and their sequence that ignores differences in type-font, size, colour, etc. This description must be compared, in some way, to one of the hundred thousand (or so) word forms stored in the head, and the best match selected. Associated pronunciation or meaning attributes must then be retrieved. Attributes relevant to the current task must be selected and used to determine the response. Each of these processes is complex. But what does introspection reveal about any of them? Nothing. The reader is conscious of, if anything, only the *results* of the process. The methodological consequence for experimental psychology is profound. We can only find out about these processes by making measures of *performance* in various reading tasks—the time taken to respond, the nature of the errors made and their probabilities, the time for which the eye fixates on particular words in a text—and then trying to work out from the pattern of performance what the underlying processes must be like.

Thus, the first point is that component processes underlying perceptual, cognitive and motor skills are simply *inaccessible to consciousness*. It might nevertheless be supposed that whatever *is* accessible to consciousness as we perform a skill, or reach a decision, must be an accurate source of evidence about what is happening in the head. This too turns out to be a risky assumption. In a provocative paper Nisbett and Wilson (1977) have reported a number of experiments of the following general form. Two large groups of student subjects are first exposed to some information; then they are asked to make a decision, or express a preference; then they are carefully interrogated about what caused them to reach the decision, or arrive at the preference. In one experiment, for example, they were shown a video of a college lecturer, then asked to indicate on a rating scale their liking for the lecturer, his clothes, his accent, etc., and then asked questions about what had caused them to give the ratings they did. The critical feature of these experiments is that the information to which the two groups were first exposed was *different* in some controlled way. It was thus possible to compare the *objectively measurable* effect on their decision of the differential information to the subjects' *subjective beliefs* about what had influenced their decision. In the college lecturer example, for instance, both groups saw the *same* lecturer, wearing the *same* clothes and speaking in the *same* accent, but in one video his manner was warm and friendly, and in the other cold and distant. Not surprisingly, students who saw the first video rated the lecturer as more likeable; but they also gave more approving ratings of his clothes and accent than the second group—even though these were objectively the same in the two videos. Clearly, the students' emotional response to the lecturer's perceived warmth/coldness had influenced their evaluation of his clothes and accent—a 'halo effect'. But in their introspective reports, all the students denied this influence, and a significant proportion claimed that their liking of the lecturer was influenced by, among other things, his clothes and his accent! Nisbett and Wilson's conclusion, which remains controversial, is that we often do not know why or how we reach decisions or make evaluations; however, a strong cultural norm dictates that we appear to ourselves and others to be rational decision makers. So we construct, unwittingly, perhaps a *rationalization* for our decision, and it is this rationalization which we report—and believe—as a causal account. Some further implications of this are pursued in Chapter 8.

The general conclusion is that introspection is both intrinsically limited and of problematic status as a tool for investigating what goes on in the head. That is why experimental psychologists have been forced to develop elaborate techniques for measuring and making inferences from performance in laboratory tasks, and measures of brain activity. Data derived from such techniques provides the basis for much of what is said in the following chapters.

One final point about introspective awareness deserves mention because of its practical consequences. It might be supposed that for information from the external world to influence one's thinking or behaviour, one has to register that information consciously in the first place. There are now numerous demonstrations that show this supposition to be wrong.

As one example, consider again the task of reading a single word. The following phenomenon, initially reported by Marcel, has been studied in a number of laboratories (see Fig. 1.1). A word, different on every trial, is flashed in the centre of the visual field followed, after a brief interval, by a superimposed pattern of letter fragments ... a 'mask'. If the interval is long, the word is clearly seen. As the interval is reduced, there comes a point where the subject not only fails to see the word, but cannot even tell whether a word was presented or not, and responds at chance level when asked to guess. Nevertheless, under these same conditions, a masked word can be shown to influence the processing of a semantically related word presented following the mask (this is called 'semantic priming') (see Fig. 1.1). It follows that the masked word is making contact with its meaning, and thus influencing performance, even though the subject cannot see the word, and does not know it has occurred! A similar paradigm has been exploited by Zajonc (1980) for showing that subjects may exhibit a preference for a stimulus that has been previously presented, even though it was initially presented so briefly that it could not be recognized. Such effects of experience on preference may be observed even when the subject cannot discriminate between stimuli that they have and have not experienced.

Thus, sensory input may influence thought and behaviour without conscious awareness of, or recollection of, that input. One medical domain where this may be of great importance is in the **use of general anaesthetics** during surgery. One standard criterion for successful anaesthesia is that the patient will *remember* nothing that happened during surgery. But the standard test is to ask the subject if he can *recall* anything that happened during his/her operation. It is possible that what the patient hears during surgery may be registered and have effects without being accessible to conscious recall. For instance, there is both anecdotal and experimental evidence that posthypnotic-like suggestions (e.g. "Pull your right ear lobe when you next hear my voice") may be successfully implanted during anaesthesia (Bennett *et al.*, 1985), that material heard during surgery is later detectable in the patients' dreams, waking fantasies and affective responses, and that playing a tape of positive suggestions to the unconscious patient about the progress of surgery and the prospects of recovery can reduce the duration of the postoperative stay in hospital (Bonke *et al.*, 1986). Yet in all these cases there was no evidence of conscious recall or awareness of the source of the information. The claim that auditory information is registered during anaesthesia in this way still rests on rather fragile evidence. Nevertheless, the mere possibility that it may be so suggests that it might be sensible for surgeons and anaesthetists either to mask the sounds of the operating theatre with earphones, or to refrain from audible commentary alarming and/or offensive to their recumbent patients. Current practice is sometimes markedly deviant from these ideals.

Neurophysiological explanations

It is difficult to state precisely when the connection between mental activity and the brain was established. Contemporary ideas about the relation can

Calibration phase

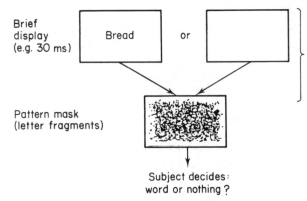

Brief display (e.g. 30 ms)

Bread   or

Pattern mask (letter fragments)

The interval between the onset of the brief display and the mask is adjusted until performance is at or close to 'chance' level: subjects are guessing whether a word was flashed or not and cannot see it when it is

Subject decides: word or nothing?

Priming phase

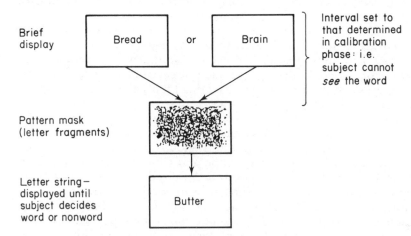

Brief display

Bread   or   Brain

Interval set to that determined in calibration phase: i.e. subject cannot *see* the word

Pattern mask (letter fragments)

Letter string— displayed until subject decides word or nonword

Butter

Result: Decision time shorter when the briefly displayed word (which the subject cannot see) is related in meaning to the letter string (as is 'bread' to 'butter')

Fig. 1.1 Marcel's (1983) experimental paradigm demonstrating semantic activation in the absence of conscious awareness. In the calibration phase, the interval between a brief display (which may or may not contain a word) and a masking display is reduced until the masking display just prevents the subject either from being able to guess accurately whether a word was presented, or from being consciously aware of it (let alone being able to report it). In the priming phase, following a masked word displayed under the same conditions as determined during the calibration phase, a letter string is clearly displayed for the subject to categorize as 'word' or 'non-word', as quickly as possible. (New items are displayed on every trial in both phases.) The average 'word' response times indicate that the *meaning* of the masked word influences processing of the letter string even though the subject cannot see the masked word or distinguish it from a blank display. (The essential outcome has been replicated in a number of laboratories. See Holender (1986) for review and critique.)

be traced back to Descartes. For him, the mind was not a function of the brain, because the brain belonged to the body and the mind was of a non-physical substance. He speculated that the mind and body communicated in a mysterious fashion via the pineal gland: the 'passions' were one instance of this influence of bodily states on the mind. (Cf. Contemporary views of the emotions in Chapter 8.) At the beginning of the nineteenth century Gall argued in detail for the dependence of mental and behavioural functions on (parts of) the brain (a view still sufficiently revolutionary that his lectures in Vienna were proscribed for materialism and denounced from the pulpit). This set the stage for a century of pioneering work, including that of the neurologist Flourens, who experimentally damaged (i.e. made lesions of) various parts of the nervous system in animals in order to determine the behavioural effects, and clinical neurologists such as Broca, Wernicke and Lichtheim, who systematically explored the correlation between the locus of damage and the effects on psychological function in human sufferers from brain trauma or disease.

Figure 1.2a shows the main gross anatomical features of the human cerebral cortex as they are defined today. A major question for neuropsychologists and neurologists has been how much specialization and **localization of function** there is within the cerebral cortex. The early phrenologists, starting with Gall, believed that highly specific traits (such as aggression and parental love) were localized in specific parts of the brain, a view in part based on dubious correlations between personality or behaviour and bumps on the head! Flourens' results led him to contradict this view and suggest that a particular brain region could contribute to many different functions. Subsequent scientific and clinical research has established that there are functions that can be localized (see Chapter 7). Some of the main sensory and output functions were localized by the end of the last century (Fig. 1.2b). However, such research has also highlighted the interaction and co-ordination of different brain areas in performing given functions, as well as the remarkable plasticity of the brain, both following injury and during development. These discoveries have been extremely important in advancing medical science, but they have not in themselves been essential for the development of psychological explanations.

Students trained in the biological sciences are prone to physiological reductionism, the belief that a truly *scientific* account of mind and behaviour must be in terms *solely* of neural structure and neural activity. Some experimental psychologists do indeed use physiological measures, such as microelectrode recording, and, like Flourens, some also look at the effects of brain lesions, or electrical or chemical stimulation on behaviour (see Valenstein, 1973). Theories about the neural substrate of visual processes, memory storage, psychotic disorders, etc., are very much a proper part of experimental psychology. What is wrong with physiological reductionism is the idea that a *purely* physiological explanation will be sufficient.

Consider the performance of a 'simple reaction-time' task: when a light comes on, the subject must press a button as quickly as he can. We are not

(a)

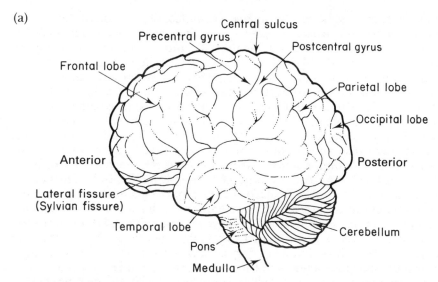

Fig. 1.2(a)   External features of human cerebral cortex and brain stem. Note the main lobes, sulci and gyri of the cerebral cortex.

(b)

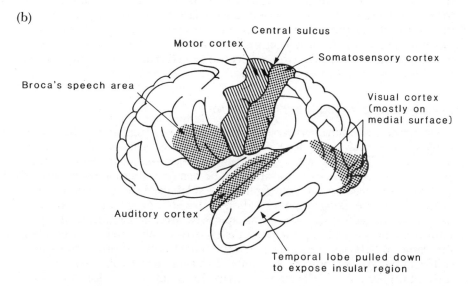

Fig. 1.2(b)   Main sensory and motor areas of the cerebral cortex. The status of Broca's speech area is now under revision (see Chapter 7).

yet remotely close to being able to give a complete description of the neural activity that occurs during the performance of even this elementary task, or as the subject prepares himself for the task. But, if we were, what would such a description look like? It would specify patterns of activity over time in vast populations of neurons in retina, thalamus, striate and other 'visual' areas of occipital cortex, inferotemporal cortex, superior colliculus, motor and premotor cortex, supplementary motor area, basal ganglia, cerebellum, brain stem, spinal cord interneurons, and, finally, motorneurons. It would specify the strengths and signs of the synaptic connections among neurons that cause and/or permit the wave(s) of activation to pass from sensory centres to motor centres. It might make reference to neurotransmitters and hormones. But, would such a description by itself constitute a *useful explanation*? No more than a description of the detailed movements of all the soldiers in an army and the communications among them would constitute a complete explanation of the army's behaviour. For one thing it would be too *large* a description to be comprehensible. For another, it would be useless without some understanding of the *functions* being carried out by particular components of the activity. For example, we would need to know that *this* part of the activity was concerned with *detecting* the signal, and *that* part with *selecting* the right index finger (as opposed to some other digit) for movement, and so on. In other words, we need a more abstract, coarser-grained, level of description for dividing the processing up into a limited number of functionally-specified components and describing their causal sequence.

Until about the middle of this century, we lacked a language for giving such an abstract functional description, other than the language of introspective mental states whose inadequacies have already been discussed. But in the last thirty years or so, it has become clear that the language of computation, or 'information-processing', can be used to describe what happens inside the head without necessarily referring either to conscious mental states or to activity in neurons.

Information-processing explanations

Many readers will have written a simple computer program in a high-level language like BASIC, FORTRAN, or PASCAL. Even those who have not done so will probably know that such a program specifies in a rather abstract way a sequence of operations to be performed on, and decisions to be taken about, a set of data (numbers, symbols) represented in a way specified by the programmer. When a BASIC program is run on a particular computer, the operations specified are carried out by electrical impulses travelling along microcircuits etched on silicon chips. But when the same BASIC program is run on a different computer or with a different language interpreter, quite different microcircuits or at least different patterns of electronic activity in them accomplish the same BASIC instruction, and different states of the computer's memory represent the same BASIC data structure. Hence, the BASIC program describes the sequence of operations to be performed and the information to be represented in an abstract way that is to a large extent *independent of the hardware that will perform the operation or store the information*. Moreover, if one observes a computer running the program, a listing of the BASIC program is likely to be more useful (at least to someone who can read a BASIC program) as a *functionally transparent explanation* of the behaviour of the computer than would be a description of the momentary states of the electronic circuitry of the computer.

In much the same way, although the brain's processing of information is clearly accomplished by patterns of neural activity, it is both possible and desirable to describe that processing at a higher level: in terms of sequences or other arrangements of abstractly characterized information-processing operations, forms of representation, and so on. As in the case of the computer, such descriptions provide a causal explanation of behaviour that is for many purposes more tractable and comprehensible than a detailed description of neural activity would be. It remains an important question how particular operations are carried out in the neural substrate, and the research of many physiological psychologists and neurophysiologists is directed towards answering such questions. The important conclusion is that physiological and information-processing accounts of what goes on in the head are not rival forms of explanation, one of which will eventually supplant the other, but rather complementary explanations at different levels of abstraction.

A 'computational' approach to mind and brain brings with it certain other advantages. There is considerable activity at present in a part of computer science known as **artificial intelligence**. The aim of research in artificial intelligence is to program computers to accomplish tasks that were previously within the competence only of humans, or at least the higher animals. Examples include recognizing spoken words, constructing a three-dimensional representation of the visual world from a two-dimensional image, and controlling the movements of an arm. An efficient strategy adopted for accomplishing such a task with a computer may be quite different from that employed in the brain. But the artificial intelligence researcher is required to explore with great precision the possible strategies for accomplishing the task, and the constraints inherent in the task, and these explorations are highly informative to the psychologist trying to ascertain how the brain accomplishes that same task.

An information-processing theory of a human skill such as spoken word recognition, since essentially computational in character, may be *simulated* on a high speed digital computer. Many information-processing models involve complex interactions among processes not readily amenable to quantification using conventional analytical mathematics: **computer simulation** may be the only way of exploring with precision the properties and predictions of such a model. As a result, such simulations are now an increasing component of research on cognitive skills.

Some philosophers and psychologists believe that a computational account of mental activity provides the means for solution, or at least clarification, of an ancient puzzle—the **'mind-body' problem**: how can mental phenomena with the unique character of conscious thought, private sensations and feelings, volition and intentionality arise out of a deterministic machine made out of interacting neurons? The basic idea is that these phenomena arise not out of some ineffable properties of neurons *per se*, but out of the way in which the computational activity carried out by neural networks is *organized*. The same organization may well be realizable (at least in principle) with quite different hardware. This view of the mind-body relationship, sometimes called 'functionalism' sees mental state terms as referring to aspects of the sort of abstract computational description introduced above (see Fodor, 1981, for an elementary brief discussion).

The claim that the brain can be characterized as a 'computational' system is not to be confused with a facile analogy between the brain and any particular type of computer. The computer now on many office desks has an information-processing architecture quite different from that of the brain. The standard digital computer of the present day has a single processor unit, and a separate passive memory store. The processor is *serial*: it can carry out only one operation at a time, but it is very fast. The processor is also *general purpose*: almost all the processing tasks done within the system have to be done by the same single processor. The brain clearly has a quite different processing architecture. Different parts of the brain carry out different kinds of processing simultaneously. Thus striate cortex extracts a certain kind of information from visual input, while the basal ganglia are (probably) concerned with movement initiation, and both kinds of processing may occur simultaneously and relatively independently. The brain may thus be seen as an interconnected network of special-purpose and partly autonomous processing modules. Within each module, too, processing is essentially parallel—millions of neurons simultaneously sending messages of excitation and inhibition to millions of other neurons. But it is slow: synaptic activation takes milliseconds compared to the nanoseconds required for execution of one instruction on a typical computer. The brain achieves its computational power through massively parallel interconnection, while the digital computer achieves its power by means of speed. In computational terms, the brain thus serves as an example of what is called **parallel distributed processing**. The storage of information is also very different in brains and digital computers. Storing two small fragments of information (e.g. two names in a data base) in a computer memory usually involves changing the contents of two different small groups of storage registers. In contrast, in the brain each name will activate large and overlapping subsets of millions of neurons, and the storage of the two memory traces presumably involves patterns of change in synaptic strength or excitability of these large and overlapping subsets of neurons.

Psychology as a branch of medicine and neuroscience

Significant components of psychological theory and psychological data are independent of mechanistic accounts of function common to the standard medical and neurosciences, but complement them in an exciting and potent way. Thus, an understanding of the effects of particular damage to the brain requires an account at a functional level of analysis in terms of impairments of particular psychological processes. Clearly, a medical scientist ignorant of psychology would be incapable of addressing problems of this sort. Indeed, such an approach would seem ill-advised since knowledge of the structure and working of the brain independent of the functional perspective ignores one of the main adaptive functions of the brain, namely the control of behavioural output.

An understanding of psychological process also has definite implications for medical practice. This is patently the case for such specialities as ophthalmology and neurology; but there are a number of ways in which psychological processes impinge on medicine in a less direct and obvious fashion. First, as noted earlier, doctors themselves are subject to the ordinary limitations of human cognition and memory; and they are, like everyone else, emotionally and intellectually vulnerable to disturbance produced by stress, tiredness, drugs, and so on. Second, these same constraints influence patients' recall and reporting of their experience of events and symptoms, as well as their appreciation of their doctor's advice and instructions. Third, peoples' emotional response to the stresses of their lives have an impact on their physical health; and an understanding of these responses is essential to the generation of effective treatments. Fourth, an appreciation of patients' emotional reaction to illness and to treatment is an essential aspect of good medical practice. Finally, forms of psychological treatment, originally developed for the treatment of psychiatric disorders, have been applied in novel ways with promising results to a range of physical disorders. Physicians working in widely differing specialities are increasingly becoming aware that the practice of their particular branch of medicine demands a sophisticated appreciation of the psychological aspects of the disorders they are concerned with and the treatments they have at their disposal.

The chapters which follow elaborate on theoretical and practical issues discussed in this introduction. The emphasis, particularly in the earlier chapters, is on psychology as a basic of medical science; but the relevance of the material to medical practice should be apparent throughout.

References

Bennett, H.L., Davis, H.S. and Gianni, J.A. (1985). Non-verbal responses to intraoperative conversation. *British Journal of Anaesthesiology* **57**, 174.

Bonke, B., Schmitz, P.I.M., Verhage, F. and Zwaveling, A. (1986). Clinical study of so-called unconscious perception during general anaesthesia. *British Journal of Anaesthesiology* **58**, 957.

Fodor, J.A. (1981). The mind-body problem. *Scientific American* **244**, 114.

Holender, D. (1986). Semantic activation without conscious identification in dichotic listening, parafoveal vision, and visual masking: a survey and appraisal. *Behavioral and Brain Sciences* **9**, 1.

Marcel, A. (1983). Conscious and unconscious perception: experiments on visual masking and word-recognition. *Cognitive Psychology* **15**, 197.

Nisbett, R.E. and Wilson, T.D. (1977). Telling more than we can know: verbal reports on mental processes. *Psychological Review* **84**, 231.

Valenstein, E. (1973). *Brain Control*, John Wiley, New York.

Zajonc, R.B. (1980). Feeling and thinking: preferences need no inferences. *American Psychologist* **35**, 151.

2

Perception: Vision, Hearing and Pain

BCJ Moore · J Atkinson

Visual perception

When we look around the world we form an immediate, clear impression of recognizable objects, coherently organized in a spatial layout. Although our eyes are constantly moving, there is no jitter or instability in what we see. At will, we can switch attention from one object to another and from one size scale to another to take in more or less detail about an object. This process of analysing and understanding incoming sensory visual signals is visual perception.

Sensory coding and how it can become distorted

In the first stage of vision, the photoreceptors signal a coded description of the image. Information is carried in the sensory code by three aspects of neural activity: its place, intensity and timing. Information is signalled by whichever fibre or set of fibres is active (**place coding**). Variations in the strength of the neural signal, brought about by changing the rate of firing, give **intensity coding**. Variations in the time pattern of neural pulses give **temporal coding**.

A good example of place coding is found in colour vision. There are three independent cone-types each of which has its own pigment, sensitive to a particular range of wavelengths. Hundreds of different colours can be specified depending on the proportion of stimulation of each of the three types of cone. Most stimuli affect all three types and to derive colour information the system must compare the levels of activity between cone types. This comparison, called the 'colour opponent' system, is carried out early in visual processing in retinal ganglion cells. Some wavelengths excite a given cell; others inhibit it. Different cells are tuned to different wavelengths for excitation and inhibition. These opponent processes can be thought of as subtraction of different cone signals. Of course, all objects have both colour and brightness; consequently, for colours to be matched, they have to have the same subjective brightness as well as carrying the same colour information.

There are a number of clinical conditions in which the sensory code is abnormal. Common forms of colour blindness, present to some degree in one out of every 15 males, are due to deficiencies in one of the cone types. In the rarer condition, retinitis pigmentosa, deficiencies in the rods severely affect vision, particularly at night. The degree of disability, which increases with age, depends on the amount of retina which is affected.

Another common form of distortion in the sensory code arises from optical anomalies of defocusing—due to the shape of the lens and cornea (Fig. 2.1). Such refractive errors seriously affect performance on tasks requiring high resolution, such as reading fine text, but have little effect on our ability to move around avoiding collision and recognizing familiar objects and people (as is the case in human infants).

★   Instant video imaging – no processing delays

★   Computerised quantification of refractive state

★   Easy to use with minimal training

★   Fast accurate results at first visit

★   Requires minimal patient co-operation and can be used with subjects of all ages

Developed at the University of Cambridge

Reference: Atkinson J, Braddick O J, Durden K, Watson P G, Atkinson S.
Screening for refractive errors in 6-9 months old infants by photorefraction.
Br. J. Ophthalmol (1984); 68: 105–122

(a)

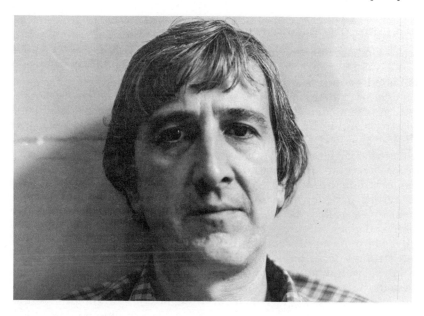

(b)

Fig. 2.1 Effects of an astigmatic refractive error on (a) text, and (b) face.

Visual feature-processing mechanisms

One way of measuring how well the visual system transmits information about the spatial layout of light and dark is to find the finest detail discriminated—a measure of **visual acuity**. Acuity is measured in terms of visual angle ($1° = 1$ cm at 57 cm; the little fingernail at arm's length subtends approximately $1°$). Various test patterns have been devised for clinical use, including Snellen letters (the letter charts viewed at opticians) and grating patterns. To resolve the detail in these patterns one needs to detect intensity differences between two locations. Generally, a limit of 1 minute of arc (min arc) bar width is taken as normal adult acuity for gratings, or 1 min arc line width of a Snellen letter.

Each retinal ganglion cell responds to visual stimuli within a limited region of space called the receptive field. Stimuli in the centre of the receptive field give responses opposite to those produced by stimuli around the edge. This is called centre-surround opponent organization. Cells respond strongly to differences of illumination or contrast between the centre and surround, and weakly to uniform illumination. This means that the signal in the optic nerve is concentrated in regions of abrupt change of contrast (edges). These edges usually carry the most important information in the image. However, we can see large areas of even illumination where there is little or no ganglion cell response, implying the existence of a filling-in process which reconstructs the region between one edge and the next. If the edge stays stationary, ganglion cells only respond for a short period of time, after which they adapt and stop responding. In normal vision, this adaptation is prevented by continuous eye movements. However, adaptation can be demonstrated in the rapid fading of an image fixed in position on the retina, e.g. an afterimage produced by a flash of light.

Many cells in the visual cortex are selectively sensitive to the orientation of lines or bars and have 'preferred' orientations to which they respond optimally. This is an example of a sensory dimension subserved by a system of neural elements, selectively responding to different parts of the range of values of this dimension. These elements are called filters or channels.

Evidence for orientation channels comes from psychophysical experiments on selective adaptation (Fig. 2.2). The usual explanation requires channels, each of which is tuned to a particular orientation. The response of a neuron as a function of orientation is called its tuning curve. The tuning curves of the channels are assumed to overlap, with perceived orientation depending on relative activity in different channels. This implies a comparison process as was also the case for perceived colour. If only one eye is shown the adapting grating, and the other eye shown the test grating, then the unadapted eye still shows the shift in perceived orientation. This **interocular transfer** means that the adapting effect must arise in structures receiving input from both eyes (and therefore must involve binocular cells). In strabismic individuals—whose eyes are misaligned—binocular cells are absent and there is little or no interocular transfer.

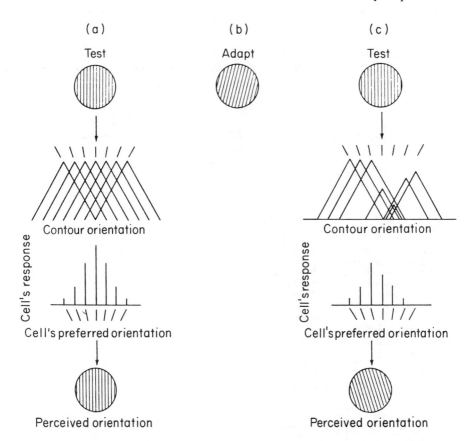

Fig. 2.2 Neural explanation of the tilt after-effect. (a) The response of the system in an unadapted state: the perceived orientation is assumed to be that of the most active channel, and corresponds to the true orientation of the test grating. (b) The effect of adapting the system with a grating of a different orientation to the test grating. The adaptation depresses the sensitivity of each channel by an amount depending on how much it has been stimulated. (c) The response of the adapted channels to the test grating. The distribution is now skewed and has a maximum response at a different orientation.

Perceived orientation can also be altered by contours which are present at the same time as the test stimulus. This effect is called **simultaneous contrast**. These effects imply mutually inhibitory interactions between orientation channels. Such interactions may also be the basis for certain geometrical illusions in which, for example, lines fail to appear parallel because of interactions with adjacent lines (Fig. 2.3).

A number of other dimensions are coded by specialized channels, including motion and size. If the contrast required to detect a grating is

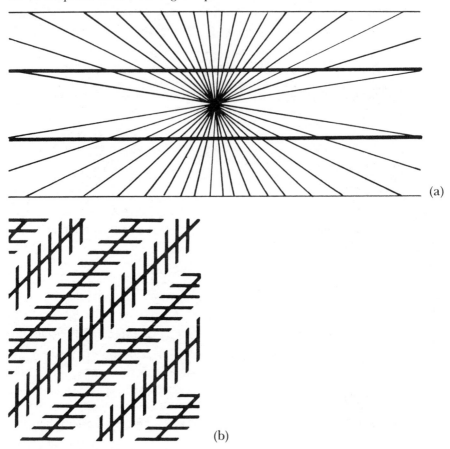

(a)

(b)

Fig. 2.3 (a) Hering illusion: the radiating lines cause the horizontal straight lines to look bowed. (b) Zoellner illusion: the long oblique lines are parallel, but look slanted with respect to each other.

measured for different stripe widths (spatial frequency in terms of bars per degree of visual angle), a contrast sensitivity function (csf) can be derived (Fig. 2.4).

Notice that adults with normal vision are less sensitive to low and high spatial frequencies than to intermediate ones. The drop at low spatial frequencies means that it can be harder to see something the closer we get to it! This is sometimes important in interpreting medical images such as ultrasound scans. To see a particular structure it may be necessary to stand further away for viewing, so as to use the sensitive intermediate spatial frequency part of the csf. Abnormalities of the csf have now been documented in a number of clinical conditions and in old age (Fig. 2.4). The practical importance of these global losses in sensitivity is now being

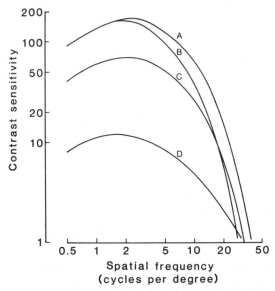

Fig. 2.4 Contrast sensitivity functions (csf). Each csf shows how contrast sensitivity varies with spatial frequency. A: Normal adult csf. B: csf attenuated at high spatial frequencies, typical of a patient with an uncorrected refractive error (such as short-sightedness) or some cases of amblyopia ('lazy eye'). C: Typical csf of a patient with glaucoma. D: csf with overall response attenuated, as in a patient with optic neuritis or multiple sclerosis.

realized and measures of contrast sensitivity are often used in addition to Snellen charts.

Feature detection and pattern recognition

If a channel is highly specific in its response it can be regarded as a feature detector. However, if such feature detectors are to be used for the recognition of objects, there must be some mechanism that recognizes a feature or object as the same no matter where it is in the field of view, what size it is, or at what angle to the eyes. The fact that we can do this is called **perceptual constancy**. One possible mechanism subserving our ability to recognize an object at various positions in space might be found in the activity of complex cells. Complex cells show selectivity for oriented bars or edges but, unlike simple cells, their responses cannot be predicted by summing areas of excitation and inhibition. The complex cell may perform logical OR operations on inputs from a set of simple cells (i.e. any one of a number of inputs can fire the cell) over a larger area of visual field. This type of OR mechanism may well operate at many levels of the visual system. Logical AND processes, where higher level features are built up by conjunction of a number of simple features, probably also operate. 'Face detectors', such as have been found in primates, probably involve a series of these AND and OR processes. Specific deficits of face recognition called **prosopagnosia** may perhaps be an example of these processes going wrong (for other examples of visual agnosia see Chapter 7).

Visual space perception

In everyday life we see in three dimensions rather than two. If a particular object is fixated in space then the image of another object, either in front of or behind the fixation object, will be on different parts of the retinae of the two eyes. The difference is called the **disparity** and is a measure of relative distance between two objects. Our ability to detect disparity can be illustrated using random dot stereograms (Fig. 2.5).

The same principle is used in 3-D films when the images to the two eyes are separated by red–green goggles. However, so that the 'stereo blind' (individuals lacking disparity detection) are not disappointed by the film, many depth cues other than disparity are used!

Two other sources of depth information come from convergence and accommodation. An object is imaged on corresponding points (zero disparity) if the eyes are converged on the object. The degree of convergence is therefore a source of distance information, as is accommodation (the degree of compression of the lens necessary to bring an image of an object into sharp focus). These processes are normally coupled so that a certain degree of accommodation accompanies a certain degree of convergence. This coupling can break down in accommodative strabismus when one eye turns in relative to the other whenever the patient attempts to converge on a nearby target.

There are many monocular cues that do not require the use of two eyes together. Some of the more important ones are **motion parallax** (relative movement of objects across the retina), **interposition** (objects occluding one another) and **texture gradients** (texture grain varying in size with distance). Normally, many cues are used together. Most natural scenes contain lots of detail, so that even when a particular object provides little depth information, its distance can be gauged from the depth of surrounding objects.

Much of the information used to interpret depth and distance is learnt through experience. Some theories of perception have assumed that it involves a kind of problem-solving; high level hypotheses are used to interpret the basic sensory information specified by visual channels. However, other theories assume that visual analysis makes use of a sequence of computational processes proceeding in an orderly way from one stage to the next.

The organization of perceptual representation

Grouping or segmenting processes are fundamental to separating one object from another and from the background. The visual system seems to

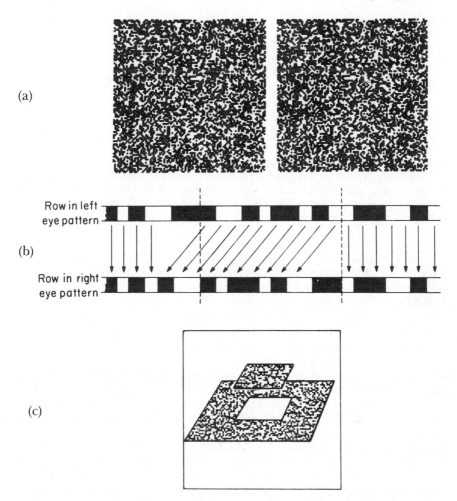

Fig. 2.5 (a) Random-dot stereoscopic pair. (b) The way in which a single row is generated. Outside the central region, the two patterns are identical random sequences; in the central region, the right eye's pattern is shifted relative to that of the left. (c) The appearance of (a) when viewed stereoscopically: the disparity of dots in the central region causes it to stand out in depth from the surround.

be particularly sensitive to certain properties of visual images which are used for segmentation. These properties have been embodied in many different psychological accounts of perceptual organization. One school of psychological thought, the Gestalt psychologists, postulated three main laws of grouping. Elements were grouped according to the laws of proximity (near one another in space and time), similarity (in shape) and good continuation (aligned). Examples of these grouping properties can be seen in Figure 2.6.

(a)   (b)

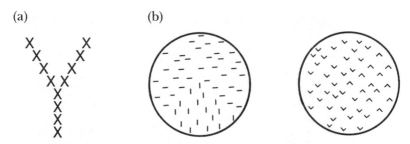

Fig. 2.6 Perceptual segmentation. (a) The figure can either be segmented into the small letters, or can be grouped into the large letter. (b) On the left, the 'pie segment' containing the vertical lines is easily segmented from the rest of the pie, although these are no physical boundaries. On the right, there is no instant perceptual segregation.

Having segmented the scene, the perceptual system must generate descriptions of shapes. This has to be done with respect to some frame of reference and ambiguities are often resolved by the frame of reference (Fig. 2.7).

Recent theories of object recognition have focused on two different levels of analysis. The first stage involves feature extraction. If an element or object differs from a whole array of objects by a single feature, then it can be very quickly picked out. This automatic unconscious, effortless perception has been called 'pop-out' or **preattentive processing** (because it does not require focal attention). Treisman has argued that there may be a number of distinct feature maps each responding to a particular stimulus dimension (probably in distinct cortical loci) and that, within a feature map, visual search operates in parallel across the whole visual field. This means that the time taken to find the odd man out (search time) will not be affected by the number of other elements or distractors in the visual field. However, the second stage of object recognition requires focal attention in order to put together the features of the object at a particular location. This will take longer the more distractors there are which have to be sequentially examined.

Tentative links can be made between these search processes and the underlying anatomy. In the primate visual cortex, two functional streams or pathways have been suggested. One, from striate cortex via V2 ending in the inferotemporal cortex, handles information necessary to recognize objects and contains feature detecting mechanisms for orientation and colour. The other handles motion information in a specialized medial temporal area (MT) and may also be involved in localizing objects in space. In addition, the inferior parietal lobule in the parietal lobe seems to be involved in focal attention, although other areas to which it connects are also implicated.

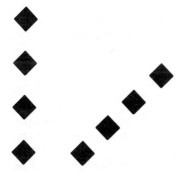

Fig. 2.7 An equilateral figure with 90° corners can be described relative to axes parallel to its sides (i.e. as a 'square') or relative to axes parallel to its diagonals ('diamond'). Here, the axis is determined by the global shape of the group rather than the orientation on the page.

Two visual systems: cortical and subcortical

Throughout the discussion so far we have been concentrating on the mechanisms of 'what' we see rather than 'where' we look, although usually in normal perception where we look is decided by what is in various locations of visual space. Consequently, it is difficult to separate completely the 'where' and 'what' processes and rather artificial to do so. However, there might be two separate but interacting visual systems that subserve these different functions. Animals with lesions in the striate cortex but intact midbrain are not totally blind: they can turn and respond to objects appearing in peripheral vision, but are unable to recognize patterns or objects. There is now an extensive literature on this 'blindsight'—visual capabilities in human patients and non-human primates lacking primary visual cortex (see Weiskrantz, 1986 and Chapter 7). Controversy concerning the relationship between the unconscious perception of these patients and conscious decision-making in normal vision is not totally resolved, partly because theories of 'consciousness' are still somewhat incomplete. However, it is clear from observations made on blindsight patients that much perceptual processing goes on continuously without focal attention and that many of our spatial localizing abilities, such as those involved in walking through a room so as to avoid collision, may be possible without cortical input.

Spatial perception and hemispheric specialization

In normal adults the contribution of each hemisphere to visual perception can be assessed by comparing the responses to stimuli projected to either side of a fixation spot. Information is only projected to the hemisphere contralateral to the stimulus. Data from perceptual tasks such as orientation discrimination, simple feature detection, and fine localization of points of light, suggest a greater contribution from the right hemisphere than the left. More complex tasks of shape recognition involve both hemispheres.

Visual perceptual development

Perceptual development can be thought of as consisting of two parts. The first involves increasing sensitivity to different aspects of objects, which implies the development of various specialized channels. The second part is the development of interpretative mechanisms to make sense of sensory information so that the child learns appropriate motor and social responses. Say, for example, an 8-month-old infant crawls confidently off the top step and falls down the stairs. What part of the child's perception is immature and leads to this fall? It could be that the visual channels used to detect depth changes are not functioning. It could be that the significance of the depth is not appreciated. Or it could be that the child has the capacity to understand a change in depth but has not linked this particular idea to the appropriate response—to stop crawling. The immaturity could be at all of these levels and subtle two-way links between sensory and motor systems need to be developed to achieve the mature response. Theories of perceptual development tend to be either neurophysiological or psychological. The former emphasize the capacity for sensory discriminations and analyse development in terms of maturation of channels; the latter postulate global mechanisms, emphasizing the interpretative aspects. Both approaches are needed for a complete understanding.

Visual development is very rapid in the first year of life. Whereas vision plays a relatively minor role in the world of the newborn, by 6 months vision is of major importance and forms the basis of later cross-modal perceptual, cognitive and social development. The newborn's sensory mechanisms or channels show high sensitivity to some aspects of stimuli (e.g. flicker) although they seem to be very broadly tuned. An adult with the visual acuity of the newborn (around 30 min arc) would be on the blind register. However, the newborn's vision is adequate for distinguishing between many large objects and is better than that needed for independent mobility in partially sighted adults. By the age of 6 months acuity is quite close to the adult's so that, if infants had the appropriate intellectual and mechanical abilities, then they could do most visual tasks except possibly read fine newspaper print and drive a car! Several underlying changes are involved in this improved sensitivity. These are differentiation of the fovea, myelination of the visual pathways, and an increase in the number of synapses and their specificity.

Sensitivity to certain aspects of the sensory input, such as orientation, disparity and direction of motion, is not present at birth but emerges in the first 3 months of life. As cortical mechanisms are necessary for detecting these aspects, it is plausible to suppose that prior to 3 months vision is largely subcortically mediated (for a more detailed review of this model, see Atkinson, 1984). As humans are somewhat less mature than other primates at birth, it is possible that human gestation has been curtailed during evolution to ensure survival of the infant with a large brain and small maternal pelvis.

Alongside changes in discriminatory capacity come changes in perceptual understanding. Although many studies show that most depth cues can be discriminated by 6–9 months of age, if we are to say that the infant 'understands' what these cues mean then we must either show that the infant recognizes an equivalence between similar depth cues or that the depth cues determine a response which is appropriate to the location in three-dimensional space. Although some researchers have claimed that the newborn's reaching behaviour is appropriate to the distance a toy is held from the baby's hand and that a 1-month-old infant will duck to avoid a looming object, the general consensus is that these responses are not reliably found until after 5–6 months of age. However, shape and size constancy seem to be found at the age of 3 months. Factors such as how the object is moved in space seem to affect the level of the infant's perceptual understanding (continuous smooth motion seems to be understood earlier than abrupt transient shifts). This principle, that the exact nature of the transition or change is an important factor in the understanding of the child, is found many times in development (see Chapter 5). It may depend on the transition triggering a switch of attention. Newborns show attention limited to the external contours of patterns (for example, the hairline in looking at a face) and ignore the inner contours (the internal features). Older infants can attend to many features either in rapid succession or even in parallel.

Acuity assessed using simple bar patterns or single letters, is close to the adult's by 3 years. However, preschool children show marked 'crowding' defects having difficulty separating one letter from the next, so that acuity for multiple letter arrays is lower than for single letters. These perceptual problems are overcome by 6–7 years.

Abnormal development

Marked refractive errors, such as astigmatism, which is very common in infants in their first year, can limit acuity, although usually these refractive errors are lessened after the first few years. Disruption of normal vision to one eye early in life can seriously disrupt development of binocular vision. The resulting 'amblyopia' means that this eye cannot perceive forms and shapes normally, although sometimes the csf for the amblyopic eye may be as good as for the normal eye.

Misalignment of the two eyes (squint or strabismus) usually results in the visual cortex not encoding the information from the deviating eye (suppression). If a squint is present early in life and left untreated until 5 years of age, surgery will be largely cosmetic with little visual recovery. Very few infants squint all of the time consistently from birth, although many will cross their eyes occasionally in the first few months. It is possible that some infants squint because of a congenital lack of potential binocular vision: for example, albinos lack the uncrossed visual pathways so that information from the two eyes is not combined in the cortex. Another group of infants develops normal binocular vision early in life, but loses it later when they develop a squint. There is a strong correlation between marked hypermetropia (longsightedness due to the optics of the eyes) in the first year of life, and subsequent strabismus and amblyopia by 4 years. What is more, if marked refractive errors are corrected in infancy, the risk of later abnormal vision is significantly reduced.

In this section, the development of visual perception has been considered largely in isolation, which may give an unrealistic picture of what happens. Perceptual, social and cognitive development are heavily interrelated, and in cases where perceptual development is abnormal (for example in a blind child), there are delays in the other aspects of development. Apart from the deleterious effects on visual development of such congenital abnormalities as cataract or strabismus, it is not known whether more subtle aspects of perceptual development are affected by environmental manipulations within an early sensitive period of life. So, although the factors leading to poor visual development are known, those contributing to an enriching or even an adequate visual environment, are not, as yet. However, given the variety of visual stimulation experienced by human infants, it would seem unlikely that there is any one ideal, narrowly defined environment.

Auditory perception

In everyday life the sound reaching our ears often arises from several different sources. Each source has its own location in space, and has its own intensity, frequency content and time pattern. At our ears the sound from each source is superimposed, and the stimulus at each eardrum is simply variation in air pressure with time (on either side of the mean value corresponding to atmospheric pressure), an apparently one-dimensional stimulus. This is illustrated in Figure 2.8, which shows the individual waveforms (plots of air pressure versus time) from several different sources, and the summation of those waveforms as occurs at the eardrum. Yet the auditory system is capable of decomposing the sound wave so each sound source is heard separately, in its appropriate place, and with its appropriate loudness, pitch, timbre (quality) and time pattern. How this remarkable feat is achieved is not fully understood. This chapter will focus on those parts of the process that are reasonably well understood and will describe how hearing impairments can affect the ability to analyse and discriminate sounds.

The action of the ear as a frequency analyser

Theoretically, any complex waveform can be represented as the sum of a series of sinusoidal frequency components, and the mathematical technique for calculating what these components are is known as Fourier analysis.

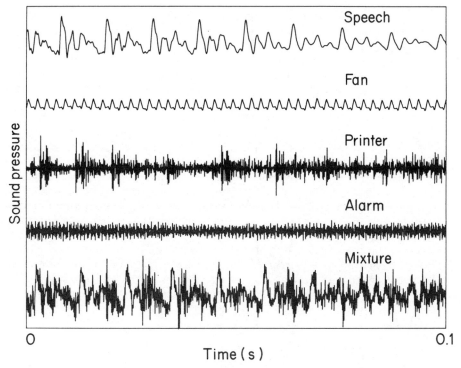

Fig. 2.8 The individual waveforms of several different sound sources (a segment of speech, a ventilation fan, a dot-matrix printer and an alarm clock ringing) and the summation of those waveforms as would occur at the eardrum. Note that in the sum, the individual waveforms are no longer discernible.

An example is given in Figure 2.9, which shows how a complex waveform can be created by summing sinusoidal components. If the waveform repeats regularly (i.e. is periodic), then the components have frequencies which are integral multiples of the repetition rate. Such components are called harmonics, and they are numbered, the lowest harmonic being called the first harmonic, the next the second, and so on. The first harmonic is also called the **fundamental frequency**. It is also possible to analyse a complex waveform by means of mechanical or electrical **bandpass filters**. If a sinusoid is applied to the input of a bandpass filter and the frequency varied while keeping the intensity constant, then the output of the filter is a sinusoid with the same frequency as the input, but the intensity varies with the input frequency. A plot of the output intensity as a function of frequency is called the filter shape. The output is greatest over a certain range (the passband) and falls off outside the passband; components outside the passband are said to be attenuated. The frequency at the centre of the passband is known as the centre frequency of the filter. Using a large number of such filters, each with a different centre frequency, it is

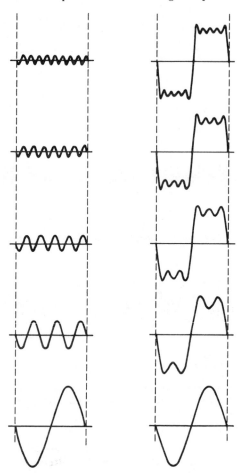

Fig. 2.9 An illustration of how a complex waveform (a square wave) can be built up from a series of sinusoidal components. The square wave is composed of odd harmonics only, and the 1st, 3rd, 5th, 7th and 9th harmonics are shown on the left. The series on the right shows progressive changes from a simple sinusoid as each component is added. Reproduced from Newman, E.B. (1948) by permission of John Wiley and Sons, New York.

possible to isolate the sinusoidal components in a complex sound, and to determine the intensity of each component (Fig. 2.10). A plot of the intensity of each sinusoidal component as a function of frequency is known as the **spectrum** of the sound.

The auditory system behaves as if it carries out a kind of Fourier analysis, but with less-than-perfect precision. In other words, it acts as a frequency analyser of limited resolution, breaking down complex sounds into their sinusoidal frequency components. The initial basis of this frequency

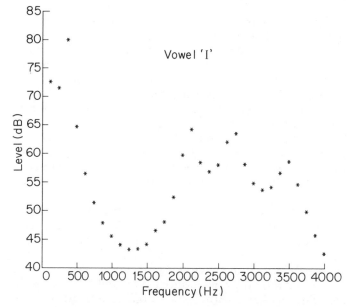

Fig. 2.10 An example of the spectrum of a complex sound, the vowel 'I' as in h*i*t. The intensity of each sinusoidal component (expressed in decibels, dB) is plotted as a function of its frequency.

analysis almost certainly depends upon processes which occur in the cochlea. Each point on the basilar membrane (BM) within the cochlea behaves like a mechanical bandpass filter. The centre frequency of the filters varies progressively with position along the BM, from low at the apex to high at the base. Thus, each frequency component in a complex sound will produce vibration at a different place on the BM. The filtering observed in the cochlea may be sufficient to account for the frequency-analysing capacity of the entire auditory system. Note that this is quite different from spatial-frequency analysis in vision which, as already pointed out, depends largely on neural processes. The tuning in the cochlea instead depends primarily on mechanical processes, although it may be partly under neural control. We are able to hear one sound in the presence of another sound with a different frequency largely as a consequence of the ear's frequency analysis. This ability is known as **frequency selectivity** or **frequency resolution**.

Measurement of the ear's frequency selectivity

Important sounds are sometimes rendered inaudible by other sounds, a process known as 'masking'. Masking may be considered as a failure of frequency selectivity, and it can be used as a tool to measure the frequency selectivity of the ear. One conception of masking, which has had some practical success, assumes that the auditory system contains a bank of overlapping bandpass filters. These filters are sometimes called the 'auditory filters'. Each filter can be thought of as corresponding to a particular place on the BM. One sound (the masker) will only mask another (the signal) if the masking sound produces an output from the filters which respond most strongly to the signal. In the simple case of a sinusoidal signal presented in a background noise (which may contain many different frequency components), the intensity of the signal relative to the background noise will be greatest at the outputs of filters with centre frequencies close to the signal frequency. It is assumed that the listener will make use of the filter whose output has the highest ratio of signal intensity to masker intensity. The signal will be detected if that ratio exceeds a certain value.

One method of estimating the shape of the auditory filter at a particular centre frequency gives curves known as **psychophysical tuning** curves (**PTCs**). The signal used is a sinusoid which is presented at a very low level, say 10 dB above the absolute threshold (the absolute threshold is the threshold for detecting the signal in the absence of any masking sound). Thus, to a first approximation, only one auditory filter will be involved in detecting the signal. The masker is either a sinusoid or a band of noise containing a narrow range of frequencies. To determine a PTC the signal is fixed in frequency and level, and the level of the masker required to mask the signal is determined for various centre frequencies of the masker. It is assumed that the signal will be masked when the masker produces a fixed output from the filter which would otherwise respond to the signal. Thus, the curve mapped out in this way represents the filter shape at the signal frequency, but the filter is plotted upside down (Fig. 2.11).

Several other methods have been used to estimate the shape of the auditory filter. Although the results from the different methods differ in detail, there is good agreement on the whole. The bandwidth of the auditory filter (the range of frequencies covered by the passband) increases with centre frequency. Above about 1000 Hz, the bandwidth is roughly a constant proportion of the centre frequency. Figure 2.12 summarizes the results of several experiments and shows how the filter bandwidth varies with centre frequency.

Frequency selectivity in the hearing impaired

There is now considerable evidence that there is a loss of frequency selectivity in listeners with hearing impairments of cochlear origin. In general, greater elevations in absolute threshold tend to be associated with broader auditory filters. However, there can be considerable variability among patients, even when the elevation in absolute threshold is similar. A common finding is that hearing-impaired listeners are unusually susceptible to the masking of medium and high frequencies by lower frequencies, a phenomenon known as the **upward spread of masking**. This may partially account for the fact that hearing aids are often most effective when they

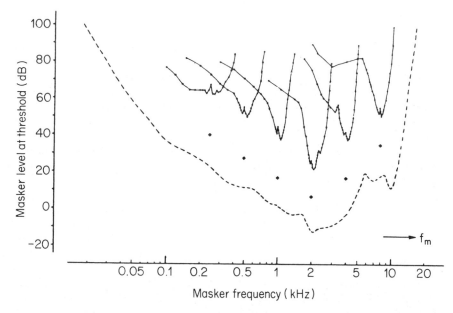

Fig. 2.11 Examples of psychophysical tuning curves (PTCs). Each curve shows results for a different signal frequency. The level of the masker (in decibels, dB) required to mask the signal is plotted as a function of the masker frequency. The level of the signal is indicated by the diamond below each curve. The dashed line shows the absolute threshold for the signal. Data from Vogten, L.L.M. (1974) by permission of Springer-Verlag, Heidelberg.

amplify high frequencies more than low frequencies. Such a characteristic will help to alleviate the effects of the upward spread of masking.

Effect of impaired frequency selectivity of the masking of speech by noise

A consequence of reduced frequency selectivity is a greater susceptibility to masking by interfering sounds. The frequency content of a sound being listened to will usually differ from that of other sounds in the environment. By making use of auditory filters tuned close to the signal frequency or frequencies, the signal will be passed but much of the background noise will be attenuated. When the auditory filters are broader than normal, the rejection of background noise will be much less effective. Thus, background noise will disrupt the detection and discrimination of sounds, including speech. Indeed, difficulty in understanding speech in noise is one of the commonest complaints among people with hearing impairments of cochlear origin. The ability to understand speech in noise decreases as frequency selectivity decreases.

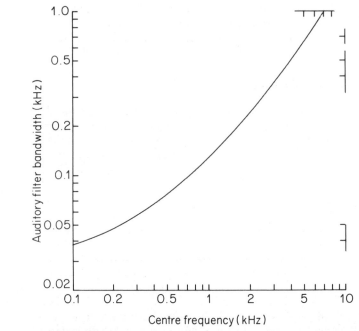

Fig. 2.12   The curve shows how the bandwidth of the auditory filter varies with centre frequency. Data from Moore, B.C.J. and Glasberg, B.R. (1983).

The perception of timbre

Timbre may be defined as the characteristic quality of sound that distinguishes one voice or musical instrument from another. Timbre depends on several different physical properties of sound, including:

1. Whether the sound is irregular, having a noise-like quality, or is periodic, having a tonal quality for repetition rates from about 20 to 16 000 Hz.

2. Whether the sound is continuous or interrupted. For sounds which have short durations the exact way in which the sound is turned on and off can play an important role. For example, in the case of sounds produced by stringed instruments, a rapid onset (a fast rise time) is usually perceived as a struck or plucked string, whereas a gradual onset is heard as a bowed string.

3. The spectrum of the sound and changes in the spectrum with time. This is the correlate of timbre which has been studied most widely.

The timbre of steady periodic sounds depends primarily on their spectrum. For example, sounds containing predominantly high frequencies have a 'sharp' timbre, whereas those containing mainly low frequencies sound 'dull' or 'mellow'. This is another example of the action of the ear as a frequency analyser. The components in a complex sound will be partially separated by the auditory filters, and the distribution of activity at the output of the filters, as a function of filter centre frequency, will determine timbre.

Timbre perception in impaired hearing

As a consequence of the reduced frequency selectivity which is associated with cochlear hearing loss, the ability to hear changes in timbre is also impaired. Thus, it will be more difficult for the impaired listener to tell the difference between different vowel sounds or to distinguish musical instruments.

The perception of pitch

Pitch is defined as that attribute of auditory sensation in terms of which sounds may be ordered on a musical scale—i.e. that attribute in which variations constitute melody. In general, any sound which is periodic will have a pitch, provided that the waveform repetition rate lies in the range 20–16 000 Hz. The pitch increases as the repetition rate increases. As described earlier, periodic complex tones, such as those produced by the human voice or by musical instruments, can be analysed into a series of sinusoidal components, a fundamental component whose frequency equals the repetition rate of the sound, and a series of harmonics whose frequencies are integral multiples of that of the fundamental (Figs. 2.9 and 2.10). Although the pitch we hear is usually the same as that of the fundamental component, the fundamental does not have to be present for us to hear this pitch; this is called the 'phenomenon of the missing fundamental'.

At this point a very remarkable aspect of human hearing should be noted. In many situations we listen to two or more complex tones simultaneously, for example, two people talking at once, or to several instruments playing together. Each tone consists of many harmonics and the harmonics of the different notes are interleaved and sometimes overlap. Yet somehow we are able to hear each note separately, grouping together all of the harmonics which belong to each tone. The apparently effortless way in which we do this might make it seem a simple task. In fact, it requires a tremendous amount of computation, as is illustrated by attempts to build computer systems to do the same thing; even the fastest and most powerful computers do not approach the abilities of human listeners in this respect.

Most modern theories of pitch perception assume a two-stage process. In the first stage the frequencies of the lower harmonics are determined. This analysis depends on the ear's filtering mechanism, but the time structure of the output from each filter is probably also important. In the second stage, which is probably located more centrally than the cochlea, some form of pattern recognizer determines a fundamental frequency whose harmonics match those of the stimulus as closely as possible. The perceived pitch corresponds to the frequency of the fundamental determined in this way. Only those components which form part of a harmonic series are classified as 'belonging' to a given tone. This provides a way of separating the components from two or more tones into groups, each group forming a harmonic series. Clearly, for these theories the resolution of individual harmonics is critical; hence, frequency selectivity probably plays a key role in pitch perception.

Pitch perception in impaired hearing

Relatively little is known about pitch perception in people with impaired hearing. Most people with cochlear hearing losses do have impaired pitch perception, but a few have almost normal abilities to detect changes in pitch. When frequency selectivity is impaired, quite good discrimination of single tones may be possible on the basis of the temporal patterns of neural activity in the auditory nerve. Only when temporal processing is also disrupted will performance become very poor. Thus, some subjects can show very broad PTCs and almost normal pitch discrimination.

The localization of sounds

Our ability to localize sounds in space is crucial to the analysis of complex mixtures of sounds. In general, it is easier to hear a given sound source, such as a voice, if it comes from a different position in space from interfering sounds. This section briefly considers the information or cues which we use to localize sounds.

Binaural cues

Slight differences in the sounds reaching the two ears can be used as cues in sound localization. The two major cues are differences in the time of arrival at the two ears and differences in intensity at the two ears. For example, a sound coming from the left will arrive first at the left ear and be more intense in the left ear. For steady sinusoidal stimulation, a difference in time of arrival is equivalent to a phase difference between the sounds at the two ears. However, phase differences cannot be used over the whole audible frequency range. Experiments using sounds delivered by headphones have shown that a phase difference at the two ears can be detected and used to judge location only at frequencies below about 1 500 Hz. This is because at high frequencies the wavelength of sound is small compared to the dimensions of the head, so the listener cannot determine which cycle in the left ear corresponds to a given cycle in the right. Thus, phase differences are ambiguous at high frequencies. On the other hand, at low frequencies accuracy at detecting changes in relative time at the two ears is remarkably good; changes of 10–20 μs can be detected, which is equivalent to a movement of the sound source of 1–2° laterally.

Intensity differences between the two ears are primarily useful at high frequencies. This is because low frequencies bend easily around the head, so that there is little difference in intensity at the two ears whatever the location of the sound source. At high frequencies the head casts more of a 'shadow', and above 2–3 kHz the intensity differences are sufficient to provide useful clues. For complex sounds containing a range of frequencies, the difference in spectral patterning at the two ears may also be important.

The idea that sound localization is based on interaural time differences at low frequencies and interaural intensity differences at high frequencies has been called the 'duplex theory' of sound localization and dates back to Lord Rayleigh. However, it has been realized in recent years that it is not quite correct. Complex sounds containing only high frequencies (above 1500 Hz) can be localized on the basis of interaural time delays, provided that they have an appropriate temporal structure. For example, a single click can be localized in this way no matter what its frequency content. Periodic sounds containing only high-frequency harmonics can also be localized on the basis of interaural time differences, provided that the repetition rate of the whole sound is below about 600 Hz. Since many of the complex sounds we encounter in everyday life have repetition rates below 600 Hz, interaural time differences will be used for localization in most listening situations.

The role of the pinna

Binaural cues are not sufficient to account for all of our localization abilities. For example, a simple difference in time or intensity will not define whether a sound is coming from in front or behind, or above or below; but people can clearly make such judgements. In recent years, it has been shown that the pinnae play an important role in sound localization. They do so because the spectra of sounds entering the ear are modified by the pinnae in a way which depends upon the direction of the sound source. This direction-dependent filtering provides cues for sound source location. The pinnae alter the sound spectrum primarily at high frequencies. Only when the wavelength of the sound is comparable with the dimensions of the pinnae is the spectrum significantly affected. This occurs mostly above about 6 kHz.

The precedence effect

In everyday conditions the sound from a given source reaches our ears by many different paths. Some of it will arrive via a direct path, but a great deal may only reach the ears after reflection from one or more surfaces. However, people are not normally aware of these reflections or echoes, and they do not appear to impair the ability to localize sound sources. The reason for this seems to lie in a phenomenon known as the precedence effect. When several similar sounds reach our ears in close succession (i.e.

the direct sound and its echoes), the sounds are perceptually fused into a single sound and the location of the total sound is primarily determined by the location of the first (direct) sound. Thus, the echoes have little influence on the perception of direction, although they may influence the timbre and loudness of the sound.

The precedence effect only occurs for sounds of a discontinuous or transient character, such as speech or music, and it can break down if the echoes are delayed sufficiently or are sufficiently intense compared to the direct sound. However, in normal conditions the precedence effect plays an important role in the location and identification of sounds in reverberant conditions. It seems dependent upon the use of two ears. When one ear is blocked room echoes become more noticeable: sounds become 'boomy' or 'muddy'.

Sound localization in the hearing impaired

Most hearing losses result in some degradation in sound localization. However, there may be considerable individual differences even in patients with similar absolute thresholds. In general, acoustic neuromas lead to greater localization problems than cochlear losses. Most patients show a reduced ability to use differences in time and intensity between the two ears. In addition, people with high-frequency hearing losses are generally unable to make use of the directional information provided by the pinnae. Hearing aid users also suffer in this respect, since, even if the microphone is appropriately placed within the pinna, the response of most aids is limited to frequencies below 6 kHz.

Perceptual organization of complex sounds

Some of the ways in which the auditory system separates simultaneous complex sounds have already been discussed. The cues used include differences in frequency content (spectrum), harmonic structure and location. This section considers further ways in which the auditory system separates mixtures of sounds and describes some general rules of perceptual organization. Note that these rules have much in common with those discussed earlier for perceptual organization in vision.

Onset disparities

Sounds in everyday life are often intermittent or interrupted. We are able to use differences in the onset times of sounds to separate them perceptually. The onset time disparities do not have to be large to be effective; about 30 ms is adequate. At such small onset disparities we may not be consciously aware that two sounds do not start simultaneously, but nevertheless we are much better at hearing the sounds separately than when they start simultaneously. Onset disparities play an important role in the perception of speech and music. Two talkers rarely produce words with exactly synchronous onsets and two musicians rarely start notes at exactly the same time—even when the musical score requires that they should! The onset disparities that occur in practice are usually sufficient to enhance perceptual separation.

Coherent variations in frequency or amplitude

The perceptual separation of simultaneous complex sounds can be considerably enhanced if the components of one of the sounds vary in frequency or intensity in a similar way; these components are then perceptually fused together and perceived as a coherent whole, separate from the remaining components. As was the case for onset disparities, this has important implications for the perception of music and speech. Musical notes often have a vibrato (regular variation of all components in both intensity and frequency), and provided the vibrato is different for different instruments, this will help us to hear the individual notes. In the case of speech, the fundamental frequency of a speaker's voice is usually continually changing. The harmonics of that voice also change in frequency in a coherent way, and this helps to fuse them together and separate them from background sounds.

These phenomena are examples of a general rule of perceptual organization which applies to both vision and hearing, and which the Gestalt psychologists called 'common fate': if two or more components of a sound or a visual scene undergo the same kind of changes at the same time, they are grouped and perceived as part of the same source or object.

Good continuation

It is a physical property of sound sources that changes in frequency, intensity, location or spectrum tend to be smooth and continuous rather than abrupt. This fact is exploited by the auditory system: a smooth change in any of these aspects is interpreted as a change within a single source, whereas sudden changes are interpreted as activation of a new source. This is an example of the Gestalt principle of 'good continuation'. As an example, a sudden change in the fundamental frequency of ongoing speech gives the impression that a new speaker has taken over from the old one.

Closure

In everyday life the sound from a given source may be frequently temporarily obscured by other sounds. While the obscuring sound is present, there may be no sensory evidence which can be used to determine whether the obscured sound has continued or not. Under these conditions the obscured sound tends to be heard as continuous because our perceptual system fills in the missing parts of the signal. The Gestalt psychologists called this **closure**. An example comes from studies of speech which is interrupted by brief silent intervals. Such speech sounds hoarse and raucous. When noise is presented in the gaps, the speech sounds more natural and continuous. For connected speech at moderate interruption rates, the intervening noise actually leads to an improvement in intelligibility. It is clear from this example that the perceptual filling-in of missing sounds does not take place solely on the basis of acoustic evidence in the waveform. Our past experience with speech and other sounds, and the context of surrounding sounds, are both of crucial importance.

General conclusions

Many different forms of information may be used to analyse a complex mixture of sounds so as to achieve the percept of several individual sources. Physical cues include differences in frequency spectrum, fundamental frequency and harmonic structure, onset disparities, changes in frequency and intensity, and sound location. We also make use of a stored knowledge of the properties of familiar sounds such as speech and music. No single form of information is effective all the time, but used together they provide an effective means of analysing and interpreting acoustic signals. People with hearing impairments of cochlear origin, which are common in the elderly, suffer from, among other things, reduced frequency selectivity. This can lead to considerable difficulty in analysing complex mixtures of sounds. A particular problem is a reduction in the ability to understand speech in noisy situations.

The perception of pain

The perception of pain differs from visual and auditory perception in several important ways. Firstly, there is no particular type of environmental energy which is the stimulus for pain, in the way that light is for vision or sound for hearing; pain can arise from many different causes, and, correspondingly, can have many different subjective qualities. Definitions of pain emphasize two main features, both of which are necessary, but not sufficient:

1. The existence of sensations associated with tissue damage, for example, strong pressure or extreme temperature
2. The existence of an emotional, aversive effect which tends to elicit behaviour aimed at stopping the conditions producing the tissue damage.

Note that the definition has both a sensory component and a component associated with mood or affect; a somatic sensation is not painful if its effects are not unpleasant.

Another important way in which pain perception differs from visual or auditory perception is that the threshold at which a stimulus becomes painful, and the degree of pain experienced at a given level of stimulation (e.g. the temperature of a heat source) can vary enormously from one situation to another and from one individual to another. Our understanding of pain perception has been increased by the application of a theory, known as Signal Detection Theory (SDT) which can be used to separate the effects of purely sensory factors from effects relating to motivation, expectation and so on. The theory applies quite generally to all of the senses, but it has proved particularly useful in the analysis of pain perception. The next section outlines the theory.

Signal Detection Theory (SDT)

Often, in the study of perception it is useful to measure a sensory threshold, for example, the threshold for detecting a painful stimulus such as a source of heat. Classically, a threshold has been considered as that magnitude of a stimulus above which it will be detected and below which it will not. However, this viewpoint is unsatisfactory: if the magnitude of a stimulus is slowly increased from a very low value, there is no well-defined point at which it suddenly becomes detectable. Rather, there is a range of magnitudes over which the subject will sometimes report a stimulus and sometimes will not. Furthermore, the proportion of times that the subject reports a stimulus of a given magnitude can be altered by non-sensory factors such as changing the instructions to the subject.

SDT explains these facts by assuming that the sensory effect, S, evoked by a fixed stimulus varies from trial to trial. S can be described in terms of a distribution with a certain mean value S_m. S_m increases with the magnitude of the stimulus, but on any given trial the value of S may be above or below that value. Even on trials when no stimulus is presented (often called 'catch' trials) there is a sensory effect which varies from trial to trial. The distribution of S on trials when a stimulus is presented overlaps with that on trials when no stimulus is presented, although the value of S_m will be smaller in the latter case. Thus, the subject can never be sure whether a given value of S arose from presentation of the stimulus or not.

SDT assumes that the subject chooses a criterion value of S, S_c. If the value of S on a given trial is greater than S_c, the subject will say "Yes, a stimulus was present", whereas if the value of S is less than S_c, the subject will say "No, the stimulus was absent". The criterion value is at the subject's disposal, and may be influenced by such factors as instructions, the probability that a signal will be presented, and the way in which responses are rewarded or punished.

SDT distinguishes two types of error. If the subject says "No" when a stimulus was present, this is called a 'miss'. The probability of a miss is equal to one minus the probability of a 'hit' (saying "Yes" when a stimulus was present). The other type of error, called a false alarm, is when the subject says "Yes" but no stimulus was present. If the subject decreases the value of S_c (i.e. becomes less cautious) this increases the probability of a hit, $P(H)$, but it also increases the probability of a false alarm $P(FA)$. If, on the other hand, the discriminability of the stimulus increases (either because of an increase in the magnitude of the stimulus, or because of an increase in efficiency of sensory processes), then P(H) may go up without any increase in P(FA); indeed, P(FA) may decrease. By measuring both P(H) and P(FA), SDT allows the calculation of two quantities. One, denoted by d′, is a measure of discriminability or sensory capacity; it is the separation between the distributions of S for stimulus and no stimulus, scaled according to the width of those distributions. The other measure, denoted by β, is related to the value of Sc. Tables exist giving the values of d′ and β for all possible pairs of values of P(H) and P(FA).

In summary, by measuring both hits and false alarms, SDT provides a means of separating sensory capacity (measured by d′) from factors relating to the subject's criterion for responding (measured by β). The following sections outline some of the factors that affect pain perception. Some, but not all, of these factors can be interpreted in terms of SDT. Later on we describe a theory which can account for many of the psychological factors which affect pain perception.

Suggestion and the placebo effect.

Severe pain can be relieved in about 35 per cent of patients by giving them a placebo, such as sugar or salt solution, in place of morphine or other analgesic drugs. Since morphine relieves severe pain only in about 75 per cent of patients, this suggests that almost half of the drug's effect is really a placebo effect. Conversely, if the word 'pain' is used in describing a procedure which is about to be administered, such as giving an injection or making an incision, the pain reported during this procedure is likely to be increased. These effects can be interpreted using SDT. Studies of pain using SDT have shown that placebos have their effect largely by increasing the criterion for reporting pain. Morphine, on the other hand, both increases the criterion and reduces sensitivity. Mentioning the word 'pain' before a procedure results in a decrease in the criterion for reporting a stimulus as painful.

Cultural and ethnic factors and past experience

Cultural background can have a strong effect on pain perception. For example, levels of radiant heat reported as painful by people of Mediterranean origin are described merely as warmth by Northern Europeans. In some cultures, religious or initiation ceremonies can involve tissue damage which would normally be regarded as excruciatingly painful, and yet those taking part show no signs of feeling pain, and sometimes appear to be in a kind of ecstasy.

The influence of past experience on pain perception is dramatically illustrated by an experiment of Melzack and Scott. They raised Scottish terriers in isolation cages, so that they did not suffer the normal bodily knocks and scrapes experienced by young animals. When mature, these dogs failed to respond normally to a variety of stimuli which would normally be regarded as painful. For example, they would sniff at a flaming match two or three times, and did not flinch when pricked with a pin. Melzack has suggested that the significance or meaning of environmental stimuli acquired during early experience plays an important role in pain perception.

Context

The context in which tissue damage occurs can have a powerful effect on the degree of pain experienced. For example, soldiers wounded in battle sometimes report feeling little pain from extensive wounds, and do not ask for medication to relieve the pain. In contrast, civilians with surgical wounds comparable to those of the soldiers often complain of severe pain, and ask for morphine. This seems partly to reflect the meaning attached to the situation. For example, Beecher pointed out that "In the wounded soldier the response to injury was relief, thankfulness at his escape alive from the battlefield, even euphoria; to the civilian, his major surgery was a depressing, calamitous event".

Attention can also have a considerable influence on pain perception. Boxers, football players and other athletes can sustain severe injuries during the excitement of the sport, without being aware that they have been hurt. In general, any situation which requires prolonged intense attention may cause wounds to go unnoticed, even when the wounds would cause considerable suffering under normal circumstances.

The gate-control theory of pain

Melzack and Wall have proposed a theory which attempts to account for a variety of psychological, physiological and clinical data on pain. This gate-control theory proposes that a neural mechanism in the dorsal horns of the spinal cord acts like a gate which can control the flow of nerve impulses from peripheral neurons to the central nervous system. Factors such as anxiety, attention, and suggestion are assumed to influence pain by acting at the earliest levels of sensory transmission. The degree of cognitive control which can be exerted depends, however, on the spatiotemporal properties of the input patterns. Some pains, such as cardiac pain, arise so rapidly that the sufferer is unable to achieve any control over them. Other pains, which increase more slowly, can be controlled by 'thinking about something else' or by other stratagems. The gate-control theory has led to several new forms of treatment of pain, including ones based on psychological methods, although neurophysiological evidence for a gating mechanism has been hard to find (see Kandel and Schwartz, 1985).

Suggested reading

Atkinson, J. (1984). Human visual development over the first six months of life: a review and a hypothesis. *Human Neurobiology* **3**, 61–74.

This article reviews recent experimental data on infant vision.

Braddick, O.J., Campbell, F.W. and Atkinson, J. (1978). Channels in vision: basic aspects. In: *Handbook of Sensory Physiology. Vol. VIII: Perception*, pp. 1–32. Edited by Held, R., Leibowitz, H.W. and Teuber, H–L. Springer Verlag, Heidelberg. Describes spatial frequency and orientation channels, particularly evidence from psychophysical experiments.

Gregory, R.L. (1971). *The Intelligent Eye*. Weidenfeld & Nicholson, London. A very readable book that argues for perception as a problem-solving and hypothesis-forming process.

Kandel, E. and Schwartz, J. (1985). *Principles of Neural Science* (2nd edn). Elsevier, Amsterdam. See the chapter by Kelly, D.D. on central representations of pain and analgesia for more information on neurophysiological mechanisms.

Marr, D. (1982). *Vision*. W.H. Freeman & Co., San Francisco. This book analyses many aspects of vision as computational processes.

Melzack, R. and Wall, P. (1982). *The Challenge of Pain*. Penguin Books Ltd., Harmondsworth, Middlesex. Provides an excellent introduction to the study of pain drawing together psychological, physiological and clinical evidence.

Moore, B.C.J. (1982). *An Introduction to the Psychology of Hearing* (2nd edn). Academic Press, London. This book describes in more detail the aspects of hearing covered in this chapter, and it includes a brief introduction to the physics of sound and the physiology of the auditory system. The appendix to Chapter 3 gives an introduction to Signal Detection Theory.

Moore, B.C.J. (Ed) (1986). *Frequency Selectivity in Hearing*. Academic Press, London. Contains a series of review chapters covering both physiological aspects and psychological aspects of auditory frequency selectivity. The chapters by Patterson and Moore, Moore and Glasberg, Tyler, and Rosen and Fourcin are particularly relevant.

Weiskrantz, L. (1986). *Blindsight*. Clarendon Press, Oxford. This book describes the remarkable visual abilities that can be found despite damage to the visual cortex.

References

Atkinson, J., Braddick, O.J., Durolen, K., Watson, P.G. and Atkinson, S. (1984). Screening for refractive errors in 6–9 months old infants by photorefraction. *British Journal of Ophthalmology* **68**, 105–22.

Moore, B.C.J. and Glasberg, B.R. (1983). *Journal of the Acoustic Society of America* **74**, 750.

Newman, E.B. (1948). In: *Foundations of Psychology*. Edited by Boring, E.G., Langfield, H.S. and Weld, H.P. John Wiley and Sons, New York.

Vogten, L.L.M. (1974). In: *Facts and Models in Hearing*. Edited by Zwicker, E. and Terhardt, E. Springer-Verlag, Heidelberg.

3

Limitations of Memory and Cognitive Performance

S Monsell

The nervous system represents and processes *information*. It continuously acquires information from the senses, combines it with information already stored in the brain to make decisions, and uses the resulting information to select and control actions and to form new memory traces. How *good* an information-processor is the brain? By certain abstract mathematical criteria of computational power, a large many-layered network of neurons has as much computational power as any other imaginable information-processor: given unlimited time there is almost no computable problem it could not, in principle, compute! But when we descend from mathematical abstraction to the concrete reality of the natural biological and social worlds, the discrepancies between the brain and an 'ideal' processor of information become all too apparent. The time taken to accomplish cognitive processes is critical in real life, and the taking of decisions and initiation of actions under time pressure results in inappropriate or inaccurate outcomes. Born of the rough and tumble of adaptive pressures during evolution, the brain's design (like that of man-made information-processing systems) is evidently a compromise among many conflicting demands and cost considerations. These include not only information-processing needs *per se*, but also constraints such as evolution in small steps from phylogenetically earlier models (rather than the option of redesign from scratch), the need to grow the brain (rather than assemble it), the need to supply it with oxygen and nutrients, the need to protect it from injury and to pass it through a small bony orifice at an early stage in its development. In addition, the adaptive pressures under which the human brain evolved to its present state were in many respects very different from the twentieth century hospital or the control room of a nuclear power station.

In short, the brain we have is far from the best of all possible brains for life in the rapidly changing, high-tech society we live in. It has major limitations of processing and storage capacity, and its 'design' results in characteristic biases, errors, and patterns of breakdown in thought and action. We are all victims of these limitations—medical practitioners included. Most people accept that a practitioner whose cognitive powers are conspicuously failing through age or illness should cease to practise. But we must also make allowance for the fact that even in his/her prime everyone is subject to characteristic failures of cognitive performance. Such failures range from the amusing or merely irritating to the catastrophic. 'Human error' is a familiar verdict in accident investigations, and could well be written on many death certificates. Furthermore, as Three Mile Island and Chernobyl remind us, these are not matters of purely local concern. In the medical context, patients are victims of cognitive failures in two ways: they suffer (even when *compos mentis*) from their own cognitive incompetence and they suffer from that of their doctors.

We cannot return our brains to the manufacturers for an upgrade, but is there nothing we can do? Knowledge about the relationship (albeit somewhat abstractedly statistical) between smoking and cancer led many doctors to give up smoking. Perhaps it is not too much to hope that knowledge about the 'built-in' limitations of human memory and processing abilities (albeit somewhat abstractly psychological) may occasionally help us to mitigate the unfortunate consequences of these limitations. That is one rationale for this chapter. The other is that some understanding of the functional components of memory and cognitive processes, and of their organization, is a prerequisite for understanding patterns of breakdown in cognitive performance that result from brain damage and disease (see Chapter 7).

Components of memory

Traditionally, from Aristotle until at least the eighteenth century, memory was conceived of as one of the four major intellectual faculties of the mind, the others being (in modern English) perception, imagination and reason. This concept of memory as a unitary mechanism is still embodied in ordinary language and continues to influence psychological theorizing; but it is wrong. In the eighteenth and nineteenth centuries, the pioneers of neurology, noticing that brain damage could result in quite selective kinds of memory disorder (as will be detailed below), speculated that different kinds of information were represented in different parts of the cerebral cortex. In the last 30 years, experiments on both normal subjects and brain-damaged patients have clearly established the existence of several distinct types and/or components of memory, although it remains a matter of intense controversy exactly how to draw the boundaries between them. Since memory is not unitary, it does not make sense to ask about the limitations of memory without specifying what kind of memory is under consideration. Thus there follows a brief survey of some of the distinctions among components of memory that we seem to need.

Working (active) memory *v* permanent (inactive) storage

Of the large amount of information stored in our heads, only a microscopic fraction is in an active, highly available, state at any given moment. This active information may include: information just acquired via the senses, information just retrieved or activated from permanent storage, and information resulting from processes that have just been carried out, such as the planning of actions. Information held in this temporary state of high availability is said to be in **working memory**. As I shall suggest below, working memory, like memory in general, is itself divisible into several subcomponents, but at least two properties appear to characterize working memory as a whole:

1. Information is lost from working memory within a matter of seconds unless maintained by an active attention-demanding rehearsal process
2. Only a very limited amount of information can be held simultaneously in working memory at one time. These properties are demonstrated in some standard tests of short-term memory function.

Free recall

If a subject is presented, just once, with a long random sequence of stimuli (usually words), and then immediately asked to recall as many as he can, without respect to their order, the probability of recalling a particular item depends systematically on the position of the item in the sequence (Fig. 3.1). The last three or four items are remembered especially well (a **recency effect**). To the subject, these last few items seem immediately available in consciousness without effort, while items from earlier in the list are recovered, if at all, as the result of a more effortful search process. William James, in his celebrated book *The Principles of Psychology* (1890), noting this distinction between the effortless availability of information from the immediate past and the struggle to recover older information, attributed it to retrieval from different memory systems, which he called 'primary' and 'secondary' memory, respectively. Are these really distinct kinds of memory? There is now good evidence that they are.

First, different variables influence the probability of recall of the last few items and of earlier items. As Figure 3.1a shows, if, between the end of the sequence and the recall attempt, the subject must perform a distracting task for only a few seconds, the recency effect is selectively abolished; recall of the final items is reduced to the level of recall of the earlier items, but recall of the earlier items is unaffected. Figure 3.1b shows the opposite pattern. The rate at which the items were presented, and the total length of the sequence both influence (as do many other variables) the level of recall of the non-final items of the list, but the size of the 'recency' effect is quite unaltered. When two measures of performance are influenced by quite different variables in this way, it is hard to avoid the conclusion that distinct storage mechanisms are involved. Notice, however, that even at the

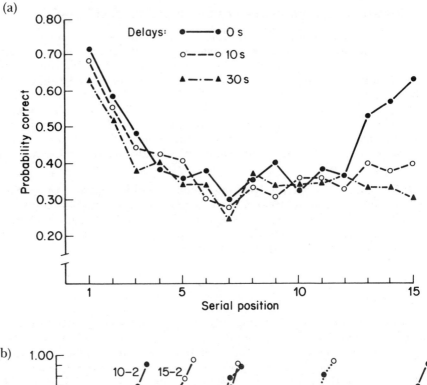

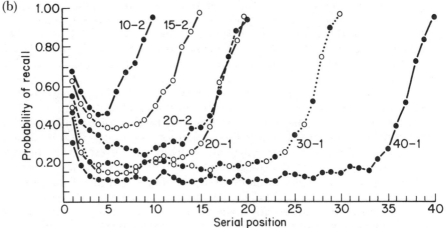

Fig. 3.1 Probability of recall plotted as a function of serial position of the item, for free recall of a word list. (a) Data showing the elimination of the recency effect by a delay occupied by an irrelevant task interpolated between the end of the sequence and recall. (Reproduced from Glanzer, M. and Cunitz, A.R. (1966) by permission of Academic Press, New York. (b) Data showing the effects of variations in the rate of presentation (1 or 2 s per word) and list length (10–40 words). (Reproduced, with

(c)

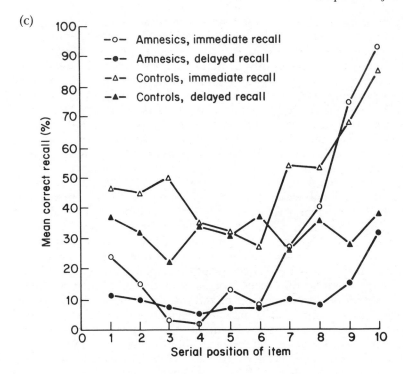

permission, from Murdock, B.B.Jr. (1962) by permission of the American Psychological Association. (c) Data comparing the performance of normal and amnesic subjects (redrawn from Baddeley, A.D. and Warrington, E.K. (1970).)

shortest delay, there is still some probability that information can be recovered from permanent storage as well as from working memory. One should not assume (though the medical literature sometimes does) that a short-term memory test (i.e. one testing retention over a short interval) necessarily tests retrieval *only* from a mechanism specialized for temporary storage.

A second kind of evidence comes from neurological patients exhibiting the **amnesic syndrome**. One of the best-studied 'pure' cases is HM, an engineering worker who, in 1953, in his late twenties, was operated upon in an experimental procedure intended to relieve his incapacitating and worsening epileptic seizures. (The procedure involved a radical bilateral medial temporal lobe resection, destroying the anterior two-thirds of the hippocampus, as well as the uncus and amygdala.) It was successful in alleviating the epileptic symptoms, but left HM with a profound memory impairment. Although he can remember events he experienced and facts he acquired up to about two years before the surgery, he can remember essentially nothing that has occurred since. He recalls nothing of day-to-day events in his own life or the world at large. He does not know what he had for lunch an hour ago, how he came to be where he now is, where he has left objects he has used recently, or that he has used them. He reads the same magazine over and over again. He has learned neither the names of doctors and psychologists who have worked with him for decades nor the route to the house he moved to a few years after the surgery. Yet, if we allow for his dislocation from that knowledge of one's spatio-temporal framework that normally underpins social discourse and one's sense of personal identity, HM is not intellectually impaired: his language comprehension and production and conversational skills are normal, he can reason competently and do mental arithmetic. His IQ (Wechsler), measured in 1962, was an above-average 117—higher than the 104 measured pre-surgery in 1953. Several pure cases like HM, resulting from a variety of traumas—anoxia, penetrating wounds, and herpes encephalitis,[1] have now been described in the literature. A somewhat larger group of Korsakoff syndrome patients have also been extensively studied: these suffer an amnesia that is usually less 'pure', because of the degenerative nature of the disease and the complicating effects of associated frontal lobe damage. Figure 3.1c shows performance by a mixed group of amnesic patients on the free recall task, compared to matched normal subjects. The patients' ability to recall the non-final items is impaired, as is performance on the final items when the recency effect has been abolished by several seconds of a distracting task. But their recency effect is normal, as are other measures of working memory (see below). This neurological dissociation supports the idea that the temporary retention of information in working memory and the permanent storage of new information depend on different brain mechanisms.

Memory span

This is another simple test of short-term memory commonly employed in a clinical setting; it is also a component of IQ tests (see Chapter 6). A short random sequence of words (e.g. digits, letter names, common nouns) is presented to the subject one at a time. The subject immediately tries to recall the sequence *in the correct order*. The length of the sequence is increased until it can no longer be reproduced without error. Memory span is normally defined as the sequence length at which the subject reproduces 50 per cent of sequences correctly. For the population at large, average span is about 7 digits, or about 5 disyllabic words. The contrast between this severe limit on our ability to reproduce a *novel* sequence and the lack of limit on our ability to reproduce a verbal sequence *after learning it* (e.g. the Lord's Prayer, the Declaration of Independence) demonstrates the **limited capacity** of working memory. But does span, like the recency effect in free recall, reflect a type of memory distinct from permanent storage? Again,

---

[1] Readers may have seen a recent Channel 4 television documentary on one such patient.

experiments on both neurological patients and normal subjects say it does. HM, for example, has a normal digit span of 7 digits, i.e. he will reproduce novel sequences of 7 digits without error on about half the trials. But an attempt to get him to learn by repetition to reproduce without error a particular list of 8 digits failed completely. (A normal subject is able to learn to reproduce such a list perfectly after only a few repetitions.) Warrington and Shallice have also described brain-damaged patients with a selective impairment of short-term memory—e.g. a span of only 2–3 digits, but normal long-term learning. Thus, there seems to be a double neurological dissociation between span and measures of long-term sequence learning. Normal performance also exhibits a double dissociation. A classic study by Baddeley showed that immediate reproduction of a short sequence of words was heavily impaired when they *sounded* similar (e.g. man, mad, map, ...) but not when they had similar *meanings* (e.g. large, huge, wide, ...). In contrast, reproduction after 20 minutes of a 10-word sequence learned through several repetitions was impaired if the words had similar meanings, but not if their spoken forms were similar. Thus, working memory and permanent storage mechanisms used for sequence-reproduction apparently use different codes. There is much other evidence that retention of verbal sequence information in working memory appears to depend largely on a **speech code**, even when presentation is visual and recall is in writing.

Distraction paradigms

A third kind of short-term memory test should be mentioned briefly. It is used, sometimes in a clinical setting, to determine the rate of loss from working memory. A subject is presented briefly with an amount of information small enough to be reproducible immediately without error— e.g. a sequence of 3 consonants. He must then perform an attention-demanding unrelated task, such as counting backwards by threes, for several seconds before being cued to recall the information. Typically, recall declines rapidly as the retention interval is increased, reaching a stable but low plateau after 20–30 seconds. Figure 3.2 shows the forgetting of a 3-consonant sequence by patients suffering from senile dementia of the Alzheimer type (SDAT) and normal elderly control subjects. Data from the latter exemplify the standard finding: a cognitively demanding distract-ing task (as in the right panel) causes rapid forgetting, while sitting in silence or merely articulating "the-the-the---" (as in the left panel) does not. Small sets of information can be maintained in working memory indefin-itely by active **rehearsal**, but when rehearsal is prevented (by the cognitively demanding task), working memory traces are rapidly displaced or over-written, leaving recall to be supported only by whatever permanent trace the subject has succeeding in forming. Typically, after several trials on similar material, the level of asymptotic recall becomes very low. This is because the formation of permanent traces sufficiently distinctive to support later recall is slow and effortful (see below). In contrast, repre-

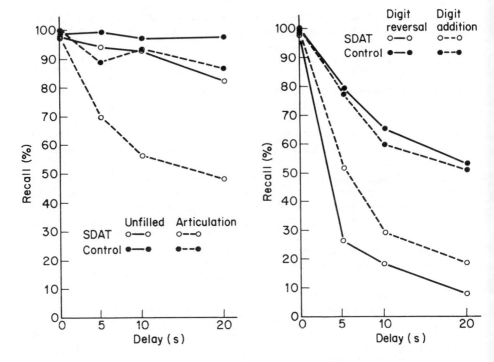

Fig. 3.2 Per cent correct recall of a three-consonant list as a function of retention interval, for patients with senile dementia of the Alzheimer's type (SDAT) and matched elderly control subjects. The retention interval was unfilled, or occupied by irrelevant articulation ('the-the-the . . .',) a digit reversal task (E: '6, 2'→S: '2, 6'), or a digit addition task (E: '6, 2'→S: '8' (Reproduced from Morris, R.G. (1986) by permission of Lawrence Erlbaum Associates, London.)

sentation in working memory seems to be an automatic consequence of attending to the material. What about the performance of the SDAT patients in Morris' experiment? They show: 1. a lower level of asymptotic recall (poorer permanent trace formation?), and 2. more rapid forgetting with tasks everyone finds distracting, and 3. rapid forgetting even with a concurrent task others find undemanding (less 'processing capacity' available for rehearsal?).

Subcomponents of working memory

That working memory and permanent storage involve distinct processes or mechanisms thus seems fairly clear. However, each is itself further divisible into components. Figure 3.3 summarizes one view of some subdivisions of working memory. As these are either of little clinical consequence, or controversial, or both, they will only be mentioned briefly.

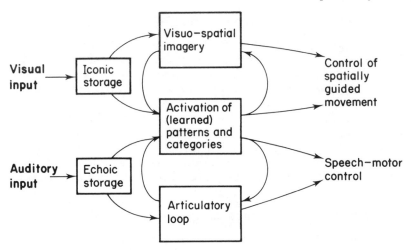

Fig. 3.3 Some hypothetical components of working memory.

Iconic and echoic memory

Information registered in the visual pathway persists for something of the order of half a second beyond the physical stimulus under normal conditions of illumination. Such persistence can be detected by various experimental techniques, and has led to the theoretical construct of **iconic memory**—a large-capacity but very short-lived 'buffer store' representing visual information prior to categorization and registration in longer-lived, but capacity-limited, forms of working memory. An analogous mechanism, which retains briefly and in relatively unanalysed form perhaps the last two-seconds' worth of speech input, has also been identified, and is sometimes called **echoic memory**. Even these distinctions are almost certainly oversimplifications. It is likely that information persists briefly at several levels in each sensory pathway.

Visuospatial *v* verbal working memory

It has become clear that we possess distinct limited-capacity mechanisms for the temporary representation and manipulation of spatial arrays or patterns, on the one hand, and verbal sequence, on the other. Rather than attempt to describe the data, I shall merely convey the basic distinction in introspective terms. Visuospatial working memory, or **imagery**, is engaged when you imagine what the Taj Mahal looks like, mentally count the number of windows in your house, or work out how many surfaces are created when a cube is cut in half along two planes (try it!); the verbal rehearsal loop is engaged when you silently rehearse a phone number you have looked up but not yet dialled, or rehearse and review an utterance you are about to emit.

Sequence retention v passive registration of the last few 'chunks'

It has recently become clear that the recency effect in free recall, and memory span, as described above, although both measures of 'working memory', may be measures of different components of working memory. As noted above, span is influenced by a number of variables, including sound similarity and the spoken duration of the words (e.g. digits versus disyllabic words), indicating that a speech coding mechanism is involved in the temporary retention of word order. But the recency effect in free recall is uninfluenced by such variables. Instead, a small (two or three) but constant number of the last few 'meaningful units' experienced seem to be retained in a highly available state by a mechanism not specific to speech.

Subcomponents of permanent storage

Permanent storage too is not a unitary system, and there is no less controversy about its components (see Squire (1987) for review). Here, briefly, are three hypothesized distinctions.

'Procedural' v 'declarative' memory

Research on profoundly amnesic patients like HM has shown that though they have become unable to learn new information in the sense of remembering new experiences, names, faces, routes, or facts, they typically retain the ability to learn skills or procedures. For example, their performance improves at a fairly normal rate from session to session if they practise on tasks such as the pursuit rotor (keeping a stylus in contact with a target moving in a roughly circular track), detecting hidden figures, or inferring the rule predicting a sequence of numbers. But they have no awareness or 'declarative' knowledge of the episodes during which they practised these skills. Brain damage may also cause the selective impairment of particular cognitive skills (as in the aphasias, agnosias, apraxias, etc.—see Chapter 7) without loss of the ability to remember episodes or facts. It seems necessary to conclude that the learning of skills or procedures ('knowing how') on the one hand, and declarative knowledge ('knowing that') on the other, depend on distinct mechanisms.

Visuospatial v linguistic memory

Normal right-handed patients with substantial temporal lobe lesions limited to the right hemisphere tend to show major impairment in learning nonsense figures, geometrical patterns, faces, and tonal melodies, but are less impaired in the learning of verbal material (rote lists, stories, etc). The converse pattern is observed with comparable left hemisphere lesions. This suggests some localization in the brain of permanent storage of different types of information. However, claims for a complete dissociation would certainly be premature.

Episodic *v* semantic memory

It seems intuitively reasonable to make a distinction between memory for individual episodes which we have personally experienced, and memory for general knowledge about the world, or our language, which, although originally derived from individual episodes, seems now represented in a form abstracted from and independent of those episodes. Some psychologists, notably Tulving, have proposed that different memory systems may be involved (rather than different kinds of information stored within the same system). However, this claim has, so far, received little experimental support.

One reason for emphasizing the distinction between working memory and permanent memory is that they limit our cognitive performance in quite different ways. The problem with working memory mechanisms is their limited capacity and lability. This causes problems when we need to keep several pieces of information 'in mind' simultaneously. Mental arithmetic is an obvious example. If you add or multiply multidigit numbers together in your head, you must temporarily store digits not yet processed, any products of the calculation to date, any 'carry' digits generated, not to mention some record of the goals of the computation and of where you have got to in it. It has, in fact, been shown (by Hitch, 1978) that a substantial proportion of the errors in such tasks can be accounted for in terms of the interval for which particular digits must be held before operating upon them, or between generating them (in the head) and saying them (aloud). Analogous problems arise in most reasoning tasks of even moderate complexity, and in interacting with complex control systems. In a later section of the chapter, I discuss the general problem of capacity limits in simultaneously processing multiple sources of information, or carrying out simultaneous tasks.

Before doing that, I will review the limitations of permanent memory for both individual episodes we have experienced and general knowledge. Here, the problem is not so much the capacity for retaining different pieces of information simultaneously (effectively infinite), but rather the severe limits placed on both the consolidation of memory traces and on the ease and accuracy of later retrieval.

Permanent memory and its limitations

The most obvious problem with memory is that we forget! The relevance of this to medical practice, as to most other areas of endeavour, is evident. Doctors are supposed to have at their command quantities of information about anatomy, physiology, histology, pathology and pharmacology—not to mention information about specific patients, colleagues, clinics, hospitals, etc. Doctors also rely heavily upon their patients' memory when taking histories and prescribing a course of treatment. A number of studies have been conducted of patients' ability to remember what a doctor has told them during a consultation. Ley (1977) reviews eleven such studies. (See also Ley, 1977). The time elapsing between the presentation of the information and its recall varied from almost no delay up to several months, and a variety of procedures were used. All the studies, even those in which patients were tested after less than an hour, found them to forget something between one quarter and three quarters of what they were told. That so much should be forgotten is not an immutable fact of life. A number of experimental attempts to improve recall in real life settings have obtained modest, but significant, improvements using fairly commonsense techniques such as repetition, explicit categorization, simplification, and conveying the most critical information first (Ley, 1977; 1982).

Learning and forgetting

In the 1880s, the pioneering German psychologist Ebbinghaus painstakingly taught himself sequences of nonsense syllables upon which he then tested himself after various intervals. He discovered a simple rule of thumb about the time-course of forgetting which still holds true: other things being equal, forgetting is roughly linear in log time (see Fig. 3.4). Thus, one forgets (on average) about as much between 15 and 30 minutes after the information is learned as one forgets between 1 and 2 days after learning. (Ebbinghaus estimated forgetting by finding out how many trials he needed to relearn the sequence.) But what causes the loss of information during the retention interval? The layman tends to assume that forgetting results principally from the decay or dissipation of memory traces in the

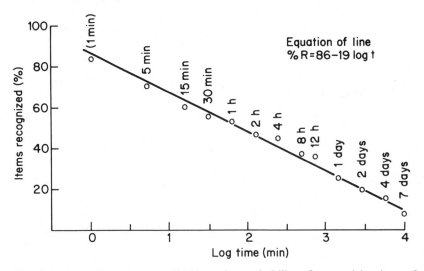

Fig. 3.4   Data (from Strong, 1913) on the probability of recognizing items from a twenty-word list previously presented just once, as a function of the interval since presentation. (Reproduced from Woodworth, R.S. (1938) by permission of Henry Holt, New York.)

brain with the passage of time. However, it is frequently the case in ordinary experience, as in the laboratory, that a fact, or name, or episode that one has 'forgotten' on one occasion can be retrieved later, perhaps when one is prompted with a suitable cue. Hence, 'forgetting' must sometimes be a matter of **retrieval failure** rather than loss from storage. It has, in fact, proved hard clearly to demonstrate *any* loss of information resulting merely from the passage of time *per se* (except when significant neurological degeneration occurs during the interval, as in dementias of the Alzheimer type). Hence, modern theories construe forgetting largely as a matter of retrieval failure.

Three major (but not independent) factors promoting retrieval failure can be distinguished; interference due to the storage in memory of other information of the same kind, the contextual specificity of retrieval, and the processing carried out at acquisition.

Associative interference

In the middle years of this century, many experiments were carried out in which a subject had to learn lists of 'paired associates'. These were arbitrary pairings of words, so that the subject might have to learn that, when presented with the cue '3', he is supposed to respond with the word 'angel', when with the cue '7', the response 'cabbage', etc. After learning such a list (List 1) to some criterion, the subject would have to learn another list (List 2). Finally, he would be retested on List 1. Two phenomena were immediately apparent. The more similar the materials of the two lists were, (a) the harder it was to learn List 2 to criterion, and (b) the harder it was to recall the appropriate items of List 1 on the final retest. These two phenomena were labelled **proactive inhibition** and **retroactive inhibition**, respectively, and much labour was expended exploring their determinants: the type of similarity between the two lists, the intervals between the two learning episodes and between them and the test, and the similarity of the material to other material previously learned. It was found that interference between the lists was most marked when the same cues were used in the two lists, paired with different responses. The associations formed in memory between a given cue and the two responses appear to *compete*. When the cue is presented, both associations are activated, but each competes with the other for control of the response.

Arbitrary paired associations between cue and verbal response were used by these researchers on the assumption that they captured and laid bare the elementary associations out of which more complex memory traces were constructed. To a contemporary eye, these experiments look rather artificial. Is associative interference an important factor in the forgetting of more natural materials?

Anderson and his colleagues (Anderson, 1980) have conducted experiments in which subjects learn a set of propositions about a group of (imaginary) people. In one experiment, for example, the propositions were noun-adjective descriptions of the form: 'the tailor is clever', 'the fireman is tall'. Subjects might learn anything from one to four properties of each person. After learning, the subject was tested by asking him to respond 'True' (i.e. I learned this) or 'False' (i.e. I did not) to test propositions, as quickly as possible. The basic finding was that average verification time increased with the number of 'facts' learned about a person. In other words, if you have learned that a particular tailor is clever, then (all other things being equal) it takes you longer to verify the proposition 'The tailor is clever' if you have also learned that he is lame and right-handed. More generally stated, the more pieces of information you have associated to X, the more interference with your ability to access one of those pieces via X. Anderson and his student Lewis extended this research further into the domain of 'natural' knowledge with an experiment in which they taught subjects a varied number of pseudofacts about historical figures already known to them. You might, for example, be taught that 'Napoleon was born in India'. The propositions to be verified in the test included actual facts ('Napoleon was an emperor'), 'experimental true' facts (i.e. the pseudofacts learned) and other false propositions, and subjects were instructed to respond 'True' to the first two. As Figure 3.5 shows, verification time increased with the number of pseudofacts learned about the person not only for the pseudofacts, but also for real facts they already knew.

In the case of ordinary experience or knowledge, the detailed associative structure of the information recorded in memory, since not carefully designed into the material by an experimenter, is often impossible to specify. Nevertheless, it can be shown that the forgetting of particular episodes or facts is dependent much more on intervening exposure to similar episodes and facts than on the passage of time between experiencing the episode (or learning the information) and the retrieval attempt. Baddeley and Hitch asked members of two rugby clubs to recall all the games they had played over the season. Naturally, some games were more memorable or significant than others, but there was also an overall trend for earlier games to be recalled with a lower probability. Is this forgetting due to the passage of time or to interference from memories of subsequent games? As many players had missed some games it was possible to separate the two effects. It turned out that with the number of intervening games held constant, there was no significant correlation between forgetting and elapsed time. Thus, the observed forgetting can be attributed largely to the number of intervening games. In another study, Baddeley and colleagues were able to attribute a substantial component of people's failure to remember where they parked on a previous visit to the Medical Research Council's Applied Psychology Unit in Cambridge to interference from memories of subsequent visits (Baddeley, 1986).

One implication of the associative interference demonstrated in Anderson's experiments may seem paradoxical: if you want to remember a fact about something, don't learn more about that something! Can it really be the case that the more information you know about X, the harder it is to remember a piece of it, given X as a retrieval cue? The answer seems to be:

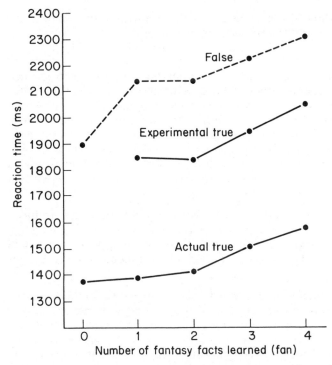

Fig. 3.5 Data (from Lewis and Anderson, 1976) on time taken to decide 'true' or 'false' of test sentences about famous figures, as a function of the number of 'fantasy facts' learned about them in the experiment. (Reproduced from Anderson, J.R. (1980) by permission of W.H. Freeman and Co., San Francisco.)

yes, but only if the several facts you learn are quite *independent* of each other. This is quite rare in practice. What happens when the facts are not independent? Subsequent researchers have conducted versions of Anderson's experiments in which the several facts learned are thematically related. (For example, 'the princess went to the shipyard'; 'the princess broke the bottle'; 'the princess received a bouquet'). Under these conditions, Anderson's effect is not observed. Hence, when one has learned the associations X→A and X→B, the effects of the interference between them can be compensated for if extra associations are available in memory linking A to B. The practical implication is obvious: try to *integrate* the various facts you know about something.

Contextual specificity of memory

The general rule is that information may be more easily recalled if the retrieval attempt is made in the same 'context' as that in which the information was acquired. 'Context' may include: material presented concurrently with the to-be-learned material, the physiological state of the individual, his mood, and the physical environment.

Some examples:

- In an experiment by Eich *et al.* (see Anderson, 1980) subjects learned word lists after smoking either marijuana or an ordinary cigarette. Four hours later they were tested again after smoking marijuana or an ordinary cigarette. Recall was significantly higher when the test was conducted under the influence of the same narcotic as at learning (even though learning was substantially worse under marijuana). Similar results have been obtained for alcohol intoxication and high levels of adrenaline. This phenomenon is sometimes called 'state-dependent learning'.

- Bower and colleagues taught subjects word lists in hypnotically induced happy or sad states and found that they recalled significantly more when tested in the same state. Similar mood-dependence appears to apply to the recall of personal experiences and childhood memories (see Bower, 1981).

- Godden and Baddeley taught word lists to divers either beneath the surface of the sea or on land, and found that average recall was improved when the divers were tested in the same environment (see Baddeley, 1982). Interestingly, this effect was not significant when memory was tested using a recognition measure (i.e. was this word on the list—yes or no?).

If one thinks of memorizing a particular piece of information as putting an isolated fragment of learning into a storehouse, like a book into a library, then these context effects might seem surprising. But that is an inappropriate metaphor for learning. To learn even a single 'item' in a list-learning experiment, let alone a 'natural fact', involves the formation of a *complex* of novel associations among elements available during the learning episode: fragments of meaning or imagery evoked by the item, its sound or appearance, and/or elements of the context. Contextual elements may both be incorporated into the trace (indeed, for some kinds of learning, they must be) and the learning context also influences the elements of pre-existing knowledge activated by an item. (For example, in the context of moving house, the word 'piano' is more likely to evoke thoughts of its weight than in a context of musical appreciation.) From this perspective, it would be surprising if contextual specificity was not observed.

What are the practical consequences of contextual specificity? If you need to be able to recall a piece of information or a procedure in only one environment and state (e.g. sober and in the operating theatre), then you should train in that environment and state. On the other hand, information you need to remember irrespective of your environment and state will most reliably be remembered if you study it in a variety of contexts. This may provide at least a partial account of the well-attested advantage of 'spaced' over 'massed' practice: given a fixed amount of time to learn something, the task is better spaced out over several learning episodes than done in one session. Spaced practice will tend to involve a greater variety of physiological and environmental contexts.

Processing at acquisition

The third major factor determining whether you will later remember material is what you do while learning it. All other things being equal, the more time you devote to learning material, the greater the probability of later recall. But much more important than the time spent is what you do with that time. One learning strategy that seems to occur naturally to people is rote rehearsal. For example, when given a series of items to memorize, as in the free recall task mentioned earlier, people tend to rehearse the last few words presented as more arrive. This rote rehearsal does improve later recall: the greater number of rehearsals received by the first few items in the sequence can be shown to account for the superior recall of the first two or three items in this task (Fig. 3.1). But rote rehearsal is relatively inefficient as a general learning strategy, even for random word lists. Much more useful is to process and elaborate the *meaning* of the material. There are numerous demonstrations that incidental learning (i.e. learning without deliberate intention to learn) of a random set of words is more effective if people are required to make judgements about the meanings of the words, rather than attend to their appearances or sounds (see Anderson, 1980, and Baddeley, 1982 for review). There are also experiments showing that merely getting people to organize and classify words by meaning can, under some circumstances, result in just as much learning (as measured by a later unexpected recall or recognition test) as trying to learn the material in anticipation of a test ('incidental' *v* 'intentional' learning).

To 'process and elaborate meaning' involves (a) making contact with a framework of pre-existing knowledge, and (b) forming a nexus of redundant associations linking the elements you want to remember to that framework and to each other. There are a number of mnemonic techniques that force you to do both. (See Morris, 1979, and Bellezza, 1981, for reviews.) For example, to use the 'method of loci', developed in classical antiquity as a technique for remembering speeches, you first learn a framework: a route through a series of locations in a familiar building or park. To learn the speech, you proceed (in imagination) through the series of locations one by one, 'placing' a bizarre image representing the next idea in your speech at each successive imaginary location. Later, when giving the speech, you follow the same route in your mind's eye, reading off the images, and interpreting them. Modern experimental work has confirmed that this and other standard mnemonic techniques, many involving imagery, can be highly effective. There has been some debate about whether the use of visual images *per se* is critical. Probably the virtue of imagery is merely that it tends to enforce *interactive* elaboration, and thus interconnection, of the elements to be learned. The construction of a story can also be an efficient mnemonic for remembering paired associates, but only if the story links the members of the pair (Bellezza, 1981). Nor does the bizarreness of the image recommended by the classical authors seem to be critical to the method of loci: perhaps it merely helps to encourage a *distinctive* elaboration.

Each mnemonic technique is specialized for a particular purpose. For example, the method of loci is designed for ensuring that a series of ideas is reproduced *without omission* and *in the right order*. It is, moreover, important that this mnemonic be reusable: a new set of images, representing another speech, can be 'placed' along the same route, with surprisingly little interference from a previous set. A rather different technique frequently recommended to medical students is the first-letter mnemonic. Shipman (1984) provides a list, from which the following example is taken. To remember the factors predisposing to carcinoma of the stomach, one learns:

> **S**pirits, **S**moking?
> **T**opographical: Japan
> **O**ther members of the family
> **M**egaloblastic anaemia, atrophic **M**ucosa, and achlorhydria
> **'A'** blood group
> **C**hronic gastric ulcer (2 per cent become malignant)
> **H**ypertrophic gastritis

The framework for this mnemonic is the spelling pattern of a word closely related to the condition, in this case 'stomach'. Provided that one does later remember the appropriate first-letter acronym, i.e. 'stomach' rather than, say, 'gastric', this mnemonic has the virtue of being *exhaustive*: it prompts you to try and recover an idea for each of the letters, and until you have, you know you've omitted something. But, as Wilding *et al.* (1986) point out, studies of the effectiveness of first-letter mnemonics have obtained mixed results, and the reason is probably the difficulty of learning the connections between the initial letters (e.g. S) and the associated terms (Spirits, Smoking). Wilding *et al.* (1986) were able to improve, significantly, the effectiveness of this mnemonic by instructing subjects to use in addition an imagery technique. (For example, it might be suggested that the letter S looks like a snake, and that the learner imagine that the winding and curling movement of the snake is like that of smoke from a cigar and the movements of supernatural spirits).

It should by now be clear that mnemonics, although they can be extremely effective, are not magical, nor are their benefits bought without costs. Mental labour must be invested to learn both the framework and the connections between what one wants to remember and the framework.

Biases and distortions in retrieval

So far we have been considering outright failures of retrieval. When we cannot recall a name or a fact, we are at least aware that memory has failed us, and will thus be prompted to resort to a colleague, a reference book, or a database, for the missing information. However, there constantly occur memory failures of a more subtle kind, in which we succeed, or at least appear to succeed, in retrieving relevant information, but the information retrieved is biased or distorted in some way.

Distortion due to pre-existing knowledge

A clinician has in his head much *general* knowledge about disease syndromes, prototypical patterns of pathology and their development, treatment outcomes, etc. Naturally, the symptoms presented by individual patients rarely fit these prototypical patterns exactly. Some depart from the prototype within what might be called 'expected' ranges of variation; others are really quite atypical. The clinician's memory has, then, to maintain two kinds of related, but (in a sense) conflicting information: on the one hand the details of *particular* patients, and, on the other, *prototypical* diagnostic patterns. Nor are these *specific* and *general* components of knowledge even logically independent, since general knowledge is, to a large extent, derived from individual instances—hence the importance attached to clinical experience.

There is ample evidence that prior general knowledge has distorting influences on either memory for, or reasoning about, particular instances. In the 1920s Bartlett found that when Cambridge undergraduates recalled an American Indian folk tale they had read, their recall tended to distort the story to bring it more into line both with the standard European 'schema' of a narrative, and with the modern taste for rational causal explanations of events. Many studies since have shown that knowledge of standard 'scenarios', such as 'eating in a restaurant' will influence the recall of particular narratives involving those scenarios. (For instance, a waiter may be 'remembered', though never mentioned.) Studies directly relevant to the medical context are harder to come by, but there is at least one study (Arkes and Harkness, 1980) indicating that when people are tested on their ability to remember details of an individual or a situation about which they have formed a diagnosis (e.g. a developmental abnormality in a child, a fault in a central heating system), they tend to forget details which were atypical or inconsistent with their diagnosis, and to 'remember' falsely details they were not told, but which are consistent with their diagnosis.

Diagnoses influence not only one's memory for past instances, but one's ability to deal effectively with present ones. There is evidence that, in forming a diagnosis, people tend to retrieve a pattern from memory that fits only a subset of the presenting symptoms, fail to check the remaining symptoms for consistency with the memorized pattern, and are reluctant to abandon their diagnosis in the face of evident contradictions. It would be comforting to suppose that professional training acts to minimize the effects of these bad cognitive habits, but there is little evidence that it does. Investigations of accidents at sea or in the electrical power industry repeatedly find that disasters happen because professional, competent, seamen and engineers lose valuable time in responding to an emergency because of adhering to hypotheses about what is going wrong that are compatible with only a small amount of the information available to them.

Distorting effects of specific knowledge upon retrieval-based generalizations

Some of the general knowledge upon which we rely in reaching decisions is acquired in the form of abstract rules or probabilistic principles, such as 'approximately 10 per cent of all males have anomalies of colour vision'. But many generalizations, especially estimates of probability, are arrived at, consciously or unconsciously, by abstracting in retrospect from our own experience of particular instances. Estimates of probabilities so derived must, perforce, be dependent on our ability to *retrieve* from memory relevant instances, and hence, as Tversky and Kahneman (1973) have demonstrated, biased by the *availability* from memory of specific instances.[2] Unfortunately, availability is determined by many factors unrelated to *representativeness*. As we have already seen, availability may depend on recency, on similarity to the present retrieval context, and on the ways in which memory for particular kinds of information is organized. Try the following example to get the flavour of the last of these. Is the letter K more likely to occur in the first position or the third position in the words of a typical English text? About two-thirds of Tversky and Kahneman's subjects said the first position. In fact, K occurs in the third position nearly twice as often as in the first. Why the misestimate? Because our mental lexicon is so organized that, as in a dictionary, words beginning with a particular letter (or sound) are much easier to *retrieve* than words with that letter in any other position.

Distortion in memory for events due to postevent questions

Research on eyewitness testimony, especially by Loftus and her colleagues (Loftus, 1979) has shown that one important source of distortion in memory for events is the questions asked of the witness. This happens in two ways. One is well known, especially to courtroom lawyers: a person in a state of uncertainty can be pushed towards one answer or another by judicious framing of the question ("You didn't feel nauseous when taking this drug before, did you?" versus "Some people feel nauseous when taking this drug. Did you?") The second is more subtle. The questions asked about a prior event at one time can considerably distort the answers given to later

[2] See Chapter 6 for discussion of other ways in which our probabilistic and deductive reasoning is non-optimal.

questions about the event. For example, in one experiment, a large group of subjects viewed a film of a traffic accident involving a minor collision between two cars. Then they filled in a questionnaire. For one group the questions included "About how fast were the cars going when they hit each other?" For another group the questions were identical, except that the word 'hit' in this particular question was replaced by the words 'smashed into'. An immediate biasing effect of this phrasing was evident in the speed estimates. The second group gave an average speed estimate about 30 per cent higher than the first. But there was also a delayed effect. One week later, the subjects were (unexpectedly) asked some more questions about the film, including the question "Did you see any broken glass?". (In fact, they had not.) Only about 14 per cent of the 'hit' subjects thought they had seen broken glass, while 32 per cent of the 'smash' subjects thought they had. Similar results have been obtained using other measures of memory for the incident, such as picture recognition or drawing. Evidently, inferences made while replying to questions either add to, or change, information stored in memory from the actual event itself. In reconstructing an event from fragments retrieved from memory, a person may be quite unable to discriminate between information derived from the event itself and that derived from postevent questions.

Limitations in processing capacity

From limitations in our ability to store and retrieve information we now turn to consider limitations in processing capacity. We cannot proceed without at least a crude starting assumption about how the brain's processing capacities are organized. In contrast to the organization of a digital computer in which the generalized processing power of a single CPU (central processing unit) is applied (sequentially) to many different kinds of computation, regardless of their content or meaning, it is clear that in most, possibly even all, cases, neurons are organized into specialized centres or 'modules' each of which is responsible for carrying out a specialized type of processing. As one example, it is the job of striate cortex (Brodman's Area 17) to provide other visual processing modules with a two-dimensional spatial map of certain primitive visual attributes of the current retinal image (see Chapter 2). Another example is provided by a rather ill-defined area of cortex around the angular gyrus in the left hemisphere. In normal right-handed people this area is clearly specialized for aspects of spoken language. The demarcation of functional modules of the brain and their anatomical localization will doubtless keep psychologists and neuroscientists occupied for centuries to come, but the general principle—of a system in which different kinds of processing are carried out in separate and partially autonomous 'modules'—seems well established. This being so, to perform one cognitive skill (rather than another) must somehow involve activating (or inhibiting) *linkages* between modules, and enabling the transmission of information among them in such a way as to carry out the appropriate specialized operations in the appropriate sequence. Given this kind of architecture, where might capacity limitations arise in task performance? There are (at least) four possibilities.

Within-module limitations on processing rate and representational capacity

Any one processing module can only do a certain amount of processing work of a certain quality in a given time. Representational limits have already been discussed; for example, we appear to be limited to representing concurrently (i.e. in active or 'working' memory) only a few seconds' worth of speech. The rate at which information can be consolidated into long-term episodic memory is also evidently very limited. So is the rate at which we can understand speech, type, etc. (In relation to the integrated circuits used in computers, individual neurons are really very slow computational devices: snyaptic activation takes something of the order of 1–10 ms in comparison to the nanosecond instruction execution times achieved in microchips. The brain achieves its computational power through massively parallel processing, but information must nevertheless be transmitted through several synaptic relays to accomplish any significant episode of processing, which is why even the simplest voluntary response to the simplest signal takes of the order of one-fifth of a second to initiate.)

Limitations on the processing of simultaneous inputs

A particular processing module may be inherently unable to process input from more than one source at a time. For example, since the late 1950s, there has been much research on people's difficulty in processing two different speech messages simultaneously. This is often, for obvious reasons, called the 'cocktail party problem'. In the typical experiment two streams of words are played to a subject simultaneously. Frequently, 'dichotic' presentation is used: one stream to the left channel of a stereo headset, and another to the right. In **divided attention** experiments, subjects have to try and process both messages. For instance, they might have to try to detect target words in either message, or remember the content of both messages. In **focused attention** experiments subjects try to extract information from one message while ignoring the other. A frequently used focused attention task is 'shadowing': the subject has to repeat back one of the two messages while ignoring the other. (An example is discussed in Chapter 9.) Such experiments (including the Corteen and Wood experiment discussed in Chapter 9) have shown that, although *words* from separate and simultaneous sources may, under some circumstances, be simultaneously identified and activate their meanings, we certainly cannot simultaneously understand the meaning of two different *sentences* at once (see Allport, 1980, for review).[3] The processing module(s) responsible for assigning a syntactic structure and an interpretation to a sentence on the basis of the meaning and syntactic class of its constituent words cannot, it seems, deal with words from more than one message at a time.

Given this limitation, it is usually necessary to *select* one of several available messages for processing. In focused attention experiments people are generally good at processing the content of one message and ignoring another, *provided that* the two messages differ in their *physical source*—i.e. the two streams of words come from different locations in space, or different voices. How does the listener succeed in preventing the words heard in the ignored message from overloading the capacity of their sentence comprehension module? We seem to have a selective filter we can 'tune' to one source. In the case of speech comprehension, a source is defined in terms of physical attributes of a speaker, such spatial location and voice pitch. In the case of vision, the source appears to be defined in terms of a spatial window or 'spotlight' whose size can be varied, depending on the scale of the objects being processed. It has been suggested that this 'spotlight' provides not only the means of *selection* of one among several available visual objects for further processing and the control of action, but also for the *integration* of the different sensory attributes of that object, like its shape and colour, that have up to that point been analysed by separate visual processing modules. (See Chapter 2.)

A general-purpose limited-capacity mechanism?

In perhaps the earliest true information processing model of human performance, published in 1958, Broadbent made a strong claim about the nature of the filter mechanism. He located it subsequent it to processes analysing 'physical' attributes (e.g. colour, movement, pitch) in parallel for all sensory input, in all modalities, but prior to a single limited-capacity mechanism which, he proposed, was necessary for any processing involving the recognition and interpretation of learned patterns like words or faces, the making of decisions, the initiation of voluntary action, and conscious awareness. The filter was obligatory, so that the limited-capacity mechanism, or 'single channel', could not process information from different sources (e.g. different sensory modalities, or different positions in space) simultaneously. Instead, the filter had to be switched successively between channels (defined in terms of physical attributes like location or voice); this switching process was held to be quite slow.

Subsequent research forced the modification of these proposals. Divided attention experiments have shown that subjects appear to be able to monitor multiple sources for word (or other learned pattern) targets as

---

[3] One qualification should be mentioned. We sometimes succeed in understanding two *short* messages presented simultaneously. This is because we can interpret the words of one message, then recover the few words of the other from echoic memory (see above) and interpret them.

readily as a single source. There is also evidence (as already mentioned, see Chapter 9) that unattended words may (sometimes) activate their meanings. As a result some theorists have placed the filter later in processing. Others, while defending the early filter, now see it as only one of several points in processing where selection takes place, and as both optional and leaky, rather than as a rigid and obligatory bottleneck.

It has nevertheless remained a popular idea among theorists that competition for a general-purpose 'single channel', 'central processor' or 'pool of (universal) processing resources' is a major cause of interference when one tries to perform two (non-automatic) cognitive tasks concurrently. The difficulty is to state in a non-circular way which kinds of processing draw upon this resource and which do not. It would hardly be satisfactory to argue only after the fact that, because two tasks do not interfere, they must involve only 'automatic' processes that do not draw upon the central resource! It has generally been assumed, from Broadbent on, that the province of the hypothesized general-purpose mechanism or resource pool is 'high-level' processes such as complex pattern recognition, translation between modalities, decision-making and the selection of action. The shadowing task discussed above appears to require all these, which is why it has been regarded as a prototypical 'attention-demanding' task.

The difficulty is that a number of cases have been experimentally studied in which it turns out that two complex tasks, both of which one would suppose *a priori* to be 'attention demanding' by these criteria, can be combined with little or no interference. For example, one might suppose that the task of sight-reading piano music was fairly similar in its general capacity demands to shadowing speech, provided that the pianist plays 'musically', i.e. with suitable dynamics and phrasing, not like an automaton. In a 1972 experiment, Allport and colleagues had university music students sight-read piano pieces they had not seen before, while shadowing a spoken passage of prose (see Allport, 1980, for a description). After only a short session of practice, no appreciable interference was observed. Sight-reading, as assessed by 'blind' judges, was no more error-prone (or less musical) with shadowing than without, nor did the number of shadowing errors increase with sight-reading, or depend on the difficulty level of the piece.

What enables this particular combination of tasks to be performed without interference? Crudely speaking, it would appear that shadowing requires analysis of *speech input*, *linguistic/semantic* coding, and *speech-motor* control processes, while sight-reading involves analysis of *visual* input (and heard notes), coding of *spatial/melodic/harmonic* patterns, and *manual* motor control. It is plausible that the two tasks can be accomplished by completely non-overlapping sets of specialized processing modules and non-overlapping connections among them. There have now been a number of other studies (see Allport, 1980; Wickens, 1984, for review) indicating that cases of task interference one might have been tempted to interpret in terms of competition for a general-purpose mechanism can better be interpreted in terms of competition for specialized processing resources.

Hence, while the hypothesis of a general-purpose central processor or pool of processing resources cannot readily be disproved, and clearly attracts some researchers because of the possibility of identifying it (in some sense) with conscious awareness, this theoretical construct is beginning to seem of dubious necessity.

Load on executive control processes?

It is necessary, however, to posit another kind of limited-capacity resource, namely, processes whose function it is to control other processes: to marshal, control the flow of information among, and monitor the specialized processing modules that contribute to the performance of a task. In cases where two tasks can be separately routed through the system, as in Allport *et al.*'s experiment, there must be executive processes to do the routing. In cases where selective filtering is required (as in the shadowing experiments), then executive processes are required to set the filter. The ability of executive control processes to handle these demands is an important source of limitation on our cognitive capacities.

Executive control, though necessary in any complex information processing system (whether a brain, a computer or an organization) may seem a rather abstract and metaphorical idea. Indeed, psychology is only beginning to come to terms with how to investigate executive control processes empirically. One way in which these processes manifest themselves is when they fail. Such failures appear to be characteristic of neurological patients with damage to the frontal lobes (see Shallice, 1982; Duncan, 1986, for review). Such patients often exhibit deficits in no specific domain of processing—such as language, or motor coordination, or spatial skills, but their behaviour in all these domains appears disorganized, not properly planned or coherently goal-directed, especially when they try to perform a *novel*, but otherwise simple, task. Components of the task may be omitted or repeated. Control of performance is readily captured by irrelevant stimuli, or by recently performed, but no longer relevant tasks. For example, a patient asked to draw a square may do so, but then write in the square a word overheard from a nearby conversation. Such patients appear to have lost control of their cognitive resources; they may even verbalize correctly what they are supposed to do ("I must press the button") while failing to do it.

'Action errors' also occur in normal people, and have increasingly come under scientific scrutiny, not least because of their role in causing accidents. Some action errors involve the mixing up of components of—or 'cross-talk' between—concurrent tasks. One nice example comes from a colleague who, completing the day's domestic tasks before retiring, found herself to have put a lettuce leaf on the doorstep and a milk bottle in the rabbit hutch. Other errors involve the 'capture' of control of performance by well-established routines when the standard eliciting conditions for those routines are present. William James described a classic instance: a man who went up to his bedroom to dress for dinner, and found himself getting into bed with his pyjamas on.

Capture errors like this indicate one of the primary functions of executive control. Our brains are learning machines. Through practice, actions and action sequences—whether overt, like changing gear, getting dressed, or brushing your teeth, or internal, like reading—which once required effortful step-by-step decision-making become automatized and 'run themselves off' when their eliciting conditions are present. But the species would have become extinct long ago if we were entirely creatures of habit, condemned to run off whatever habitual routines were triggered by the external stimuli. One function of executive control mechanisms is to inhibit or override these habitual couplings of action to environmental conditions, and organize our processing resources to produce novel actions to those same conditions, and to allow the establishment of new habits (Shallice, 1982). However, it is clear that the capacity of executive control mechanisms is limited. If this capacity is pre-empted by other demands, habitual routines will tend to grab control. Indeed, both systematic diary studies of everyday action errors, and accident investigations indicate that capture errors are especially likely to occur when the perpetrator is intensely preoccupied with another task or train of thought.

Stressors, arousal, and performance breakdown

The conception of the brain as a set of linked (capacity-limited) specialized processing modules coordinated by (capacity-limited) executive control processes will help us to understand the effects of stressors on cognitive performance. But an additional idea is needed: namely, that particular processes might be more or less strongly energized as a function of global **arousal** or 'activation'.

Classically, the effects of stressors have been interpreted by relating them to their effects upon a global 'arousal' mechanism, where the level of arousal is held to increase or decrease the efficiency of the whole range of different processes. (See Eysenck, 1984; Hockey, 1984, for review.) Arousal has been held to be increased by: sensory input, especially noise; incentives; knowledge of results (i.e. being told how well you are performing); time of day (arousal increases throughout the day, apart from a 'post-lunch dip'); unsatisfied biological drives like hunger, thirst and sex; drugs like the amphetamines. Arousal has been held to be reduced by sleep deprivation, sensory deprivation, and drugs like chlorpromazine. The physiological mechanism usually assumed to underly arousal has been the non-specific effects of ascending reticular activation upon cortical activation. Physiological measures such as pupil dilation have been offered as indices of arousal.

The relation between arousal and performance is, according to this classical theory, described by an inverted-U shaped function sometimes known as the **Yerkes-Dodson law** (after the psychologists who first noted it in 1908): at low levels of arousal, performance increases with arousal, but at high levels, performance deteriorates with additional arousal. Thus, moderate levels of noise may increase performance, but high levels impair it. Particular tasks are held to have optimal levels of arousal. Thus, a boring task like proof-reading benefits more from increasing the level of arousal than a more demanding (and hence intrinsically arousing) task like memory span and hence shows a different pattern of time-of-day effects. Individuals are also held to differ in their intrinsic arousal levels as a function of personality: people with an extroverted personality are supposed to require more external stimulation to maintain their arousal at an optimal level than introverts.

Parts of this story work quite well. One kind of evidence that supports mediation of the effects of these stressors via a common arousal mechanism is that deterioration in performance due to a 'de-arousing' stressor can be compensated for by the application of an 'arousing' stressor. This is illustrated by the data in Figure 3.6 which shows the number of errors and the number of 'lapses' (unusually long reaction-times) in successive 10-minute periods of a serial choice reaction task: one of five lights was illuminated, the subject responded as quickly as possible by touching a stylus to the corresponding contact, which caused that light to go out and the next light to come on, and so on. Sleep-deprived subjects (under-aroused) exhibit a marked deterioration of performance over time compared to control subjects. However, this deterioration is much less marked if noise or knowledge of results (both arousers) is added.

However, this unitary arousal theory leaves certain basic questions unanswered. Major impairment of performance by sleep-deprivation seems limited to boring repetitive tasks like serial reaction, and only after several minutes of performance. Why is there no effect during the first few minutes, and why has it proved so hard to detect any effect of comparable amounts of sleep deprivation on performance of interesting and variable tasks like playing table tennis or darts? Secondly, the arousal theory gives no explicit account of why performance *deteriorates* at high levels of arousal instead of continuing to get more and more efficient. Moreover, the physiological basis of cortical activation is now known to be much more complex than I have so far suggested (Robbins, 1986; see also Chapter 8). There certainly exist diffuse projections from sub-cortical to cortical areas whose function appears to be general activation or potentiation of cortical mechanisms rather than the transmission of specific information: damage to these systems produces a general deterioration of function across the whole array of cognitive skills, not in one specific domain. However, these projections comprise several distinct sub-systems, characterized by (among other things) different neurotransmitters (hence, differential responses to different drugs), and, perhaps, different functions.

A possible solution to these difficulties, summarized in Figure 3.7, is to assume that global variations in performance efficiency depend not only on the level of activation in one or, more probably, several basic arousal mechanisms responsible for *energizing* specialized processing modules, but also upon the efficiency of the executive control mechanisms that *co-ordinate* them. Low levels of arousal may reduce the efficiency with which

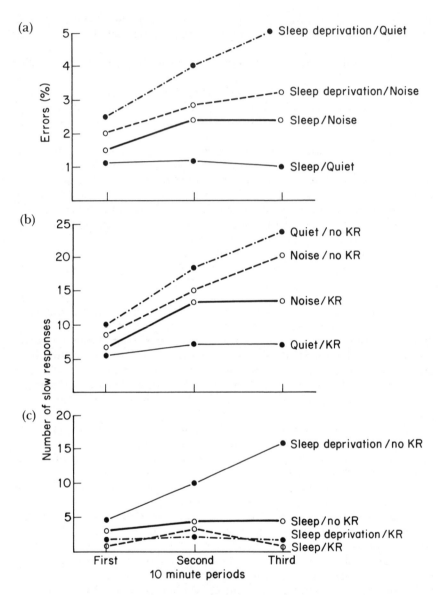

Fig. 3.6   Data (from Wilkinson, 1961; 1963) on the interacting effects of 32 hours without sleep, 100 dB 'white' noise, and knowledge of results (illumination of a 'correct' or 'error' light), on the number of errors and slow (>1.5 s) responses in successive ten-minute periods of performance on a serial five-choice reaction task. Reproduced from Eysenck, M.W. (1984) by permission of Lawrence Erlbaum, London.

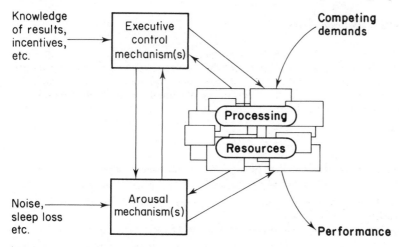

Fig. 3.7   A simple framework for the effects of stressors upon cognitive performance.

both individual processing resources and executive control processes operate. However, executive control processes can also, for short periods of time, marshal extra resources to overcome this deficit. There is evidence that making a 'mental effort' is associated with a reduction in the resources available for simultaneous performance of a secondary task. At high levels of arousal, as individual processing modules become more and more activated they become harder to control, in part because as irrelevant automatized routines become more activated they are more prone to seize control, in part because high arousal levels may cause more 'neural noise' or uncontrolled cross-talk between modules. The task of executive control becomes even harder when the environment is presenting numerous competing demands.

As the load on executive processes exceeds their capacity, the selectivity of processing begins to break down, and coherent performance progressively disintegrates. There is indeed evidence that under conditions inducing high arousal levels, people are more distractable by sources of information irrelevant to the task in hand. These distractors may involve the physiological consequences of high arousal levels (heart-pounding, sweating, blushing) and cognitive reactions both to these and to performance failure (loss of self-esteem, fear of the consequences). In the extreme state (known colloquially as 'panic'), processing resources are switched rapidly and involuntarily among competing demands, regardless of whether they are relevant or irrelevant.

Suggested reading

Citations in this chapter have, of necessity, been restricted largely to review chapters or books in which the theories or evidence discussed are reviewed at greater length. These sources would therefore be the first place to look for more extended discussion, and to locate citations of relevant experiments or theoretical discussion, including some mentioned here.

On memory:
Anderson, J.R. (1980). *Cognitive Psychology and its Implications*. W.H. Freeman and Co., San Francisco.
Especially good on the structure of the information stored in permanent memory and how this can make sense of the various factors influencing forgetting.

Baddeley, A.D. (1982). *Your Memory: A User's Guide*. Penguin Books Ltd., Harmondsworth, Middlesex.
The gentlest introduction, and lavishly illustrated.

Wingfield, A. and Byrnes, D.L. (1981). *The Psychology of Human Memory*. Academic Press, New York.

Zechmeister, E.B. and Nyberg, S.E. (1982). *Human Memory: an Introduction to Research and Theory*. Brooks/Cole, New York.

Memory is also covered in more general textbooks on cognitive psychology (e.g. Eysenck, 1984; Smyth *et al.* 1987). Readers wishing to get into the more technical recent literature might use as entry points the reviews of Johnson and Hasher (1987) for long-term memory, and Monsell (1984) and Baddeley (1986) for working memory.

On attention and processing limitations:
Allport, D.A. (1980). Attention and performance. In *Cognitive Psychology: New Directions*, pp. 112–153. Edited by Claxton, G. Routledge and Kegan Paul, London.
An excellent survey of changing perspectives on the problem of capacity limitations.

Eysenck, M.W. (1984). *A Handbook of Cognitive Psychology*. Lawrence Erlbaum, London.
A undergraduate text on cognitive psychology.

Kahneman, D. and Treisman, A. (1984). Changing views of attention and automaticity. In *Varieties of Attention*, pp. 29–61. Edited by Parasuraman, R. and Davies, D.R. Academic Press, New York.
Sophisticated but useful review on selective filtering.

Wickens, C.D. (1984). Processing resources in attention. In *Varieties of Attention*, pp. 63–102. Edited by Parasuranam, R. and Davies, D. R. Academic Press, New York.
Sophisticated but useful review on dual task performance.

Readers wanting to get into the recent primary literature might do so via recent reviews by Johnston and Dark (1986) and Wickens and Kramer (1985), and the conference proceedings edited by Posner and Marin (1985).

References

Allport, D.A. (1980). Attention and performance. In *Cognitive Psychology: New Directions*, pp. 112–153. Edited by Claxton, G. Routledge and Kegan Paul, London.

Anderson, J.R. (1980). *Cognitive Psychology and its Implications*. W.H. Freeman and Co., San Francisco.

Arkes, H.R. and Harkness, A.R. (1980). Effect of making a diagnosis on subsequent recognition of symptoms. *Journal of Experimental Psychology: Human Learning and Memory* **6**, 568.

Baddeley, A.D. (1982). *Your Memory: a User's Guide*. Penguin, Harmondsworth, Middlesex.

Baddeley, A.D. (1986). *Working Memory*. Oxford University Press, Oxford.

Baddeley, A.D. and Warrington, E.K. (1970). Amnesia and the distinction between long- and short-term memory. *Journal of Verbal Learning and Verbal Behaviour* **9**, 176.

Bellezza, F.S. (1981). Mnemonic devices: classification, characteristics and criteria. *Review of Educational Research* **51**, 247.

Bower, G.H. (1981). Mood and memory. *American Psychologist* **36**, 129.

Duncan, J. (1986). Disorganization of behaviour after frontal lobe damage. *Cognitive Neuropsychology* **3**, 271.

Eysenck, M.W. (1984). *A Handbook of Cognitive Psychology*. Lawrence Erlbaum, London.

Glanzer, M. and Cunitz, A.R. (1966). Two storage mechanisms in free recall. *Journal of Verbal Learning and Verbal Behaviour* **5**, 358.

Hitch, G.J. (1978). The role of short-term working memory in mental arithmetic. *Cognitive Psychology* **10**, 302.

Hockey, R. (1984). Varieties of attentional state. In *Varieties of Attention*, pp. 449–83. Edited by Parasuraman, R. and Davies, D.R. Academic Press, New York.

Johnson, M.K. and Hasher, L. (1987). Human learning and memory. *Annual Review of Psychology* **38**, 631.

Johnston, W.A. and Dark, V.J. (1986). Selective attention. *Annual Review of Psychology* **37**, 43.

Kahneman, D. and Treisman A. (1984). Changing views of attention and automaticity. In *Varieties of Attention*, pp. 29–61. Edited by Parasuraman, R. and Davies, D.R. Academic Press, New York.

Ley, P. (1977). Psychological studies of doctor-patient communication. In *Contributions to Medical Psychology*, pp. 9–42. Edited by Rachman, S. Pergamon Press, Oxford.

Ley, P. (1982). Satisfaction, compliance and communication. *British Journal of Clinical Psychology* **21**, 241.

Loftus, E.F. (1979). *Eyewitness Testimony*. Harvard University Press, Cambridge, Massachusetts.

Monsell, S. (1984). Components of working memory underlying verbal skills: a 'distributed-capacities' view. In *Attention and Performance X*, pp. 327–50. Edited by Bouma, H. and Bouwhuis, D.G. Erlbaum, London.

Morris, P.E. (1979). Strategies for learning and recall. In *Applied Problems in Memory*, pp. 25–57. Edited by Gruneberg, M.M. and Morris, P.E. Academic Press, London.

Morris, R.G. (1986). Short-term forgetting in senile dementia of the Alzheimer's type. *Cognitive Neuropsychology* **3**, 77.

Murdoch, B.B. Jr. (1962). The serial possition effect of free recall. *Journal of Experimental Psychology* **64**, 483.

Posner, M.I. and Marin, O. (1985). *Attention and Performance XI*. Erlbaum, Hillsdale, New Jersey.

Robbins, T.W. (1986). Psychopharmacological and neurobiological aspects of the energetics of information processing. In *Energetics and Human Information Processing*, pp. 71–90. Edited by Hockey, G.R.J., Gaillard, A.W.K. and Coles, M.G.H. Martinus Nijhoff, Dordrecht.

Shallice, T. (1982). Specific impairments of planning. *Philosophical Transactions of the Royal Society, London* **B 298**, 199.

Shipman, J.J. (1984). *Mnemonics and Tactics in Surgery and Medicine* (2nd edition). Lloyd-Luke, London.

Smyth, M.M., Morris, P.E., Levy, P. and Ellis, A.W. (1987). *Cognition in Action*. Erlbaum, London.

Squire, L.R. (1987). *Memory and the Brain*. Oxford University Press, Oxford.

Tversky, A. and Kahneman, D. (1973). Availability: a heuristic for judging frequency and probability. *Cognitive Psychology* **5**, 207.

Wickens, C.D. (1984). Processing resources in attention. In *Varieties of Attention*, pp. 63–102. Edited by Parasuraman, R. and Davies, D.R. Academic Press, New York.

Wickens, C.D. and Kramer, A. (1985). Engineering psychology. *Annual Review of Psychology* **36**, 307.

Wilding, J., Rashid, W., Gilmore, D., and Valentine, E. (1986). A comparison of two mnemonic methods in learning medical information. *Human Learning* **5**, 211.

Wingfield, A. and Byrnes, D.L. (1981). *The Psychology of Human Memory*. Academic Press, New York.

Woodworth, R.S. (1988). *Experimental Psychology*, p. 55. Henry Holt, New York.

Zechmeister, E.B. and Nyberg, S.E. (1982). *Human Memory: an Introduction to Research and Theory*. Brooks/Cole, New York.

4

The Development of Social Relationships in Infancy and Childhood

MPM Richards

Developmental issues

The task of the developmental psychologist is a daunting one. The aim is to provide an account of how a single cell, newly formed at conception, can develop into a feeling, thinking person who can categorize and form concepts, reflect on their own actions and those of others, communicate these thoughts and feelings and, more generally, live as part of a very complex social world. It is these characteristics which mark us off to a greater or lesser extent from all other animal species and a good way to begin this discussion is to look at developmental issues in broad evolutionary terms. It appears that it is through our capacity to form social relationships that we come to possess the human characteristics described above. In human development there is a relatively long period of immaturity in which infants and young children are dependent for all their needs on others. Close social relations are characteristic of this dependency, and it is probable that the evolution of the specifically human psychological attributes has been made possible by prolongation of human immaturity and the opportunities this provides for developing close social relationships and for learning about the complex social world our species inhabits. The point can be made in another way. Ours is a cultural species and each generation must learn afresh the attitudes, values, knowledge and information about the world that makes social life possible. This information is not transferred genetically but via social relationships. So, human infancy and childhood can be viewed as an adaptation to cultural life, providing the settings in which the information is passed to each new generation and by which specifically human attributes are acquired.

This process of acquisition is not unidirectional where a child passively picks up information and learns from the environment, but it is an active and interactive process by which a child structures the world and selectively attends to it. The nature of this interactive process is perhaps most obvious in cognitive development (see Chapter 5) where the world is perceived via a child's conceptualization of it—objects have a meaning for a child as they become identified and categorized. But the same process can be seen in social development. Here, a child is not the passive recipient of the social attentions of others but may demand attention or ignore approaches and generally plays a part in forming his own social world from the first days after birth.

A mother's responsiveness to her baby is influenced by the particular patterns of sleeping, waking and crying her baby exhibits (Bernal, 1972). Such mutual responsiveness may also be seen at a more detailed level of interaction. When feeding, babies do not suck at a steady rate but have bursts of sucking separated by pauses. Careful observation of feeding sessions shows that mothers are much more likely to talk to their babies and to jiggle them during the pauses than the bursts of sucking, thus demonstrating the interdependence of the behaviour of the two partners. Such observations have led to the speculation that this mutual patterning of infant and maternal behaviour may provide the baby with an opportunity to learn the basic rule of conversation—you listen while your partner talks and vice versa (Kaye, 1982).

It is all too easy to see an infant simply as an immature adult yet to grow up. Psychologists, like parents, have tended to pay attention to each new sign of increasing maturity—the first attempt to sit up, a new tooth or a first word—and to view childhood simply as a preparation for adulthood. However, the world of infants and children is very unlike that of adults and to survive in that world requires very different skills from those needed by an adult. An infant must be adapted for the world of infancy as well as having the capacity to grow up. An example of this is provided by feeding. Infants are adapted to feed on a liquid diet by sucking. The shape and musculature of the mouth as well as the capacity to turn towards a point of stimulation on the cheek (at least when hungry) make obvious sense for a newborn that lives on milk, as do many other aspects of neonatal behaviour and physiology. But as development proceeds, new features such as the eruption of teeth and the capacity to chew become apparent which allow the diet to be broadened to include solid food. Parallel changes are found in the digestive system. In the same way, the appearance and behaviour of a developing child change so evoking new responses in social encounters and the ability to sustain much more complex and varied social actions. As the social world of the child changes, new and appropriate social capacities emerge. So, while a newborn can only sustain rather brief social interactions involving little more than visual regard of an adult's face, an infant at a couple of months can engage in a sustained game involving smiling and looking away. By 6 months, a whole range of vocal and visual signals are being used in complex games like peek-a-boo (Trevarthan, 1977).

Clinicians and parents often share an interest in **developmental prediction**. How will this infant turn out? Will this active crying baby grow up to be an equally active and demanding toddler or teenager? What are the long-term consequences of damage to the brain that might be seen in an ultrasound scan of the head of a preterm baby? Developmental prediction is a difficult and uncertain process. This is not only because at any age events may occur which may influence the outcome, but also because the changing nature of a child and a child's world means that similarity in psychological functions and abilities across the age range may be much more apparent than real, making it very difficult to know what infantile characteristics to measure as the precursor of the later ability. For example, if we are interested in the prediction of IQ, we need to find behavioural items in infancy that might be equivalent, in some sense, to those that are used in IQ tests at later ages. Items reflecting verbal abilities are an important component of most IQ tests but what measures can be used in the preverbal child? Developmental tests used in the first year of life rely heavily on motor abilities and aspects of social behaviour and it is perhaps for this reason that correlations with later IQ are low and remain so until the ages at which verbal abilities may be directly tested (Bayley, 1968).

An analogy with the development of animals may make the issue clearer as some animals change in form and behaviour through the life cycle in more dramatic ways than in our own species. Let us suppose that we are interested in the speed of flight of butterflies. Given a batch of caterpillars could we select ones likely to be fast flyers when mature? The temptation might be to take those which crawled fastest, but there seems no particular reason for that choice given that quite different structures are used for crawling in caterpillars and for flying in butterflies. And so with infants; we can assess infant behaviour in a wide variety of ways, but given the fundamental changes of the developmental process, it is not surprising that predictions of later behaviour from infancy are in general very poor—at least if we exclude cases of gross pathology. Given these difficulties, at least in early infancy, assessments of the social environment are as good predictors of later behaviour as any behavioural assessment we can make at that time, once gross pathology has been excluded.

The next point to be discussed at this stage is the importance of **cultural diversity**. Here, once again, we are dealing with a consequence of the fundamental importance of culture to human life. Cultures vary widely in different parts of the world and they may change rapidly over time. What we refer to as culture is not simply a matter of such things as a common language and shared beliefs and attitudes, but also involves all sorts of social arrangements—the nature of marriage and household organization, the spacing of children and the provision of childcare and education, for instance. All of these profoundly influence the world of each individual in a society, including of course, infants and children. Too often, psychologists and other social scientists refer to *the* child and *the* mother as if they were cultural universals with little regard to the diversity that exists within and between societies. Of course, some general statements can be made. For example, the majority of children in all human societies begin to speak (however this is defined) at some point in their second year of life and most children in most societies are cared for in their early years of life by women. But generalities like these hide variation and diversity. Not only is this diversity interesting in its own right but appreciation of it may help us to disentangle developmental processes. For example, as we will see below, attachment theorists like John Bowlby have claimed that a rather limited number of infant signals play a basic role in the formation and modulation of mother-infant relationships. Crying is one of these behaviour patterns and indeed there are a large number of studies carried out in Europe and North America which attest to its potency as an important cue that is used by caretakers in structuring their caretaking (e.g. Bernal, 1972). When babies cry, caretakers respond with a greater or lesser delay depending on a number of factors such as the time, place, attitude of the caretaker. Usually, crying babies are picked up and often they are fed. The pattern would seem to be a very general one and so it is not surprising that theorists came to regard crying as one of the basic signals by which infants can express their needs as well as one of the key elements in the developing relationship of mother and child. However, a consideration of other societies shows that crying only comes to have this very central role because of the way in which we order the lives of young children. In particular, in our society mother and infant are often separated—they usually sleep in separate rooms and it is unusual for a baby to be carried around all day by a mother—so that an infant cue that can be perceived at a distance is of particular importance.

Among the !Kung people of the Kalahari desert, social relationships are arranged rather differently from Western Societies. This is a gathering and hunting society in which people live in small groups, of perhaps a dozen or twenty people, made up of couples with their children and other relatives. In this society, mother and baby are seldom separated, babies are carried on a sling on the mother's body and they sleep beside her at night. Unless babies are hurt or ill, they seldom cry. The nipple is always close and often can be reached by the baby's own actions. If not, the baby's movements serve as a signal to the mother who will shift the sling or her position to enable the baby to suckle. In this society, an infant's crying is not a fundamental regulatory signal in the early interactions (Konner, 1972).

Under the social conditions of !Kung society an infant of a few weeks of age is likely to be sucking at the breast several times each hour. Indeed, it may be misleading to talk of feed times here as the process is really a continuous one. This stands in great contrast to what can be seen in our own society. Here, some babies are 'demand' fed and others are fed to varying degrees by the clock. But in almost all cases, it is possible to recognize distinct mealtimes which usually occur at 3–4 hourly intervals during the day and less frequently at night. Clearly, this is unlike the !Kung pattern which provides a very different experience for the babies.

As this example should make clear, we must set aside generalizations which are based on a knowledge of our society alone. This example also provides evidence of the **adaptability** of infants (and their caretakers)—the fact that they can grow up and thrive under a very wide range of conditions. This should lead us to take with a pinch of salt a good deal of the more prescriptive advice offered by doctors, nurses and other professionals or which we can find in the many manuals produced for parents in our own and other societies.

Cultural diversity raises a whole range of interesting questions: How far do variations in caretaking patterns matter in terms of developmental outcomes? Are they related to differences in adult behaviour? Unfortunately, the ethnocentricity that has so often characterized psychology has meant that all too few studies have explored cultural variation. But where this has been done many interesting differences in the behaviour of children and adults have been found. The widespread practice of restraining babies for at least part of each day by swaddling them or strapping them into cradle boards provides an example here. Cradle board use has been studied in a native American society, the Navajo (Chisholm and Richards, 1978). Babies are often propped up in their cradle boards beside the mother while she works. During these periods there is a great deal of social interaction between the babies and older siblings and other children, not least because the baby's face is the height of a small child—indeed these Navajo babies have much more social contact with both adults and children than babies in our own society. On the assumption that a lot of practice and exercise are necessary for satisfactory motor development, it has often been thought that babies brought up with a cradle board would be delayed in walking and the achievement of other motor milestones. Work with Navajo children and other societies that use cradle boards shows this not to be the case. Equally unconvincing are the claims that cradle board use leads to an adult emotional pattern of being easily frustrated and given to sudden outbursts of anger.

One of the many difficulties in using cultural comparisons to seek simple cause and effect relationships between aspects of child care and the developmental environment and adult characteristics, is that societies differ in so many ways. Suppose we did find a difference between Navajo and British adults in an aspect of behaviour. We might be tempted to relate this to cradle board use. However, without further evidence we could equally attribute it to any other difference between the societies, such as patterns of play among the children or diet. Here, a within-group comparison may be more helpful: a comparison of Navajo children with varying experience of cradle board use, for example, may be more illuminating for unravelling developmental processes. Indeed, it is on the basis of comparisons of this kind that the statement of the lack of retardation of motor milestones is made.

In this introductory section some general developmental issues have been outlined. Now, as an example of developmental work I will deal with three specific topics will be dealt with in a little more depth. These are the growth of social relationships in infancy (including attachment theory), the effects of parental divorce and separation on children, and gender identity.

Sex and gender

The most obvious social division in society is that between men and women. From birth, or before (see below), an individual is labelled as female or male and thereafter development proceeds within one or other gender. This labelling becomes part of ourselves so that we think of ourselves and see the world in gender terms. A simple thought experiment will illustrate the point: is it possible to think of a person without thinking of them as male or female?

Given the importance of gender in our lives, and its political significance, it is not surprising that there are strongly held positions about the development of **gender identity**—the process by which we become boys or girls and women and men. There are those who see it as a matter of biological determination; that is a process which is set inevitably in train at conception by the chromosomal make-up of the zygote—XX or XY. In effect, this view draws no distinction between sex (based on anatomical and physiological features) and gender (based on attitudes and behaviour). But as the case of transexuals shows, sex and gender may not always go together. These individuals behave and are seen as belonging to one gender while their chromosomes, physiology and anatomy (unless altered by surgical and hormonal means) would indicate the other. At this point, I should perhaps mention another matter which sometimes causes confusion. Choice of sexual partner, whether homosexual or heterosexual, represents a different dimension than the distinction between genders. Within each gender there are some who choose sexual partners from among their own gender rather than from the other. But patterns of homosexual behaviour tend to be gender-specific—gay men and lesbian women have rather different patterns of relationships. So, while the homo-sexual-heterosexual dimension has nothing to do with gender *per se*, particular patterns of homosexual behaviour may be characteristic of each gender.

In contrast to those who believe that anatomy determines gender, there are others who take an opposite position which claims that gender is largely or wholly a matter of 'conditioning' or other such learning. This view would, at least in its extreme form, deny any role for anatomy or physiology and would see the newborn (or fetus) as being completely labile and capable of being shaped into either gender. The position adopted in this chapter is to suggest that gender is not an *inevitable* consequence of biological endowment. During development, gender identity is formed through complex social and psychological processes. Usually, an initial decision about an individual at birth confers gender. It happens when someone, usually a midwife or doctor, on the basis of the form of the external genitalia, identifies the baby as a boy or girl. Thereafter, the child is treated as a girl or boy and, with the development of self-awareness, comes to see themselves and to behave in gendered terms consistent with that first labelling. As that first label is given on the basis of anatomical characteristics, the gender identity will be consistent with the sex. What gender identity will mean will vary widely from culture to culture as well as for individual reasons. So that attitudes or behaviour that are seen as typically male in one society might be regarded very differently elsewhere. This point will be elaborated further. Also, there may be an individual divergence from the path of development typical for a particular society. The case of the transexual who takes a conscious decision to move from one gender to another has already been mentioned. Such an individual in changing gender from male to female may undergo genital surgery to produce an outward female form (Morris, 1974). Why some individuals make such decisions is not understood. Despite the usual description of this operation as a 'sex change', according to the terminology used here, it is part of a change of gender, not sex. The other departure from the usual path of development which has been much studied are individuals who at birth, usually because of abnormal genital anatomy, are assigned to the gender which does not correspond to their chromosomal sex. For some of these children, after a period of rearing in one gender, a change is made. Such examples allow us to study the process of the development of gender identity, albeit in unusual and atypical individuals (Money and Ehrhardt, 1972).

With the growing use of techniques for the diagnosis of fetal genetic disorders, the sex of an individual may be known early in pregnancy. In Britain, if this information becomes available parents are usually asked whether or not they want to be told and about half opt to know it. Those who do come to know the sex, may name the baby in pregnancy and begin to perceive it in gendered terms. One study (Katz Rothman, 1986), indicates that the fetal movements may be perceived differently once the sex is known: those of a male fetus are seen as being 'stronger', 'more powerful', 'thrusting' and in other ways consistent with cultural stereotypes of male behaviour. If, for cultural or individual reasons, parents want a child of a particular gender, fetal diagnosis and abortion may be used to achieve their goal (Levidow, 1987).

Leaving aside the cases of prenatal knowledge, the usual decision point is at birth. Thereafter, the treatment of boys and girls will diverge according to the customs, traditions and beliefs of the society. In early infancy, differential treatment may be very obvious, as with the genital mutilation which is practised in some societies, or it may be more subtle as with small differences in holding, touching and feeding patterns. Because gender differences tend to be taken for granted, such differences may not be apparent without systematic observation. In North America, genital mutilation in the form of postnatal male circumcision is widespread, not only in the Jewish community where it has religious significance, but much more widely. The operation to remove the foreskin from the penis is usually carried out without anaesthesia and produces changes in the sleep/wake patterns, alertness and other aspects of behaviour which may be apparent many days later (Bernal *et al.*, 1976).

As children grow up through the preschool years, behavioural differences between girls and boys tend to become more obvious. For example, many studies have been made of patterns of play and social interaction in nursery schools. In general, these show that boys spend more time in play with larger objects (e.g. building bricks and push toys) while girls are more often seen in the activities that involve fine motor coordination. Boys more often seek out and choose the company of other boys while girls seem much less concerned about the gender of their play companions. Girls spend more time than boys in the company of the teachers and nursery nurses. However, we should not overestimate these differences and it is important to emphasize that all children are likely to engage in all activities. The differences described here are in terms of the average times spent in the various activities (Henshall and McGuire, 1986).

While it may be easy enough to chart the behaviour of girls and boys and to describe differences, it is another matter to explain how these differences arise. In the case of the nursery, we may notice that the adults present are almost always women, and that we can observe them treating the boys and girls somewhat differently. For instance, they may be more tolerant of rough behaviour from boys than girls, or they may be more likely to suggest to a girl that she sits at a table and takes part in the paper-cutting activity going on there. Such differential treatment might lead to the conclusion that it is this that gives rise to the observable differences in behaviour. However, we may also observe the children making choices and expressing preferences along gender lines. These, of course, might be the result of previous differential treatments. The problem, when viewed in these terms, becomes like the infinite regress of images in two mirrors. Instead, psychologists have begun to analyse the *process* of development which they assume to be a continuing interaction in which each gender is seen and treated somewhat differently, but equally where each gender acts and behaves in a somewhat different way. Sometimes, as in the case of circumcision, when a specific event is involved, its consequences can be followed by comparing the behaviour of circumcised and non-circumcised infants.

Within (and outside) the home it is usually mothers rather than fathers who look after children. Despite much discussion and speculation in Britain and elsewhere about the symmetrical family and a growing involvement of fathers in childcare (Lewis and O'Brien, 1987) the usual pattern of the division of domestic labour has changed little in recent years. While more women are working outside the home, the effect on domestic tasks is small (Henwood *et al.*, 1987). (See Table 4.1.)

While in most societies most of the domestic work is done by women, there are considerable variations in the patterns of the domestic division of labour. For instance, in many Eastern Mediterranean and Middle Eastern societies, men and women live in very separated social worlds. In these societies, women have a relatively low level of participation in the labour force (apart from agricultural work), and they are often withdrawn from school at an early age to do domestic work so that female illiteracy is higher than male, the reverse of what is typical in industrialized countries in Northern Europe or North America. But when we view such a society we must be careful not to interpret everything as we would do in our own.

Table 4.1 Division of domestic labour %

Task		Women working full-time	Women working part-time
Household shopping	Mainly men	4	4
	Mainly women	52	64
	Shared equally	43	32
Preparation of evening meal	Mainly men	11	4
	Mainly women	61	79
	Shared equally	26	15

(From Jowell and Witherspoon, 1985)

Despite what I have said about the division of labour, the proportion of women in most professions—medicine, law, teaching, publishing etc.—is much higher in a country like Turkey than in Europe or North America (Kâğitçibaşi, 1982). The reason for this is that among middle class families, education—for both genders—is highly prized and employment opportunities are not as constrained by gender stereotypes as they are in Europe. Cheap domestic labour allows middle class mothers to work outside the home as they can pay for childcare and other domestic work. In such societies there are close male-male and female-female friendships as well as family alliances. Rules of behaviour in public differ. While there is frequent physical contact—hugging, holding hands, etc—between men in public as a display of friendship, such behaviour between a married couple would be frowned on, again the reverse of what we may observe in Northern Europe where a public display of physical touching between men is usually interpreted as a sign of homosexuality.

In different societies children will observe and experience a somewhat different gender divide and will learn a pattern of both public and private behaviour which is appropriate to their community.

Theories of the process of the development of gender identity are diverse and there is no one overall approach that has wide acceptance among psychologists. Theories may be grouped into three broad categories, although increasingly positions are being constructed which involve more than one of these.

One important family of theories is derived from the psychoanalytic tradition (e.g. Chodorow, 1978). These are built around the observation that the child's first (love) relationship is with the mother and so, while a girl may develop her gender identity by a process of identification with someone emotionally close to her, a boy must construct his identity by perceiving what is unlike the mother or by identification with a typically more distant and intermittently present father. Most of these theories also embody a notion of the differential power of men and women in the world; men as the economically and politically powerful gender active in the world outside the home and women as predominant in the personal, private and emotional world of the home—a view which, we should notice, may be ethnocentric. These relations may be represented by the symbol of a phallus and the fear of its loss and this may be seen more literally in terms of children's knowledge of genital sex differences and the boy's fear of losing a penis and the girl's belief that she may have lost hers in early infancy.

The second type of theory was originally derived from the work of Piaget by Kohlberg (1966). He pointed out that almost any theory of gender development must necessarily involve a basic understanding by the child that the social world is divided into two genders and that he or she belongs to one of these. Kohlberg stresses the cognitive basis of such a position in that it requires a child to structure and make sense of his own experience of the social world.

The third group of theories is based on learning processes—identification, modelling, reward and punishment. In contrast to the cognitive view—'I am a girl and so I want to do girl things and be seen as a girl'—the simplest learning theory position would state that, 'I find girl things rewarding and therefore I want to do more girl things'. Clearly, both the psychoanalytic and cognitive views involve learning processes and today few would ascribe to a view of gender development which is a 'pure' learning theory position.

Social relationships at birth

In 1948 when the National Health Service was founded, nearly half of all births occurred at home; today the proportion has dropped to a few per cent. The same trend may be seen in almost all parts of the industrialized world. One exception to this in Europe is The Netherlands where nearly half all births are still conducted by midwives at home. So, birth outside a hospital has become a rarity. Not only has the place of birth changed but so has its conduct. Labour is 'managed' so that its timing and duration are often controlled by drugs. Physiological parameters, such as the uterine contractions and the fetal heart rate, are often monitored by electronic devices. Similar changes have occurred in antenatal care. Fetal growth is often followed by ultrasound scans, and this technique and others, such as amniocentesis and chorionic villus sampling, are used to diagnose genetic and other fetal pathologies so that abortion may be offered when these are detected.

Many have indicated the way in which such techniques have altered the psychological experience of pregnancy and birth for mothers and their partners. For most, gone are the days when they would deliver at home in their own bed (where, in all likelihood, the child was conceived) attended by their familiar midwife and surrounded by their own family. Hospital births not only usually involve much more medical intervention but take place in a strange place where the mother is likely to be attended at various times by a large number of different people. She is less likely to feel in control of what is happening to her and at ease socially. As some women have come to resist these changes, the question is raised of possible longer term psychological consequences. These are difficult areas to investigate but there are some indications that the extent to which a woman feels in control during her labour is linked to the probability of her being depressed in the post-partum period (Oakley, 1980).

Specialized neonatal units

Perhaps even more dramatic than these changes in maternity care, has been the development of specialized neonatal units. Since the late 1950s, with a growing understanding of neonatal physiology, specialized units for the care of sick and preterm babies have been set up in most large obstetric hospitals. In Britain, nearly one-fifth of all babies are admitted to a specialized neonatal unit. While for most this is for a matter of hours or days, for a small group, mainly of very low birth weight babies, such units may be their home for several months.

As specialized neonatal care developed, fears began to be expressed about the possible damaging effects of the separation between newborn and parents that usually followed an admission to a neonatal unit. The separation arose partly because visiting by parents tended to be restricted and because neonatal units were centralized in large hospitals, so many infants, but not mothers, might be transferred considerable distances from outlying hospitals. Even when the parents were able to get to the neonatal unit, the baby might be in an incubator and handling was generally discouraged because of fears of infection. Parents often found this separation stressful and some paediatricians noticed that, at least in a few instances, there were long-term difficulties in the relationship between parent and child following separation. Claims were made about a possible association between separation and child abuse. While psychologists had a good deal of evidence to call on when discussing separation later in development, very little work had been done in the neonatal period. One reason for this was that the predominate view about separation stemmed from John Bowlby's **attachment theory**. This theory (which will be discussed in the next section) presented a picture of attachment between the mother (or mother figure) developing over the first year of life. Separation was held to be generally damaging and was thought to produce long-lasting effects because it interrupted or broke an existing attachment. From this perspective, if an attachment had yet to be formed, as during the newborn period, separation was held to have little consequence. Indeed, that was a widespread view of the baby in a neonatal unit: parents could simply 'pick up' on their relationship with their babies once they were fit and well and discharged home.

Bonding

In the early 1970s, two American paediatricians, Klaus and Kennell, published their theory of **bonding** (see Klaus and Kennell, 1982). This claimed that the period of the first couple of days after birth was of crucial

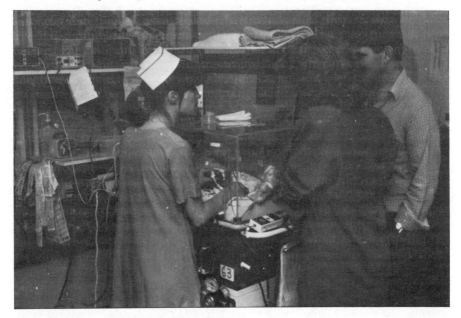

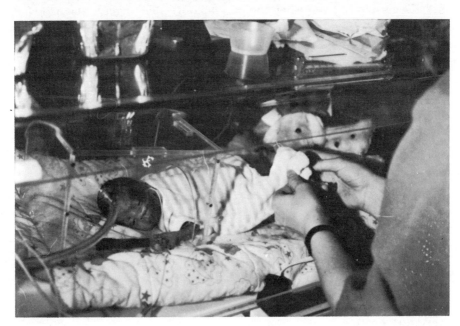

Fig. 4.1   Views of parent-child interaction in a neonatal unit. Handling the baby was once discouraged because of fears of infection but parents often found this separation stressful. Can the parents just 'pick up' on their relationship with their baby when well enough to go home?

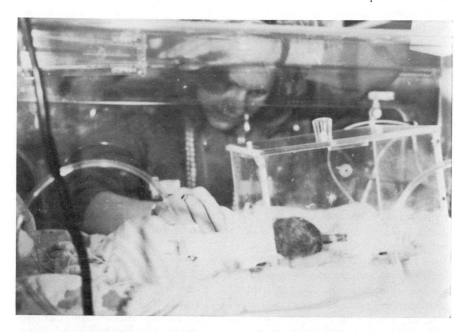

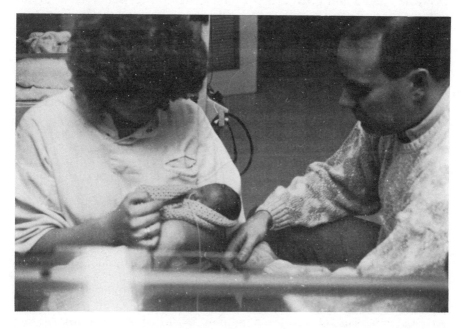

Photographs courtesy of Dr C. Morley, Rosie Maternity Hospital, Cambridge.

significance for the formation of subsequent relationships. On the basis of extrapolations of animal evidence and observations they had made in neonatal nurseries, they suggested that in the period immediately after birth, mothers (and they later included fathers) were in a particular psychological state which made them especially able to form a bond with their baby. If there was separation during this 'sensitive period' they suggested that there would be long-term deleterious effects on the parent-child relationship. These claims sparked off a large research effort which has examined the effects of separation and has led both to a much better understanding of the psychological processes involved as well as to modified policies in neonatal units which aim to reduce separation as far as possible and to provide various kinds of help and support for parents.

First, it is perhaps worth making a few comments about the way evidence from animal species was used in this debate because it illustrates some very general points about the difficulties in using animal analogies for human behaviour.

In the original account of the bonding process, the analogy was drawn with the behaviour of sheep and goats. In both these species, as is well known to shepherds, the removal of the newborn kid or lamb from the mother can result in a rejection at a later reunion. This, so the argument ran, demonstrated a process widespread in animal species and humans. However, sheep and goats are not phylogenetically closely related to our own species and consideration of the differences between their ecology and social behaviour and our own shows the process by which the offspring and mother begin their social relationship is unlikely to be the same in the two cases. Sheep and goats live in large social groups, both in the wild and after domestication. They have a restricted breeding season so that many young are born into the flock at the same time. Lambs and kids are mobile almost immediately after birth. There is, thus, the problem of mothers and offspring maintaining contact. Also, from the point of view of natural selection, a mother should not waste her milk feeding the offspring of others. What seems to happen is that in licking the young in the period after the birth, the mother places a scent marker on her offspring. Thereafter, she rejects young that do not have her own scent label (Sluckin *et al.*, 1983).

Most human generations were spent living as gatherers and hunters. There is little known of the social life of such early human groups, but on the basis of our knowledge of contemporary societies of this kind, it seems likely that groups were small and births were widespread throughout the year. Given these considerations and the point that the human baby cannot move around independently, there seems no reason why selection should favour a process by which mothers should reject an infant who has been separated from them, or indeed, one who is not their own. Given the potential dangers of childbirth, it might make a lot of sense for infants to be fostered, especially by close relatives. In short, the social situation is quite different in the two cases and so it seems unlikely that a common process would be found. Indeed, it is not a matter of chance that the example of sheep and goats was used in this instance, as rarely has the rejection of separated newborns been described in other species. As suggested, it is an adaptation only likely to be found in species that live in large social groups, have a restricted breeding season and mobile young. To draw the point more widely, we should be very cautious of extrapolations concerning social behaviour without an analysis of the social organization of the two species involved. And we should always be sceptical of parallels drawn with animal species that are not clearly related.

Testing the bonding hypothesis: separation

Since the publication of Klaus and Kennell's ideas, many human observational and experimental studies have been carried out to test what has become known as the bonding hypothesis. As it is ethically unacceptable to separate mothers and babies as part of a research study, the experimental design most often adopted has been to take a situation in which separation is already occurring and to introduce as an experimental intervention added contact between mother and infant. Given that, especially in the United States, hospital policies for full term normal babies as well as those in neonatal units often involved a good deal of separation, it has proved relatively easy to set up such studies. Where such designs proved difficult to implement, observational studies comparing hospitals where there were varying degrees of separation have been used. However, designs of this kind suffer from the obvious difficulty that there may be significant differences in the population of women using the two hospitals or the hospitals may vary in other aspects of their organization or the care they provide that might account for any differences found in the mother-infant relationships. The ideal we should always aim towards is random allocation to groups in order to avoid bias.

The main conclusion arising from this research is that there are differences between separated and non-separated groups but these tend to be relatively short-lived; that is to say by a year, or perhaps a good deal less, it ceases to be possible to demonstrate differences (Goldberg, 1983; Richards, 1983). The main differences that have been described have been in the quality of the mother-infant relationship, the mother's feelings about looking after her baby and in the incidence and duration of lactation. There is a tendency after separation for mothers to be somewhat distant from their babies—to spend slightly less time with them and perhaps to be a little slower in responding to them should they cry. Asked about their feelings, mothers said it took them longer to feel that their babies belonged to them and they were less confident about coping with them when they returned home. But these differences are transient and soon fade as mother and infant spend time together. One very consistent finding has been that early separation tends to reduce the incidence and duration of breast-feeding. This finding is in line with other evidence that suggests that the frequency and intensity of the sucking stimulus in the neonatal period may set the course of a lactation. There are fewer studies of fathers, but these suggest that increasing fathers' contact with their babies in the neonatal period may be associated with greater social involvement with them some weeks after birth (Rödholm, 1981).

Although the effects of early separation are by no means permanent, there are short-term effects, and in individual cases where these may be coupled with other social and psychological problems, such as a lack of social support or ambivalent feelings towards the baby, there may be serious consequences. There are several ways in which separation can be reduced. It may be possible to reduce admissions to neonatal units. It has been found that admissions for observation and for a number of minor procedures can be avoided without detriment to the infant's health, thus preventing separation (and incidentally reducing health service costs). Evidence indicates that several procedures may be carried out on normal lying-in wards without any untoward effects for the babies (Richards and Roberton, 1978). Given our system of centralizing neonatal special care so that such care is not available in all maternity hospitals, some admissions are bound to involve separation. This can be minimized by providing accommodation in units for parents and making sure that wherever possible mothers and babies are admitted together. Where a mother cannot stay in a unit—she may herself need hospital care elsewhere or have other children to look after at home—open-door visiting policies have been instigated and positive support and encouragement to visit are given.

Policies for neonatal care have to be made in the context of our understanding of the parental psychological processes following birth. The parents' need to be involved in the care of their child—and to feel that the baby is theirs must be recognized so that they do not feel mere spectators in the neonatal unit. Nursing routines may need to be modified to allow for this involvement in caretaking although it is not always easy for nurses to change their role from caretakers to supporters of parents. Sometimes parents may hold back from their babies, not wishing to become too involved in case their baby does not survive. Here, understanding, counselling and support may be crucial. Throughout pregnancy many parents have anxieties that their baby may be malformed. If a baby is removed quickly at birth to be taken to a neonatal unit without giving the parents a chance to make a careful examination, parents may come to feel their worst fears have been realized. As one might expect, studies have shown that parents need clear information and they provide justification for the practice adopted in many units of giving parents a polaroid photograph of the baby when rapid admission of the baby to another hospital is essential for medical reasons (Jacques *et al.*, 1983).

Observational work has shown that preterm babies do not have the same capacities as full term infants for engaging in reciprocal interaction. Their behaviour is often unpredictable and their social signals hard to read (Goldberg and Divitto, 1983). Not surprisingly, parents can find them disconcerting and unrewarding as social partners. Knowledge of these early patterns of interaction allows us to provide appropriate support until the infant reaches a level of behavioural maturity sufficient to engage fully in social exchanges. With present day techniques of neonatal care, infants born as early as 24 weeks of gestation are surviving. Such babies need long periods of hospital care and experience shows that it is as important to understand their psychological needs and those of their parents as it is to offer appropriate physiological support.

In summary, the development of neonatal paediatrics has created new situations for parents and their small and sick offspring. The bonding hypothesis served to draw our attention to the potential difficulties and to encourage new research. This has led to a much better appreciation of the social and psychological context in which early relationships are formed, which has permitted the development of appropriate psychological care as a part of neonatal paediatrics.

Attachment theory

Bowlby's theory of attachment has proved to be a major influence on both psychological research and social policy concerning parents and children. It deals both with the process by which babies form social attachments and the consequences of breaks in such attachments (Bowlby, 1969; 1973). Bowlby describes **attachment** as the affectional tie the infant forms to another person (usually the mother, in his view) and he claims that a satisfactory attachment is necessary to ensure satisfactory mental health in adulthood.

Bowlby's theory draws on animal ethology and psychoanalysis as well as some elements from cybernetics. He postulates that attachment originates with a number of specific behaviour patterns of the infant—sucking, crying, clinging, smiling and following—which bring it and the caregiver together and keep them close. Through this close contact the infant's generalized social responsiveness becomes more specific so that the care-taker is individually recognized and responded to. Towards the end of the first year of life when the attachment is formed, the baby will deliberately seek and remain close to the attachment figure. Operating in the opposite direction to draw the infant from the mother, is the infant's need to explore. Bowlby sees the balance between these opposing needs operating in the manner of a cybernetic control system so that a particular infant at a specific time will have a goal set to balance the two at an appropriate level.

The usual way in which attachment has been assessed in the laboratory is by Ainsworth's **'strange situation'** (Ainsworth *et al.*, 1978) which is used for infants aged from about 1 year to 18 months. Mother and baby are observed in a playroom equipped with toys. First the two are observed alone together to see whether the infant approaches the toys or remains close to the mother. Then a stranger enters and sits by the mother and tries to engage the infant in play. The mother leaves the room for 3 minutes. She then returns and is reunited with her baby. Both stranger and mother then leave for a brief period. The stranger returns and finally the mother comes in and picks up the baby. Most infants play with the toys in the initial part of the session. They protest when the mother leaves and fail to be comforted by the presence of the stranger. By the point of the mother's second departure, most infants are crying and they cling tightly at the final reunion. However, behaviour does vary widely. By using a combination of measures of behaviour in each phase of the test, children are classified as securely attached, avoidant (those who show much disturbance at the mother's departure and either ignore or are ambivalent towards the mother at her return) and an ambivalent group (who show elements of both avoidance and attachment). In most samples of normal European or North American children, about 70 per cent show the secure pattern, about 20 per cent are avoidant and 10 per cent are ambivalent.

While no one doubts that infants form relationships with their social companions and caretakers, many rather different criticisms of attachment theory have been put forward. As we have already seen, the ways in which specific patterns of infant behaviour may be used to mediate the caretaker-infant relationship may vary from culture to culture so that Bowlby's list of five patterns may not have the universal quality he claimed. Indeed, some on his list such as following and clinging probably owe more to his interest in animal ethology than studies of mother-infant interaction. Other critics have been concerned with the relationship between measures of attachment obtained in laboratory tests and what can be observed in everyday situations (Sawalsky *et al.*, 1987). The different measures do not always correlate, suggesting that attachment may not be a unitary concept.

The other side of Bowlby's work is about the effects of separation on development. His claim was that breaks in attachment would have long-term, if not permanent, effects on adult mental health and, in particular, on the capacity to form love relationships. Here, Bowlby was drawing on a much older idea that may be found in Freud as well as even earlier writers that the mother-child relationship is the first love relationship and that a satisfactory first love relationship is necessary to form the capacity to develop later ones. While it is easy enough to observe the distress of a young child separated from an attachment figure, whether separations have long-term consequences is much more controversial. For example, studies of children who go to hospital suggest that long-term effects may be confined to those who are repeatedly separated (Rutter, 1981). Rutter in his review of the evidence also shows that the quality of the child's relationship with the attachment figure prior to separation and the nature of the separation experience (for example, a hospital stay usually has a very different meaning for a child than a pleasurable holiday with grandparents) may have very significant effects on outcomes.

Effects of parental divorce and separation on children

The study of the effects of divorce on the social development of children is important both for practical reasons and because it may serve to highlight other shortcomings of attachment theory.

As was mentioned in the last section, a child's response to a separation may have a lot to do with how and why that separation occurs. For example, studies of the effects of parental divorce suggest that it is more upsetting in the longer term than the death of a parent (Rutter, 1981). To understand this difference we need to examine the meaning of the two events from the child's point of view. Most children deeply resent their parents' marital separation and often feel betrayed that their parents have chosen to do something they experience as so hurtful. At divorce, a child may be faced with the realization that his parents may not see his interests as paramount, whereas a child can usually understand that the separation imposed by a death does not involve a parental choice. But this is not the sole difference between divorce and parental death. On the whole, children are in a better financial situation after a death than a divorce and are more likely to remain in close contact with their wider family in the former case (Burgoyne *et al.*, 1987).

Another shortcoming of attachment theory that is of particular relevance, is the concentration on the single relationship of mother-child. While it is certainly true that in our society most child care is provided by mothers, the importance of the psychological role of other family members—fathers, sisters, brothers, grandparents and so on—is increasingly recognized. At divorce, most children remain with their mothers, and their fathers generally become an intermittent presence in their lives or disappear altogether. Thus, divorce is a situation in which we often observe psychological disturbance in children despite the continuity of the mother-child relationship. The situation of divorce highlights the role of continuity and change in relationships with other family members including the wider kin group of grandparents and others, in a child's psychological wellbeing.

Current British estimates suggest that about one-quarter of babies born are likely to experience a separation of their parents before they reach school-leaving age. Or, to look at it in another way, about 160000 divorces are granted annually in England and Wales and in 60 per cent of cases there are children in the family. These figures represent the result of 25 years of a rising divorce rate, and an increasing tendency to divorce early in a marriage. The greatest likelihood of divorce in childless couples now occurs in the fourth year of marriage, whereas for couples with children, it is in the eleventh year. These figures also emphasize the extent to which young children are caught up in divorce.

It is important to notice that these figures refer only to divorce. From a child's point of view, however, the most significant event is likely to be the parents' separation, not when a court pronounces a decree absolute. Separation may precede divorce by several years. Indeed, it has been suggested that divorce has become less the formal mark of the end of a marriage and more a first step towards remarriage. Remarriage rates have risen alongside the divorce rate, indicating that the present statistics are not evidence of a fall in the popularity of marriage. Indeed, as great a percentage of the adult population currently marries as at any previous time for which we have records.

There is a shift towards a pattern of several marital partners in a lifetime.

A third of all marriages involves at least one spouse who has been married before, and in a fifth of divorce cases, this is a second or subsequent divorce for at least one of the spouses. This implies that, for a minority, childhood will involve two or more divorces with, presumably, a growing collection of step-parents. Second marriages are more likely to end in divorce than first marriages. These statistics on divorce mean that there are fundamental changes in family life which, potentially at least, could have profound effects on the development of children.

One of the most detailed studies of the reactions of children to separation and divorce was carried out in Marin County, California by Wallerstein and Kelly (1980). Like many studies, it draws upon a sample of parents and children who went to a helping agency so may not be typical of the divorcing population as a whole. However, comparison with other work suggests the results are fairly typical with regard to the children's reactions.

Preschool children frequently appear to be very sad and frightened when their parents separate, they become very clinging and demanding. Bedtime fears and a refusal to be left alone, even for a few minutes, are not uncommon. Some children attending school or nursery may become very anxious about going there, and may protest strongly when left alone. Vivid fantasies about abandonment, death of parents or injury are not infrequently encountered. Increased levels of aggression towards other children may occur as well as fights and quarrels between siblings.

With somewhat older children grief and sadness are still a prominent feature of the usual reaction to parental separation but anger is more marked than with the younger children. This anger is usually directed at the parents, especially at the parent with whom the child is living. In most cases (about 80 per cent in Britain) this will be the mother who, regardless of the actual history, may be blamed by the child for everything that has happened. The absent father may be idealized (again, often regardless of the actual situation), and the mother is held responsible for driving him away. Children, especially in the age group 7–8 years, may express a very strong yearning for their fathers.

The pre-adolescents may show very much less outward sign of their pain and distress and they often seek distraction in play and other activity. These older children may find it very difficult to talk about what they are feeling. Underneath, however, anger is again common, and the children may align themselves very strongly with one parent and perhaps refuse to see the other. Adolescents may show overt depression. They may 'give up' on their family and withdraw into other relationships outside the home. Worries about their own relationships, sex and marriage may be prominent on the surface.

It is often claimed that children may hold themselves responsible for the break-up of their parents' marriage and feel very guilty about this. However, such reactions do not seem to be common. Much more frequent is anger towards the parents for separating. Children of all ages commonly express the wish that their parents be reunited and they blame either or both of them for the split. For adults, it is perhaps more comforting to avoid recognizing that most children do not want their parents to separate and may feel that their own parents have not taken their interests into account. As often seems to occur with this topic, our own feelings may get in the way of seeing the problems clearly. We may, therefore, tend to continue to emphasize the supposed guilt of children, rather than recognizing that they are angry at what their parents have done to them.

The effects described above are the immediate reactions of children to parental separation. Usually, they are seen in an acute form for a matter of months and then begin to subside. The precise time course is variable. Much may depend on factors such as the atmosphere in the home before the break, the quality of the relationship with each parent and how these change after the separation. Some researchers have suggested that the pre-separation turmoil in the home may be one of the most damaging parts of the process for children, and this is certainly something that children will describe later as being very upsetting. The Marin County study found that half of all the children in their sample had witnessed violence between their parents. While no evidence about pre-separation violence seems to exist for Britain, there is little to suggest that the California figures would not apply here. The study also found that the children's degree of upset was strongly influenced by their understanding of what was going on. Those who received clear explanations of what was happening, and could talk to their parents about it, fared best. However, those in this latter position were a depressingly small minority.

One of the problems for children involved in parental separation is that the parents themselves are likely to be depressed or anxious and have little energy to cope with their children's problems. The self-confidence of parents may be low and they may withdraw from social contacts. Friends and relatives may be avoided by the parents and the children become cut off from familiar people. Another pattern that is reported is a postseparation period for one or both parents of a very active social and sexual life with many partners. This is something that adolescents in particular find distressing. The separation itself may be a long, drawn out process with many comings and goings. In some cases, even when the spouses have set up home with new partners, they seem to find it very difficult to detach from their original marital relationship.

The parents' coping abilities are also likely to be reduced by money and housing problems. A separation almost always means a drop in living standards and it is commonly followed by a move of house. In about two-thirds of all cases a woman with children will be dependent on state benefits for at least a time after separation. For some, the parents' divorce will mark the start of a period of prolonged poverty. Moving house, with the attendant loss of friends and change of school, is something that many children find upsetting at the best of times, but its effects can be far more serious if it is coupled with a break-up of the parents.

The evidence about the longer-term effects of a divorce or separation on children is uncertain. As has been mentioned, the loss of a parent through a marital separation is much more likely to cause long-term problems than a loss through death. This may be because of the events that are likely to have preceded the break-up, or because the child experiences a feeling of intentional abandonment. The evidence suggest that long-term ill effects are reduced if a child remains in contact with both parents after a break.

For children, the longer-term problems that have been associated with divorce and separation of their parents are depression, low self-esteem, problems in heterosexual relationships (especially in girls), difficulties in parenthood and an increased likelihood of divorce in their own marriages.

In the past, there was much discussion about the relative merits of a bad marriage or a divorce for children. Whatever the outcome of this debate, its conclusions now seem largely irrelevant. The raised divorce rate and studies of attitudes towards marriage suggest that bad marriages are much less likely to be tolerated today. It is also likely to be true that the period of friction before an actual separation occurs may tend to be shorter. In effect, as divorce and marital separation have become more common, the phenomenon itself has changed. A sample of children taken in the 1950s whose parents had divorced was probably very different from one which might be gathered today. This means that we should not perhaps place too much reliance on the older research as it may be a very poor guide to what is going to be the long-term outcome for the present generation. One thing, however, is certain. The 'clean break' that many parents hope a divorce will bring is a fantasy, at least as far as children are concerned. For them, there is always some carry-over from the past. While it is undoubtedly the case that some divorces help children, it is often the case that adults improve their own situation at the expense of their children.

The current situation of children whose parents are separating gives several causes for concern. For both parents and children, a marital separation is strongly associated with a variety of morbidity, yet it is an event to which our health and welfare services have a very fragmented and confused approach and it is seldom seen as a priority area. Nevertheless, successful support for parents and children is likely to be a very effective form of preventive medicine and social work. For many people, the needs are fairly straightforward and are primarily an opportunity to talk over what has happened to them. People want a chance to discuss their problems and simple counselling can often be very effective. Extensive training is not required for people to become adept at offering this kind of help. One important thing that can be achieved through discussion is that parents can be helped to separate their own needs from those of their children. Unless these two are kept separate, children may suffer as their parents act out the fears, desires and anger that often predominate at a separation.

Conclusion

This chapter has ranged widely in order to indicate some of the scope of developmental research on social relationships. Perhaps the main conclusion in this area of work is that if we wish to understand the psychological processes involved in our social relationships, behaviour must be analysed within the social context in which it occurs.

Suggested reading

Archer, J. and Lloyd, B. (1982). *Sex and Gender*. Penguin Books, Harmondsworth, Middlesex.
A good general introduction to gender, its development and sexuality.

Burgone, J., Ormrod, R. and Richards, M.P.M. (1987). *Divorce Matters*. Penguin Books, Harmondsworth, Middlesex.
A survey of the social and psychological effects of separation and divorce.

Dunn, J. (1977). *Distress and Comfort*. Fontana, London.
A description of the emotional life of babies.

Goldberg, S. and Divitto, B.A. (1983). *Born too Soon: Preterm Birth and Early Development*. W.H. Freeman & Co., San Francisco.
Brings together clinical, psychological and practical information about preterm babies and their care.

Kaye, K. (1982). *The Mental and Social Life of Babies*. Tavistock Publications, London.
A wide ranging discussion of the growth of parent-child relationships.

Klaus, M.H. and Kennell, J.H. (1982). *Parent-Infant Bonding*. Mosby & Co., St. Louis, Missouri.
A view of early separation by the authors of the bonding hypothesis.

Lewontin, R. (1982). *Human Diversity*. W.H. Freeman & Co., New York.
A clear account of human genetics and evolution.

Lieberman, P.H., Tulkin, S. and Rosenfeld, A. (1977). *Culture and Infancy*. Academic Press, New York.
This brings together research conducted in several cultures and provides a view of cultural diversity.

Macfarlane, A. (1977). *The Psychology of Childbirth*. Fontana, London.
Deals with both parental feelings and the psychology of the infant.

Parke, R.D. (1977). *Fathers*. Fontana, London.
A description of fathers' roles in the lives of their children.

Richards, M.P.M. (1980). *Infancy*. Harper & Row, London.
An introductory account of the psychology of the first two years of life.

Rutter, M. (1981). *Maternal Deprivation Reassessed* (2nd edn). Penguin Books, Harmondsworth, Middlesex.
A comprehensive review of the research on the effects of separation of mothers and children.

Stern, D.N. (1977). *The First Relationship: Infant and Mother*. Harvard University Press, Cambridge, Massachusetts.
A detailed analysis of early social interaction.

References

Ainsworth, M.D.S., Blehav, M., Waters, E. and Wall, S. (1978). *Patterns of Attacı ment*. Erlbaum, Hillsdale, New Jersey.

Bayley N. (1968). Behavioral correlates of mental growth: birth to thirty-six year *American Psychologist* **23**, 1.

Bernal, J. (1972). Crying during the first 10 days of life and maternal response *Developmental Medicine and Child Neurology* **14**, 362.

Bernal. J.F., Brackbill, Y. and Richards, M.P.M. (1976). Early behavioural diffeı ences: gender or circumcision? *Developmental Psychobiology* **9**, 89.

Bowlby, J. (1969); (1973). *Attachment and Loss*: Vol 1 *Attachment*; Vol 2 *Loss*. Pengui Books, Harmondsworth, Middlesex.

Burgoyne, J., Ormrod, R. and Richards, M.P.M. (1987). *Divorce Matters*. Penguiı Books, Harmondsworth, Middlesex.

Chisholm J.S. and Richards, M.P.M. (1978). Swaddling, cradleboards and thı development of children. *Early Human Development* **2/3**, 255.

Chodorow, N. (1978). *The Reproduction of Mothering*. University of California Press Berkeley.

Goldberg, S. and Divitto, B.A. (1983). *Born too Soon: Preterm Birth and Earl Development*. W.H. Freeman & Co., San Francisco.

Goldberg, S. (1983). Parent-Infant bonding: another look. *Child Development* **54** 1355.

Henshall, C. and McGuire, J. (1986). Gender development. In *Children of Socia Worlds*, pp. 135–67. Edited by Richards, M.P.M. and Light P. Polity Press Cambridge.

Henwood, M., Rimmer, L. and Wicks, M. (1987). *Inside the Family: Changing Roles oj Men and Women*. Family Policy Studies Centre, London.

Jacques, N.S., Hawthorne Amick, J.T. and Richards, M.P.M. (1983). Parents and the support they need. In *Parent-Baby Attachment in Premature Infants*, pp. 100–28. Edited by Davis, J.A., Richards, M.P.M. and Roberton, N.R.C. Croom Helm, London.

Jowell, R. and Witherspoon, S. (1985). *British Social Attitudes*. Gower, London.

Kăğitçibaşi, C. (1982). *Sex Roles, Family and Community in Turkey*. Indiana University Turkish Studies, Bloomington, Illinois.

Katz Rothman, B. (1986). *The Tentative Pregnancy*. Viking Penguin, New York.

Kaye, K. (1982). *The Mental and Social Life of Babies*. University of Chicago Press, Chicago.

Klaus, M.H. and Kennell, J.H. (1982). *Parent-Infant Bonding*. Mosby & Co., St. Louis, Missouri.

Kohlberg, L. (1966). A cognitive-developmental analysis of children's sex-role concepts and attitudes. In *The Development of Sex Differences*, pp. 82–172. Edited by Maccoby, E.C. Tavistok Publications, London.

Konner, M.J. (1972). Aspects of the developmental ethology of a foraging people. In *Ethological Studies of Child Behaviour*, pp. 285–304. Edited by Blurton-Jones, N. Cambridge University Press, Cambridge.

Levidow, L. (1987). Sex Selection in India. *Science on Culture*. Pilot issue. Free Association Books, London.

Lewis, C. and O'Brien, M. (1987). *Reassessing Fatherhood*. Sage, London.

Money, J. and Ehrhardt, A.A. (1972). *Man and Woman, Boy and Girl*. Johns Hopkins University Press, Baltimore.

Morris, J. (1974). *Conundrum*. Faber and Faber, London.

Oakley, A. (1980). *Women Confined*. Martin Robertson, London.

Richards, M.P.M. and Roberton, N.R.C. (1978). Admission and discharge policies for special care units. In *Separation and Special Care Units*, pp. 82–114. Edited by Brimblecombe, F.S.W., Richards, M.P.M. and Roberton, N.R.C. Clinics in Developmental Medicine. No. 68. Heinemann Medical Books, London.

Richards, M.P.M. (1983). Parent-infant relationships. In *Parent-Baby Attachment in Premature Infants*, pp. 82–110. Edited by Davis, J.A., Roberton, N.R.C. and Richards, M.P.M. Croom Helm, London.

Rödholm, M. (1981). Effects of father-infant contact on the interactions 3 months after birth. *Early Human Development* **5**, 79.

Rutter, M. (1981). *Maternal Deprivation Reassessed*. Penguin Books Ltd., Harmondsworth, Middlesex.

Sluckin, W., Herbert, M. and Sluckin, A. (1983). *Maternal Bonding*. Blackwell, Oxford.

Suwalsky, J.T.D., Klein, R.P., Zaslow, M.J., Rabinovich, B.A. and Gist, N.F. (1987). Dimensions of naturally occurring mother-infant separations during the first years of life. *Infant Mental Health Journal* **8**, 3.

Trevarthan, C. (1977). Descriptive analysis of infant communicative behaviour. In *Studies in mother-infant interaction*, pp. 227–70. Edited by Schaffer, H.R. Academic Press, London.

Wallerstein, J. and Kelley, J. (1980). *Surviving the Breakup*. Grant MacIntyre, London.

5

Cognitive Development in Infancy and Childhood

DA Frye

Our abilities to think, reason and form concepts undergo systematic changes during our lifespan. These changes are particularly prevalent early in childhood. Because the changes affect how thought is organized, they can make a fundamental difference to all aspects of children's understanding. For example, many advances can be found in the child's ability to think about other people and social relationships. Children also make dramatic progress in their ability to conceptualize the physical world. Cognitive development is the study of the changes in the child's understanding of the physical world.

Two major changes in the child's understanding of the world will be considered in this chapter along with a brief discussion of language acquisition. The first change, the **object concept**, is a development that belongs to infancy and the first two years of life. This concept refers to the baby's understanding of the spatial and temporal characteristics of the objects that constitute the world. Do babies, like adults, divide the world into solid objects that continue to exist even when they are out of sight? The second development, **conservation**, occurs at 6 or 7 years of age. Conservation makes possible the understanding that there are various physical constancies in the world. So, for instance, the child recognizes that the quantity of a liquid does not change as its shape changes. Types of conservation include number, continuous quantity, weight, density and volume.

Development

The object concept, language acquisition and conservation are thought to be universal developments found with every normal child, and they clearly represent fundamental changes. For these reasons, there can be a tendency to classify them as a predetermined part of the child. Of course, the nature-nurture issue has application to all developments, whether they be perceptual, social or cognitive. Nature versus nurture is really the issue of why developmental change occurs at all. Is development mostly a function of nature, an innate part of the child, something that will eventually unfold by virtue of maturation? At the other extreme, the child could enter life with relatively little endowment, and development would result principally from the experiences encountered in the world. Most modern theorists believe development must be some interaction of the two.

Figure 5.1 portrays one model (McCall, 1981) of the interaction between nature and nurture necessary to account for human development.

The model shows the interaction between nature and nurture to be complex. Each will have a different weight in the interaction at different

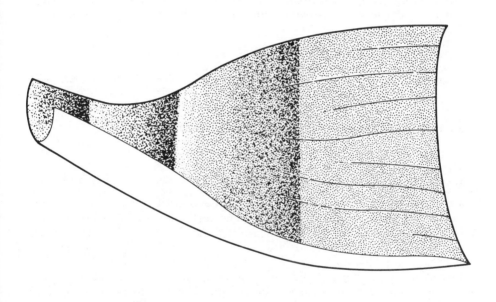

Birth——————————— 2 years ——————————— Childhood

Fig. 5.1 The 'trough' characterization of development. In the model, the shape and tilt of the trough represents the genetic disposition of the species, while the grooves mark individual differences due to genetics. Development is signified as a ball rolling from left to right down the trough. The different shadings show the different stages of development that all members of the species pass through. The environment is represented by a wind that can affect the path of the rolling ball. As can be seen, development is relatively channelled in infancy, but is more susceptible to environmental influences later. (Adapted from McCall, R. (1981). Reproduced by permission of University of Chicago Press, Illinois.

points of development. Early on, because the trough is narrow, development will be channelled, it will proceed along much the same course for all individuals, even if they are being raised in a wide variety of environments. The environment (i.e. the wind) can alter the rate of development, but it is unlikely to change the outcome. In the periods following infancy, development becomes much more susceptible to environmental influence. Now, not only can the rate of development change, but the outcome can be affected as well. Winds across the trough, if strong enough, have the potential for altering individual differences within the species.

In general, this model provides a broadly accurate depiction of development. Development during infancy has shown itself to be remarkably tolerant to variations in the environment. Thereafter, the variations have demonstrable effects. At no point is it possible to say that development is due solely to nature or solely to nurture. The developments discussed in this chapter—object permanence, language acquisition and the various forms of conservation—are all outcomes of the interaction between the two.

Cognitive development in infancy

Early perceptual-motor development

Immediately after birth, babies make active motoric responses and show evidence of the five senses. Perhaps their most highly organized behaviour is exhibited in reflexes. If the area around a newborn's mouth is touched, it will turn its head to suck on the object. Very little or no experience is necessary for this complete response to be shown. Similarly, an object placed in the newborn's hand will elicit a grasping response. Babies' senses are equally active: newborns will startle when exposed to a loud noise; and their eyes can follow the movements of large objects. They are soon even able to discriminate and react to familiar smells.

In spite of these early abilities, all of the newborn's sensory and motor systems undergo considerable development during the first months of life. In this chapter, particular attention will be given to developments in the visual system and in prehension (the baby's ability to grasp and manipulate objects). Object permanence involves both of these systems and it is typically tested by having infants attempt manually to retrieve an object from a place they have seen it hidden. In addition, vision and prehension are the best studied perceptual and response systems, respectively, in infant development.

Vision changes rapidly in the first several months of life (see Chapter 2).

Before the age of about 2 months, the baby's gaze is strongly attracted to areas of high visual contrast, boundaries between light and dark. The infant's acuity, or ability to see fine detail, is poor compared to what it will be just a few months later. Although the child will be able to track the movements of large objects, it is not until 2 months that smooth pursuit of the movement of small objects in the visual field becomes possible. Similarly, recognizing the patterns on objects, rather than just their shapes or outline, does not begin to occur until about the same time. All of these changes may be related to foveal vision becoming more important as a part of a neurophysiological shift from the subcortical to cortical visual systems.

These early changes in vision may be best illustrated by the **externality effect**. Figure 5.2 shows the fixations and eye movements 1-month olds and 2-month olds follow for simple geometric figures such as polygons. This information was obtained by a technique called infrared corneal scanning which uses infrared lights reflected off the baby's eye to determine exactly where the child is looking. The change between 1 and 2 months is obvious. At the earlier age, children scan the outer boundary of the objects almost exclusively. They do not cross over the external boundary to scan the internal features of the figures that have them. By 2 months, however, the externality effect has disappeared. Infants will now spend much of their time scanning the internal features of displays, especially if they contain areas of high visual contrast.

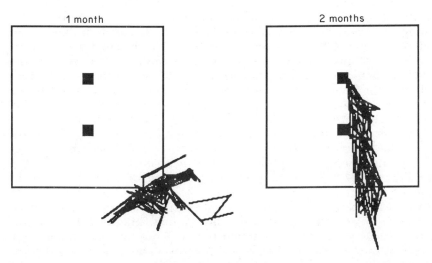

Fig. 5.2 The typical change in visual scanning patterns between 1 and 2 months of age as described by the externality effect. Before 1 month, infants very seldom cross over the external boundary of a figure to scan its internal features. (Adapted from Salapatek, P. (1975). Reproduced by permission of Academic Press, New York.)

The externality effect is not limited to geometric figures. If a line drawing of a face is shown to a 1-month old then, just as with the polygons, the baby will not attend to the internal features of the face. By 2 months, the effect is not found. It is of interest that there are other changes that occur at this same time. At about 2 months, babies first exhibit 'social smiles': they smile spontaneously when confronted with a passive human face. The development would seem to be related to the changes in visual perception because babies of this age will also now show smiles to line drawings of faces. In fact, the stimulus needs only to have rudimentary drawings of eyes enclosed in a round outline to be effective.

The baby's ability to recognize patterns also improves dramatically from 2 months on. For example, by 2 months, the infant will be able to discriminate between the bull's eye and the normal drawing of a face shown in Figure 5.3. Pattern discrimination in infancy is usually determined in one of several simple ways. With **habituation**, the baby is repeatedly allowed to look at one stimulus until his or her attention to it decreases, then the second stimulus is shown. If the baby's attention increases to the second stimulus, then it is clear that the child discriminates between the two. It is also possible to do a **paired preference test**. Here, the baby is presented with both stimuli simultaneously. If the child shows a reliable preference for looking at one over the other, then it is again clear that the child can discriminate between the two.

Results comparing drawings of faces to stimuli like the bull's eye initially led to the conclusion that infants had a very early ability to perceive faces. However, when the normal versus scrambled faces in Figure 5.3 were compared (Fantz *et al.*, 1975; Maura and Bonera, 1981) it was not until 2 months of age that infants showed a preference between the two. This finding illustrates an inescapable problem with habituation and paired preference tests. Although they can establish that the child sees a difference in two displays, they do not necessarily reveal what difference the child is using to make the discrimination. In this case, it appears that before 2 months the infant is using some criterion like internal contrast in the figure, since infants do not discriminate drawings of normal and scrambled faces, but they prefer them both to simple figures like bull's eyes. By the time babies are 4 months old, however, they prefer looking at normal rather than scrambled or inverted faces. Six- and 7-month olds can discriminate among facial photographs of people who look very similar. (See Fagan (1979) for a comprehensive account of face perception in infancy.)

Like visual perception, prehension goes through a set of identifiable changes during the first six months of life. At first, infants will more or less do two things with objects, although they will do those two things very reliably: if an object makes contact with the baby's hand, the baby will grasp it; and it if touches the baby's mouth, the baby will suck on it. These reactions start out as being separate. Over the course of the first several months, they come to be combined. If an object is placed in the baby's hand, it can be grasped and transported to the mouth. If it is in the baby's

Fig. 5.3 Before 2 months of age, babies given a paired preference test between the bullseye and normal face, look more at the face, yet when the normal and scrambled faces are paired, the preference disappears. These results demonstrate the importance of visual complexity for early visual preference. (Adapted, in part, from Maurer, D. and Barrera, M. (1981). Reproduced by permission of the University of Chicago Press, Illinois.)

mouth, it will be found and grasped. The coordination of prehension and sucking depends on experience, but it is built out of responses that were present at birth.

Until 3 or 4 months, vision does not seem to contribute to these responses. Even though the baby may be holding a toy or small object, the child does not typically look at that object, it is just moved to the baby's mouth. By 4 months of age there is a change. Now babies not only watch a grasped object, they also spend a significant amount of time gazing at their own hands. What is of crucial interest at this point is that vision and prehension are not coordinated. If an object is shown, babies at this age will be unable to reach out and grasp it. It is only at 5 months that **visually directed reaching** becomes common. This landmark development makes it possible for babies to reach for any object they see. It marks the beginning of vision's dominance over the child's manual responses. Interestingly, this development seems to depend on the children having experience with seeing their hands and objects in the same visual field. (White's (1975) classic monograph describes this series of developments admirably.)

Six-month olds exhibit remarkable strides in development. Their visual acuity and detection of visual patterns is reasonably close to that of the adult. They can easily reach out and grasp objects. Their reaches will be accurate. They will not reach for objects that are far beyond the length of their arms. In spite of these impressive abilities, there is evidence that babies do not yet exhibit object permanence.

Object permanence

The study of the object concept or object permanence was initiated by the renowned Swiss psychologist Jean Piaget. In carefully observing his own three children, Piaget was led to the conclusion that babies do not begin life with the common understanding that objects in the world are three-dimensional solids that have independent existence. Instead, Piaget concluded that babies start off believing that objects only exist when they are being directly acted on or, in other words, that 'out of sight is out of mind' for young babies. Consequently, Piaget argues, infants must construct the concept of the object over the course of development.

Object permanence has traditionally been studied through some very simple hiding tasks. It must be remembered that 6-month olds can see well and are capable of reaching for objects under the direction of vision. They are also able to solve partial hiding tasks. If a toy the baby is interested in is partially covered by a cloth in front of the child, 6-month olds will easily be able to retrieve the toy. They fail total occlusion hiding tasks however: when the cloth completely covers the toy, 6-month olds are unable to retrieve the object. Their typical reaction is important. It is not that they become upset. When the toy completely disappears under the cloth or some other cover, the baby's attention simply moves to something else.

The total hiding task is solved at approximately 8 months. Piaget argues that this development signals the beginning of object permanence. Now, when the toy is hidden, the baby will have very little difficulty uncovering and retrieving it. This advance is accompanied by a strange error, the **AB error**. The effect can be demonstrated using two hiding covers, one on each side of the child as shown in Figure 5.4. The object is hidden at the first place or A, several times. Since this is merely a total covering task, the infant solves it. On a subsequent trial, the toy is moved, within plain sight of the baby, to B. Eight-month olds reliably return to A to look for the toy. They will make this error several times in a row and will often be surprised when they fail to find the toy. After they finally find the toy at B, it can be hidden there several times, then moved back to A, and the babies will search at B expecting to find the toy.

Piaget theorizes that infants younger than 8 months do not find a completely covered toy because they do not realize that the object continues to exist when it disappears. A change in memory may underlie the new development. If the child can remember the toy while working to remove the cover, then the total hiding task can be solved. Of course, this change is limited. In the AB task, memory seems to mislead the child. Even though

Fig. 5.4 An 8-month-old searching at the wrong hiding place on the B trial of the AB task. (Photograph by Linsley J. Barbato.)

the toy can be seen to disappear at B, the child searches at A. This pattern of results would seem to indicate that although there is a change in memory capacity at 8 months, the contents of the new memory cannot be modified very quickly. Whenever the toy disappears at a new place, the child can remember that it still exists, but for several trials the previous contents of memory cause the child to search at the old place.

Infants continue to fail the AB task for the next several months. By the time they are about 1 year of age, they have no trouble with it at all. There are several more complicated hiding tasks—tasks in which the infant cannot watch the movements of the object directly—that are solved over the course of the second year. In Piaget's estimation, babies do not have complete object permanence until they are approximately 2 years old (see Piaget's *The Construction of Reality in the Child* (1954) for a complete description of the theory). At 2 years, they will search for an object at the place they last saw it disappear. If they have not been given information about the location, they will systematically search the possible hiding places. Even if they have difficulty finding the toy, they will, like adults, necessarily assume that it continues to exist and can be eventually found.

Other research on object permanence

Research over the past twenty years has generally come to the conclusion that Piaget underestimated the abilities of the infant. This research indicates that object permanence is likely to be present very early. Indeed, object permanence may well be a part of the innate endowment of the child since, without it, the child lacks a very basic understanding of the world. According to this view, Piaget may have formulated an inaccurate estimation of the child's cognitive development because of the type of tasks he used to assess object permanence.

Bower was among the first to take up the study of object permanence after Piaget (the research is fully described in Bower's book, *Development in Infancy* (1982)). Bower suspected that Piaget's hiding tasks may have not done justice to the infant's abilities because they required a manual response from the child. Bower invented his **tracking studies** as one way to circumvent this difficulty. In a tracking study, the infant merely watches an out-of-reach object as it moves on a path across the visual field. In the middle of the field there is a barrier that the object must pass behind. The crucial question in this task is whether the infant looks ahead in order to anticipate the reappearance of the object from behind the barrier. If so, then there is evidence the child knew the object continued to exist when it was out of sight behind the screen.

Bower first tried the tracking task with babies as young as 3 months. Initially, the results looked promising. The infants did seem to anticipate the reappearance of the object from behind the screen. However, when a control condition was imposed, in which the object was stopped before the barrier, the infants still seemed to look ahead! In other words, they did not track the object with complete accuracy at this age even when it moved and stopped in sight. Similar tests with 5-month olds showed an intelligible pattern of results. These infants stopped tracking if the object stopped in sight; and they anticipated the reappearance of the object if its path sent it behind the barrier.

Some attempt has been made to determine if the disparity between the hiding and tracking results is due to the baby having to make a manual response in one and not the other. Of course, we know that 5-month olds can reach out and pick up an object they see, but they still may have trouble removing a cover in the constraints of the hiding task. Bower devised two other tasks to address this question. The first was to hide the object by turning out all the lights in the room rather than using a cover; and the second was to 'hide' the object underneath a transparent cover like a drinking glass. Of course, if it is the manual response that is the difficulty then 5-month olds should solve the first task, but fail the second. Unfortunately, the studies that have tested these manipulations are not in full agreement. It is probably fair to say, however, that the disparity between the hiding and tracking results cannot solely be accounted for by the difference in manual response.

Bower's studies have raised the possibility that object permanence may be present earlier than Piaget believed. Certainly, the results of both Piaget's and Bower's studies highlight the difficulties of research with infants and the need for multiple tasks to test for important developments. Bower's results do not support the view, on the other hand, that object permanence is present from birth. This extensive line of research has established that the object concept is something the infant must develop. Subsequent research will presumably settle just when the first signs of object permanence appear and the course the developments take after that.

Object permanence and nature versus nurture

Throughout the discussion of object permanence reference has been made to ages for developmental milestones (e.g. solving the total hiding problem at 8 months), as if all babies mastered the task at precisely that time. Actually, the dates represent averages and there is considerable individual variation. Studies of the AB error have found, for instance, that various babies start to commit the error from as early as 6½ months to as late as 9 months, although they all do show it at some point. What is important is not that the rate of development is constant for all babies, but that all babies go through the same sequence of developments.

As has been discussed, differences in development can be a function of the innate endowment of the child, the environment, or, more likely, an interaction of the two. Questions of this type are usually addressed by just two basic experimental tools and their variants. These are **training** and **deprivation studies**. The logic for the two is very similar. Children are either provided with a superabundance of experience or, through some accident, crucial experiences are withheld from them. If, in either case, development is affected, it is clear that the environment is playing an important role. On the other hand, if development is not accelerated or impeded, then there is good reason for believing that the sequence is determined by the child's endowment.

For obvious reasons, it is ethically preferable to do training, rather than deprivation studies with children. There have been times, however, when what might be called 'natural deprivation' studies occurred. Thalidomide babies provide such an example for object permanence. Thalidomide is a sedative which was prescribed in the 1960s before its serious side-effects were known. When given early in pregnancy, it sometimes led to congenital limb deficits—arms, legs or both—in the child. A number of these children were born before the drug was withdrawn from the market. Of course, one of the many developmental questions these children pose is what will their object concept be, given that many of them will not have any experience with prehension.

Studies of these children over the course of infancy found, rather remarkably, that their development of the object concept did not suffer greatly. In fact, at 2 years they may have been only a month or two behind their normal counterparts on the object permanence hiding tasks. The

Thalidomide babies solved these tasks by removing the covers with their mouths or feet. This finding might seem to indicate that, since the deprivation condition had little effect on the development of object permanence, it must be under genetic control. However, careful observation of these babies over the first two years led to a different conclusion. It became evident that the babies were not really being deprived of experience manipulating objects. All along they actively sought to play with objects, but used other parts of their bodies instead of their hands.

These results, besides pointing out a common difficulty with deprivation studies, are consistent with the notion that development in infancy is channelled. Infants can be exposed to wide variations in rearing conditions and still reach the same developmental endpoint. What is more, they clearly show the obstacles to unravelling nature versus nurture. What first appeared to be genetically driven was found to have a large environmental component, reinforcing the point that it is the interaction of the two influences that is most important.

Language acquisition

Theories of language acquisition provide one of the best examples of the full extent of the nature-nurture debate. The acquisition of language is in itself a remarkable process. At birth, of course, babies show no detectable comprehension of spoken language. Yet, by 2 years of age, virtually all children will be able to comprehend and produce simple utterances sufficiently well to communicate with those around them. The initial theories of how this change occurs took very prominent positions at either end of the nature-nurture continuum. All the subsequent research has pointed to a much more complex interaction.

Skinner in his 1957 book, *Verbal Behavior*, advanced a strong nurture or empiricist explanation for the acquisition of language. Skinner was writing at a time when learning theory was the dominant voice in psychology. A serious objection against learning theory, as it was then construed, was that it could not explain the complicated human activity of language. Skinner's book set about explaining language, or verbal behaviour, in learning terms. His account of the acquisition of language was relatively straightforward. Young babies naturally produce sounds of which adults, and especially caregivers, try to make sense. Adults will *shape* the baby's behaviour, by showing increased attention to certain sounds, in order to have the baby produce sounds that more closely resemble adult language. When the infant produces a word like 'more' or 'milk', then the favourable effects that follow the use of the word serve to establish it in the child's vocabulary. From then on, the common beneficial effects of language drive the acquisition process.

Skinner's explanation was soon opposed by Chomsky (1959). Chomsky advanced the view that the essential features of language must be innate, part of the nature of the child. He tried to rebut Skinner's theory on a wide variety of grounds. Several points in Chomsky's rebuttal questioned the plausibility of Skinner's theory. It is known that adults rarely speak in complete, well-formed utterances. Chomsky found it difficult to believe that this linguistic environment was sufficient to provide the appropriate reinforcement contingencies to enable all children to learn language by the time they were 2 years of age. Chomsky also argued against Skinner on logical grounds. Chomsky had the crucial theoretical insight that language is creative. One of the central characteristics of language is that it permits an infinite number of new, yet meaningful utterances. It is difficult to see how Skinner's theory of reinforcement might account for the generation of novel utterances.

Chomsky argued that it is possible for language to be creative because it is rule governed. The rules, essentially, are just the rules of grammar. Grammar dictates how words can be combined into meaningful sentences, but it does not put an upper limit on the number of combinations that can be made, the number of meaningful things that can be said. Children provide some evidence that language is rule governed. Young children will occasionally say things like, "He goed to the shop". This utterance is of course wrong, but it shows an attempt to follow a rule. It is not likely to be something the child has heard before, nor is it something the child would be reinforced for saying. Chomsky's view of the acquisition process is that the very basic rules of grammar are innate. Because these rules are inborn, they enable the child to take in and decode linguistic input from the environment, thus allowing the child to gain a complete command of the language. Chomsky believed that without the grammatical rules being innate the child would never be able to acquire language.

One of the benefits of Skinner's and Chomsky's disagreement is that it forced researchers to begin to examine how children actually acquire language. This topic has been the subject of considerable investigation over the past thirty years. A number of the basic facts of the acquisition process have been settled. Babies begin to produce streams of speech sounds, babbling, at about 5–6 months of age. They typically speak their first words when they are nearly 1 year old. For the next six months, they will only speak in single-word utterances, and their vocabularies will be limited to approximately five or six words. Common words at this point are "mummy", "daddy", "dog" and "ball". At a year and a half, there is a remarkable change. Now children begin to combine words into two-word utterances. At this same time, their vocabularies explode. Table 5.1 displays all the two-word utterances of a child in this period. It is not unusual that by 2 years the child will have a vocabulary of nearly two hundred words. (See de Villiers and de Villiers for more detail on the acquisition process.)

Neither Skinner's, nor Chomsky's position has been endorsed by the further research on child language. Contrary to Skinner's views, it has been very difficult to observe occasions when parents appear to shape their infant's language production. More often, they will attend to what the baby tries to say, even if the child adopts an incorrect linguistic form. On the other hand, there are only a small number of language effects that fit a strong version of Chomsky's maturational view. For example, although

Table 5.1   All of the two-word utterances made by one boy in the two-word period. Adapted from Braine (1976) by permission of the Society for Research in Child Development.

More car	No bed	Other bib	Boot off
More cereal	No down	Other bread	Light off
More cookie	No fix	Other milk	Pants off
More fish	No home	Other pants	Shirt off
More high	No mama	Other part	Shoe off
More hot	No more	Other piece	Water off
More juice	No pee	Other pocket	Off bib
More read	No plug	Other shirt	
More sing	No water	Other shoe	Airplane by
More toast	No wet	Other side	Siren by
More walk			Mail come
	All broke	See baby	Mama come
Byebye back	All buttoned	See pretty	What's that
Byebye Calico	All clean	See train	What's this
Byebye car	All done		Mail man
Byebye papa	All dressed	Hi Calico	Mail car
Calico byebye	All dry	Hi mama	Our car
Papa byebye	All fix	Hi papa	Our door
	All gone		Papa away
Down there	All messy		Pants change
	All shut		Dry pants
	All through		
	All wet		

profoundly deaf children begin to babble in the middle of the first year just as hearing children do, feedback seems to be important for the maintenance of this behaviour, because deaf children stop babbling in a month or two whereas the hearing children do not. It has also been discovered that the baby's linguistic environment may not be as complicated as Chomsky assumed. Adults adopt a particular style when speaking to infants. They tend to use simple, well-formed, complete sentences. The existence of this type of input weakens the argument that language could not be acquired unless the rules were innate.

By 3–4 years of age, children are speaking in full multiword utterances. Most of their speech now conforms closely to the normal rules of grammar. Whilst it is logically defensible to argue that the rules of grammar are innate and merely just take a period of time to emerge, this does not provide a very helpful explanation of how language is acquired. Of course, Skinner's account is also incomplete, since it neglects some of the crucial features of language and has not been borne out by the research. Any adequate theory of language acquisition is likely to need to incorporate both cognitive and social developments. Children must have a basic understanding of the world, such as that of object permanence, to name and talk about objects. They will also have to be somewhat accomplished socially, because language is at its heart a means of communicating with other people. All of these considerations point to the conclusion that a full explanation of language acquisition will be highly complex. That complexity should not come as a surprise, since language itself is one of the most complex abilities humans have.

Cognitive development in childhood

In Piaget's theory of cognitive development (Table 5.2), object permanence is a part of the Sensorimotor Period which lasts from birth to the end of infancy at 2 years. The next period, the Preoperational Stage, covers the ages from 2 to 6 or 7 years. Concrete Operations comes into effect from 7 to 12 years of age. The final period of development, Formal Operations,

Table 5.2 Piaget's theory of cognitive development listing the names, average ages and representative developments from the four major periods of development

Sensorimotor	Birth to 2 years	Object permanence
Preoperational	2 to 5 or 6 years	Class inclusion
Concrete Operations	6 to 12 years	Conservation
Formal Operations	12 years on	Logical reasoning

commences at about 12 years and is thought to last for the remainder of the lifespan. Conservation, the development to be discussed next, defines the break between the Preoperational and Concrete Operational periods. When the children can solve the conservation tasks, they have entered Concrete Operations.

Conservation

While it may be easy to believe that babies lack some basic understanding of the physical world, it becomes much more difficult to believe the same thing of 3-, 4-, 5- and 6-year-olds. These children, of course, understand object permanence. They have acquired language and can carry on conversations with adults and peers. They are adept at play, are starting to use their imaginations, and are beginning to form social relationships with children of their own age. Nonetheless, the research on conservation would suggest that in several ways these children have an understanding of the physical world that is fundamentally different from that of the adult.

Conservation problems take a variety of forms. Two of the simplest are conservation of discontinuous quantity and conservation of continuous quantity. Figure 5.5 shows the displays used in each of these tasks. In conservation of discontinuous quantity or number, the child is shown two equal rows of, say, seven small objects. After the child agrees that both rows have the same amount, one of the rows is transformed either by lengthening or shortening it. The child is then asked again whether the two rows have the same amount or whether one has more. The continuous quantity task begins with two identical beakers containing equal amounts of water. The transformation this time is for the water from one beaker to be poured into a different shaped container e.g. a graduated cylinder. As usual, the

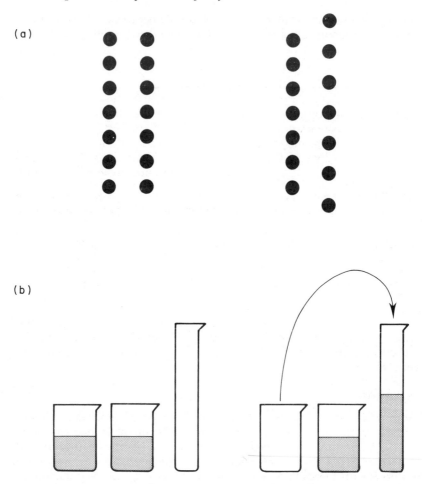

Fig 5.5 Illustration of the procedures for the conservation of (a) discontinous quantity (number) and (b) continuous quantity tasks. The displays on the left and right are before and after the transformation. For each display before and after the transformation the child is asked, "Is there the same amount in this row (or container) as the next to it, or does one have more that the other."

child is asked before and after the transformation if the amounts are the same or not.

Children younger than 6 or 7 years of age fail both of these tasks. They do not seem to realize that the amount does not change with the rearrangement. In other words, they do not conserve quantity across the transformation. There are similar conservation tasks for weight, density and volume. These tasks pose the questions that if the shape of some object, like a piece of plasticene, is changed, Will it still weigh the same?

Will it still float (or not) in some other material? and Will it still displace the same volume when immersed in a liquid? Children entering school will fail all of these conservation tasks. In fact, these tasks are much more difficult than the two testing quantity. Their solution may be delayed several years until ages 8, 9 or even 10 years.

Why do young children have such an odd view of the world that they believe that the quantity of something changes if its physical arrangement changes? Piaget concluded that **Preoperational** children make these errors because they can only consider single dimensions at a time. So, in the continuous quantity task, the child uses the height of the water column to compare the quantities. It can be observed that children do often make reference to this dimension. If the display is returned to its original arrangement, the child will revert to saying that the quantities are the same. In comparison, the **Operational** child is thought to be able to consider two dimensions simultaneously. They can conserve because they know that the water in the graduated cylinder is higher, but that the cylinder is much narrower, so the quantity need not have changed. They appreciate that the change in one dimension is compensated for by the change in the other.

Piaget's explanation of conservation, then, is of the same general type as his explanation of object permanence. A change in the child's cognitive abilities makes possible a change in the child's understanding of the world. The change is a developmental one that occurs for all children. A problem with this explanation for conservation is that the various conservation tasks are solved at different times. If a cognitive change is responsible, then should not all the tasks be solved at the same point in development? One possible rationale for why this is not the case is that all the tasks require simultaneous consideration of two dimensions, but the dimensions are more difficult to identify for certain tasks. It is more difficult to see the dimensions relevant to the weight of plasticene than to see how height and width affect the quantity of water. Even if this explanation is plausible, Piaget's theory loses some of its elegance in not being able to give a strong account of the observed delays.

Much like object permanence, the subsequent research on conservation has questioned whether young children are really as bad at understanding these aspects of the physical world as Piaget claimed. Questions about the conservation tasks have been raised in many forms. One of the most recent has been Donaldson's argument (from her book, *Children's Minds* (1978)) that young children may have no difficulty conserving, but that they are misled by the social context of the standard conservation task. Specifically, Donaldson argues that it is actually the social sophistication of the young child that causes the difficulty in the standard task. In the standard task, the child is asked and must answer the very same question about quantity twice in a row. This pattern does not agree with what is normally done in a conversation. Donaldson hypothesizes that although young children can conserve, when confronted with the quantity question twice in a row, they think that the experimenter cannot reasonably be asking about quantity the second time, so they answer the question in regard to the dimension that has changed in the display and appear to fail the task.

Donaldson tested this hypothesis with the aid of a hand puppet named Naughty Teddy. The logic of the experiment was that if the transformation of the display seemed to be an accident, then the experimenter's second quantity question would be in a context that made sense, and the children would answer it correctly. One group of 4-year-olds was given a standard conservation of discontinuous quantity task where the experimenter transformed the display. In another group, the children were first told that Naughty Teddy might disrupt the games they were playing. When it came time for the transformation, the experimenter put on Naughty Teddy and had the puppet change the display. The quantity questions were the same for both groups. The results supported Donaldson's hypothesis. Twenty per cent of the children in the standard condition conserved, whereas 50 per cent in modified condition answered correctly.

Moore and Frye (1986) have qualified Donaldson's study by repeating it with several new conditions. The new conditions tested the effect with a larger number of objects in the display and with a transformation that actually changed quantity. The point of these conditions was to see if the Naughty Teddy context was always better than the standard. Donaldson's discontinuous quantity task had four objects in each of the two rows. Moore's included groups that were shown seven objects per row. In the new quantity changing transformation, an object was added into the middle of a row without changing its length. As children typically understand the effects of an addition before they understand conservation, they can be expected to do well on this test. The results of the experiment are shown in Table 5.3. They indicate that Moore replicates Donaldson's results for four objects. With the seven objects, however, Naughty Teddy does not seem to produce performance that is any better than in the standard context. Even more striking are the results for the addition transformation. Here, the children in the standard group recognized that the addition resulted in one row having more objects than the other. The children in the Naughty Teddy context, in contrast, performed very poorly. They said that the rows had the same amount after the addition.

Donaldson's results establish that social context exerts a considerable influence on children's performance in cognitive tasks. Moore's results, especially for the addition transformation, illustrate that the effect of the modified context is not always predictable, and does not necessarily give a more sensitive assessment of the child's abilities. Taken as a whole, these results certainly do not indicate that young children can conserve. If anything, they show that, since the inability to conserve and social context interact, neither of these constraints on development can be dismissed. All cognitive tasks must be carried out in some social context so we need to be mindful of the possible effects of the context. On the other hand, young children's difficulties with conservation do not seem ascribable solely to the social context, so conservation would appear to require an explanation in terms of cognitive development.

Table 5.3 The results from Moore and Frye's Naughty Teddy experiment showing that the modified context only improved conservation responses with 4 and not 7 counters for the usual length change transformation. For the addition transformation that changed the quantity, the modified context actually produced worse performance. (Reproduced from Moore, C. and Frye, D. (1986) by permission of Elsevier Science Publishers, Amsterdam.)

	Length change		Addition	
	'Same' (correct)	'More' (incorrect)	'Same' (correct)	'More' (incorrect)
Standard				
4 counters	8	22	1	29
7 counters	10	20	5	25
Naughty teddy				
4 counters	17	13	11	19
7 counters	6	24	23	7

N = 30 in each condition for each transformation.

Conservation and nature versus nurture

Conservation is another topic that has been taken up in the nature-nurture debate. The issue was raised mainly by theorists who usually place primary emphasis on experience and the environment. Their chief tool in this case was to perform an extensive array of training studies. The general rationale was to give children as young as 3- and 4-years old explicit training in conservation either by exposing them repeatedly to the conservation tasks or by more complicated procedures which highlight the inconsistencies of non-conservation. The prediction was that, if conservation were largely due to learning (i.e. nurture), then it would be possible to produce conservation in very young children.

The conservation training studies helped to define how training studies should be designed. A good training study will have three phases: pretest, training and post-test. The pretest phase will uncover the subjects' initial conservation abilities. For the training phase, the children will be randomly divided into control and training groups. After the training has been done, all of the subjects are given the post-tests. The difference between the control and experimental groups will reveal if the training has had a significant effect.

It is not enough, however, just to test the children on the tasks on which half of them have been trained. It is important to test for **generalization**. If the children have been trained on conservation of discontinuous quantity, then they should also be tested on continuous as well as discontinuous quantity tasks. **Retention** must be assessed too. The subjects should be tested immediately after training and several months later. Both of these requirements are designed to assess whether the children actually learned to conserve. For example, it is possible to pass many conservation tests merely by learning to say 'same' whenever a conservation question is posed. Generalization and retention tests help to guard against superficial solutions to the tasks.

The conservation training studies met with some success (e.g. Silverman and Rose, 1982). The age at which children would conserve could be lowered, but usually only by a year or two. The training generally was not effective for 3- and 4-year-olds. The advances that did occur seemed to represent real gains in conservation, rather than the learning of specific verbal responses or some other shortcut tied to the experimental situation. Reasonable generalization from training on one conservation task to performance on others has been found. Retention of the gains is usually very good. It has also been discovered that those children who are at the transition point before training, because they are almost ready to conserve on their own, are the ones who benefit most from the training. This finding again fits the picture of an interaction between nature and nurture. It shows that the effect of an environmental event will differ depending on the current developmental status of the child.

Implications of Concrete Operations

If children begin to conserve because of some general change in their cognitive abilities, as has been argued, then it might be expected that the change would have consequences outside of conservation. In fact, the change to concrete operations has been found to have effects in domains as diverse as children's understanding of causality and their conception of emotion. Examples of children's thoughts about morbidity and mortality are given below to illustrate these changes.

Research into children's understanding of phenomena like illness and death is usually done merely by asking children a series of questions to see if their answers are different at different ages. For example, in the case of illness, children have been asked, "If you sat next to someone with a toothache, do you think you would catch it?" The particular ailments asked about were a cold, a toothache and a scraped knee. Children younger than about 6 years consistently say that all three of these could be caught by sitting next to someone who had them. Children older than 6 understand that only the cold is infectious. A somewhat similar effect can be found if children are told a story about an old person dying and then questioned about it. Young children tend to deny the propositions that everyone will die someday and that death is irreversible. Again, their answers to these questions change sharply between the ages of 5 and 7 years.

These results are reminiscent of non-conservation to the extent that it seems the children are forming judgements on relatively superficial grounds. Just as they tend to judge quantity by single salient physical characteristics, like the length of a row or the height of a water column, their judgements of illnesses seem to be dominated by the most salient feature of infection, i.e. the effect of physical proximity. Their initial rejection of the universality and irreversibility of death may be similar to their belief in the mutability of quantity. Although they have said the quantity is more when it is poured into the graduated cylinder, it can be made to be the same amount again just by pouring back in the original container. With both illness and death, young children have been found to supplement their explanations of these phenomena with references to notions of punishment. They will say people become ill or die because they must have been bad. These thoughts tend to disappear at the same time of the other changes, but they have obvious implications for the care of young children who are ill.

It is always important when two developments co-occur to consider the possibility that they are merely coincidental. It is conceivable that the change in the child's thinking about morbidity and mortality at 6 or 7 years is unrelated to Concrete Operations. The strongest evidence that they are related could be obtained in a modified training study where children would be trained on one developmental task, say conservation, to see if it automatically affected the other task, their understanding of illness or death. These studies have not yet been conducted. Nevertheless, it has been found that children's performance on conservation tasks is a better predictor of their answers to the morbidity and mortality questions than is their age. This result would indicate that these developments are probably related to Concrete Operations.

Summary and conclusions

The two major cognitive developments discussed in this chapter form the core of the child's understanding of the physical world. The acquisition of object permanence during infancy establishes that there is an outside world. In the first two years of life, babies come to recognize that objects are separate, three-dimensional entities that have independent existence. Conservation during middle childhood shows that there are other physical constancies to be found. Conservation builds on object permanence. Four- or 5-year-old children who do not conserve quantity, nonetheless know that when objects in a row are spread out they are still the same objects. What they will understand at 6 or 7 years is that, despite the change in appearance of the display brought about by the transformation, the number of counters remains the same. This new understanding will ultimately be followed by conservation of continuous quantity, weight, density and volume.

Skinner's and Chomsky's opposing views of language acquisition illustrate the extremes in the nature versus nurture debate. Nature versus nurture also has application to object permanence and conservation. In general, later researchers have argued that Piaget placed both of these cognitive accomplishments too late in development. Bower and Donaldson have shown that it is possible to find some evidence of the two somewhat earlier on. None of the later research has, however, shown them to be primarily a function of nature *or* nurture. All evidence points to the conclusion that they are some interaction between the two. The goal of developmental psychology is to discover the specifics of that interaction. Training and deprivation studies are the basic research tools available for unravelling the interaction. Both rely on manipulating experience to see the effect on developmental outcome. Obviously, training studies, like the ones done with conservation, are to be preferred on ethical grounds to those requiring deprivation; but occasionally, informative, unintentional deprivation studies occur, as in the case of object permanence and the Thalidomide babies, or speech sounds and deaf infants.

Finally, some attention has been given to the view that object permanence and conservation are the consequence of more general cognitive changes. A change in memory capacity may underlie early changes in object permanence. Children should be able to conserve when they can consider changes in more than one dimension of a display. If these cognitive changes are to be viewed as general, then they must have wider application than just to object permanence and conservation. Shifts at 6 or 7 years in children's understanding of morbidity and mortality would seem to indicate that the change in thought at that time is not limited to conservation. Of course, a single cognitive change cannot be the full explanation even for conservation because the solution of the different conservation tasks is distributed over several years. Thus, even though the cognitive changes cannot be the entire explanation, they are certainly essential for explaining several of the major steps in the child's development.

Suggested reading

Bower, T.G.R. (1982). *Development in Infancy*. W.H. Freeman & Co., San Francisco.
Bower's report of his experiments and theory of development in infancy including his studies of object permanence.

de Villiers, P. and de Villiers, J. (1979). *Early Language*. Fontana, Glasgow.
A good introductory survey of the important findings in the language acquisition research.

Donaldson, M. (1978). *Children's Minds*. Fontana, Glasgow.
Donaldson's very clear presentation of the argument for recognizing the importance of social factors in experiments on cognitive development.

Fagan, J. (1979). The origins of facial pattern recognition. In *Psychological Development from Infancy*. Edited by Bornstein, M and Kessen, W. Erlbaum, New Jersey.
An excellent review of the experiments on perception of faces in infancy.

Piaget, P. (1954). *The Construction of Reality in the Child*. Basic Books, New York.
The book in which Piaget presents his original observations on object permanence.

White, B. (1975). The initial coordination of sensorimotor schemes in infancy. In *Developmental Psychology*. Edited by Sants, J. and Butcher, H. Penguin Books Ltd., Harmondsworth, Middlesex.
An excellent research monograph on the early coordination between vision and touch in infancy.

References

Braine, M.D.S. (1976). Children's first word combinations. *Monographs of the Society for Research in Child Development* **41**, 164.
Chomsky, N. (1959). Review of Skinner. *Language* **35**, 26.
Fantz, R., Fagan, J. and Miranda, S. (1975). Early perceptual development as shown by visual discrimination, selectivity and memory with varying stimulus and population parameters. In *Infant Perception: from Sensation to Cognition*. Edited by Cohen, L. and Salapatek, P. Academic Press, New York.
Maurer, D. and Bonera, M. (1981). Infants' perception of normal and distorted arrangements of a schematic face. *Child Development* **52**, 196.
McCall, R. (1981). Nature-nurture and the two realms of development: A proposed integration with respect to mental development. *Child Development* **52**, 1.
Moore, C. and Frye, D.A. (1986). The effect of experimenters intention on the child's understanding of conservation. *Cognition* **22**, 283.
Salapatek, P. (1975). Pattern perception in early infancy. In: *Infant Perception: From Sensation to Perception*. Edited by Cohen, L. and Salapatek, P. Academic Press, New York.
Skinner, B.F. (1957). *Verbal Behavior*. Appleton-Century-Crofts, New York.
Silverman, I. and Rose, A. (1982). Compensation and conservation. *Psychological Bulletin* **91**, 80.

6

Intelligence and Reasoning

NJ Mackintosh

Intelligence testing

Intelligence testing differs from most other branches of psychology. This is not only because of its controversial social implications, but also because its central aim has been to measure differences between people rather than to elucidate the nature of intelligence by appropriate experimental or theoretical analysis. Psychologists who have devised intelligence or IQ (intelligence quotient) tests have often, like many of us, held certain preconceptions about the nature of intelligence. Some of the most influential figures in the history of IQ testing, such as Spearman and Burt in Britain, and Jensen in the USA have assumed that one can distinguish between native endowment and acquired skills, or between underlying capacity and the diverse array of achievements that may depend on this capacity. They have contrasted tests of intelligence or ability with tests of attainment or achievement, defined intelligence as 'innate general cognitive ability', and argued that this unitary ability enters into practically everything that we do. This everyday definition of intelligence is hardly surprising, but it is worth contrasting with Piagetian views of intelligence or cognitive development (see Chapter 5). According to Piaget, the young child's understanding of the world is strikingly different from the adult's. Children progress through a succession of different stages before learning to interpret the world in ways which adults take for granted. Our intelligence, therefore, is not a single entity with which we are endowed at birth, but rather a series of competences or skills, acquired by lengthy interactions with our surroundings. It will be worth bearing this contrast in mind throughout this chapter.

The origins of IQ testing

In order to understand the nature of modern IQ tests, it is necessary to know something of their origins and development. And it will help to understand this development if we consider, in principle, how one might set about measuring a characteristic such as intelligence. One way to start would be with a theory. Armed with a detailed psychological theory of the nature of intelligence, one going well beyond the simple idea that it is innate general cognitive ability, which specifies the operations or processes involved in thinking, reasoning or problem solving, we could devise tests specifically designed to measure these postulated processes. A second, more empirical alternative would be to assemble a large group of people, some of whom were, by general consent, exceptionally intelligent, others of average intelligence, and yet others exceedingly unintelligent. We could then administer a battery of tests, without necessarily knowing whether they were all good measures of intelligence. We should soon discover which ones were, however, since they would be those which discriminated between our three groups. By discarding those tests on which the more and less intelligent members of our original group obtained similar scores, we should end up with a smaller set of tests with some claim to being successful tests of intelligence.

It is not difficult to see the drawbacks associated with each of these strategies. On the one hand, we may not have a good psychological theory of the processes involved in intelligent behaviour; on the other, we may be unable to agree whether one person is more intelligent than another. But these problems are hardly confined to the measurement of intelligence, and the only solution will be to rely on both approaches, so that one may complement the other.

In practice, the development of intelligence tests began (in the nineteenth century) with the former, theoretical approach, which was seen to fail. It then turned to a largely empirical approach, which appeared to succeed. As a consequence, IQ tests developed as a technology rather than as a branch of theoretical or experimental psychology, and is a monument to the statistical and methodological sophistication of its practitioners, but even to this day rests on distinctly shaky theoretical foundations.

Francis Galton, a first cousin of Charles Darwin, was the first person to attempt to measure differences in intelligence. In his book *Hereditary Genius,* published in 1869, he tried to show that certain kinds of talent ran in families, but recognized that he needed some better yardstick of talent than worldly eminence or success. So, he set to work to devise some simple measures of mental ability. Like other empiricists, he assumed that mental ability rested on knowledge, which comes from the senses, and "the more perceptive the senses are of difference, the larger is the field upon which our judgment and intelligence can act". The finer the discriminations of which the mind is capable, the richer that mind will be, and a test of sensory discrimination will therefore be a good measure of intelligence.

Galton's lead was followed by a number of psychologists who put together a number of tests, popular in the new laboratories of ex- perimental psychology, such as the threshold for discriminating differ- ences in weight or time, two-point tactile threshold, and reaction-time for responding differentially to different lights or tones. But the death knell for this approach was the publication of a paper by Wissler (1901), which reported two singularly embarrassing findings. Employing the newly invented procedure for calculating correlation coefficients, Wissler found no correlation between the performance of American college students on these various tests; a person good at one task was not necessarily any good at any of the others. Even if one of the tests was a good measure of intelligence, they could not all be, for all tests that measure the same thing should correlate with one another. Worse still, however, *none* of the tests correlated with college grades (although a student's grades in one subject did tend to correlate with his grades in another). On the reasonable assumption that grades do bear some relation to intelligence, the implication was that performance on the psychological tests did not.

Notice how an attempt to base the measurement of intelligence on a psychological theory (albeit one which we should nowadays reject) foundered because it failed to satisfy the requirements of the second, empirical approach, by failing to agree with an independent criterion of intelligence. It is time to turn to this second approach and to the work of the French psychologist, Alfred Binet, who was largely responsible for its success.

Binet was charged by the French Ministry of Public Instruction with the task of identifying any child, who "because of the state of his intelligence was unable to profit, in an average measure, from the instruction given in the ordinary schools", so that such a child could be placed in a special class or school designed to alleviate his or her difficulties. In other words, Binet's task was to devise tests which would identify educationally handicapped or subnormal (ESN) children so that they could be given remedial teaching, or assigned to ESN classes or schools. It is a use to which IQ tests have been put to this day.

Instead of basing his tests on any formal psychological theory, Binet took the more commonsense view that a child's level of intelligence was best assessed by his ability to answer a whole range of everyday questions and solve a wide variety of puzzles. So his tests required children to name parts of their body, count backwards from 20, give the meanings of some simple words, or draw a picture from memory. More important, he saw that the proof that such items constituted a test of intelligence rested on demonstrating that they correlated with some independent criterion. The problem, of course, is to find such a criterion: if we had one, after all, why should we need a new measure of intelligence? Binet's insight was to see that, since he was dealing with young children, age provided just the criterion he needed. By and large, as children grow older, they become able to solve more demanding intellectual tasks. Children do not come into the world fully equipped with an adult's cognitive skills; a long process of development is necessary before they think and reason like adults (see Chapter 5). A good test of intelligence, therefore, is one which older children find easier than younger.

By contrast with earlier attempts to measure intelligence, Binet's approach was pragmatic and atheoretical. But he did, of course, have certain theoretical preconceptions, and it is worth noting how sharply they differed from those of other IQ testers. Binet acknowledged that children develop and change, that his tests did not necessarily measure children's innate endowment, but only their current level of intellectual functioning, and he regarded it as of the utmost importance that a good intelligence test should contain a diverse array of items, because intelligence might be manifested in a variety of different ways.

Binet and Simon (1905) developed a series of tests, of progressively greater difficulty, each appropriate for a different age group. By giving the tests to large samples of children, they found that a particular set of questions was answered correctly by the average 6-year-old, but not by many 4-year-olds, and was therefore an appropriate 6-year-old test. If a child of that age could not answer these questions correctly, he was by definition below average; if he could answer not only these but also the questions in the 8-year-old test, he was above average. In this latter case, his mental level or mental age was that of an 8-year-old.

The concept of mental age is still sometimes used, most commonly in the context of mental retardation or handicap, but in the American translation and extension of his tests, the Stanford-Binet test, Binet's term was replaced with the **intelligence quotient** or **IQ score**. A child's IQ score was defined as his mental age divided by his chronological age, the whole multiplied by 100. Thus, the IQ scores of children of different ages could be directly compared (even if they were based on the answers to different questions), and the average IQ of the population would, necessarily, be 100. In fact, however, IQ is no longer calculated in this way. One problem is that the definition worked only for children up to the age of 18 or so. Beyond this age, there is little further increase in the complexity of intellectual puzzles that people can solve, i.e. no increase in mental age. The consequence will be that the average IQ of 40-year-olds will be half that of 20-year-olds. In 1939, the Wechsler intelligence scales introduced the calculation of IQ simply as a statistical norm. For any given age group, a test given to a large, randomly chosen sample of the population will give a distribution of raw scores approximating to that shown in Figure 6.1. The mean of these raw scores (80 in the figure) will be said to correspond to an IQ, for that age group, of 100. The dispersion of scores round this mean is measured in **standard deviations** (approximately 67 per cent of scores will fall within +/− 1 standard deviation of the mean); and the convention that 1 SD = 15 IQ points means that a raw score of 100 will correspond to an IQ of 115 and so on.

Modern development of IQ tests

Binet's independent criterion of intelligence was age. But this is hardly sufficient. One problem, already noted, is that it does not continue to increase at the same rate after the age of 18 or so: the average 30-year-old does not obtain substantially better scores than the average 20-year-old. So how do we devise adult IQ tests? The answer is, in effect, by extrapolation. To the extent that we can discern what makes an item hard in a 12-year-old's test (the rarity of a word in a vocabulary test; the number of transformations applied to the terms of a series completion task), we can

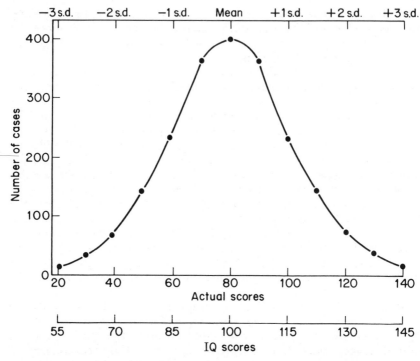

Fig. 6.1 Hypothetical distribution of scores on a hypothetical IQ test for a given random sample of the population, illustrating how raw scores on the test are converted to IQ scores. A raw score of 80, which is the mean for this population, is said to correspond to an IQ of 100, and IQs greater or less than 100 are calculated by measuring the standard deviations (SDs) of raw scores, and by adopting the convention that the standard deviation of IQ is 15.

extrapolate to create yet harder items for adult tests. But there are other, obvious reasons why age cannot be the only criterion. Children do not develop only in intelligence. They grow taller and heavier as they grow older, but no one has seriously proposed that a ruler or a pair of scales would make a good IQ test. There must be other criteria. Binet acknowledged that he would expect some agreement between the results of his tests and other indices of a child's performance at school. Modern IQ tests are 'validated' by correlating their scores with various measures of school achievement. These correlations, whether with formal tests of reading or mathematics, or with the results of exams such as CSE or 'O' levels, are typically in the range 0.40–0.70 (Jensen, 1980; Mackintosh and Mascie-Taylor, 1985). These are substantial, although not perfect correlations, but this is probably as it should be. We do not doubt that there are many reasons why a child may do well or badly at school; native ability is only one such reason and, if this is what IQ tests purport to measure, they ought not to predict school achievement perfectly.

Binet also, of course, had internal criteria, in the sense that he held views, as we have seen, about the nature of intelligence or intellectual competence. He believed that a test of intelligence should measure a variety of everyday skills and accomplishments, a child's vocabulary, counting and drawing, as well as psychological processes such as short-term memory, measured by the digit-span test, or comprehension, measured by requiring a paraphrase, in the child's own words, of a passage read out to him. Binet's influence has been such that the most influential of modern IQ tests, the Stanford-Binet and Wechsler tests, have faithfully followed him. The Stanford-Binet is a translation and extension of Binet's tests, first published in the USA in 1917, but revised several times since. The Wechsler tests, the **Wechsler Adult Intelligence Scale** or **WAIS** and the **Wechsler Intelligence Scale for Children** or **WISC**, although based on tests first published in 1939, are largely the product of the years since World War II.

The Wechsler tests consist of 11 subtests, shown in Table 6.1, divided into six 'verbal' and five 'performance' subtests. The former include general knowledge (information), questions about social competence and the meanings of proverbs (comprehension), mental arithmetic, as well as vocabulary and digit-span. The performance part of the test requires the child to see what is missing from line drawings of more or less familiar objects (picture completion), arrange pictures to tell a story, arrange coloured blocks of wood so as to make certain designs, and so on.

These are hardly the sorts of questions one would expect to see in a test purporting to measure native intelligence. They seem remarkably diverse, and, in many cases, tests of knowledge rather than ability. The test constructors have argued that a child's knowledge reflects his intelligence because intelligence was needed in order to acquire that knowledge. But, a more important point is that one fundamental requirement for the inclusion of an item in an IQ test is that it should agree with other items in the test. A particular item will be included provided that it correlates with other items measuring intelligence; in a sense it hardly matters what the first item is measuring provided it is something that correlates with intelligence. This is also the answer to the question about the diversity of items in standard IQ tests: whatever the apparent diversity of form or content, the fact remains that all items in the test will correlate with all others. The correlation matrix for the 11 subtests of the WAIS or WISC

Table 6.1 Subtests comprising Wechsler Adult Intelligence Scale (WAIS) and Wechsler Intelligence Scale for Children (WISC)

Verbal	Performance
Information	Picture completion
Comprehension	Picture arrangement
Arithmetic	Block design
Similarities	Object assembly
Vocabulary	Coding
Digit Span	

shows that the average correlation between each possible pair of subtests is greater than 0.50 (Table 6.2c). It is precisely this fact that has encouraged some IQ testers to argue that their tests are measuring a single underlying general ability.

There is, no doubt, an element of circularity here. If one criterion employed in the selection of items guarantees that they will all correlate with one another, it is hardly surprising that they do. What is surprising, however, is the range of items for which this holds true. One could not have predicted, in advance, that the correlation between scores on the blocks design and information subtests of the WAIS, or between vocabulary and picture completion, would be about 0.60.

Given that such apparently diverse subtests correlate with one another, it is not surprising that entire tests should do so, and indeed that one criterion for accepting a new IQ test should be that it correlate with accepted existing tests. This may seem not only circular but a guarantee of stagnation. If existing IQ tests have got it wrong, how will we ever break out of the circle? But, once again, this ignores the remarkable diversity of tests that will satisfy this criterion. The Stanford-Binet and Wechsler tests are broadly similar, both consisting of a number of different subtests weighted towards vocabulary, comprehension and verbal definitions, and both administered individually by the examiner to one tester at a time. It is perhaps not surprising that they should correlate about 0.80. But the majority of tests are paper and pencil, multiple-choice group tests, administered by the examiner to large numbers of people at once. Many group tests consist of a series of questions all of the same general class, for example vocabulary or word definitions, analogies or series completions, or diagrammatic, non-verbal tests such as Raven's Matrices (Fig 6.2). Remarkably enough, in the population as a whole, scores on Raven's Matrices correlate about 0.60 not only with such diverse tests as the Stanford-Binet and Wechsler scales, but also with a simple vocabulary test. Although it is true that a new test would not count as an IQ test if it did not correlate with existing tests, it remains an empirical fact that such a wide range of tests should satisfy this requirement. Those who argue that IQ tests do not really measure intelligence are faced with a dilemma: if they do not, then either intelligence cannot be measured, or there must exist some other set of tests that do measure it, but which do not correlate with existing IQ tests. Given the wide range of tests that all correlate with another, it is hard to imagine what new tests would satisfy this requirement.

General intelligence or diverse abilities?

The correlations between various IQ tests or subtests are substantial but by no means perfect. They cannot, therefore, all be measuring exactly the same thing. One school of thought, however, has followed the British psychologist, Charles Spearman (1927), in concentrating on the fact of overall correlation, and inferred that even if each test or subtest measures some special factor, they must also all be measuring a single general factor

Table 6.2 Correlation matrices for different IQ tests.
The number in each cell represents the correlation between the scores obtained on the test in that row with the test in that column.

(a) Hypothetical correlation matrix consistent with Spearman's g

Test	1	2	3	4	5	6
1	–					
2	.72	–				
3	.63	.56	–			
4	.54	.48	.42	–		
5	.45	.40	.35	.30	–	
6	.36	.32	.28	.24	.20	–

(b) Hypothetical correlation matrix consistent with Thurstone's independent abilities

Test	1	2	3	4	5	6
1	–					
2	.72	–				
3	.63	.56	–			
4	.15	.10	.05	–		
5	.10	.05	.00	.72	–	
6	.05	.00	.05	.63	.56	–

(c) Observed correlation matrix for some subtests of WAIS

Test	I	V	C	B	P	O
Info	–					
Vocab.	.81	–				
Comp.	.71	.71	–			
Blocks	.60	.56	.47	–		
Pictures	.64	.62	.53	.69	–	
Objects	.54	.48	.42	.69	.66	–

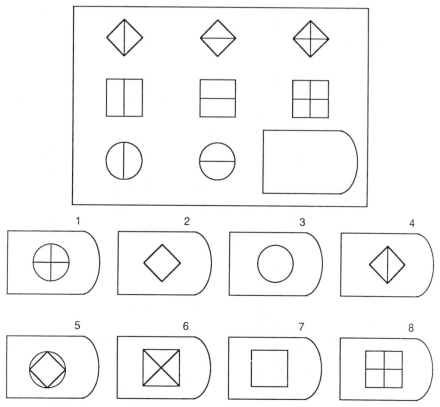

Fig. 6.2   An example of the type of item that appears in Raven's Matrices. The testee is required to select, from the 8 numbered alternatives below, the one which best completes the pattern or matrix shown above.

common to all tests. This general factor or *g* is then what we mean by intelligence, and it is variation in *g* that is responsible for the variation in people's ability over the whole range of IQ tests. A different school, following the American psychologist Lewis Thurstone (1938), has concentrated on the imperfection of the correlations between different tests, and argued that there is a diverse set of largely independent abilities that go to make up what we loosely refer to as intelligence. The statistical technique of **factor analysis** has been wielded in an attempt to resolve this issue, but has failed singularly to do so.

Factor analysis is simply a way of interpreting correlation matrices of the kind shown in Table 6.2, and the nature of the dispute between Spearman and Thurstone can be understood by reference to this Table. According to Spearman, tests correlate with one another because they are all measuring the same thing; some tests will be better measures of *g* than others, and will therefore show higher intercorrelations, and it will always be possible to order a set of tests (from better to worse measures of *g*) such that the size of the correlations between them decreases as one goes down or across the correlation matrix. Table 6.2a illustrates such a pattern of correlations. If, on the other hand, there are a number of independent abilities, as Thurstone maintained, we should expect to see clusters of high correlations (between tests measuring the same ability) separated by low correlations (between groups of tests measuring different abilities). Table 6.2b illustrates this, but it is important to recognize that even if such a pattern were observed, it would not necessarily tell us *what* these various abilities were. We should need a theory of intelligence to interpret the factors. In practice, the correlation matrix of most IQ tests reveals a picture somewhere between these two extremes, as can be seen in Table 6.2c, the observed correlation matrix from some of the subtests of the WAIS. All correlations are substantial and significant, as Spearman requires, but there is a clear suggestion of two clusters of high correlations, between Information, Vocabulary and Comprehension, on the one hand, and Blocks Design, Picture Completion and Object Assembly, on the other, separated by rather lower correlations between the first group and the second. Factor analysis of the Wechsler scales does indeed, as Thurstone requires, yield at least two factors, labelled verbal and performance (although these labels have little theoretical significance); but these two factors will not be independent, as he also requires, since the correlations between verbal and performance subtests are far from zero.

The notion that a person's intelligence can be summed up in a single number, his IQ score, rests on accepting something like Spearman's position, that the single most important determinant of performance on any set of tests is that person's level of general intelligence or *g*. To the extent that Thurstone is right, one and the same IQ score may be achieved in a variety of different ways: one person may be better at one group of tests and worse at another; a second may show the reverse pattern of abilities. We know that this is partly true. Men and women, for example, tend to differ in their pattern of abilities, with women usually obtaining rather higher average scores on verbal tests than men, but lower scores on tests of spatial ability. This alone is enough to show that we can break *g* down into at least some component parts, a conclusion of considerable relevance for clinical or educational practice. Here, it is often less important to know about a patient's or child's general level of intellectual competence, than about their specific pattern of strengths and weaknesses. Nevertheless, it would be quite wrong to assert that different abilities are completely independent: the overall positive correlation between all IQ tests shows that there is a strong tendency for people good at one to be good at others. Either all tests are measuring, *in part*, a single underlying ability, or the various abilities happen to go together.

Test reliability: stability and change in IQ

IQ tests should be reliable. The **reliability** of a psychological test is a measure of the consistency of the scores it assigns to people: a test purporting to measure intelligence should not give someone an IQ of 125 today and only 85 tomorrow. Reliability is measured by the correlation between two scores on the same test. Some tests, such as the Stanford-Binet, are issued in two 'parallel' forms, each containing the same kinds of items, and one can correlate scores obtained on one form on one day with those obtained on the other on another day. In other cases, one can measure 'split-half' reliability by correlating scores obtained on the odd-numbered items in a test with those obtained on even-numbered items. Typical reliabilities for IQ tests assessed in either of these ways are between 0.85 and 0.98.

What of reliability over the longer term? If IQ tests purport to measure innate ability rather than a heterogeneous collection of acquired skills and knowledge, one might expect IQ scores to remain stable over relatively long periods: a child's IQ at one age should accurately predict his IQ several years later, or even into adulthood. In practice, although IQ scores obtained before the age of 4 or 5 years do not predict later IQ particularly well, after that age IQ scores are relatively stable: children's IQ scores at age 7 correlate about 0.70 with their scores at age 17. It is perhaps not very surprising that no test given to infants or children at the age of 2 or 3 years will predict their later IQ: the moderately high correlations observed after that age with later IQ attest to the long-term stability of *something* being measured by these tests. But, it is important to realize that such correlations are consistent with substantial changes in individual cases. From a correlation of 0.70 between IQ at 7 and 17 years, one can predict that, approximately, one child in three will show a change in IQ of at least 10 points between these ages, and one in twenty a change of 20 points or more.

Changes in IQ in old age

Earlier IQ correlates with later IQ well beyond the age of 17. But, it has long been thought that there are substantial changes in IQ as people grow older. Evidence of such changes comes from the standardization of any IQ test. The WAIS, for example, is standardized on a large cross-section of the population, stratified by sex, age, class, region of the country and so on. Within each age band, the mean score is set to an IQ of 100 (thus guaranteeing stability of IQ across ages), but the raw scores required for an IQ of 100 decline with age, thus revealing, apparently, a real decline in intelligence. Figure 6.3a shows this decline for the verbal and performance halves of the WAIS-R. For any one over the age of 30, it seems a depressing picture. Although one may expect to retain one's general knowledge, vocabulary and verbal comprehension tolerably well into old age, more abstract, problem-solving skills seem to decline inexorably from an astonishingly early age.

This picture, although entirely typical of many other studies, is in fact quite misleading. The real implication of these data is optimistic rather than pessimistic. What they actually demonstrate is an increase in IQ

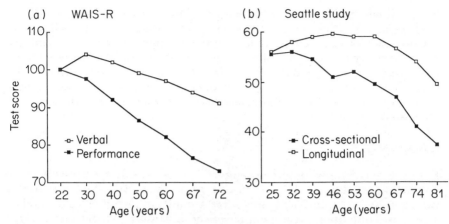

Fig. 6.3 Changes in IQ with age. (a) Estimated mean IQ of the different age groups in the standardization sample for the revised version of the WAIS (WAIS-R, 1981) (b) Cross-sectional and longitudinal estimates of total IQ from the Seattle longitudinal study (Schaie, 1983).

between generations, rather than a decrease in IQ with age. The data of Figure 6.3a are misleading because they are cross-sectional: they were obtained, at a given point in time, from groups of people of different ages. In other words, the reason for the difference between 20- and 70-year-olds may be that one group was born in 1960 and the other in 1910. The 70-year-olds might have obtained equally low scores if they had been tested at age 20 in 1930. Indeed, this turns out to be the case. Although it was at one time fashionable to make dire predictions about the declining national intelligence, there is actually good reason to believe that national intelligence (or at least IQ) has been increasing for the past 50 years or more, not only in Britain, but also in the USA and Japan (Flynn, 1984; Lynn and Hampson, 1985). The increase, moreover, has been particularly marked in non-verbal, rather than verbal, IQ. It is this increase in the average IQ of 20- and 70-year-olds between 1930 and 1980 that is shown in Figure 6.3a.

The conclusion is confirmed by longitudinal rather than cross-sectional studies, that is to say by following people as they grow older and recording their IQ at different ages. Although no study has gone to the heroic lengths of following up a group of 20-year-olds at ten-year intervals until they are 70, it is still possible to get a long-term picture by combining cross-sectional and longitudinal designs. Data from one such study are shown in Figure 6.3b (Schaie, 1983). The cross-sectional data give a picture much like that of the cross-sectional data of Figure 6.3a: a steady decline in measured IQ from the age of 20. But, the longitudinal data suggest that IQ may actually continue to increase until the age of 50 or so, and only starts to decline after the age of 60. There are problems with longitudinal studies associated with the difficulty of keeping track of one's complete sample, and the possibility that the attrition is not random. But, there can be little doubt that the longitudinal data of Figure 6.3b give a more accurate impression of changes in IQ with old age. It is worth noting that even the decline after age 60 needs careful interpretation. There is some evidence to suggest that IQ only starts to decline within about 5 years of death. Since a higher proportion of any group of 60- or 70-year-olds will die within the next 5 years than a similar group of 40-year-olds, what appears to be a moderate decline in all 60-year-olds may really reflect only a decline in those shortly about to die.

Heritability

Both the correlations observed between scores on different tests and the long-term stability of IQ scores are important. But they are hardly sufficient to establish that IQ measures a single, inborn intellectual ability. The most contentious argument advanced in support of this claim is that IQ is said to be largely genetically, rather than environmentally, determined.

Stated thus, the claim is merely misleading, not because the available evidence disproves it, but because the evidence is concerned with a slightly different issue, namely the **heritability** of IQ. Heritability is a term from population genetics whose meaning is this: the heritability of a given characteristic in a given population is the proportion of variance in that characteristic in that population ascribable to genetic differences between members of that population (to simplify, we may assume that the remainder of the variance is attributable to environmental differences). The heritability of IQ, therefore, refers to the extent to which differences in IQ are due to genetic differences between members of a particular population. It is a statistic specific to a given population at a given time, being dependent on the genetic make-up (or diversity) of that population and the extent to which its members have different environmental experiences. In the limiting case, for example, if there is no variation in relevant environmental circumstances (where 'relevant' means those circumstances that affect the characteristic in question) its heritability must be 1.0.

It is worth following this argument through, since it may help to dispel some myths. It is commonly implied that a belief in the heritability of IQ is a mark of extreme political reaction. One could plausibly argue, on the contrary, that the heritability of IQ has probably increased in most industrial societies in the past hundred years, and that this is a consequence of modest increases in social justice. In a society where the heritability of IQ is low, there must be marked differences in relevant environmental circumstances. It is hard to believe that educational opportunity is not one of those circumstances. Where a substantial proportion of the population receives no schooling at all, and only a small proportion receives any after the age of 12, differences in IQ are likely to reflect these educational differences. Increases in equality of educational opportunity will decrease the importance of this source of differences in IQ, and therefore *increase* its heritability.

The argument seems plausible, but remains entirely hypothetical: there are no data to say what the heritability of IQ was a hundred years ago. Indeed, it is a moot point whether there are any data which would provide an accurate estimate of the heritability of IQ today. How are the relative contributions of heredity and environment to differences in IQ to be estimated? In animal or plant breeding, experimental intervention allows one to manipulate one factor while holding others constant. People cannot be manipulated in this way. So we must rely on natural observation or natural experiment. We can try to determine how closely particular groups of people resemble one another, by calculating correlations between their IQ scores. We know that the correlation between pairs of people chosen at random will be zero. If the correlation between genetically related, individuals is significantly greater than zero, then, other things being equal, this implies that IQ has some heritability. Conversely, if people who share similar environmental experiences resemble one another in IQ, this implies, other things being equal, a significant environmental effect. The problem is that in neither case will other things be equal. In most, if not all, human societies genetic relatedness and shared environmental circumstances go hand in hand. Members of a family are genetically related to one another, but they also tend to live together.

Although, therefore, the correlation in IQ between members of the same family, such as parents and their children or brothers and sisters, is quite substantial (usually somewhere between 0.40 and 0.60, Bouchard and McGue, 1981), there is no way of knowing whether this is because they share their genes or their environment. Nor is this problem really solved (although many people act as though it were) by studying such special groups as identical (MZ) twins. It is true that MZ twins resemble one another as closely in IQ as in many other respects, but it is also easy to show that they also share more of their life together than do other brothers and sisters or even than fraternal (DZ) twins. So, even though the IQ correlation for MZ twins is usually 0.80 or more, and even though this approaches the correlation between the same person's score on an IQ test on two separate occasions, it does not provide unequivocal evidence of a significant genetic effect.

In order to disentangle genetic and environmental causes of variation in IQ, it is essential to break the natural covariation between genetic relatedness and shared environments that the structure of human societies imposes. We cannot do this by experimental manipulation, but we can rely on some natural experiments—for example, when children are adopted and brought up by someone other than their biological parents. We can ask two sorts of questions in these cases. Do biologically related people who have never lived together resemble one another in IQ? Do biologically unrelated people who live together resemble one another? An affirmative answer to the first question implies a genetic, and to the second an environmental, effect on IQ.

The most dramatic version of an adoption study is where MZ twins are separated and brought up apart. It is also, not surprisingly, the rarest, and the data are therefore sparse. There have been four published studies of separated MZ twins (Burt, 1966; Juel-Nielson, 1965; Newman, Freeman and Holzinger, 1937; Shields, 1962) ranging from 12 to (supposedly) 53 pairs, and a fifth study is currently underway in the USA. All have reported substantial correlations between the IQs of the separated twins, ranging from about 0.60 to 0.80. The higher number is not much lower than the correlation between MZ twins living together; but even the lower figure suggests that IQ may have substantial heritability. Indeed, if the twins were separated immediately after birth, if they were brought up in completely uncorrelated environments which spanned the range of environments to be found in the population at large, and if one could safely generalize from twins to the rest of the population, these numbers would give one a direct estimate of the heritability of IQ. Only one published study, that of Burt (1966), has claimed to satisfy these empirical concerns, but it is now clear that this is because Burt fraudulently invented his data (Hearnshaw, 1979); free from the constraints of the real world, Burt simply fabricated data that appeared to resolve, once and for all, the issue of the heritability of IQ. In practice, natural experiments are inevitably imperfect. It is rare enough for a mother of MZ twins to give up one or both for adoption; it is even less likely that she will do so in such a way as to satisfy the concerns of social scientists. Excluding Burt, the largest published study of separated twins is that of Shields (1962) (a total of 40 pairs, 3 of whom were excluded from most analyses). Shields' exemplary reporting of the details of each case makes it clear that the twins were only rarely separated at birth, several lived together before separation or were reunited after separation for several years, while for the large majority 'separation' consisted of one twin being brought up by the mother and the other by another relative (e.g. aunt or grandmother).

Exhaustive analyses of these three published studies have convinced some environmentalist critics (e.g. Kamin, 1974, 1981) that they fail to prove any heritability for IQ. Their inevitable imperfections certainly mean that they cannot provide a reliable or precise estimate of heritability. But it requires a remarkable degree of scepticism to insist that they are consistent with a heritability of zero. 'Separated' twins may have been brought up in similar, even in related families, but the resemblance in their IQ scores is greater than that typically observed for brothers and sisters brought up in the same family, and is substantially greater than that observed for unrelated, adopted children brought up in the same family (for whom the correlation ranges between 0.10 and 0.40, Bouchard and McGue, 1981). It is difficult to reconcile this with a heritability of zero.

Nevertheless, studies of small numbers of separated identical twins hardly provide the most secure base from which to infer the heritability of IQ in the population as a whole. Other types of adoption study may at least offer larger samples. What, for example, is the correlation between an adopted child's IQ and that of his biological parents with whom he has never lived? The data from three relatively large American studies are shown in Table 6.3. These correlations, although somewhat smaller than

Table 6.3 Correlations between the IQ scores of adopted children and those of their biological mothers and of their adoptive mothers

Study	Correlation with adopted child's IQ	
	Biological mother	Adoptive mother
Skodak & Skeels (1949)	0.31	0.04
Scarr & Weinberg (1977)	0.32	0.23
Horn, Loehlin & Willerman (1979)	0.31	0.17

those typically reported between parents and their children living together, are all significantly greater than zero, the value predicted, other things being equal, if the heritability of IQ really were zero. Yet again, however, the data must be treated with caution. Just as the resemblance between MZ twins brought up apart may be partly attributed to the correlation between their supposedly separated environments, so here the resemblance between adopted children and their parents with whom they have never lived may be partly attributed to **'selective placement'**. Although these children did not go to live with relatives or friends, the adoptive families selected for them by adoption agencies were not chosen at random; such agencies usually, and no doubt rightly, attempt to match the child to the home. They are likely to choose an adoptive family that shares at least some of the characteristics of the child's biological parents, for example in terms of parental occupation and level of education. This will produce a correlation between biological and adoptive families in at least some factors likely to affect IQ, so that any resemblance between the child and his biological parents may be due not to the genes they have in common but to the environmental influence of the adoptive parents (which happens to resemble that which would have been provided by the child's biological parents).

There is, however, a flaw in this argument. As Table 6.3 shows, adopted children tend to resemble their biological parents *more* than their adoptive parents. The environmentalist's argument implied that the correlation between child and biological parent is mediated, because of selective placement, via the adoptive parent. But whatever the degree of selective placement, it is difficult to see how a weaker correlation between children and their adoptive parents could be sufficient to explain a stronger correlation with their biological parents. If children resemble their biological parents, even when they have been separated from them since the age of 6 months or younger, the only reasonable conclusion is that IQ has at least some heritability.

It is worth ending on a cautious note. At best, any estimate of the heritability of IQ is no more than that, an estimate, possibly valid for a given population at a given time, not a universal eternal truth. And any precise, numerical estimate of the heritability of IQ will be seriously misleading, because the precision will give the wholly unwarrantable impression that the data from such natural experiments as we have are sufficient to bear the weight of the sophisticated biometrical analyses to which they have been subject. But the data range from the imperfect through the seriously flawed to occasional outright fraud, and the application of the biometrical analysis requires a whole host of arbitrary, simplifying assumptions. Depending on the assumptions made, and the particular data set analysed, one can generate estimates for the heritability of IQ ranging from zero to over 0.80. In the absence of better data and better justified assumptions, the only conclusion that is justified is that the heritability of IQ in modern industrialized societies probably lies somewhere between 0.20 and 0.70, with no particularly good reason for believing that a figure near the middle of this range is more likely than one nearer either extreme.

Environmental effects on IQ

No scientist, even the most ardent hereditarian, has doubted that a child's IQ is affected by the circumstances of his life. There is a significant environmental contribution to variations in IQ but attempts to measure or specify that contribution more precisely have not been notably successful. It is a simple matter to establish correlations between the circumstances of a child's life and his IQ. Children's IQ scores are directly correlated with their parents' income and occupational status, with the neighbourhood and type of accommodation in which they live, with the number of other children in the family (children in smaller families having higher IQs), and with their birth order (first-born children having higher IQs than those born subsequently). There are also correlations between children's IQ scores and the way they are treated by their parents, with higher IQs being associated with higher parental expectations, greater pressure to achieve, more involvement with the child's activities, better provision of toys, and greater stress on talking to, rather than on punishing, the child. Not all of these correlations are large: they range from about 0.20 to 0.50, with considerable variation from one study to another (Rutter and Madge, 1976; Mascie-Taylor, 1984), but between them, one might have thought, they must account for much of the observed variation in IQ. Unfortunately, that conclusion is unwarranted.

The first problem is that, as must be obvious, several of these factors are not independent. Parental income and occupation are themselves correlated, and correlate with neighbourhood and types of accommodation. In most modern industrial societies, middle-class parents have smaller families than working-class parents, and they also interact with their children in characteristically different ways, being more likely to talk with them, and less likely to resort to physical punishment. There is no reason to suppose, therefore, that each of these factors makes an independent contribution to IQ. Parental income may correlate with IQ, for example, not because money buys a high score on IQ tests, but because it is correlated with other factors, such as space, toys, leisure and style of parental interaction, that do have an effect on IQ. Fortunately, there are statistical solutions to this problem: a multiple regression analysis allows one to estimate the contribution of each of a number of intercorrelated factors when the contribution of the others has been allowed for. In effect, it estimates how much additional variation is accounted for by each additional factor. Such regression analyses suggest that the social and demographic factors alone (parental status, family size etc.) correlate about 0.30 to 0.40 with IQ, and that the addition of the more psychological factors (style of parental interaction etc.) brings the correlation up to about 0.50 to 0.60.

This is a sizeable correlation, and if it represented a direct causal contribution to variation in children's IQ scores, we should be in a position to explain much of that variation. But, the most important lesson to learn in social science is that a correlation between A and B does not prove that A causes B; B might cause A; both A and B might be caused, independently, by a third variable, C. Thus, parents who talk a lot to their children and have high expectations for them may not be causing their children's high IQ, they may be responding to it: clever children may raise one's expectations for them and be more rewarding to talk to. Similarly, if IQ is partly heritable, the reason why parental occupation is correlated with children's IQ scores may be that parents with high occupational status also have high IQs and their children inherit their IQ. It is not clear how some of these possibilities are to be disentangled; but some questions might be answered by looking at adoptive families to see what factors there are correlated with the adopted child's IQ. Several studies have established that children adopted into 'good' homes end up with IQ scores higher than would have been expected had they been brought up by their biological parents (see Table 6.4) but, there is little analytic evidence to establish what factors make for a 'good' adoptive home, and the magnitude of the correlation between home background and child's IQ is substantially lower in adoptive families than in biological families.

Table 6.4 Evidence for the effect of adoption on adopted children's IQ scores

Study	IQ of adopted child	Comparison statistic	
Skodak & Skeels (1949)	106.0	IQ of biological mother	85.7
Scarr & Weinberg (1976)	109.0	estimated IQ of population from which adopted child came	90.0
Schiff *et al.* (1978)	110.6	IQ of half-sibling brought up by biological mother	94.7

All three studies obtained measurements of IQ scores of adopted children, and in all cases they average over 100. This is suggestive evidence that adoption into 'superior' homes raises IQ, but what is needed is some estimate of the IQ scores the children might have obtained if they had not been adopted. The most convincing evidence is provided by Schiff *et al.* who obtained IQ scores from half-siblings of the adopted children who had been brought up by their natural mothers.

Group differences in IQ: test bias and 'culture-fair' tests

Almost from the outset, IQ tests revealed substantial differences in the average scores obtained by different groups: middle-class children obtained, on average, higher scores than working-class children; urban children higher scores than rural; and, in the USA, Whites higher scores than Blacks. Few aspects of IQ testing have been responsible for more notoriety and controversy. Further, the controversy is heightened by the suggestion, implied in the preceding discussion, that some of this difference between, say, social classes may be genetic in origin. Many regard this as a deeply offensive proposition and it is worth noting that there is little *direct*, although considerable indirect, evidence to support it. But it should not be misunderstood. It does not imply that different social classes are genetically distinct castes, and it certainly does not rule out the possibility of social mobility. Indeed, it is the existence of social mobility that probably provides the basis for, and certainly provides the best evidence for, a genetic difference in IQ between classes. We should never forget that children do not resemble their parents *very* closely in IQ: the typical parent-child correlation is only about 0.40 to 0.50. This means that many sons will have substantially higher or lower IQs than their fathers. The important observation, confirmed in both British and American studies, is that these differences in IQ are associated with social mobility: sons with higher IQs than their fathers are more likely to end up in higher status jobs, those with lower IQs are more likely to end up in lower status jobs (Waller, 1971; Mascie-Taylor and Gibson, 1978). The implication is that the correlation between social class and IQ is not simply a consequence of a middle-class upbringing being good for your IQ; it is renewed in each generation because a child's IQ partly determines his eventual occupational status.

The most common reaction to the observation of group differences in average IQ is that they are the fault of the tests, proving, if further proof were needed, that IQ tests are biased. But what does this mean? A test purporting to measure intelligence would be biased against a particular group, if it could be established that it underestimated that group's true level of intelligence. But, without some independent, true measure of intelligence, it is difficult to see how this could ever be established. We can, of course, ask whether one kind of IQ test is biased against a particular group by comparison with another kind of test (see below); and we could also ask whether IQ tests in general underestimated a particular group's academic or scholastic attainment. This last question certainly needs to be answered if IQ tests are to be used in educational assessment. The answer is, in fact, quite clear: IQ tests predict school attainment for Black or working-class children just as well as for White, middle-class children, and there is no evidence that they systematically underestimate their performance. If anything, the opposite is true: if we take a Black, working-class child and a White, middle-class child with the same IQ, the chances are that the Black child will do worse rather than better at school.

This does not, of course, prove that IQ tests necessarily provide a fair assessment of the 'real' intellectual potential of Black, working-class children. Their level of achievement at school might simply be an even more biased measure of that. The problem is that we have no other measure of 'real' intellectual potential: indeed, it is a myth to suppose that there could be such a thing. All we can measure is intellectual attainment, that is to say, performance on various intellectual tasks, which will almost certainly include IQ tests, or tasks that correlate rather well with them. This point is equally relevant to a second argument about bias. The reason why, say, Black, working-class children obtain low scores on IQ tests, it is claimed, is because the tests simply measure culturally acquired knowledge as opposed to real intellectual potential. If all that is being said is that performance on an IQ test depends on past experience and the opportunity to learn, there would be no sense in disputing it. Of course, IQ scores are affected by environmental circumstances, but to say that this is due to bias in the test, as though it were the test's fault, implies that there might be some other kind of IQ test of which this were *not* true and which would measure real intellectual potential divorced of all past experience; and that is a myth.

It is, of course, a myth that has sometimes been propagated by IQ testers themselves, especially by those who have devised so-called **'culture-fair' tests**, such as Cattell's culture-fair tests or Raven's Matrices, where the materials, abstract diagrams or patterns, are intended to be equally unfamiliar to all and therefore not to favour children from some backgrounds over those from others. The non-verbal or performance parts of tests such as the WAIS or WISC, especially a test such as the blocks design, are similarly supposed to be less culturally loaded than tests such as vocabulary or information. But the distinction cannot really be sustained. There is some suggestion that the difference between middle- and working-class children is more pronounced on verbal than on non-verbal tests, but differences between at least some ethnic groups are equally great on either, and there is absolutely no reason to suppose that one is better proof of a real difference in inborn intellectual potential than the other. Recent immigrants from the Indian sub-continent to Britain, for example, obtain IQ scores some 20 points below the White mean on tests such as Raven's Matrices; after 5 years of schooling in Britain, their scores are indistinguishable from those of White children (Ashby, Morrison and Butcher, 1971; Mackintosh and Mascie-Taylor, 1985). Cross-cultural studies from other countries have confirmed that the experience of formal schooling has dramatic effects on abstract problem-solving (Cole and Scribner, 1975).

Non-verbal, or culture-fair tests may not be testing for specific items of culturally acquired information, such as knowing the meaning of the word 'sudorific' or the distance from London to New York, but this does not mean that the ability to answer them is part of the child's native endowment developing regardless of his experience. The study of cognitive development has revealed that children's understanding of the world and their entire way of thinking change quite dramatically over the first ten to fifteen years of life (see Chapter 5). One aspect of this change is an increase in abstraction: the transition from Piaget's Concrete Operational to his Formal Operational stage involves an increasing ability to understand the formal, abstract principles underlying problems, divorced from any concrete instantiation of them. It follows that supposedly culture-fair tests—precisely because they present formal, abstract problems, in the hope that the material, being equally unfamiliar to all, will be equally fair to all—will reward those children who have learned to solve abstract problems and discriminate against those who have not.

Intelligence and problem-solving

IQ tests have proved relatively successful in measuring reliable and stable differences between people—differences that are undoubtedly correlated with differences in educational attainment and, to a lesser extent, occupational attainment—but they have been notably less successful in telling us very much about the nature of intelligence. Factor analysis suggests that we should distinguish between various aspects of intelligence, verbal, spatial, non-verbal reasoning etc. But useful as this is for certain diagnostic purposes, the fact remains that the isolation of these factors has depended solely on patterns of correlations, on finding that people who are good at one kind of verbal IQ test, vocabulary, are also good at another, such as verbal analogies, but not necessarily so good at Raven's Matrices or a spatial rotation task. Factor analysis can never explain what spatial intelligence *is*, what processes are available to the successful spatial reasoner that are not available to others, and what we might do to improve people's spatial skills.

To understand the nature of intelligence or problem solving, we need to adopt a rather different strategy, even though data from IQ tests will almost certainly provide valuable information. The psychological study of problem-solving has been much influenced by work in artificial intelligence (AI). The attempt to program computers to solve even simple problems has proved illuminating because it forces one to specify every step in the solution, and because most success has attended programs which break problems down into smaller units. A flow diagram, such as that shown in Figure 6.4, illustrates in very general terms the steps that are likely to be followed. It may seem to be little more than commonsense, but several points are worth noting: that the problem will not be solved unless it is correctly represented, unless the solver looks for evidence that will disconfirm erroneous hypotheses, and unless he can generate new hypotheses when old ones fail.

Failure to solve a particular problem can often be traced to a failure in one or more of these stages. The way that we represent a problem is influenced by our preconceptions or prior expectations; if these were appropriate there would, as we say, be no problem to solve. IQ tests abound in examples. Given the letters of the alphabet arranged as in Figure 6.5, and the instructions to continue with the next six letters, above or below the horizontal line as appropriate, most people start searching for

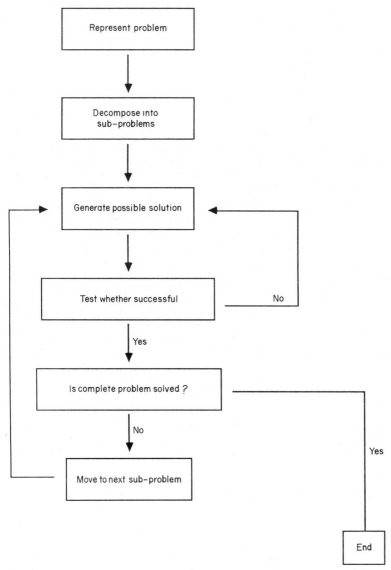

Fig. 6.4 Schematic flow-chart of steps involved in solving a problem.

a pattern to the numerical sequence, noting that a single letter above the line is followed by three below, two above etc. There may or may not be a solution to be found along these lines, but a rather simpler description is that letters without curves go above, and those with curves below the line. But our reluctance to abandon a general way of representing a problem even when it fails is apparent from repeated attempts to find new sequences.

Fig. 6.5 A catch problem: continue the series by putting the next 6 letters of the alphabet above or below the line as appropriate (from Weinman).

Often, the failure arises because we do not even notice that our initial solution is inadequate, because we fail to look for evidence that would disconfirm it. A simple demonstration of our penchant for confirmatory over disconfirmatory evidence is provided by the following task devised by Wason (Wason and Johnson-Laird, 1974). You are shown the four cards illustrated in Figure 6.6, and told that all cards have a number on one side and a letter on the other. Your task is to test whether the following proposition is also true: all cards that have a vowel on one side have an odd number on the other. Which cards would you need to turn over in order to test the truth of this proposition? (Try it before reading further.)

Virtually everyone correctly turns over Card A (if it had a 2 on the other side the rule would be violated). Most people correctly realize that they do not need to turn over Card B. It is the two numbered cards that generate errors. Some people want to turn over Card 1, but the proposition would be equally true whether an A or B appeared on the other side. Worst of all, very few people turn over Card 2, but the proposition would be falsified by finding an A on the other side. The error of commission, turning over Card 1, seems to be a matter of looking for quite unnecessary confirmatory evidence: the proposition would no doubt be confirmed by finding an A on the other side, but it could never be disconfirmed. But the even more common error of omission, failing to turn over Card 2, seems equally indicative of a penchant for confirmatory evidence: we do not turn over the card, because nothing that we found on the other side could possibly *confirm* the proposition, it could only disconfirm it.

All cards have a letter on one side and a number on the other.

A	B	1	2

Which cards do you need to turn over to check whether the following statement is true ?

If a card has a vowel on one side, it has an odd number on the other.

Fig. 6.6 Wason's 'four-card' trick (from Wason and Johnson-Laird, 1972).

The difficulty of this problem, which is solved correctly by less than 20 per cent of university students, provides further illustration of a point already made. The problem is couched in abstract terms, about letters and numbers and a wholly arbitrary rule relating them, and it is, in part, this that makes it so difficult. If it is presented in a more realistic, concrete form, it suddenly becomes easy. You are asked to believe (what was once true) that the rule for 1st and 2nd class post is that only unsealed envelopes (and postcards) are allowed to go 2nd class; sealed envelopes must have a 1st class stamp. Which of the envelopes shown in Figure 6.7 need checking (by turning over) to make sure that no one is trying to cheat the post office? Here, most people (over 80 per cent of students, at least) can see that they need to turn over the first and fourth envelopes, and that if someone wants to waste their money by affixing a 1st class stamp to an unsealed envelope (the second and third) that is their problem. But, it should not take too much reflection to see that the logical structure of this problem is exactly the same as that of the four cards. The dramatic change in difficulty suggests that Piaget was too optimistic in supposing that the transition from Concrete to Formal Operations is at all straightforward. Few of us can be relied on to solve abstract, arbitrary problems, whose logical structure is in fact quite simple; and that, no doubt, is why IQ tests contain such problems. A further implication, however, is that our ability to solve the concrete, realistic version of such a problem is unlikely to involve any elucidation of its underlying formal structure.

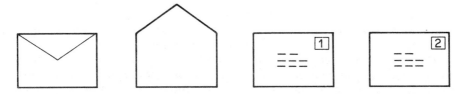

If an envelope is sealed, it must have a first class stamp.

Fig. 6.7 'Realistic' version of Wason's problem.

Medical diagnosis and decision-making

A doctor making a diagnosis or recommending treatment is trying to solve a problem. Given this set of symptoms, what is the most probable cause? Given this set of probable causes, which treatments are indicated, and which, if any, strongly contraindicated? Part of his problem of course, may be lack of information or specialized knowledge. The GP must consult experts for laboratory tests or information about rare symptoms, but at least part of the difficulty is more mundane than this, and may reflect some of the issues outlined above.

Both diagnosis and selection of treatment may be influenced by irrelevant preconception. The problem, in other words, may be misrepresented. In one study (McNeil, Parker, Sox and Tversky, 1982), three groups of people were asked to choose between two treatments for lung cancer, either radiation or surgery. The information on which they had to base their decision was the immediate and longer term survival rates: approximately 10 per cent of patients, they were told, die during or shortly after surgery, but the survival rate after two years is higher than with radiation treatment, even taking these initial deaths into account. This undoubtedly represents a genuine dilemma of balancing long-term benefit against short-term risk, but the study found that decisions were affected by two quite irrelevant factors. Asked to choose between surgery and radiation, only 25 per cent of the sample chose radiation. When they were simply labelled Treatments A and B (but with exactly the same information about life expectancies), 43 per cent of the sample chose Treatment B (radiation). Secondly, when the life-expectancy data were given in terms of survival rates, for example that 90 per cent of patients survive surgery and 35 per cent are still alive four years later, 76 per cent recommended surgery; but if the statistics were given in terms of death rates (10 per cent dying from the operation and 65 per cent dead within four years), only 57 per cent recommended surgery. The authors suggest that the contrast between 10 per cent dying immediately from surgery against 0 per cent dying immediately from the radiation treatment must have seemed more marked than the contrast between 90 per cent and 100 per cent survival rates. Both doctors and research students were just as much swayed by these apparently irrelevant aspects of the task as were the patients. Neither a training in statistics nor practice in recommending treatments seems to render one immune to these sorts of preconceptions.

Diagnosis is no exception to the general rule that it is difficult to apply the formal rules one has learned to rather arbitrary, unfamiliar problems. Students who have learned formal logic, and scientists who should be familiar with the importance of disconfirming hypotheses, are not much better at solving Wason's problem than anyone else. Similarly, students who have learned statistics are not necessarily much better at applying what they have learned. Thinking statistically is not necessarily a matter of applying statistical formulae, calculating correlation coefficients or performing an analysis of variance. Consider the data shown in Figure 6.8 (Tversky and Kahneman, 1974). A hospital has admitted 100 patients, some displaying symptom A, others not; over the next month, some of the 100 develop disease B, others do not. From the incidence of symptom and disease shown in Figure 6.8, is symptom A an indicator of disease B? Far too many people say that it is, having been misled by the large number, 60, in the top left cell, of patients with both symptom and disease, as opposed to the small number, 5, of those who have neither. But, this is irrelevant and ignores the difference in base rates (more patients had the symptom than not; more went down with the disease than not). The critical comparison is that of 75 patients who developed the disease, 60 (or 80 per

Symptom A

		YES	NO
Disease B	YES	60	15
	NO	20	5

Is Symptom A an indicator of Disease B ?

Fig. 6.8 A 2×2 table showing the hypothetical incidence of Symptom A and Disease B in 100 hospital patients.

cent) had the symptom, and exactly the same percent (20 of 25) of those who did *not* develop the disease also had the symptom. Having the symptom does not increase the chances of developing the disease, or, put another way, the symptom does not raise the *relative risk* of the disease (see Chapter 10). The problem is one of thinking in terms of probabilities and conditional probabilities, i.e. of thinking statistically.

The problem is sometimes even worse, for if it coincides with their preconceptions, people can see a correlation which is objectively not there. This means that clinicians may continue confidently making erroneous diagnoses, not only failing to look for evidence that might contradict their diagnosis, but failing to *see* it even when it is forcibly brought to their attention. Some forms of psychological diagnosis, for example projective tests, are notoriously susceptible to this sort of preconception. The Rorschach ink-blot test, which requires the patient to 'interpret' various bizarre patterns, supposedly like ink-blots, is said to reveal all manner of psychopathology, but few objective assessments have been able to document these claims. In the draw-a-man test, the patient is asked to draw a picture of a man, and is said to reveal, unwittingly, his anxieties or pathology in the type of picture he produces. It is widely claimed that the drawings of people with paranoid tendencies, for example, will unduly emphasize the eyes. Several objective studies have found no evidence to support this claim, but have failed to shake the confidence of many clinicians. Some insight into the reason for their persistence is provided by the following study (Chapman and Chapman, 1969). The experimenter prepares on cards a large set of drawings, some of which have large, emphasized eyes, most of which do not. Each card also bears a brief description of the person who supposedly drew it, that he is cheerful and extroverted, or lacks self-confidence, or is abnormally suspicious of others, etc. These descriptions are carefully assigned to the drawings to ensure that there is absolutely no correlation between the paranoid description (abnormally suspicious) and the over-emphasized eyes. But, when people are given the set of cards to look through and asked to report any tendency for any particular description to go with any particular drawing, 80 per cent claim that the emphasized eyes were more likely to have been drawn by the paranoids. Even if the experimenter arranges a *negative* correlation between the two, over 50 per cent still claim to have seen a positive correlation.

Computer-aided diagnosis

What, then, is the solution? Even if formal teaching in statistics does not always ensure that the student will think statistically, or apply his formal knowledge to unfamiliar problems, one can only hope that drawing attention to common sources of error may guard some people against them. But there is another strategy—that of providing the diagnostician with more dispassionate, statistical and logical assistance in the form of a computer program. Computer-aided diagnosis, it is obvious, will be no better than the information and rules built or fed into the program. There is no suggestion that the computer is about to take over from the skilled expert. But a computer program can, in principle, contain the most sophisticated information available to experts in the field; it can also, and this is the point of present concern, be programmed to be less susceptible to preconception, less confounded by poor statistical thinking, and more willing to consider alternative hypotheses and to look for evidence that will disconfirm one or more of them. The aim of the program is not, as with much research in artificial intelligence, to simulate the behaviour of skilled diagnosticians or to test theories of how they make their diagnoses. It is designed more as an aid to the less skilled practitioner, making available to him the expert's information, and allowing him to benefit from the application of formal rules of inference which, although known in principle and no doubt followed intuitively by the expert, are not easily made explicit.

Many such programs are now available. One such is MYCIN, designed to diagnose the cause(s) of infections, particularly bacteraemias, and to recommend appropriate treatment (Shortliffe, Davis, Axline, Buchanan, Green and Cohen, 1975). One problem in this area is that the initial signs of infection may require treatment before laboratory tests have had time to identify the organism(s) responsible; another is that the attendant doctor or surgeon may not be particularly well qualified to make the necessary diagnosis; given the proliferation of new antibiotics, it is no wonder that there should be concern about their misuse. A simplified, schematic representation of MYCIN's program is shown in Figure 6.9. The computer receives information about the patient, and combines this with its knowledge base, both static and dynamic, to make inferences or draw conclusions in accordance with a set of inference rules (**judgmental knowledge**). The knowledge base comprises both general, static information in the form of lists of infections, pathogenic and non-pathogenic organisms, and antibiotics, and dynamic information about the relationships between

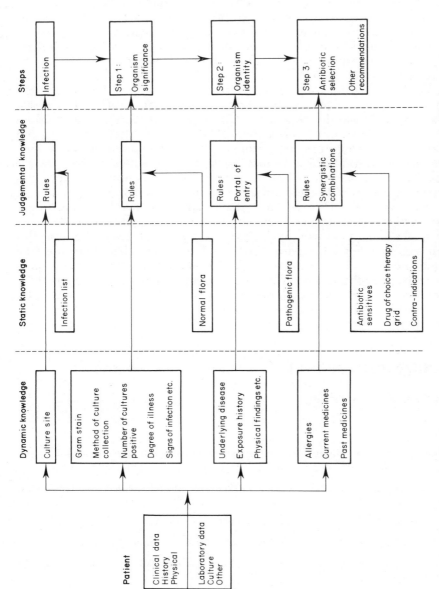

Fig. 6.9 A simplified, schematic representation of how MYCIN selects an antimicrobial treatment.

infections and infecting agents, treatments and consequences. The doctor using the program provides information about the patient, such information about the infection as is available, and the computer provides a list of potential infective agents, assigning a probability to each, and then, on the basis of further information about the patient's medical history, recommends various treatments. The doctor is invited to reject any treatment thought to be unsuitable, and the computer will provide a second-best list of treatments, and so on.

MYCIN's diagnoses and suggested treatments compare favourably with those of acknowledged experts. Five experts from Stanford University, where MYCIN was developed, and five from other American universities were given the same information as MYCIN on fifteen patients and evaluated the program's conclusions. A majority of both groups agreed completely with MYCIN's initial assessment of whether there was a significant case for treatment; a majority of the Stanford doctors also agreed with all MYCIN's identifications of the infecting organism, and with 91 per cent of MYCIN's recommended treatments; the other experts were less enthusiastic, a majority agreeing with only 91 per cent of MYCIN's diagnoses and 73 per cent of its choices of treatment. If nothing else, this indicates that not all experts agree, and therefore that there must be legitimate grounds for disagreement. But MYCIN's performance is quite creditable, and the virtue of computer programs is that everything in them is explicit, so that it should, in principle, be possible to specify why MYCIN makes errors, and to program them out.

Suggested reading

For the history of IQ testing:

Fancher, R.E. (1985). *The Intelligence Men: Makers of the IQ Controversy*. Norton, New York.

Representative statements of the extreme hereditarian and environmentalist viewpoints, together with some flavour of the controversy, are provided by:

Eysenck, H.J. and Kamin, L.J. (1981). *Intelligence: The Battle for the Mind*. Pan Books, London.

An orthodox account by a staunch defender of IQ testing is:

Jensen, A.R. (1981). *Straight Talk About Mental Tests*. Methuen, London.

Two edited books which contain a number of papers on problem solving and reasoning are:

Johnson-Laird, P.N. and Wason, P.C. (1977). *Thinking: Readings in Cognitive Science*. Cambridge University Press, Cambridge.

Kahneman, D., Slovic, P. and Tversky, A. (1982). *Judgment Under Uncertainty: Heuristics and Biases*. Cambridge University Press, Cambridge.

References

Ashby, B., Morrison, A. and Butcher, H.J. (1970). The abilities and attainments of immigrant children. *Research in Education* **4**, 73.

Binet, A. and Simon T. (1905). Methodes nouvelles pour le diagnostic du niveau intellectuel des anormaux. *L'Annee Psychologique* **11**, 191.

Bouchard, T.J. and McGue, M. (1981). Familial studies of intelligence. *Science* **212**, 1055.

Burt, C. (1966). The genetic determination of differences in intelligence: a study of monozygotic twins reared together and apart. *British Journal of Psychology* **57**, 137.

Chapman, L.J. and Chapman J.P. (1969). Illusory correlation as an obstacle to the use of valid psychodiagnostic signs. *Journal of Abnormal Psychology* **74**, 271.

Cole, M. and Scribner, S. (1975). *Culture and Thought*. Wiley, New York.

Flynn, J.R. (1984). The mean IQ of Americans: massive gains 1932–1978. *Psychological Bulletin* **95**, 29.

Galton, F. (1869). *Hereditary Genius*, Macmillan, London.

Hearnshaw, L.S. (1979). *Cyril Burt: Psychologist*. Hodder and Stoughton, London.

Horn, J.M., Loehlin, J.C. and Willerman, L. (1979). Intellectual resemblance among adoptive and biological relatives: the Texas adoption project. *Behavior Genetics* **9**, 177.

Jensen, A.R. (1980). *Bias in Mental Testing*. Methuen, London.

Juel-Nielsen, N. (1965). Individual and environment: a psychiatric-psychological investigation of MZ twins reared apart. *Acta Psychiatrica Scandinavica* (Supplement 183). Munksgaard, Copenhagen.

Kamin, L.J. (1974). *The Science and Politics of IQ*. Erlbaum, Hillsdale, New Jersey.

Kamin, L.J. (1981). *Intelligence: The Battle for the Mind*. Pan Books, London.

Lynn, R. and Hampson, S. (1986). The rise of national intelligence: evidence from Britain, Japan and the United States. *Personality and Individual Differences* **7**, 23.

Mackintosh, N.J. and Mascie-Taylor, C.G.N. (1986). The IQ question. In *Personality, Cognition and Values*, pp. 77–131. Edited by Bagley, C. and Verma, G.K. Macmillan, London.

McNeil, B.J., Panker, S.G., Sox, H.C. and Tversky, A. (1982). On the elicitation of preferences for alternative therapies. *New England Journal of Medicine* **306**, 1259.

Mascie-Taylor, C.G.N. (1984). Biosocial correlates of IQ. In *The Biology of Human Intelligence*, pp. 99–127. Edited by Turner, C.J. and Miles, H.B. Eugenics Society, London.

Mascie-Taylor, C.G.N. and Gibson, J.B. (1978). Social mobility and IQ components. *Journal of Biosocial Science* **10**, 263.

Newman, H.H., Freeman, F.N. and Holzinger, K.J. (1937). *Twins: A Study of Heredity and Environment*. University of Chicago Press, Chicago.

Rutter, M. and Madge, N. (1976). *Cycles of Disadvantage*. Heinemann, London.

Scarr, S. and Weinberg, R.A. (1976). IQ test performance of black children adopted by white families. *American Psychologist* **31**, 726.

Scarr, S. and Weinberg, R.A. (1977). Intellectual similarities within families of both adopted and biological children. *Intelligence* **1**, 170.

Schaie, K.W. (1983). *Longitudinal Studies of Adult Psychological Development*. Guilford, New York.

Schiff, M., Duyme, M., Dumaret, A., Stewart, J., Tomkiewicz, S. and Fiengold, J. (1978). Intellectual status of working-class children adopted early into upper-middle-class families. *Science* **200**, 1503.

Shields, J. (1962). *Monozygotic Twins Brought Up Apart and Brought Up Together*. Oxford University Press, Oxford.

Shortliffe, E.H., Davis, R., Axline, S.G., Buchanan, B.G., Green, C.C. and Cohen, S.N. (1975). Computer-based consultations in clinical therapeutics: explanation and rule-acquisition capabilities of the MYCIN system. *Computers in Biomedical Research* **8**, 303.

Skodak, M. and Skeels, M.H. (1949). A final follow-up study of one hundred adopted children. *Journal of Genetic Psychology* **75**, 85.

Spearman, C. (1927). *The Abilites of Man*. Macmillan, London.

Thurstone, L.L. (1938). *Primary Mental Abilities*. University of Chicago Press, Chicago.

Tversky, A. and Kahneman, D. (1974). Judgment under uncertainty: heuristics and biases. *Science* **185**, 1124.

Waller, J.H. (1971). Achievement and social mobility: relationships among IQ score, education, and occupation in two generations. *Social Biology* **18**, 252.

Wason, P.C. and Johnson-Laird, P.N. (1972). *The Psychology of Reasoning*. Batsford, London.

Wechsler, D. (1939). *The Measurement of Adult Intelligence*. Williams and Wilkins, Baltimore.

Wechsler, D. (1981). *Wechsler Adult Intelligence Scale—Revised*. The Psychological Corporation, Cleveland.

Wissler, C. (1901). The correlation of mental and physical tests. *Psychological Review Monograph Supplement* **3**, 6.

7

Clinical Neuropsychology

R McCarthy

Impairments of cognitive function are seen following a wide range of cerebral disorders. With relatively circumscribed conditions, such as embolic stroke or cerebral abscess, highly specific or selective impairments may occur. In more widespread pathology (such as that observed following severe closed head injury, or in the degenerative or dementing illnesses) there may be multiple and extensive cognitive deficits. The precise pattern and extent of cognitive dysfunction shown by any individual patient is often of considerable clinical significance since it may be a guide to the location, type, and extent of neuropathology. The patterns of deficit shown by individual patients have also been of considerable importance in the development of psychological accounts of cognitive function (see Chapters 2 and 3).

Clinical neuropsychology is concerned with the evaluation of cognitive function in people with suspected or confirmed neurological disease. The results of these clinical investigations serve a number of purposes: aiding diagnosis, monitoring change in function, and as a guide for developing appropriate rehabilitation programmes. Neuropsychological investigations are often required in the initial stages of the diagnostic process, when, for example, it is necessary to determine whether a particular patient's difficulties are likely to be due to a primary neurological deficit rather than to a psychiatric disturbance. Selected tests can also be used to monitor change in function in order to establish whether a condition is progressive, or whether a particular therapeutic intervention has proven satisfactory. The results of clinical assessment can be used as a guide to the pattern and severity of an individual's difficulties, and this information can then be taken into account when patient management and rehabilitation programmes are devised.

The human brain is highly differentiated in terms of its functional organization. It appears to differ from that of other primates in that it has processing systems which are only represented in one cerebral hemisphere as well as systems which are duplicated in both cerebral hemispheres. Although the human cerebral hemispheres are very similar in size and shape there are crucial differences in the functions that they subserve. The pattern of the cerebral organization of function appears to be very similar in the vast majority of people. In all cases, primary sensory and motor functions appear to be duplicated in both cerebral hemispheres. Asymmetrical organization of function is found in systems that are implicated in more 'cognitive' aspects of information processing. For approximately 95 per cent of right-handers and 70 per cent of left-handers, major language and literacy skills are dependent on the integrity of the left hemisphere. The right hemisphere is involved in perceptual, spatial and non-verbal processing. For most of the remainder of the population this pattern appears to be reversed, although a very small proportion of individuals may have bilateral organization of some cognitive skills. Damage to the left hemisphere sustained in infancy and early childhood appears to increase the incidence of bilateral and right hemisphere speech representation. Evidence for these patterns of functional asymmetry has been drawn from sources including studies of patients who have received unilateral administration of the barbiturate sodium amytal during angiography and patients who have received unilateral electroconvulsive therapy (ECT).

Lateral asymmetries of function are frequently discussed in terms of the **dominance** of one hemisphere with respect to language and linguistic skills. The division of function between the cerebral hemispheres is also sometimes discussed in terms of a dichotomy between the 'verbal' left hemisphere and the 'non-verbal' right hemisphere. These distinctions are something of an oversimplification since many, if not all, everyday tasks would appear to require the interaction of both sides of the brain operating as a total system. However, they are often useful as a 'shorthand' means of describing the specializations of the cerebral hemispheres in a clinical context. For example, it is occasionally necessary to decide whether the risks involved in a particular neurosurgical procedure on one side of the brain are justified (e.g. in the removal of slowly growing neoplasms, or elective surgery for epilepsy). In such cases, it is essential to take into account whether the site of operation is likely to involve the 'dominant' or 'language' hemisphere rather than the 'non-dominant' or 'non-verbal' hemisphere since the adverse consequences of language impairment are frequently both personally distressing and socially isolating. Even in the absence of a clinical language deficit, impairment of verbal memory resulting from damage to the left hemisphere is considerably more of a handicap than is an impairment of non-verbal memory resulting from damage to the right.

The remainder of this chapter will provide an overview of some of the more important neuropsychological syndromes and consider their diagnostic significance. Some brief methods of assessment will be described and the anatomical correlates of particular types of impairment will be specified where known. In the case of asymmetrically organized functions, the commonest pattern of laterality will be assumed, that is left hemisphere dominance for language.

Neuropsychological deficits can be considered in terms of whether dysfunction of bilaterally symmetrical or more lateralized systems is implicated. In considering the types of disorder that are observed it is useful to draw a broad distinction between the following levels of disturbance which can arise as a result of cerebral damage:

1. Deficits in maintaining alertness
2. Deficits arising in previously well-established cognitive skills
3. Deficits in learning and memory
4. Deficits in problem solving.

Alertness

Impairments in alertness are seen in the context of a wide range of acute and chronic neurological conditions. Head injury may give rise to an acute impairment of alertness and the rate at which patients recover to a normal level of alertness appears to be a good indicator of subsequent recovery. In chronic conditions, the patient's level of alertness may either be consistent or it may fluctuate over time, as in some cases of obstructive hydrocephalus and in many toxic states. Widespread, chronic and progressive slowing of cognitive performance is seen in the syndrome of frontosubcortical dementia which is associated with degenerative conditions such as some forms of Parkinson's Disease and Wilson's Disease. Generalized slowing of performance is also, unfortunately, an all-too-common side-effect of many anticonvulsant medications which are in current use.

The patient's ability to maintain a reasonable level of alertness may be monitored by simple timed tasks such as counting forwards up to 30, (which most normal people can achieve in under 30 sec) or reciting well-known series, such as the months of the year or the alphabet. Such tests may not be feasible with language disordered (aphasic) patients and timed paper and pencil tests (letter or number cancellation, or writing as many Xs as possible) can also be used. Such tests, while simple, are particularly useful clinically for monitoring changes in a patient's level of alertness over time.

Impairments in previously well-established cognitive skills

Selective impairments in previously well-established cognitive skills often have very precise significance for the localization of cerebral pathology. The following account provides a very brief summary of relatively common patterns of deficit in the skills of visual object recognition, visuomotor co-ordination, literacy and language processing.

Visual object recognition

As discussed in Chapter 2, the processes involved in object recognition are complex and they appear to require the integration of a number of diverse processing systems. The selective breakdown of these systems leads to different patterns of deficit which may provide a useful clinical guide to the localization of lesions. The major stages of processing which give rise to specific patterns of deficit are the sensory level (cortical blindness), the perceptual level (apperceptive agnosia) and the semantic (meaning) level (associative agnosia).

Cortical blindness

Damage to striate and circumstriate cortex, or to the geniculostriate projection systems to the primary visual cortex, may result in partial or complete cortical blindness. The severity of the defect, and the part of vision which is affected varies according to the site of the lesion. With unilateral lesions the visual field contralateral to the lesion site is impaired. These deficits can extend to one whole half of the visual field (hemianopia), occupy a single quadrant of the visual field (quadrantinopia), or be restricted to a small portion of vision (scotoma). These visual field defects are not necessarily absolute in that they may affect one aspect of visual functioning, whilst leaving other aspects intact. For example, some patients may selectively lose their colour vision in one visual field, and others may lose their ability to locate stimuli in space or to discriminate shapes, again showing the deficit on one side of vision alone.

Bilateral visual field deficits resulting in cortical blindness occur in patients with bilateral damage to the major visual pathways and to striate and circumstriate cortex in the occipital lobe. As with hemianopic deficits, cortical blindness is not necessarily absolute and may selectively affect particular aspects of visual processing, leaving other aspects intact. In severe cases, the patient may be left with only one residual component of visual sensory analysis. The evidence indicates that there may be a highly selective loss, or selective preservation of the ability to perceive colour, locate stimuli in space, discriminate form, or detect movement. Perhaps the most dramatic example of the selective preservation of a component of early visual processing has been documented in patients with circumscribed striate cortex lesions. These patients may show preservation of the ability to locate visually presented stimuli, yet they claim not to experience 'seeing' anything. When the patients are asked to guess where a stimulus has been presented they may do so, at normal levels of accuracy, whilst insisting that they have seen nothing. This phenomenon has been termed 'blindsight', and contrasts with the complementary syndrome of 'visual disorientation' in which patients can see, and identify stimuli, but are incapable of locating them in space.

On the basis of evidence from patients with unilateral or bilateral visual field deficits it has been argued that early visual sensory processing is subserved by bilaterally symmetrical systems. Since specific types of visual processing impairment can be confined to one half of vision, they must be organized in a way that reflects the topographical distribution of stimulation at the level of the retina. They are said to be retinotopically or topographically organized processing systems. The evidence indicates that there are a number of these retinotopically organized processors in both right and left hemispheres which are dedicated to the early visual analysis of different sensory properties. Thus, there are bilateral processing modules for processing sensory attributes such as colour, location, form, and motion.

From a clinical perspective selective impairments of early visual processing may appear quite bizarre and some care is needed in their assessment. The commonest areas of difficulty (colour, location, shape) can be evaluated using simple tests. Colour discrimination can be investigated using coloured wools, or paint samples and localization is assessed by asking the patient to point to visual targets. The ability to perceive and discriminate forms can be evaluated by asking the patient to decide whether a shape is present or absent from a 'noise field' (Fig. 7.1 (a)), or whether a given shape is a square or a rectangle using stimuli matched for total flux (Fig. 7.1 (b)).

Perceptual analysis of visual objects

Selective impairments in perceptual analysis can occur following circumscribed cerebral lesions. The patient may be able to recognize and discriminate between simple, prominent visual stimuli but has difficulties in interpreting more complex stimuli such as 'sketchy' or degraded drawings. The type of error made by the patient is typically one of confusing the object in the picture with a visually similar item: thus a picture of a book might be confused with a picture of a brick, or a drawing of handcuffs might be identified as a pair of spectacles. Patients with impaired perceptual analysis often complain of 'poor eyesight' but may nevertheless function adequately on standard tests of acuity.

In a group study of patients with unilateral lesions, Milner (1958) found that performance on the McGill Anomalies test which uses relatively complex pictures was specifically impaired by right temporal lobe lesions. Subsequent work using fragmented stimuli, and objects photographed from unusual angles (Fig. 7.2) has shown that the highest incidence of impairment occurs, in fact, in patients with right parietal lobe lesions (Warrington, 1982). This right hemisphere syndrome has been identified with the pattern of deficit originally characterized by Lissauer in the latter half of the nineteenth century as **apperceptive agnosia**. This syndrome provides one example of a **non-retinotopic** visual processing skill. It may be observed in both visual fields in patients who do not have a hemianopia, and more critically, it can be documented in the intact right visual field of patients whose right hemisphere lesion has given rise to the syndrome. Thus, despite visual information being available to the undamaged left

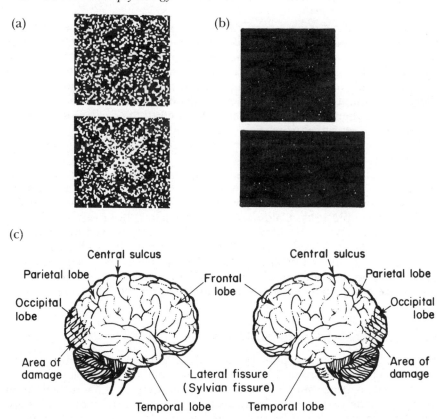

Fig. 7.1 (a) Example of stimuli for making judgments about the presence or absence of a shape against a 'noise field'. (b) Example of square and rectangle matched for total flux. (c) Areas of damage implicated in visual sensory impairments. (Stimuli reproduced by permission of Warrington, E.K.)

hemisphere, the patient still has difficulty on tests of perceptual analysis due to a lesion affecting the right hemisphere of the brain.

More detailed investigation of single cases with the syndrome of apperceptive agnosia has shown that all aspects of visual sensory processing (shape, colour, movement, location) may be entirely normal in the right visual field. The right hemisphere lesion appears to affect a specific processing system which is necessary for the perception of objects in terms of their volume and structure. This aspect of perception cannot be achieved on the basis of sensory information alone. For example, the normal individual has no difficulty in going 'beyond the information given' when looking at a fragmentary or incomplete stimulus. It is possible to 'filter out' irrevelant sensory information, and 'fill in' any gaps so as to perceive a coherently structured object. These filtering out, and gap-filling processes appear to require the ability to refer incoming sensory informa-

(a)

(b)

(c)

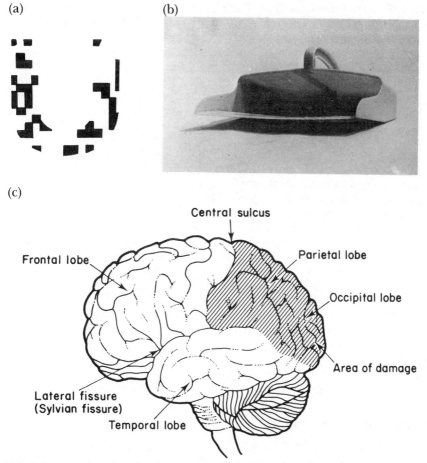

Fig. 7.2 (a) Example of a fragmented letter stimulus. (b) Unusual angle photograph. (c) Area of damage implicated in apperceptive agnosia. (Stimuli reproduced by permission of Warrington, E.K.)

tion to a 'vocabulary' of visual knowledge in which the volume and structure of familiar objects is represented. Difficulties with these types of perceptual analysis and processing are revealed by tests making use of fragmentary or distorted test stimuli. (Warrington, 1982.)

Assignment of meaning to visual objects

The assignment of meaning to an object can be disrupted independently of any impairment in visual sensory processing and perceptual analysis. Patients who are unable to assign meaning to visual objects not only fail in naming an object which they can see but, in addition, are unable to demonstrate the object's use, or to allocate a visually presented object to a class of objects of the same type. For example, the patient may be unable to name a razor when it is shown, to mime its use, or recognize that a visually presented electric razor and a safety razor are the same type of object. At the same time the patient may have no difficulty in describing or miming the function of an object when told its name, and may also be able to identify it on the basis of touch. Patients with impaired ability to assign meaning to visually presented objects are not affected by the visual complexity of the stimulus material and pictures may be recognized as well or as poorly as real objects. These patients can be considered to show a deficit in a specific (visual) component of their data base of 'factual' knowledge, or their visual 'semantic memory' (see Chapter 3).

Following Lissauer's nineteenth century terminology, difficulty in assigning meaning to visual objects which cannot be accounted for in terms of language difficulties, or more global intellectual deterioration is termed **visual associative agnosia**. A severe visual associative agnosia may present a significant handicap in everyday life, but this is extremely uncommon. Milder forms of the deficit have been documented in patients with damage to the posterior sectors of the left hemisphere. In single case studies of patients with a severe and selective visual associative agnosia, the lesion has involved the left occipital and posterior temporal lobes. A magnetic resonance imaging (MRI) scan of one patient who showed the syndrome of visual associative agnosia in a particularly selective form is shown in Fig. 7.3 (a) together with a lateral view of the left hemisphere showing the lesion in a schematic form (Fig. 7.3 (b)).

In testing for this syndrome, tasks which may be useful include those requiring the patient to recognize pictures, to mime the use of objects or to match two visually dissimilar but conceptually similar items (Fig. 7.3 (c)).

Visuomotor co-ordination

In everyday life we are continuously required to act or perform a series of actions in a spatial context. Patients with cerebral damage may be impaired in these abilities and the precise type of deficit varies according to the site of the patients' lesions. The following components of processing will be considered here:

a) The distribution of attention
b) The analysis of spatial co-ordinates
c) The programming of action

Fig. 7.3   (a) MRI scan of visual agnostic patient showing left occipitotemporal lesion with sparing of the splenium. (Reproduced from McCarthy, R.A. and Warrington, E.K. (1986) by permission of British Medical Association Publications, London.) (b) View of lateral aspect of left hemisphere showing site of lesion in (a). (c) Example of task requiring patient to match visually dissimilar but conceptually similar stimuli.

(a)

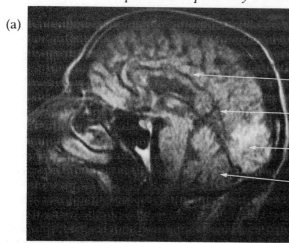

Corpus callosum

Splenium

Area of damage

Cerebellum

(b)

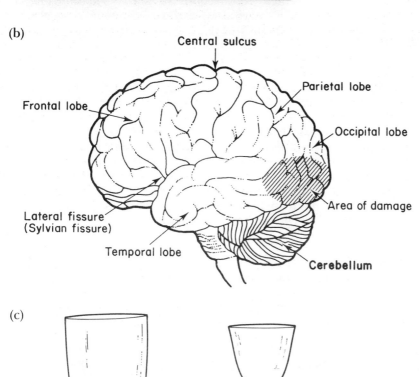

Central sulcus

Parietal lobe

Frontal lobe

Occipital lobe

Area of damage

Lateral fissure
(Sylvian fissure)

Temporal lobe

Cerebellum

(c)

Collectively these deficits, particularly those arising at levels (b) and (c) are sometimes referred to in the neurological literature as 'constructional apraxia'.

The distribution of attention

Unilateral cortical and some unilateral subcortical lesions can affect the ability to distribute attention evenly across space. Patients may ignore or be less attentive to the half of space which is contralateral to the site of their lesion. This syndrome, termed unilateral **neglect**, may be shown on visual, tactile, auditory, or motor tasks and individual patients differ in the type of task which is affected and the severity of their impairment. Surprisingly, neglect may not necessarily be confined to external space but may involve the individual's ability to distribute attention across a memory image. Bisiach *et al.* (1981) found that certain patients would ignore one half of a scene when describing their recollections of a city square from one viewpoint. When the patients were asked to describe the square again from the opposite perspective they showed neglect of the side they had previously described and recalled those parts of the scene which they had omitted on the first occasion.

Clinically, neglect syndromes are more frequently observed following right hemisphere lesions than following damage to left hemisphere. The deficit is most common following damage to the right parietal lobe, although there are cases on record with frontal lobe and basal ganglia lesions. Visuospatial neglect is most easily tested by asking the patient to cross out lines scattered across a page. Neglect is shown by the patient ignoring one side of the page. Alternatively, tests of line bisection or drawing tasks may be used. Testing for neglect in other modalities may be more problematic since attentional impairment may be confused with primary sensory or motor deficits. Both behavioural and electrophysiological measures may be required for adequate diagnosis.

Spatial analysis

The ability to evaluate the spatial relationships between stimuli or of a visual array of stimuli is essential for the performance of many visuomotor tasks. Impairment at this level of processing can occur quite independently of impairment of gross localization abilities (seen in the context of visual disorientation syndromes). Thus the patient may have no difficulty in pointing to targets, but may be impaired in analysing their position relative to other targets, or in evaluating their orientation in space. Selective deficits in spatial analysis are associated with lesions of the posterior right hemisphere. Since these deficits are *not* specific to one visual field it is inferred that right hemisphere systems are responsible for this form of processing (i.e. that this is yet another example of a **non-retinotopic** visual skill). Impairments in spatial processing can be assessed by comparatively simple tasks such as asking the patient to count scattered dots or to judge the position of stimuli such as in the position discrimination task shown in Fig. 7.4, which requires the patient to decide which of the two dots is centrally located in a square. (Warrington and Rabin, 1970.)

Fig. 7.4   Example of dot location test of spatial anaysis: the patient must point to the square in which the dot is centrally located. (Test stimuli reproduced by permission of Warrington, E.K.)

The programming of action

The processes involved in performing an action can be subdivided into those which are part of the programming of the action in which the form and function of the action is specified, and into processes of movement implementation in which muscle groups are co-ordinated and activated in accordance with the central programme. This section will be concerned with the programming stage. Patients with focal cerebral lesions may show difficulties in the programming of voluntary action as is shown by their impairment on tasks requiring them to perform actions on command. Disorders of implementation tend to affect the same muscle groups in a predictable and reliable manner. A deficit may be considered to be one of programming rather than implementation because the deficits are typically inconsistent and are dependent on the conditions in which the movement is required. A minor alteration in task parameters, such as embedding an action in a more familiar context, or requiring the patient to copy a movement, rather than recall it voluntarily, will result in the movement being executed quite normally. Disorders of movement programming have been termed the **apraxias**. The apraxias can be subdivided into two major forms of apraxia involving the limbs, and a third type which is specific to oral, thoracic, and tongue movements.

Apraxias involving the limbs are usually tested by requiring the patient to perform actions with the arm, hand or fingers; there does not appear to be any advantage in testing the lower limbs since it has been established that the same patients show impairment on actions with both upper and lower limbs. In one subtype of limb apraxia, **ideational apraxia**, the patient has particular difficulty in using real objects despite being able to identify them. For example, one patient described by Poeck (1985) attempted to use a tin-opener by beating it against the side of a tin. In less severe cases the impairment can be elicited by pantomime tasks, such as asking the patient to show how a comb, hammer, or toothbrush should be used. The patients' errors frequently take the form of using a body part as the object, raking their fingers through their hair, striking the desk with a fist, or rubbing the index finger along the teeth. Such patients may be quite normal in imitating actions made by the examiner, and even have no difficulty in copying complex novel actions. The deficit in ideational apraxia therefore appears to be one of recalling, or organizing the actions which are appropriate to particular objects, rather than a deficit in the co-ordination and organization of movements *per se*.

In the second major subtype of limb apraxia, **ideomotor apraxia**, the patient is disproportionately impaired in performing unfamiliar or novel actions, whether tested by spoken command (e.g. 'place your thumb and your little finger together'), or by copying of the examiner's actions. In severe cases, even a simple novel hand posture may be impossible to imitate, although milder deficits may be elicited by requiring the subject to imitate, or learn a series of different hand postures (Fig. 7.5). This syndrome appears to reflect the patients' difficulties in assembling a novel motor programme.

Both the ideational and the ideomotor forms of limb apraxia are associated with damage to the left hemisphere. They are one of the most common signs of left hemisphere damage and may be present in up to 50 per cent of patients with acute unilateral lesions. Within the left hemisphere, chronic apraxia is associated with lesions to the parietal lobe (Fig. 7.5). In patients who are not hemiparetic (e.g. as a result of damage extending into primary motor cortex), both right and left hands are usually affected to the same extent: the apraxia is bilateral. In the case of a patient with a hemiparesis, the difficulty in performing tasks with their non-dominant hand may often simply be dismissed as 'natural' clumsiness, until it becomes obvious that they have particular problems in rehabilitation. Unilateral apraxias affecting the non-dominant hand alone are also on record: in these patients the lesion affected the corpus callosum and appears to have 'disconnected' the communication channels between the action programming systems of the left hemisphere and the right hemisphere systems which are implicated in the control of action implementation by the left hand.

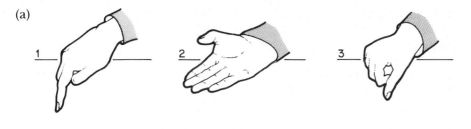

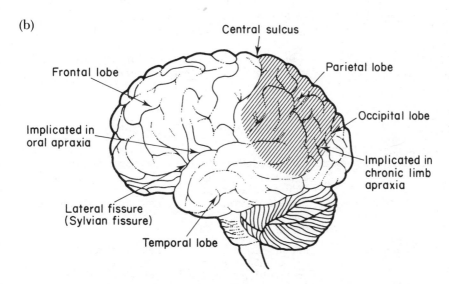

Fig. 7.5 (a) Sequence of hand postures used to test for ideomotor apraxia. (b) Lateral view of left hemisphere showing regions implicated in chronic limb apraxia and oral apraxia.

The syndrome of **oral apraxia**, in which oral, laryngeal and thoracic movements are affected is distinguished from the limb apraxias. In oral apraxia, the patient may be unable to smile, protrude the tongue, open or close their mouth, sneeze, yawn or cough on command, although all gestures are possible spontaneously. This may give the impression of an unwillingness to co-operate with routine physical examination. Patients with this syndrome may also have difficulty in learning or imitating a series of oral movements, despite being able to perform similar or identical actions spontaneously. For example, the patient may have no difficulty in performing the complex actions which are required for speech or eating. These difficulties in the voluntary production of oral movements have a very precise significance for localization, and are associated with damage to the insula of the left hemisphere.

Literacy skills

Dyslexia

The dyslexic syndromes can be subdivided into the following four main sub-types (see also, Table 7.1):

a) *Impaired visual analysis*: A specific difficulty in the visual analysis of printed words.
b) *Surface dyslexia*: Overreliance on the commoner print-to-sound rules of the language and difficulty in reading words which do not obey them.
c) *Semantic dyslexia*: The patient is unable to understand a word, despite being able to read it.
d) *Phonological dyslexia*: The patient has difficulties in working out the pronunciation of new words on the basis of print-sound rules.

Table 7.1   Dyslexia

Type	Characterization	Lesion/localization
Impaired visual analysis		
a) word-form dyslexia	Letter-by-letter reading effects of word length, failure to read script	Left occipital lesions
b) neglect dyslexia	Real word errors, transforming one side of the target	Left neglect: right parietal Right neglect: left parietal
Surface dyslexia	Inability to read rule-breaking words (e.g. yacht) but can read non-words (e.g. YOT)	Left temporal + degenerative dementing diseases
Semantic dyslexia	Patient can read rule-breaking words but cannot comprehend them	Degenerative dementing diseases
Phonological dyslexia	Patient can read familiar words (e.g. yacht) but cannot read non-words (e.g. YOT)	Left hemisphere: no precise localization
Word category dyslexia	As in phonological dyslexia with additional difficulties in reading specific categories of word	Left hemisphere: extensive lesions

Impaired visual analysis
Of the visual dyslexias, perhaps the most common is the syndrome in which patients lose their ability to recognize words as whole units—**word form**

dyslexia. It is characterized by the use of a reading strategy in which the patient attempts to read words by spelling them out letter by letter. As a consequence there is a direct relationship between the number of letters in a word, and the length of time it takes to read it. Whilst this letter by letter strategy is partially effective (although laborious) for clear and simple print, the patient may show particular difficulty in reading cursive hand-writing which can rarely be analysed letter by letter because the individual letters are almost illegible in isolation. Since this disorder is often seen in the context of preserved fluent handwriting, it is often called 'dyslexia without dysgraphia'. The critical site in this type of dyslexia appears to be in the occipitoparietal or occipitotemporal areas of the left hemisphere.

Other patterns of visual dyslexia also occur, and may have clinical localizing significance. **Neglect dyslexia** affects the patient's ability to read one side of a word accurately and is characterized by the production of an alternative real word of approximately the same length as the target word (e.g. gouge→ rouge; scintillate→ fascinate). This deficit is similar to the other neglect syndromes in being more common following right hemisphere lesions (giving left-sided neglect).

Surface dyslexia

Many words in English (and in other languages) can be read according to predictable correspondences between print and pronunciation. This can be demonstrated by reading 'non-words' such as 'bope', or 'rean' which most people can pronounce appropriately to rhyme with 'hope' or 'bean'. Some dyslexic patients are overdependent on these common 'rules' for convert-ing print into pronunciation. So, if the patient is asked to read rule-following, regular words (such as hope or bean) they perform quite normally. However, they make mistakes on rule-breaking, irregular words (e.g. love, busy or yacht). In reading this type of word the patient treats them as if they did follow the commoner rules (for example: love→ lowve, busy→ buzzie, yacht→ yakt). The patient's reading speed may be entirely normal, and novel (or non-words) and unfamiliar words may be read as quickly, and in the same way as more common words. This syndrome has been labelled **surface dyslexia** because the patient's reading shows an over-dependence on the superficial letter-sound correspondences of the language, rather than using a deeper or more comprehensive analysis of the printed word. This type of dyslexia has also been termed **phonological reading**. This syndrome been documented both in patients with extensive left hemisphere lesions, and in cases of progressive degenerative illness resulting in global language comprehension impairment. The involvement of left temporal lobe structures appears to be important in all cases.

Semantic dyslexia

In some patients the ability to read many words which break the common print-to-sound rules may be preserved, despite failure to comprehend them. The syndrome is termed **semantic dyslexia** because the patient's reading impairment affects the ability to extract meaning from the printed word. This phenomenon is actually quite common in the dementing illnesses and it has been exploited by Nelson in a clinical test of premorbid intellectual level (Nelson, 1982). The National Adult Reading Test or NART reading test gives an estimate of 'premorbid' vocabulary, working on the assumption that if a patient can read an irregular word such as LEVIATHAN, or SIDEREAL then it is likely to have been in their vocabulary prior to the onset of dementia. Scores on this test can be contrasted with the patient's current level of performance on tests of comprehension or intellectual function (e.g. IQ tests, see Chapter 6). In the case of a discrepancy between scores on the NART and the patient's current scores on intellectual tests, then the clinician may suspect a dementing illness.

Phonological dyslexia
In this syndrome the patient is unable to make use of common print-to-sound rules in order to read novel words or non-words (such as bope or rean). It is termed phonological dyslexia because the patient is impaired in deriving sound or phonology on the basis of printed letters. For many patients with phonological dyslexia, reading appears to be carried out by a 'naming' process in which it is necessary to access the meaning of a printed word prior to its pronunciation. This method of reading can be highly efficient, indeed, for some individuals the term 'dyslexic' seems almost a misnomer since their only practical handicap may be in the development of a new pronunciation vocabulary on the basis of sight information alone.

More commonly, patients who are impaired in reading non-words have additional difficulties in reading certain types of common word. These impairments selectively affect the patient's ability to read words with particular types of meaning, or which belong to a particular grammatical class. Some patients, **deep dyslexics**, are only able to read words with a concrete, imageable meaning (such as book, table, house), and they may be almost incapable of reading more abstract words (idea, reason, wish). This difficulty in reading abstract words usually occurs in conjunction with difficulties in reading verbs, adjectives and the 'little words' or grammatical words of the language such as function words (e.g. 'if', 'and', 'of', 'for', and 'by'). Some patients may also make errors of meaning in reading aloud (such as gnome→fairy and evil→Nazi). Word category effects are not confined to those observed in 'deep dyslexia'. Abstract words may be read more accurately than concrete words, or the deficit may be selective to the grammatical words of the language.

In terms of the localizing significance of these disorders the critical lesion sites appear to implicate posterior regions of the left hemisphere. Patients with word category impairments, such as 'deep dyslexics', have typically shown extensive left hemisphere pathology (Table 7.1).

Dysgraphia

Acquired disorders of spelling and writing—the dysgraphias—are as varied in their manifestations as the dyslexias. Indeed, there are some striking parallels in the types of deficit which can be observed. Nevertheless, the deficits in reading and writing frequently dissociate in individual patients.

The following four subtypes of dysgraphia will be considered:

a) Overreliance on sound-to-spelling rules resulting in impairment on words which do not obey the rules.
b) Impaired ability to translate sound into print resulting in impaired writing of new words or non-words.
c) Impairment in translating 'spelling' into writing (or speaking).
d) Disorders of the writing process.

Overreliance on sound-to-spelling rules
In some patients, there may be an overreliance on the commonest sound-to-spelling rules resulting in failure of words which are irregular or rule-breaking. This deficit is apparent even with very common words (e.g. yes→yess, said→sed), and indeed it is essential that common words be used in assessment of this syndrome since overreliance is a type of error most people make when faced with a word which they do not know how to spell. For the patient, the spellings of even common words have become unfamiliar and hence they rely on this form of spelling.

Impaired ability to translate sound into print
In this syndrome the individual is unable to write non-words or familiar words by translating them directly from sound. **Phonological dysgraphia**, like its reading counterpart, phonological dyslexia, may not be a significant handicap in everyday life. Some patients have additional difficulties in writing words with specific types of meaning (abstract or concrete words) or words which are 'grammatical'.

Translating spelling to writing (or speaking)
Having obtained the correct spelling from one's 'mental dictionary' it is necessary to retain it for long enough to write it (or spell it aloud). It is very common to find that patients 'jumble' or misorder the letters of words, suggesting that there is a problem in the way the translation process operates.

Writing disorders
Writing dysgraphias implicate a specific disorder at the level of programming the actions required for the formation of written words and letters. Some patients are unable to recall the actions required to construct a specific letter, others have difficulty in maintaining the fluency of their writing. Other 'graphic' skills such as drawing may be relatively well preserved. These disorders are thought of as being a very specific type of action programming deficit (an apraxia: see above).

The anatomical correlates of the dysgraphias are poorly specified, and at present it is only certain that they are more likely to implicate left hemisphere pathology than right.

Dyscalculia

Despite the frequency with which members of our culture are required to operate with numbers, and the comparatively high incidence of calculation disorders in patients with cerebral lesions, the dyscalculias have received comparatively little attention in neuropsychological research. For some patients the primary difficulty may be one of a specific dyslexia for numbers: they may be unable to read individual numbers, or have difficulty in reading longer number strings extending into the 'hundreds' or 'thousands' or in reading or understanding arithmetic signs. For other cases, the disorder implicates processes of calculation, rather than 'reading', and their deficit can be elicited using simple mental arithmetic problems (e.g. 'what is the sum of $15 + 23$?'). These dyscalculic deficits can occur as a completely independent impairment in patients with adequate language, memory, and problem-solving skills. Simple calculations can be failed for a number of reasons: the patient may be unable to automatically retrieve the sum of '$5 + 3$' and may have to resort to a counting strategy, other patients may have difficulty in holding in mind the various substages of the calculation and so 'lose track'. The dyscalculias are most commonly observed in patients with damage to the posterior sectors of the left hemisphere.

Disorders of language

Disorders of language were amongst the first of the neuropsychological syndromes to be studied in any detail. Paul Broca described several patients who had lost the ability to speak but who were able to comprehend what was said to them. Subsequently, Karl Wernicke described a complementary pattern of language disorder in which patients were unable to comprehend spoken language, but were able to produce fluent speech. These two patterns were associated with different lesion localizations. Impaired speech, with intact comprehension was observed in patients with anterior lesions of the left hemisphere, whereas impaired comprehension with relatively intact speech was correlated with damage to the left temporal lobe. The labels 'Broca's aphasia' and 'Wernicke's aphasia' are still often applied to patients showing these patterns of deficit (see Goodglass and Kaplan, 1972).

Discrepancies between speech production and speech comprehension can be clinically useful since they provide an approximate guide to the localization of brain damage. Patients with poor speech fluency, but adequate comprehension are likely to have lesions more in anterior regions of the left hemisphere. Conversely, patients with fluent (or even excessively fluent) speech and poor comprehension are likely to have lesions in more posterior areas of the left hemisphere. However, the categorization of patients into 'Broca's' and 'Wernicke's' subtypes is only possible in a minority of cases with acquired language disorders. It has become increasingly clear that an adequate analysis of aphasia needs to take account of the various components of language processing which can be disrupted by cerebral disease. This type of approach has the advantage that individual patients' impairments can be documented and where appropriate, this information can provide guidance in patient management or therapy. More precise documentation of specific types of language processing impairment has also led to a greater refinement and accuracy in clinicoanatomical correlations.

The various disorders of language, the **aphasias**, will be considered from the perspective of whether they primarily affect language:

a) Perception
b) Comprehension
c) Retrieval
d) Speech production

These deficits can be further sub-classified according to whether they primarily affect language units at the level of the single word, or whether higher order combinations (e.g. sentences) are implicated. This chapter will focus on deficits which arise at the level of the single word.

Language perception
The global impairment of language perception occurs in the rare syndrome of 'pure word deafness' in which the patient is able to perceive and comprehend environmental sounds and may understand the written word, but is unable to perceive language. Recent work indicates that this syndrome is typically the consequence of a more general impairment of auditory sensory analysis (and in particular the temporal resolution of acoustic information) which is most obvious or pronounced in the context of the complex task of language perception (see Chapter 2). Bilateral temporal lobe (auditory cortex) lesions have been observed in such cases.

Difficulties in discriminating similar sounding words can occur as a selective deficit without necessarily giving rise to 'deafness' for language. The patient may have difficulty in deciding whether successively presented stimuli are the same or different (e.g. choke—joke; cap—gap; lid—lit; bag—back). However, despite these difficulties patients are still able to make use of the redundancy of spoken language and of contextual information in order to compensate for their impairment. This type of impairment in word-sound discrimination is reported to be most common following left temporal lobe lesions, although less severe deficits may also occur following anterior left hemisphere damage.

Language comprehension
The familiarity or frequency of a word is critical in determining whether it will be understood by patients with language comprehension impairments (sometimes termed word meaning deafness). Studies of groups of aphasic

patients have shown that the comprehension of familiar common words (such as baby, table, sit, think, bread) is more likely to be preserved than the comprehension of less familiar, rare words (such as aeon, spurn, quay, concept, tirade). There are vast individual differences in familiarity with the words of the language, such differences relating to scores on IQ tests (see Chapter 6). Sensitive tests of comprehension are therefore graded in difficulty so that they can be adjusted to take account of these differences and are tailored to the premorbid level of the patient. The tests that are used include word definition and word-picture matching tasks taken from standard tests of intelligence.

Word frequency is not the only determinant of comprehension success or failure: patients may show selective difficulties with certain categories of word. These patients have been studied in some detail because of the valuable information which they can provide with respect to the organization of the memory systems responsible for the representation of verbal knowledge. A failure to comprehend abstract words (e.g. advantage, knowledge, indignation) is not uncommon: they are in some respects more 'complex' in their meaning than are concrete words (e.g. harp, garage, pencil). Selective impairment of the concrete word vocabulary is less common, but it is important to be aware of such deficits in patient diagnosis. Impairment of the concrete word vocabulary appears to indicate that the organization of abstract and concrete words may be different in the verbal knowledge base since there is no way in which these deficits can be dismissed as a simple artifact of task difficulty. These impairments can be quite dramatic. For example, a patient studied by Warrington (1975) produced the following definitions of concrete words:

HARP	To measure with
GARAGE	Don't know
PENCIL	Cutting tool

These contrast with his evident ability to define abstract words:

ADVANTAGE	gain you get
KNOWLEDGE	Making oneself mentally familiar with a subject
INDIGNATION	Not happy about something, to get angry about something.

Deficits in the comprehension of concrete words can be even more specific: patients may show a selective deficit in the comprehension of body parts and colour names. The selective impairment of knowledge of animate things, with preserved knowledge of inanimate things is also on record as is the converse, namely knowledge of inanimate things such as household objects being impaired whilst categories such as plants, animals and foods were preserved.

There is a considerable body of evidence that indicates that impairments of single word comprehension are associated with left temporal lobe pathology.

Word retrieval

Difficulty in retrieving words occurs as a selective impairment in the syndrome of **amnestic** or **nominal aphasia**. As with word comprehension impairments, word retrieval difficulties are critically influenced by the frequency or familiarity of the word to be retrieved. In severe cases, the patient's speech may be restricted to a few high frequency generic terms such as 'thing', but in milder cases only the fringes of the patient's vocabulary may be affected. Word category effects may also be observed in patients with word retrieval deficits. Thus, selective impairment and selective preservation of grammatical categories, such as nouns and verbs, is on record, together with preservation and loss of even more specific concrete word categories such as the selective loss of the proper name vocabulary or the selective impairment of the names of fruit and vegetables.

Word retrieval deficits are frequent in all types of language dysfunction. As an isolated sign they imply damage to the left temporal lobe. Word retrieval deficits, often attributed to 'poor memory', are also quite common as an early sign of degenerative neurological illness.

Speech production

Once a word has been retrieved, it has to be converted into a series of laryngeal and oral movements so that it can be produced. This is a complex process which can be disturbed in a variety of ways and two major syndromes will be considered in this section. First, the patient may have problems in selecting and ordering the specific articulatory 'programmes' for speech production, giving rise to errors such as trouble→skrubble; fascinate→fashingstate (termed **phonemic paraphasias**.). For some patients, the deficit, termed **conduction aphasia**, is largely restricted to tasks in which they are required to repeat single long (polysyllabic) words, or short, familiar clichés spoken by the examiner. Their spontaneous speech may be relatively unimpaired. By contrast, in other cases, **transcortical motor aphasics**, repetition of polysyllabic words and clichés may be normal, but spontaneous speech may be seriously contaminated by phonemic paraphasic errors.

Impairment in the repetition of single polysyllabic words and clichés is associated with left parietal lobe lesions. The occurrence of phonemic paraphasia in spontaneous speech with preserved repetition has less certain anatomical correlates, although it may possibly be associated with more anterior left hemisphere lesions.

In the second major type of speech production deficit, the individual sounds of words may be 'programmed' accurately, but there is disruption in the timing and co-ordination of tongue, lips, and larynx movements. These movements must be very strictly organized in order to work together to produce a coherent word (try pronouncing words such as 'shuttlecock' or 'trampoline' slowly to yourself in order to get some impression of the complexity of the movements and movement co-ordinations which are required). Patients with a speech production disorder of this type have distorted and laboured speech which may seem childlike and, in some cases, can even give the impression of a foreign accent. They have just as much difficulty with spontaneous speech as with repetition tasks. The deficit has been labelled **apraxia of speech** or **cortical dysarthria**. This syndrome is distinguished from cases of poor speech production due to muscular paralysis in which error types are predictable and consistent. In apraxia of speech, the patient's errors are typically inconsistent, a particular sound may be produced accurately in one context but not in another. This syndrome has a very precise localizing significance and implicates anterior left hemisphere regions, specifically, the insula, operculum, or white matter deep to these areas.

The main subtypes of language disorder, together with a note of their probable localizing significance are given in Table 7.2.

Table 7.2   Language dysfunction

Cognitive function	Syndrome	Lesion/localization
Perception	Pure word deafness	Bilateral temporal lobe lesions
	Word sound discrimination	Left temporal lobe
Comprehension	Word meaning deafness	Left temporal lobe
Word retrieval	Nominal or amnestic aphasia	Left temporal lobe
Speech production	Phonemic paraphasias	
	a) repetition	Left parietal?
	b) spontaneous speech	Left frontal?
	Apraxia of speech	Left hemisphere: insula, operculum

Disorders of memory

It is not uncommon for patients with neurological disease to complain of a deterioration in their memory. Indeed, memory impairment is often the first symptom noticed by patients and their families in the early stages of cerebral degenerative illnesses (e.g. the dementias). Memory deficits are also a frequent complication of closed head injury and a variety of more focal neurological conditions such as a stroke or tumour. Poor memory is by no means confined to neurological conditions, and one of the tasks of the clinician is to differentiate between the types of memory impairment which are due to factors such as stress, or depression, and those which can be attributed to a primary neurological deficit. For example, the types of memory loss which feature in fictional and newspaper accounts of 'amnesia', in which the individual appears to have forgotten his identity, and his past history, are typically the consequence of a psychiatric, rather than a neurological disturbance. Similarly, the patient who is able to give a detailed account of all the instances in which memory failure has occurred is usually describing a stress-related pattern of memory failure, rather than a neurological deficit.

Another guide to the differential diagnosis of neurological and non-neurological disorders of memory is the type of deficit shown by the patient. A global deficit on all tests which appear to have a 'memory' component, occurring in the context of near normal functioning in everyday life is strongly suggestive of a psychiatric source of deficit, rather than a neurological one. Neurological deficits can be global, but it is more usual for them to affect certain types of memory function more than others. The complaint of 'poor memory' can refer to disorders which affect a variety of distinct memory systems and it is important to determine the type of deficit as well as the severity of impairment. Memory deficits can result in a difficulty in recalling words for use in conversation. They can also give rise to a difficulty in recognizing the meanings of words or the significance of familiar objects. Other patients may be impaired in retaining verbatim information, such as spoken instructions or lists, and other cases may have difficulty in keeping a useful record of events and occurrences.

Disorders which implicate a deficit in assigning meaning to words or objects (namely word-meaning deafness and visual associative agnosia) and specific difficulties with word retrieval are often described by patients as a 'memory impairment'. These deficits implicate a disorder of the type of memory system which experimental psychologists have termed **semantic memory**. The study of patients with specific deficits in deriving meaning from visual or auditory information is perhaps the strongest source of evidence for the independent existence of semantic memory systems (see Chapter 3). As shown in Table 7.3, there are two further types of memory impairment which have both theoretical and diagnostic significance:

a) Impairment of short-term memory
b) Impaired memory for events

Short-term memory

Psychologists have distinguished a separate short-term memory system which is thought to be limited both in its capacity, and in the time over which it can store information without being aided or boosted by rehearsal processes. Its operation in everyday life is typified by one's ability to retain only a few names when introduced to a group of people, or in retaining a telephone number for long enough to dial it. Clinically, the capacity of short-term memory is assessed by the digit-span task: the normal repetition span being 7 ± 2 items for numbers. The duration of storage is measured using the retention with distraction technique (see Chapter 3).

Deficits in the capacity and the duration of auditory verbal short-term memory are commonly observed in the context of language disorders, or in cases of extensive degenerative disorders. However, the selective impairment of auditory verbal short-term memory has also been reported in a

Table 7.3 Types of memory and memory disorder

Type	Duration characteristics	Specificity	Lesion/localization
Short-term	Transient, labile	Modality specific	Auditory: left parietotemporal (angular gyrus) Visual: left occipitotemporal
Events/episodic	Long-lasting, flexible modifiable	Material specific	Verbal: left hemisphere Non-verbal: right hemisphere Global: bilateral medial temporal or diencephalic damage
Facts/semantic	Very long-lasting	Modality, material, and category specific	Visual: left occipitotemporal Verbal: left temporal lobe

small number of intensively studied single cases. These patients may have digit or letter span capacities restricted to *one* item when auditory presentation is used. However, they may have near-normal spans (of four or five items) for the same type of material when it is shown visually. These findings indicate that the very limited capacity of their short-term memory is specific to auditory presentation. It is also specific to verbal auditory information: patients may have no difficulty in retaining a series of familiar environmental sounds (animal noises, traffic noises etc.). In addition to a limited capacity for auditory verbal information these patients may also be incapable of retaining even a single auditory item following five seconds of distraction indicating that the duration of their short-term memory is also impaired.

Despite this severe impairment of short-term memory for auditory verbal material, such patients do not necessarily have difficulties with everyday conversation, and may even score normally on many formal language comprehension tasks. Thus, they may discriminate normally between word sounds (indicating good language perception, see above) and have a good vocabulary, even when tested by asking them to generate names in response to long spoken sentences such as "what is the name of the thin grey dust that remains after something has burned, such as a cigarette." They may even be able to point to the appropriate picture when asked which picture matches 'the dog is being followed by the man', when the picture choice is intentionally a highly confusing one (e.g. a man following a dog vs. a dog following a man).

However, these patients do show impairments in understanding unfamiliar or complex instructions. Their difficulties appear to arise in those situations in which 'backup' from an accurate record of the spoken information is required to permit a 'second chance' for hearing the message. This is exploited in the Token Test in which the patient is asked to carry out an unpredictable set of actions with an array of tokens varying in shape, colour and size (e.g. before picking up the red square to touch the yellow triangle). Patients with impaired auditory verbal short-term memory do badly on instructions, such as these, which convey a lot of critical information in a single auditory message. All of the patients with a selective impairment of auditory verbal short-term memory on record have had lesions located at the parietotemporal junction of the left hemisphere in a region termed the angular gyrus.

The selective impairment of visual-verbal short-term memory is somewhat less well established than is the complementary auditory-verbal deficit. This is because testing for the disorder requires information to be presented rapidly in order to preclude the 'translation' or recoding of visual-verbal material into a speech based representation. When material such as letters or digits are presented briefly (in a tachistoscope), certain patients show a disproportionate impairment in recalling or recognizing the stimuli. Patients have been reported with a visual letter and digit span which is reduced to one item; their lesions were in the occipitotemporal region of the left hemisphere (Kinsbourne and Warrington, 1962).

Deficits in learning and memory for events

The ability to remember occurrences such as a meeting with a friend, recalling the conversation that took place, and subsequently recognizing the face of his or her companion are all examples of memory for events. Memory for events is often termed 'episodic memory' in the psychological literature. This type of memory can be selectively and globally disrupted in the amnesic syndrome, resulting in the patient's inability to recall the occurrences of a few moments ago and an inability to plan for the events of a few moments hence. In severe amnesic disorders the patient may fail to recall or recognize any information following a few minutes' interruption. For example, it is quite characteristic for patients to react to their examiners as if they were complete strangers if they return to the room following a few moments' interruption in the course of a testing session. They may also have considerable difficulty in learning the name of their hospital, and may never learn the names of doctors or nurses caring for them.

In the case of a global deficit in memory for events, the patient is typically impaired in the ability to recall or recognize the events of the past **retrograde amnesia** and is impaired in the acquisition of new information **anterograde amnesia**. Both anterograde and retrograde impairments may vary in their severity, and the clinical impression is that they are typically similar in degree in the individual patient.

An adequate quantitative measurement of the patient's knowledge of events of the past, their retrograde knowledge, has proven extremely difficult to achieve. A number of formal techniques for measuring retrograde amnesia have been developed, based, for example, on recall of newsworthy events, the identification of famous faces, or the details of old television programmes. However, the problem has been that, for any test in which normal people show forgetting as a function of time, amnesics fail to score. When the test difficulty is adjusted so that the amnesic patients are capable of scoring, the test is no longer sensitive to normal forgetting. More recently, there has been an increasing interest in attempts to quantify the detail and accuracy of patients' recall or recognition of personal, autobiographical events, rather than in using the somewhat artificial stimulus 'events' provided by occurrences in politics and the media. The evidence indicates that, although severely amnesic patients may retain a skeletal autobiography, it is typically without the normal level of detail and, on questioning, cannot be elaborated.

There are fewer methodological problems in testing patients' ability to acquire new events. Patients can be presented with stimulus material in a controlled fashion and subsequently tested for their ability to remember the items. The use of different types of material allows the clinician to evaluate whether specific types of memory are particularly impaired. In global amnesia, patients show equivalent levels of deficit for recall and recognition of a wide range of materials (when compared with control subjects). They show a disproportionate degree of impairment and may even perform less well when attempts are made to aid their memory by the use of 'mnemonic' techniques such as the generation of a visual image, which aids normal memory dramatically.

Despite this loss of anterograde and retrograde event memory, other forms of 'memory' may be preserved in cases with a selective amnesic impairment. The distinction between the tasks that amnesics can, or cannot perform has challenged theoretical interpretations of the syndrome. Amnesic patients may show a normal short-term memory, both on measures of capacity (measured on the digit- letter- and word-span tasks) and duration (as measured by the retention with distraction technique). Their ability to recall the meanings of words, even for those acquired during a period for which they have a dense retrograde amnesia for events, may be entirely normal. Amnesic patients may also be able to acquire novel skills, or to improve and develop skills which they already possess. For example, patients with musical ability may be capable of learning new tunes.

Performances on a number of other tasks may also be preserved. Perceptual learning may be normal in these patients, as shown by their ability to show savings on the identification of incomplete or fragmentary stimuli (words or pictures) which may persist for months (Fig. 7.6). Both normal and amnesic patients require a less 'complete' version of an 'incomplete' stimulus for it to be identified on a second exposure. The reproduction of a word on the basis of its first three letters test is another example of a task in which the amnesic patient may show normal levels of retention. The patient is shown a list of words, and subsequently tested for retention with the first three letters of the stimulus: (e.g. depart—dep?). Under such conditions the amnesic patient may treat the word completion task as a guessing game, and may perform at least as well as neurologically intact subjects under the same circumstances.

Fig. 7.6 Sequence of degraded words used in testing for residual learning in amnesic patients. (Test stimuli reproduced by permission of Warrington, E.K.)

The critical sites of damage which have been implicated in the amnesic syndrome correspond to those which were previously thought to be important in emotion, namely the Papez circuit including the hippocampus, fornix, mamillary bodies and the medial thalamus (see Chapter 8). As was pointed out by Milner and her colleagues, bilateral damage to the medial surfaces of the temporal lobes may result in a dense and severe amnesic syndrome (e.g. case H.M.). Paradoxically, in the condition which has produced some of the most severe cases of amnesia, the Wernicke–Korsakoff syndrome, the lesion site may be restricted to a small diencephalic area. In the Wernicke–Korsakoff syndrome, which arises as consequence of thiamine deficiency (usually, but not invariably, in the context of chronic alcohol abuse), damage may be confined to the mammillary bodies and a very restricted area of the medial thalamus (the subependymal zone).

There have been a number of theories of the amnesic syndrome which have attempted to account for patterns of preserved and impaired function. One hypothesis (discussed in Chapter 3) is that amnesic patients have specific difficulties with those types of memory which require the use of explicit, or **declarative knowledge** and preservation of the ability to use **procedural memories** ('knowing how'). However, amnesic patients may exhibit relative preservation of certain types of information which would be considered as belonging to the declarative domain such as the personal 'facts' of their skeletal autobiographies, One patient has been described who was even able to retrieve and define vocabulary items which had been introduced into the language during the period for which he had a dense retrograde amnesia. The patient was able to define words such as 'AIDS', or 'Thatcherism' whilst failing to recall even the most salient personal events (such as the death of his mother). This evidence of preservation of one component of 'declarative' knowledge in amnesia together with the observation that non-amnesic patients may have a highly specific impairment within the 'declarative' domain (such as a loss of verbal or visual factual knowledge), indicates that the procedural/declarative dichotomy is likely to require refinement in the future.

Other theorists have suggested that amnesics are impaired in their ability to make use of some form of active memory processing such as performing searches of memory for recall. One development of this framework is the hypothesis that amnesia represents a **disconnection** or failure of communication between active cognitive memory processing systems and a factual knowledge base (Warrington and Weiskrantz, 1982). Amnesic patients with this syndrome would be expected to be able to use active cognitive processing in tasks other than those involving memory. Similarly, the integrity of a factual knowledge base would account for a patient's ability to show preserved vocabulary and personal 'semantic' knowledge. On this account, many of the preserved abilities of amnesic patients can be viewed as reflecting a type of 'learning' that does not require active cognitive processing: their impairments arise when the active cognitive system and the factual knowledge systems are required to interact in order to establish new memories. According to this interpretation, the failure of amnesics to benefit from mnemonic techniques such as imagery would be attributed to the demands which such operations place on the interaction between the two types of system.

Milner and her colleagues originally reported that damage to the left hemisphere resulted in impairment of verbal memory, with sparing of memory for non-verbal material such as patterns and faces. Damage to the right hemisphere resulted in the opposite pattern of deficit with selective impairment of non-verbal material and specific preservation of memory for verbal material. This pattern of preserved and impaired skills has been replicated in many experimental studies of patients with unilateral lesions. Warrington (1984) has reported the results of an investigation of a large sample of patients with unilateral lesions using a recognition memory test for words and faces. She has shown that performance on these tasks may be a very reliable indicator of the lateralization of damage to the brain. Patients with more diffuse cerebral disease may also show patterns of highly selective memory impairment which may suggest differential severity of involvement of the right or left hemispheres.

In considering the anatomical basis of memory deficits, Milner and her colleagues initially placed considerable emphasis on the role of the temporal lobe, and particularly on the role of the hippocampus. Subsequently, it has become clear that other structures are necessarily involved in a wide range of learning and memory tasks. For example, in recent years there has been increasing emphasis on the importance of the integrity of frontal lobe systems in normal memory functioning. Selective and isolated memory difficulties may arise following damage to the frontal regions of either the right or the left hemisphere which appear to reflect disorganization in the processes which are responsible for the active selection of memory representations. In the extreme case, this may give rise to **confabulation** in recall in which the patient blends together a number of unrelated real experiences, or confuses them with imagined experiences. Confabulation in recall may be sufficiently bizarre for the examiner to suspect a deficit. In other cases, repeated testing may be necessary in order to reveal inconsistencies in the patient's story.

The types of memory deficit which have been discussed in this chapter, together with a guide to their significance for localization are summarized in Table 7.3.

Deficits in problem-solving

It is not merely sufficient to have an adequate set of cognitive skills at one's disposal, they have to be harnessed appropriately according to demands of the situation, used flexibly, and integrated according to a coherent plan. For many familiar situations this integration and modulation of cognitive processing appears to be relatively 'automatic' (see Chapter 3): we are able to store a 'programme' (sometimes called a schema or script) which can call up the relevant component skills appropriately and at the correct time. To take the example of someone driving to work: the overall programme of action would include information about the route to be followed, but it would also include instructions to carry out spatial operations, or to execute actions. Although these components of the overall programme can often be executed 'automatically' without demanding a significant amount of attention, there are many circumstances in which functioning on 'autopilot' would be disasterous. When following a new route, or when a crisis occurs at some point in the journey it is possible to reorganize one's pattern of action appropriately to cope with changing situations: we are able to engage in problem-solving activities.

The ability to 'switch' from habitual and practised routine and to modify action in accordance with novel circumstances is a hallmark of the problem-solving processes which are an essential component of adaptive behaviour. Problem-solving is required in a wide range of situations, including practical routines (such as driving) and social interaction, as well as abstract intellectual reasoning tasks. Impairments in flexible problem-solving are relatively common in patients with neurological disease. As a selective impairment, which cannot be attributed to a deficit in alertness, previously well-established cognitive skills, or the ability to retain the relevant information, these disorders appear to implicate frontal lobe dysfunction.

In an influential series of clinical case reports, Luria (reviewed in Luria, 1973) described a range of difficulties observed in the context of frontal lobe lesions. Patients were described as having impaired ability to plan their actions, or to modify their behaviour in accordance with task demands. In some cases, having produced one action or pattern of action the patient would tend to repeat it over and over again—a phenomenon termed **perseveration**. This can be considered as an extreme form of failure in flexibility in problem-solving. The circumstances need not necessarily be those of a well-defined problem. For example, in patients with large destructive lesions, Luria described instances in which the instruction to draw a circle resulted in a series of overlapping spirals which continued until the pencil was removed from the patient's hand. In other patients, perseveration was shown as an inappropriate persistence in a particular line of thought, or in shifting from one line of reasoning to another.

A variety of tests have been devised in order to evaluate the difficulties in problem-solving which are seen following frontal lobe lesions. Abstract reasoning skills, such as those required to classify and organize one's knowledge of the environment are frequently described as being impaired in these patients. The two most widely used tests of abstraction are the Weigl sorting task and the Wisconsin Card Sorting task. In the Weigl sorting task the patient is presented with tokens which vary in colour (red, green, yellow, blue) and in shape (square, circle, triangle). They are asked to sort the tokens 'into groups so that the ones that are alike in one way are together'. If the patient achieves one classification they are then asked to 'sort them the other way'. Patients may show marked difficulty with this task and either fail to achieve a single classification, or have difficulty in shifting from their first classification to another. The Wisconsin task is a more complex version of the Weigl test. The patient is required to classify cards bearing symbols which vary in colour, shape and number. Therefore three rather than two sorting criteria are required. The patient classifies a series of cards by matching them to one of four 'key' cards. These cards might consist of one yellow circle, two blue triangles, three red squares, and four green stars. The order in which a set of classifications is required is predetermined, and finding the required classification principles has to be done on the basis of systematic search strategies starting from an initial hypothesis. The patient is told whether a particular decision is right or wrong. Following a sequence of correct responses, the sorting criterion is changed and the sorting task is continued. The sorting criterion may be varied for up to twelve 'shifts'. Patients with frontal lobe lesions, particularly those affecting the left frontal lobe, may have difficulty with this task and tend to perseverate with one sorting principle, even when they have been told it is wrong.

The patient's ability to cope with a novel problem can be affected by a number of different factors: three important components are concentration, evaluation, and planning. The ability to concentrate and to generate sufficient effort for a specific problem may be impaired, resulting in distractible, and erratic performance, particularly on 'boring' tasks; 'interesting' tasks may be performed at a normal level. Failure to take account of the whole of the problem resulting in impulsive responding has been documented on the 'cognitive estimates test' devised by Shallice and Evans (1978). In this test, the patient is asked to make appropriate guesses to questions such as 'what is the weight of a full pint bottle of milk', or 'how fast can a racehorse gallop'. More recently Shallice and McCarthy have developed a specific test of planning, the Tower of London task (see Shallice, 1982), which requires the patient to plan several moves in advance of an action (Fig. 7.7). In this test the patient is required to move beads placed on three sticks so as to progress from a specific starting position to a particular target position. The subject can only move one bead at a time, and must always move the beads between the supporting sticks of the apparatus. In the easier problems, the solution is an 'obvious' one, and the only limitations are on the order in which the beads are moved. In more complex problems, the subject has to plan in order to move away from the final goal position in order to solve the problem. Patients with left frontal

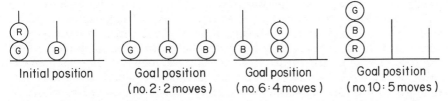

Initial position   Goal position (no. 2 : 2 moves)   Goal position (no. 6 : 4 moves)   Goal position (no. 10 : 5 moves)

Fig. 7.7 The 'Tower of London' problem showing initial position and three goal positions. (Reproduced by permission of *Philosophical Transactions of the Royal Society*.)

lesions were particularly poor on problems of this type being both slow and inaccurate.

Shallice (1982) has argued that many of the symptoms of impaired reasoning and problem-solving which are associated with frontal lobe pathology can be considered as disorders of the ability to control the selection of appropriate programmes for action (schemas). Patients with frontal lobe lesions have difficulty in selecting non-obvious or non-habitual patterns of action and once a particular programme has been triggered, they may have difficulty in stopping it. They are also unduly affected by environmental influences, and have difficulty in concentrating and in deriving abstract principles from 'concrete' instances. Shallice suggests that this difficulty may be due to a deficit in the operation of a 'supervisory attentional system'. This system is responsible for modulating and integrating the selection of action programmes under conditions in which the influence of habitual patterns of action or automatically 'attractive' or distracting sources of stimulation has to be suppressed or inhibited. The supervisory attentional system can effectively turn off a particular action programme, and direct processing appropriately: it therefore plays a crucial role in planning. On this account, the supervisory attentional system provides one way in which the executive control processes, which were discussed in Chapter 3, could influence the selection of actions, or programmes of action. The supervisory attentional system theory seems a promising approach to the understanding of at least some of the deficits in reasoning and problem-solving which are shown by patients with frontal lobe lesions.

Conclusion

In this chapter, the major neuropsychological syndromes have been discussed from a clinical, diagnostic perspective. The nature and significance for localization of brain damage of different patterns of impairment are summarized in Table 7.4.

Due to the problems caused by an ageing population, and the continual improvements in medical and surgical treatment of cerebral disease and trauma, there is a large and growing population of patients with neuropsychological disorders. The four major components of cognitive function which have been considered in this chapter, namely alertness, cognitive skills, memory, and problem-solving, may all break down in patients with cerebral disease. In clinical practice, it is usual to examine for disorders using the sequence in which the four components have been discussed in this chapter (i.e. in alphabetical order: A–C–M–P). Thus, one would first establish that a patient was alert enough to cope with evaluation of various cognitive skills, and then establish that these skills were adequate prior to evaluating those memory or problem-solving abilities which are dependent on the integrity of particular types of skill. Such a sequence of testing

Table 7.4 Summary of major neuropsychological syndromes

Function	Test	Diagnostic implications
Alertness	Timed tests of counting, cancellation	General cerebral trauma, subcortical damage, toxic states, metabolic disturbances
Cognitive skills	Specific tests for object recognition, spatial analysis, action organization, language, literacy	Lesions in more posterior sectors of cerebral hemispheres
Memory: short	Digit/word span	Left posterior
Memory: events	Acquisition of new information, recall of 'old' events	Global: Temporal lobes, diencephalon Material specific: unilateral cerebral lesions
Memory: facts	Knowledge of meaning	Left temporal lobe
Problem-solving	Planning, reasoning	Frontal lobes

would provide a logically organized diagnostic assessment and a coherent starting point for the management and possible rehabilitation of the individual patient's cognitive deficits.

Suggested reading

General reading:

Broadbent, D.E. and Weizkrantz, L. (Eds) (1982). *The Neuropsychology of Cognitive Function*. The Royal Society, London. Also published as: *Philosophical Transactions of the Royal Society of London, Series B*, **298**, 1.
This volume consists of a collection of papers from many of the major workers in neuropsychology. It provides an excellent and broad ranging survey of the area in readable form.

Ellis, A. and Young, A. (1988). *Cognitive Neuropsychology*. Lawrence Erlbaum Associates, London.
This text provides an evaluation of the implications of selective impairments of cognitive function for theories of normal information processing.

Specific topics:
Vision/Object Recognition
Warrington, E.K. (1985). Agnosia, the impairment of object recognition. In *Handbook of Clinical Neurology 1 (series 2)*. Edited by Friedriks, J.A.M. Mouton, the Hague.
Reviews work on visual sensory processing and its relationship to object perception and object recognition.

Language:
Coughlan, A.K. and Warrington, E.K. (1978). Word comprehension and word-retrieval in patients with localized cerebral lesions. *Brain* **101**, 163–85.
Discusses testing methods and their significance for localizing pathology.

Literacy skills:
Ellis, A. (1983). *Reading Writing and Dyslexia*. Lawrence Erlbaum Associates, London.
This book provides an overview of the complex dyslexic syndromes. Chapter 4 gives a particularly useful and clear summary.

Margolin, D. (1984). The Neuropsychology of Writing and Spelling: semantic, phonological, motor and perceptual processes. *Quarterly Journal of Experimental Psychology* **36A**, 459.
A very comprehensive review of the literature on the acquired dysgraphias.

Spatial processing:
De Renzi, E. (1982). *Disorders of Space Exploration and Cognition*. John Wiley and Sons, Chichester.
Pages 84–170 give a useful survey of the evidence for deficits in spatial processing, and also consider unilateral neglect of space.

Apraxia:
Roy, E. (Ed) (1982). *The Neuropsychology of Apraxia and Related Disorders*. Elsevier, North Holland, Amsterdam.
This book provides an up-to-date summary of the research on apraxia. The Chapters by Basso *et al.* and by De Renzi are particularly clear and informative.

Smith, M. and Wing, A. (Eds) (1984). *The Psychology of Human Movement*. Academic Press, New York.
The chapter by Wing 'Disorders of Human Movement,' pp. 269–98, provides a very readable introductory discussion of the various forms of acquired movement disorder.

Memory:
Warrington, E.K. and McCarthy R.A. (1986). Disorders of memory. In *Diseases of the Nervous System 2*. Edited by Asbury, A.K. McKhann, G.M. and McDonald, W.I. Heinemann Medical Books, London.
This chapter attempts to bring together evidence for the various forms of memory deficit which are observed in patients with cerebral disease and discusses their significance for the localization of damage, and their implications for theories of memory organization.

Weiskrantz, L. (1982). Comparative Studies of Amnesia. In *The Neuropsychology of Cognitive Function*, pp. 97–110. Edited by Broadbent, D.E. and Weizkrantz, L. The Royal Society, London.
Discusses the relationship between experimental studies in animals, and the clinical observations of memory disorder in the amnesic syndrome.

Frontal lobe disorders:
Stuss, D. and Benson, D.F. (1986). *The Frontal Lobes*. Raven Press, New York.
This book gives a thorough and detailed review of studies of frontal lobe dysfunction. It is particularly useful for its discussion of theories.

Shallice, T. and Milner, B. (1982). In *The Neuropsychology of Cognitive Function*, Edited by Broadbent, D.E. and Weizkrantz, L. The Royal Society, London.
The chapter by Shallice 'Specific Impairments of Planning' pp. 199–210, gives a review of the 'Supervisory Attentional System' model of frontal lobe function. Milner provides a review of evidence for asymmetry of function in the frontal lobes and some cognitive effects of frontal lobe lesions in Man, pp. 211–66.

References

Bisiach, E., Capitani, E., Luzzati, C. and Perani, D. (1981). Brain and the conscious representation of outside reality. *Neuropsychologia* 19, 543.

Goodglass, H. and Kaplan, E. (1981). *The Assessment of Aphasia and Related Disorders*, Lee and Febiger, Philadelphia.

Kinsbourne, M. and Warrington, E.K. (1962). The localising significance of limited simultaneous form perception. *Brain* 85, 461.

Luria, A.R. (1973). *The Working Brain*. Penguin Books, Harmondsworth, Middlesex.

McCarthy, R.A. and Warrington, E.K. (1986). Visual associative agnosia: a clinico-anatomical study of a single case. *Journal of Neurology, Neurosurgery and Psychiatry* 49, 1233–40.

Milner, B. (1958). Visual deficits produced by temporal lobe excisions. *Proceedings of the Association for Research into Nervous and Mental disease* 36, 244.

Nelson, H.E. (1982). *The National Adult Reading Test*. NFER, Windsor, England.

Poeck, K. (1985). Clues to the nature of disruptions of limb praxis. In: *Neuropsychological Studies of Apraxia*, pp. 99–110. Edited by Roy, E. Elsevier, North Holland, Amsterdam.

Roy, E. (Ed) (1985). *Neuropsychological Studies of Apraxia*. Elsevier Science Publishers, North Holland, Amsterdam.

Shallice, T. (1982). Specific impairments of planning. In *Neuropsychology of Cognitive Function*, pp. 199–209. Edited by Broadbent, D.E. and Weizkrantz, L. The Royal Society, London.
Also published in: *Philosophical Transactions of the Royal Society of London, Series B* 298.

Shallice, T. and Evans, M. (1978). The involvement of the frontal lobes in cognitive estimation. *Cortex* 14, 294.

Warrington, E.K. (1975). The selective impairment of semantic memory. *Quarterly Journal of Experimental Psychology* 27, 635.

Warrington, E.K. (1982). Neuropsychological studies of object recognition. In: *The Neuropsychology of Cognitive Function*, pp. 15–33. Edited by Broadbent, D.E. and Weiskrantz, L. The Royal Society, London.

Warrington, E.K. (1984). *Recognition Memory Test*. NFER, Windsor.

Warrington, E.K. and Rabin, P. (1970). Perceptual matching in patients with cerebral lesions. *Neuropsychologia* 8, 475–87.

Warrington, E.K. and Rabin, P. (1971). Visual span of apprehension in patients with unilateral cerebral lesions. *Quarterly Journal of Experimental Psychology* 23, 423.

Warrington E.K. and Weiskrantz, L. (1982). Amnesia a disconnection syndrome? *Neuropsychologia* 20, 233–49.

8

Emotion and Conditioning

TW Robbins

Emotion

Motivation and emotion

Terms such as motivation and emotion are frequently used in everyday descriptions of behaviour—often in related contexts—but their exact meanings are seldom made clear. Motivation can be linked to physiological concepts such as homeostasis—a view made plausible by the behavioural (as well as physiological) responses that an animal may make in order to reduce a particular body deficit in, for example, sodium ions, calories or extracellular fluid. However, there are many examples of motivated behaviour that do not satisfy any obvious homeostatic need, such as the ingestion by rats of non-caloric solutions of saccharin, as well as other examples that will be considered below. In psychological terms, motivation is a process that generally contributes not only to the intensity or energetics of behaviour (that is, the speed or force of responding), but also to its selection or direction (for example, the decision to approach food and eat, rather than to approach water and drink).

Emotion is perhaps best understood as a collection of responses that can vary along several dimensions. The most obvious dimension is that of verbal report (e.g. 'I am angry' or 'I feel afraid') which enables the subjective experience or introspection of the subject to be communicated (see Chapter 1). A second important dimension is that of the non-verbal behaviour of the subject. Overt behavioural signs of fear and escape may be shown, for example, by a patient who has an intense fear, or phobia, of spiders. These behavioural signs may of course be more subtle. Someone feeling anxious or frustrated may exhibit 'nervous pacing' or general restlessness which appear to be emotional responses to the situation without apparently being directed towards any particular aspect of it. Behavioural measures of emotion can be measured objectively and relatively easily in animals, but tend to be recorded anecdotally in humans, particularly in the clinical situation. Facial expressions are also important behavioural manifestations of emotion, as Charles Darwin himself appreci-ated in a famous monograph. There is evidence that the same facial expressions represent the same emotions for people from widely different cultures. A third important dimension of emotion is the physiological responses that are shown to emotional stimuli, including changes in indices of autonomic nervous system (ANS) activity, neuroendocrine output, (for example, of the pituitary–adrenal axis), muscular tension and desynchron-ization of the cortical electroencephalogram (EEG).

Measurement of emotion

An example of typical results produced by stressful, emotionally arousing stimuli is shown in Figure 8.1. In this study, volunteer subjects were shown either a harrowing film depicting some primitive 'subincision' rituals, or a neutral control film ('Corn-Farming in Iowa'). Measures were made of the subjective responses of the subjects, but also of skin conductance and heart rate. It can be seen from the figure that not only were these indices generally elevated during the stressful film, but they also showed phasic increments in response to specific incidents in the stressful film. The skin conductance responses were often rather slow in latency and certainly came after the subject's subjective appraisal of the event. There was a correlation of +0.545 between heart rate and skin conductance scores, which for 50 subjects is highly significant and presumably reflects a general arousal of the sympathetic division of the ANS. (See LeDoux (1986) for a recent discussion of the organization and function of the ANS.)

When the different forms of emotional response are measured together the indices often correlate quite well, but sometimes they do not. The generalized sympathetic arousal seen in Figure 8.1 was almost certainly accompanied by changes in other variables not measured in that study, such as increased respiratory rate and release of adrenaline from the adrenal medulla, which form part of what Cannon termed the **emergency reaction**. However, there is evidence that autonomic responses do not always covary. Work by the Laceys indicated wide individual differences in measures of autonomic function, suggesting that sympathetic arousal was expressed idiosyncratically in different people. This important observation shows the necessity of monitoring several different indices of emotion.

The theoretical importance of multiple measures immediately becomes apparent when behavioural and physiological indices of emotion are compared. Another study measuring the effects of emotionally-loaded slides showed that it was possible to decide what type of slide material (nudes, pleasant landscapes, severe injuries) had been shown on the basis of the subjects' facial expressions, although again there were wide indi-vidual differences, women, for example, being more expressive than men. The surprising result, however, was that the less externally expressive individuals often proved to be those with the greatest physiological

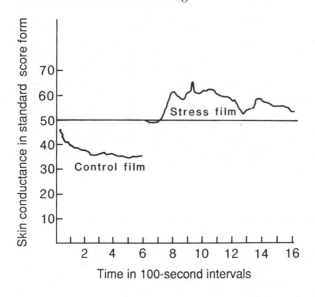

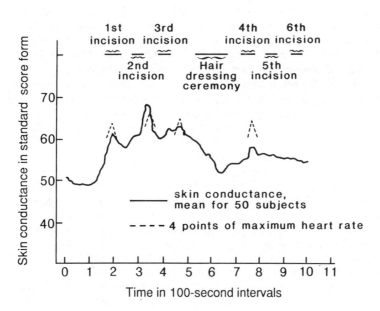

Fig. 8.1 Effects of stressful films on the skin conductance response. The lower panel shows the effects of specific stressful events ('incisions'). (Reproduced from Lazarus, R.S., Speisman, J.C., Morakoff, A.M. and Davison, L.A. (1962) by permission of the author and American Psychological Association.)

responses. This dissociation extended to the subjects' subjective response to the slides: those less capable of describing their reactions were often those with the greatest physiological reactions (see Buck, 1986). These results have implications for theories of emotion in showing that emotion can consists of a number of partly independent response systems which are only loosely tied to subjective responses. They have implications for those subjects who may be predisposed towards psychosomatic illness, a topic to be considered below. They also have practical and social implications, because the somewhat controversial use of 'lie detectors' essentially depends upon the interpretation of physiological responses to leading questions that are not apparent in the facial or verbal responses of the interrogated subject.

Distinguishing among the emotions

The evidence from subjective experience and the existence of different forms of emotional behaviour, together, argues strongly that there are qualitatively different emotional states, such as fear, anger, love, and sadness, but there has been only limited evidence to suggest that these subjective states have distinct physiological correlates. The presence of heightened respiratory rates in patients with a phobia for spiders presented with the phobic stimulus, or of a cardiac response to the presentation of a pleasant scene, indicates that there are physiological responses to emotional events: but this does not in itself show that these responses differ qualitatively according to the type of emotion subjectively experienced. Early evidence suggested, for example, that adrenaline secretion was linked to both pleasant and unpleasant conditions. The results of other studies, however, suggested that different emotions could be correlated with different **patterns** of autonomic responses, when a large number of these were monitored.

Ekman *et al.* (1983) have recently shown that it is possible to differentiate the emotions, to some extent, according to patterns of physiological responses. Professional actors were instructed to either produce, muscle by muscle, the facial expressions which correspond to different emotions, or re-live previous emotional experiences corresponding to the same emotions, while different indices of their autonomic activity were being monitored. In fact, measures of ANS activity in both conditions led to similar results. Figure 8.2 shows the different pattern of responses in the directed facial expression condition for six of the emotions and two of the physiological responses (heart rate and skin temperature). Anger and fear produced equivalent changes in heart rate, but only anger affected skin temperature. The use of actors and controlled test situations had helped to eliminate the variability in the measures seen in earlier studies. Furthermore, merely mimicking the facial expression of specific emotions such as anger was shown to produce the same pattern of ANS responses as thinking about an episode that had caused anger. Thus, part of the pattern of ANS activity could be used to differentiate the emotions, at least for

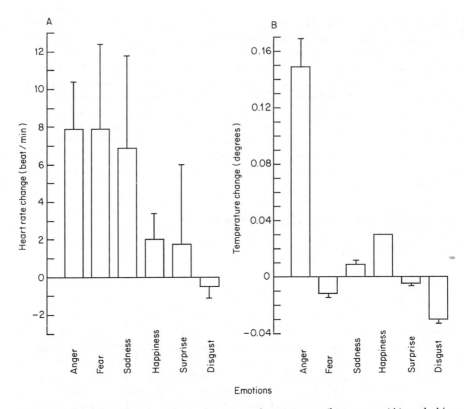

Fig. 8.2   Patterns of change in two autonomic measures (heart rate (A) and skin temperature (B)) can distinguish some of the emotions. (Redrawn from Ekman, P., Sorenson, E.R. and Friesen, W.V. (1983). Reproduced by permission of *Science* and, The American Association for the Advancement of Science.)

some subjects, in certain situations. What is not understood at present is how these very different response systems are co-ordinated; how their co-ordination develops or is learned; and the conditions which lead to their loss of co-ordination.

Functions of the emotions

The results of the Ekman *et al.* study have implications when considering the possible functions of the physiological responses in emotion. Some of these may well have adaptive significance, as suggested by Cannon's emergency reaction which was held to produce metabolic and other changes to facilitate flight or fight in aversive situations. The emergency reaction could be interpreted simply as an effect of the high levels of arousal that can result from aversive situations. However, the findings shown in Figure 8.2 suggest that the adaptive responses could provide a more precise tuning according to the requirements of the situation than would be provided by a general arousal of the ANS. The fact that reliving the subjective experience of emotions can apparently produce a patterned ANS response would also suggest that this experience has, potentially, an adaptive role.

The physiological responses also provide bodily or visceral feedback to the brain (via visceral afferents, or by blood-borne hormones passing through the blood–brain barrier) which may provide information about emotional state, or serve to intensify it. The feedback may be important for motivating learning about emotional situations and what to do in them. This motivation of actions may enable communication of emotional states that serve important social functions, as, for example, in courtship and the display of aggression. The possibility of visceral feedback that can be sensed by the brain also raises the question of the causal relationships which can exist between subjective experience and bodily reactions.

Theories of emotion

A commonsense view of emotion is depicted in Figure 8.3. There is a phase of cognitive evaluation or appraisal of the situation, leading to subjective feelings of emotion, which in turn lead to emotional behaviour and adaptive physiological responses appropriate to the situation.

James–Lange theory

The commonsense view suggests that conscious emotional experience causes emotional responses. However, this commonsense view was rejected by William James in 1884. Considering the evidence from clinical anecdote, introspection, and what little was known about brain function, he turned around the causal sequence to propose, instead, that it is the physiological and behavioural responses to emotional situations that are the substrate of emotional experience. Running away from mad bears is not caused by fear; it is the running (among other responses) that causes the fear. In support of this claim, James could also have referred to the emotional experiences that many report to occur well after traumatic events, such as accidents and battles, and the behaviour they elicit. James had a neurological mechanism for his theory. He supposed that, following the perception of the emotion-eliciting event by the sensory regions of the cerebral cortex, motor areas and descending projections are excited to produce changes in skeletal muscle activity and visceral responses by the activation of either innate predispositions or learned associations. Sensory nerves in the skeletal muscle and visceral organs provide feedback to the central nervous system, and it is the perception of this, at the cortical level, that leads to emotional experience (see Fig. 8.3). James saw no need to postulate a specific centre in the brain for the emotions and indeed, at the time of his theory, there was little evidence to support the existence of such a centre.

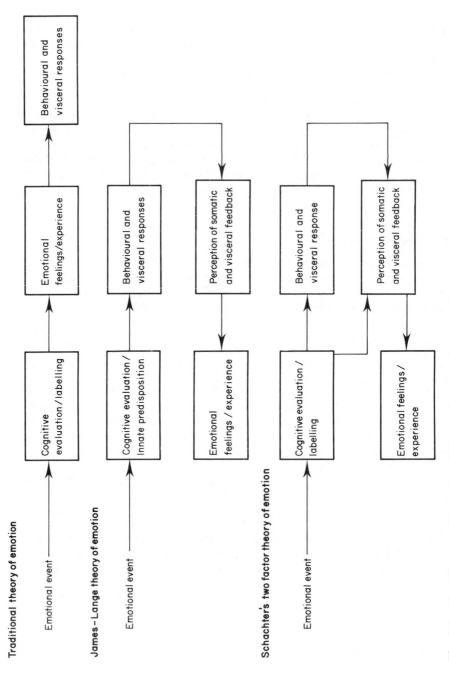

Fig. 8.3   Flow diagrams illustrating different theories of the emotions.

The neurologist Lange, published, apparently independently, a similar version of James' theory in 1885. Although often referred to as the James–Lange theory, there are differences between the two formulations. Lange failed to specify a feedback mechanism by which visceral changes could be perceived as emotional feelings, and concentrated instead on the peripheral manifestations of emotion, an emphasis which could be said to represent the origins of psychosomatic medicine.

Cannon's criticisms

Taking account of accumulating evidence of specific subcortical regions in emotional behaviour in man and animals, and of apparent shortcomings in the peripheral feedback hypothesis, Cannon criticized the James–Lange position on five major grounds:

1. Total separation of the viscera from the central nervous system does not eliminate emotional behaviour
2. The same visceral changes occur in very different emotional states and in non-emotional states
3. The viscera are relatively insensitive structures
4. Visceral changes are too slow to be a source of emotional feeling
5. Artificial induction of visceral changes typical of strong emotions does not produce these emotions.

The impact of these criticisms on the status of the James–Lange theory has been less devastating than was originally thought. Criticism 2 has already been invalidated because of the results of Ekman and colleagues described above. Criticism 1 has also been negated to some extent. To substantiate this criticism, Cannon depended too much upon the results of animal experiments in which no deficits in behavioural measures of emotion were found following decerebration or total sympathectomy. However, this is irrelevant to the main point of the James–Lange position that *emotional experience* depends upon the visceral feedback, because there is no reason to assume that changes in *behaviour* necessarily reflect *emotional experience*. In fact, studies by Hohmann of emotional experience and expression in human paraplegics reinforce this point by demonstrating striking dissociations between emotional behaviour and conscious experience. Hohmann studied paraplegics who had received surgery of the spinal cord at different levels. These subjects, for example, reported acting in an angry way without feeling angry. The emotional experiences lacked the 'heat' and intensity they had experienced prior to their operations. There was a marked reduction in the reported emotional experiences for anger and fear that was monotonically related to the level of cord transection (Fig. 8.4). Those subjects with the highest transections, and consequently the least visceral feedback, exhibited the greatest reductions in intensity of experienced emotion.

The paraplegic subjects presumably still acted emotionally because of prior learning about the form of behaviour that is appropriate to particular

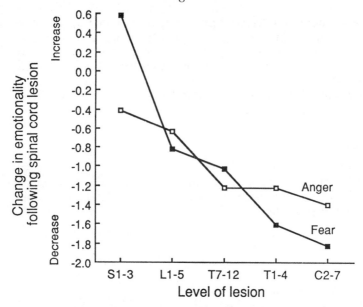

Fig. 8.4 Subjective responses in paraplegic subjects. S = Sacral spinal cord injury. L = lumbar. T = thoracic and C = cervical. (Data of Hohmann, redrawn from Schachter, S. (1966). Reproduced by permission of the author, editor and Academic Press, Orlando.)

situations. Sympathectomized dogs have been shown to continue to make responses to escape shock, although they are deficient in learning new responses. These results suggest that visceral feedback may aid the learning of emotional behaviour, but is less important for its maintenance. It seems possible that conditioning mechanisms can also be invoked to diminish the power of Cannon's fourth criticism. Anticipation of previously experienced visceral feedback could perhaps enable rapid emotional experience, as well as emotional behaviour.

Hohmann's results are also relevant to the evaluation of the negative evidence that Cannon used in support of his fifth criticism, that artificial induction of visceral changes did not always lead to emotional experience. Experiments in which human volunteers were injected with agents such as adrenaline failed to induce convincing reports of emotion in those subjects. Instead, they claimed to feel 'as if' they were angry or happy, without actually experiencing these feelings. These subjective reports parallel, of course, those of the paraplegics, though for different reasons. Whereas the paraplegics had deficient visceral feedback, they were still confronted by situations that caused them to act emotionally. In contrast, the volunteers receiving adrenaline exhibited visceral responses, but experienced these in situations that generally did not elicit emotion.

Schachter's two-factor theory

The realization that emotional feelings may depend jointly upon visceral feedback and an appropriate environmental or cognitive context for emotion, led Schachter (see Schachter, 1966) to propose a new, two-factor theory of emotion which added a cognitive factor to the James–Lange formulation (see Fig. 8.3). According to this view, the subject receives a relatively undifferentiated feedback from the periphery which he or she interprets according to the cognitive features of the situation. Schachter and Singer (1962) reasoned that the earlier failures to observe experimental induction of the emotions resulted from the failure to control adequately the subject's cognitive appraisal of the situation. Thus, a subject receiving adrenaline in an experimental context, where he or she probably knows what type of peripheral sensations to expect, may well be unlikely to experience these sensations as emotion. The subject would have many reasons for interpreting and 'labelling' the sensations differently. The subjects' introspections may, for example, be of the form, "I feel that my heart is racing, but it must be because of the drug that I've been given as part of this experiment".

Schachter and Singer designed an experiment to test two predictions of the two-factor theory: (1) reducing the availability of suitable labels or reasons for the bodily symptoms of increased sympathetic arousal will enhance the intensity of experienced emotion and (2) the type of emotion experienced will be determined by the cognitive context of the situation. This experiment was based on deceiving volunteers into believing that they were helping in the evaluation of the effects of a new vitamin, when in fact they were receiving adrenaline or placebo treatments. Schachter and Singer manipulated the amount of information that different groups receiving adrenaline were given about its expected effects. One group ('ignorant') was told that the injection would have no side-effects. The second group ('misinformed') was told to expect parasympathetic side-effects such as numbness of the feet and itching. Only the third ('informed') group were told to expect the symptoms of hand tremor, palpitations and flushing that commonly result from the release of adrenaline. The placebo group received injections of saline and the same instructions as the 'ignorant' group. Each of the four groups was further divided into two conditions which varied the cognitive context of the situation. Subjects in both conditions were tested in the presence of an experimental 'stooge' who, in one condition acted angrily, and in the other, euphorically. The complete design is made clear in Table 8.1. One of the main experimental measures was self-report ratings. For example, response to the question "How good or happy would you say you feel at present?", the scale varied from a value of 0 ("I don't feel at all happy") to 4 ("I feel extremely happy"). The other main measure was a behavioural one based on the type and intensity of activities viewed through a one-way screen, unknown to the subject. Pulse rate was also measured both prior to and following the injection, and these measurements confirmed that

Table 8.1   Design of Schachter and Singer's experiment

Group	Condition
Placebo	Euphoric
	Angry
Adrenaline informed	Euphoric
	Angry
Adrenaline misinformed	Euphoric
	Angry
Adrenaline ignorant	Euphoric
	Angry

adrenaline had its expected effects and that they were similar in magnitude across the experimental groups.

Although there were some puzzling aspects of the data, the results generally supported both of the predictions. For both the self-report and the behavioural variables, the groups ignorant or misinformed of the effects of adrenaline exhibited and experienced more intense signs of emotion than the informed group. The subjects' behaviour and reported experience also differed between the two contextual conditions produced by the stooge's antics, so that they felt and acted angrily in the anger condition and euphorically in the euphoria condition.

Schachter and Singer's experiment has been much discussed and criticized. There have been several attempts to replicate the main findings, not always successfully (see Reisenzein, 1983). There is some doubt that the *type* of emotional experience can be so easily determined by manipulation of the cognitive context, but it is likely that such manipulation can influence the *intensity* of the reaction. For example, the magnitude of the behavioural, subjective and physiological responses to emotionally-loaded slides have all been shown to be affected by the type of information the viewer is given before their presentation (see Buck, 1986).

Applications of Schachter's two-factor theory

Schachter's two-factor theory has been used to explain results in diverse areas of research into motivation and emotion. For example, Valenstein (1973) has pointed out that the effects of electrical stimulation of the brain via implanted electrodes in both man and animals seem to depend as much on the nature of the test context as on the precise intracerebral location of the electrode. A rat that is stimulated to eat following electrical stimulation of the hypothalamus, may drink instead if water is made available. Presumably, the electrical stimulation results in a central elicitation of non-specific arousal that circumvents or 'short circuits' the normal route by which visceral afferent information (e.g. from the ANS) is received centrally.

Schachter himself saw applications of his theory in the areas of drug abuse and obesity. The experimental observations of the subjective effects of adrenaline described above have clear relevance to understanding the subjective effects of abused drugs. Marijuanah intoxication has been suggested to depend importantly upon social context: textbook pharmacological accounts of the drug's effects are hard to distinguish from those attributed to nausea and yet its presumably identical symptoms are perceived pleasurably in a conducive social context.

Obesity

Schachter thought that in obese subjects eating is less dependent than normal upon the interoceptive, visceral cues that lead to feelings of hunger and satiety, and more dependent upon such factors as the time of day, and other exteroceptive cues, such as the smell and taste of food. There is now less emphasis upon this so-called 'externality hypothesis' of overeating and obesity, but Schachter's theorizing and experiments have stimulated much research into the types of situation which trigger overeating in overweight subjects.

Although it is common clinical knowledge that overeating can occur in conditions such as bulimia nervosa and forms of depression (see Bruch, 1973), there has been little experimental evidence in favour of a role for non-specific emotional factors in overeating. Part of the reason for this has been that the means of inducing anxiety or fear in experimental subjects have been somewhat crude: threatening people with injections of formalin or electric shocks, for example, may not be the most effective way of producing the appropriate emotional state! Slochower (1977) has described experiments which overcome this problem. She induced anxiety in her subjects by increasing their level of ANS arousal while manipulating cognitive factors to prevent the subjects using 'labels' to rationalize their internal feelings, the approach also used in the earlier experiments of Schachter and Singer.

Obese and normal weight subjects volunteered for an experiment apparently concerned with physiological measures of thought. In fact, the most important variable monitored was the number of cashew nuts eaten by the subjects from the bowls liberally available in the testing situation! All subjects wore equipment suitable for the recording of physiological indices, including heart rate. The subjects also received feedback of ostensibly their own heart rate via headphones. Actually, the two groups, of obese and normal weight subjects, were further divided into a 'labelled arousal' and an 'unlabelled arousal' condition. Subjects in both conditions were, in fact, receiving false biofeedback in the form of a recording of very fast heart rates. In the labelled arousal condition, the subjects were assured that the apparatus was faulty and that the feedback was thus false. However, subjects in the unlabelled arousal condition were given no such assurance. Previous research and the results of the questionnaire given to the subjects after the experiment confirmed that this unlabelled condition produced greater levels of experienced anxiety.

The results of the experiment are shown in Figure 8.5. The amount eaten was generally similar in the obese and normal weight groups and was unaffected by labelled arousal. However, in the unlabelled arousal condition, the obese subjects, remarkably, ate five times as much as the subjects of normal weight, who actually responded to this condition with reduced levels of eating. The results suggest that the obese subjects reacted to induced anxiety by overeating, whereas subjects of normal weight responded by reducing their food intake. In subsequent experiments, Slochower extended these results to less artificial conditions. In one study, obese medical students were found to eat more than normal weight students prior to important examinations, although there were no differences between the two groups during periods of less anxiety.

There would seem to be at least two possible explanations of overeating in the obese. First, it is possible that the obese subjects are less able to discriminate between their internal bodily states than subjects of normal weight. This explanation, of course, would be in agreement with Schachter's externality hypothesis. According to the clinician Bruch, this lack of discrimination could result from faulty training in infancy. For example, babies given food when they show signs of distress might never learn to distinguish adequately the internal sensations of hunger from those of anxiety. Thus, eating becomes a natural response to stressful situations later in life. There is, at present, only limited evidence to support this suggestion. A second possibility is that the eating functions as a **coping response** to reduce stress. Presumably, subjects of normal weight utilize other coping responses, for example, pacing or combing their hair. This speculation is supported by some additional data from the Slochower experiment on 'the physiology of thinking'. Self-reported anxiety ratings taken after the experiment showed that there was a significant, though small, correlation between the amount of subjective anxiety reduction and the amount eaten in the obese group.

Psychopharmacology of anxiety

Another possible application of Schachter's two-factor theory of the emotions can be found when considering the psychopharmacology of anxiety. At present, the benzodiazepine class of drugs (which includes chlordiazepoxide (Librium) and diazepam (Valium) is the one most widely used in the treatment of anxiety because of the relative safety of these compounds. There are, however, some disadvantages to their use. These include not only mild dependence and withdrawal symptoms, but also clear evidence of impairment in learning, attention and memory, which may

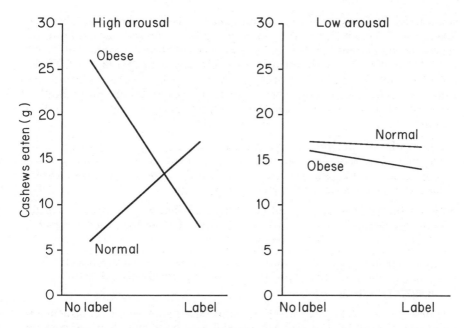

Fig. 8.5 Effects of 'labelled' and 'unlabelled' arousal on eating in normal weight and obese subjects. (Redrawn from Slochower, J. (1977). Reproduced by permission of the author and Elsevier Science Publishers, Amsterdam.)

arise partly from their sedative action. Thus, they are not necessarily the drugs of choice when treating certain forms of anxiety. For example, propanolol and related β-adrenoceptor blocking drugs are often used in the treatment of **somatic** forms of anxiety, where the symptoms often present in the form of anxieties about bodily feelings, such as palpitations, hyperventilation or sweating, rather than specific worries about life situations or events (**'psychic anxiety'**). The β-blockers block peripheral sympathetic activity (although some of them also penetrate to the CNS and also block central β-adrenoceptors). This contrasts strongly with the action of benzodiazepines, which facilitate neurotransmission at the GABA-receptor complex in the CNS at specific benzodiazepine receptors (see Kandel and Schwartz, 1985).

Tyrer (1976) compared the effectiveness of diazepam and propanolol, as well as a placebo, in the treatment of groups of subjects exhibiting either predominantly psychic or somatic forms of anxiety. The study used different subjective and psychological indices. The former included subjective ratings of bodily symptoms, and also the scores by the clinician of the subjects' responses on the Hamilton Anxiety Scale. This scale has questions about both somatic and psychological symptoms that can be scored separately. The results of the comparison between the drugs are shown in Table 8.2, from which several conclusions can be drawn. According to the scores on the Hamilton Scale and the subjective ratings, diazepam is clearly effective in treating both forms of anxiety, while propanolol is effective only for somatic anxiety. However, whereas propanolol significantly reduced the pulse rate in both psychic and somatic conditions, diazepam had no effect. Several important theoretical inferences can be made from these results:

1. Blockade of peripheral sympathetic activity may be sufficient for reducing anxiety, but only in the somatic condition. This result is consistent with a James–Lange view of the emotions if the β-blocker is actually having most of its effect peripherally.

2. Even though the peripheral symptoms are blocked by propanolol for subjects in the psychic condition, this failed to reduce their subjective anxiety.

3. In contrast, diazepam reduced subjective anxiety both in subjects of the somatic and psychic conditions without markedly affecting their peripheral symptoms.

These latter two points show that the James–Lange theory is insufficient to account for all of the results. It would appear that the benzodiazepines work by affecting some of the cognitive processes involved in anxiety. An interesting further question is whether benzodiazepines influence the initial evaluation of stimuli causing anxiety, or alter the subject's interpretation of perception of his or her peripheral feedback. The fact that the pulse rate was unaffected by diazepam in the psychic condition is most consistent with the latter possibility. Overall, however, these psychopharmacological

Table 8.2 Summary of Tyrer's comparison of diazepam and propanolol

	Placebo		Diazepam		Propanolol	
	Somatic	Psychic	Somatic	Psychic	Somatic	Psychic
Hamilton scale						
(i) Psychological	43.0	38.2	25.1	21.2	28.1	42.8
(ii) Somatic (mean scores)	22.1	22.0	12.2	8.3	25.3	28.3
Subjective rating of bodily symptoms (mean ± SD)	3.0	2.3	1.8	1.1	1.9	2.4
	0.6	0.2	0.8	0.4	0.7	0.6
Physiological measures e.g. Respiratory rate (breaths/min)	20.6	18.5	18.6	18.8	18.8	17.4
Pulse rate (beats/min)	86.5	76.5	82.5	75.5	60.9	63.5

results support Schachter's general point about the importance of cognitive factors in the interpretation of bodily states.

Conditioning

Cannon's criticism of the James–Lange theory that peripheral responses are too slow to mediate emotional responses can be well understood from the perspective of a phobic subject's immediate emotional reaction to a feared stimulus. However, mechanisms of conditioning enable the subject to form expectancies and thus anticipate emotional events. The fears directed to specific stimuli by phobic individuals suggest that they may have learned avoidance responses, through processes of conditioning.

One form of conditioning that has been related to the induction of phobias is called classical or Pavlovian conditioning. Dogs were found to salivate in the presence of a conditioned stimulus (CS) that was presented just prior to food (the unconditioned stimulus, or US) (see Fig. 8.6). The salivation which normally occurs in response to the presentation of food, as the unconditioned response (or UCR), had thus been conditioned to the presentation of the stimulus which predicted food, to become the conditioned response (CR). More recent work has shown that the representation of the CS in the brain appears to substitute for that of the US, and so elicits the salivation response with which the US is connected. Successful conditioning depends upon rather precise temporal relations between the

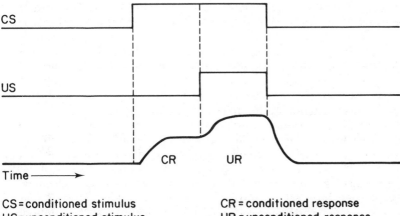

CS = conditioned stimulus   CR = conditioned response
US = unconditioned stimulus   UR = unconditioned response

Fig. 8.6 Temporal relationships or sequencing of stimuli and responses in classical (Pavlovian) conditioning. Note the smaller size of the conditioned response relative to the unconditioned response. The CS could be, for example, a bell; the US food; and the CR and UR, salivary responses. The CR develops after a certain number of pairings of the CS and US in this manner.

CS and US, with the former preceding and sometimes overlapping the US. This temporal relationship is, of course, consistent with a predictive role for the CS (see Mackintosh (1983) for a fuller account and Davey (1981) for an elementary one).

Salivating in anticipation of food has the adaptive advantage of facilitating efficient mastication and digestion. In fact, salivation is but one of a number of reflexes of what Pavlov called the 'cephalic phase' which serves this same general function. For example, the secretion of insulin can be conditioned to stimuli that predict food before it has even been digested, which may aid the utilization of glucose. This, of course, is generally beneficial, but can have disadvantageous consequences, as exemplified by the enhanced insulin response shown to food by obese subjects (see Robbins, 1986). By the same token, although aversive reactions to stimuli have an even more obviously adaptive function, if conditioning has been excessive or inappropriate, they could have unfortunate consequences such as the irrational fears of phobic individuals.

Conditioning of phobias

There was an attempt in the 1920s to condition phobic reactions in a human infant ('Little Albert') by the behaviourist J.B. Watson and his collaborators that would now seem ethically dubious. They tried to condition fear in Little Albert towards an innocuous white rat (CS) by pairing it with an unpleasant noise (US) which caused startle and signs of anxiety in the infant. The attempt was partly successful, but controlling or monitoring the early experiences of human subjects is, of course, a difficult undertaking and other investigators such as Minecka (1987) have since studied phobias in subhuman primates. She studied the emotional reactions of either laboratory-reared or wild rhesus monkeys to novel toy snakes and found that fear reactions were only evident in the wild-reared animals. This result would suggest that the wild monkeys had previously acquired the fear reaction as a result of their experience, and the lack of such responses in the laboratory-reared animals argues against such responses resulting from an innate fear response.

One problem for a conditioning account of phobic reactions by monkeys to snakes is that it would seem unlikely that the animals would gradually learn such aversions by experience. If monkeys had to learn by trial and error that snakes were potentially highly dangerous, this might prove to be too severe an adaptive pressure! This problem can be overcome by postulating **vicarious conditioning**: perhaps a monkey gains its fear of snakes by observing the behaviour of its parents towards such stimuli. (It is relatively easy to see how similar vicarious conditioning could occur in children.) To test this idea, Minecka *et al.* (1987) made a video-recording of the fear reactions of the parents of monkeys, and then spliced the video-tape to make it appear that the reaction was in response to specific stimuli, such as toy snakes. By showing young monkeys the altered video-tape of the parents' responses, the investigators were able to induce signs of anxiety to these previously innocuous stimuli in laboratory-reared animals, thus supporting the hypothesis that phobic reactions can arise from vicarious conditioning.

Phobic-like reactions have also been induced in normal human subjects with classical conditioning techniques, using skin conductance as the measure of learning. Ohman and his colleagues (1985) presented a pictorial slide as a CS which was paired with a mild electric shock as the US. Subjects were divided into several groups which varied (i) the number of pairings of the CS and US (1 or 5) and (ii) the nature of the slide CS (for half the subjects the CS was a picture of a potentially phobic stimulus (a snake), whereas for the remainder of the subjects it was a 'neutral' stimulus (a picture of a house). Following the pairing stage, the conditioned skin conductance response was measured to the CS, in the absence of the shock (that is, in **extinction**). To provide a baseline against which the strength of conditioning could be assessed, some subjects received no pairings of CS and US in the initial stage, but merely a similar number of presentations of the CS. The skin conductance responses to those stimuli were then compared directly with those in the conditioning groups. As can be seen in Figure 8.7, for both the phobic and neutral conditions, the strength of the skin conductance response was much greater in the conditioning group than in the CS alone group. This result indicates that the enhanced CS response in the conditioning group could not simply be accounted for by the response to the CS itself; for these non-phobic subjects the picture of a snake alone, unsurprisingly, produced no skin conductance response. However, it is possible that the larger response in the conditioning group arose not because of the association *per se*, but because the experience of a shock sensitizes the subject to respond to the snake stimulus, for example, by increasing his or her non-specific arousal. In order to control for this possibility, it is necessary to have further sensitization control groups which are exposed to the shock alone, before being exposed to the stimulus acting as the CS in the other groups. This group therefore receives the same number of shocks as the conditioning groups, but there is no pairing between the CS and US. Figure 8.7 shows that **sensitization** was insufficient to account for the size of the skin conductance response shown by the conditioning group in the phobic condition, but might well have accounted for the apparent conditioning seen to the neutral CS. Finally, it is important to note that similar results were found for the 1 and 5 pairings; Figure 8.7 shows the results from only one pairing of the CS and US.

The main conclusions that can be drawn from this experiment are:

1. A skin conductance response can be conditioned to a stimulus associated with shock in normal human volunteers.

2. A single pairing of the CS and US is sufficient for this form of conditioned response to develop.

3. Certain stimuli (in this case, a snake) are easier to condition than others to the US. This result is consistent with the evidence that phobias are

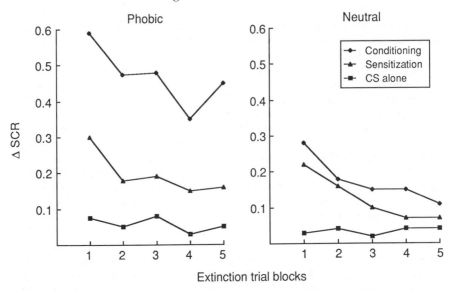

Fig. 8.7 Extinction of skin conductance responses (SCR) in groups of human volunteers conditioned to phobic or neutral stimuli (Conditioning), given unpaired presentation of phobic or neutral stimuli (sensitization) or given the conditioned stimulus alone (CS alone). (Redrawn from Ohman, A., Dimberg, U. and Ost, L-G. (1985). Reproduced by permission of the authors and Academic Press, Orlando.)

most often seen to biologically relevant stimuli, such as snakes or spiders, open spaces or large social groups, rather than to man-made, though dangerous, stimuli such as guns or motor cars. Seligman (1971) has proposed that, for adaptive reasons, conditioning between certain types of stimuli occurs more readily than between others, a principle he describes as **biological preparedness**.

While the results of the skin conductance experiment show the possible importance of Pavlovian conditioning in the establishment of fear in humans, it does not by itself illustrate all of the conditions that must be met for successful conditioning to occur. To do this, it is necessary to extrapolate from the results of other experiments conducted with infrahuman species (Mackintosh, 1983). These experiments have shown that the nature of the predictive relationship or **contingency** between the CS and US is as important as the pairing of the stimuli in close temporal association. Although a potential CS could be paired many times with the occurrence of the US, there may be occasions when it is not followed by the US and the correlation between the two would thus be weakened. Pavlovian conditioning most effectively occurs when there is a positive temporal correlation between the CS and US. This fact has led some to consider Pavlovian conditioning to reflect the formation of expectancies, so that when a CS occurs, the subjects expect the US because of the predictive capacity of the CS.

If Pavlovian conditioning always involves the formation of expectancies, it might be expected that manipulating the expectancies would affect the strength of the CR. However, this does not appear always to be the case for the conditioning of the skin conductance response. In an extension of the experiment described above, Hugdahl and Ohman examined the effects of verbal instructions on the strength of the CR. Prior to the extinction trials, one group was told that the CS would no longer be followed by the shock and was therefore now 'safe', whereas the other group received no such instructions. The results showed that the instructions reduced skin conductance conditioning to neutral stimuli, but had no effect for the phobic stimulus condition. This suggests that manipulating the cognitive aspects of the situation by giving instructions has no effect on conditioning of the phobic stimulus, a result that corresponds to the clinical experience that phobias are irrational and resistant to cognitive factors.

Although Pavlovian conditioning can perhaps lead to the formation of expectancies that are perceived consciously, it is clear that some conditioning can occur somewhat automatically, below the level of consciousness. This is reminiscent of some of the evidence described in Chapter 1 in which the phenomenon of 'semantic priming', and also the development of an emotional reaction or preference for a stimulus can be shown to occur unconsciously without the need for cognitive inference (see Zajonc, 1980). Thus, it is likely that some emotional responses may be triggered with or without the mediation of cognitive processes of stimulus evaluation or appraisal, and that phobias may not require cognitive mediation.

A phobic stimulus may elicit escape responses, but the phobic individual will also avoid those places or situations in which such stimuli are likely to occur; someone who is frightened of spiders avoids dark cellars. This avoidance behaviour represents a different type of conditioning called **instrumental** (and sometimes **operant**) conditioning, and occurs when there is the formation of a link between an action and its consequences. Mowrer's two-factor theory of anxiety suggests that first there is Pavlovian conditioning of particular CSs and physiological responses which leads to the emotional state of anxiety, and this is followed by a stage in which the subject strives to reduce his or her anxiety by making an avoidance response (see Gray, 1988). There are many other examples of such interactions between Pavlovian and instrumental contingencies, and some of these will be discussed in the more detailed account of instrumental conditioning below.

Treatment of phobias using conditioning principles

According to Mowrer's two-factor theory of anxiety, part of the persistence of phobias may arise from the phobic individual, through efficient avoidance behaviour, never allowing his or her anxiety to dissipate in the presence of the CS. If the continued presentation of the CS no longer predicted an unpleasant event, then the phobic CR itself would be expected to extinguish (c.f. Fig. 8.7). This principle has guided the design of three forms of behaviour therapy for phobias, **flooding**, **modelling** and **systematic desensitization**. Each of these involves the subject being subjected to exposures of the phobic stimulus.

In flooding, the patient is literally 'thrown into the deep end': agoraphobics, afraid of open spaces, are taken to the centre of a busy junction, where it is assumed that this fear will extinguish. In modelling, therapists gradually introduce the subject to the feared stimulus by their own example: a therapist may handle a snake in the presence of phobic subject afraid of these animals, in order to demonstrate that they provide no danger.

Systematic desensitization, introduced by Wolpe, involves more complex principles. In imaginal desensitization, a subject imagines his or her own list of feared situations in ascending order. The therapist then leads the subject gradually through this hierarchy, while the subject is experiencing deep muscle relaxation. The theory is that the subject is then exposed to the phobic stimulus in conditions which are incompatible with anxious behaviour, so that it rapidly extinguishes. This deliberate opposition of a positive state (the pleasant experience of relaxation) and an aversive one is sometimes called **counter-conditioning**.

Behaviour therapy is effective and preferred to pharmaceutical treatments for simple phobias. However, there is some doubt about its exact mechanism of action. For example, some clinical trials have provided evidence that, for desensitization, neither the element of relaxation, nor the use of an imagined hierarchy, are necessary conditions for success. The utility of other forms of behaviour therapy for agoraphobia, sometimes in conjunction with cognitive therapies, that do not necessarily follow from the classical Mowrer two-factor theory are also currently being explored (see Rachman, 1983).

Anxiety as a conflict

Most forms of anxiety do not involve such specific and intense fears as phobias. Several theorists, including Freud, have suggested that conflict is at the core of neurotic anxiety. This has led to the design of animal tests of anxiety for evaluating potential new anxiolytic drugs which involve a conflict between appetitive and aversive states. The Geller–Seifter conflict test is carried out in a test chamber which is supplied with a dispenser for delivering small food pellets and a lever that the hungry animal (generally rats) can press to earn food. An instrumental contingency can be arranged between lever-pressing and the delivery of food, so that pressing occasionally results in the delivery of a food pellet. The main feature of the conflict test is to introduce a signalled period in which every lever-press earns a food pellet, but is also punished by the delivery of a mild electric shock to the feet through an electrified grid. The suppression of lever-pressing behaviour that occurs in the conflict period can be seen in the example shown in Figure 8.8 and is accompanied by hesitant behaviour on the part of the animal, which includes aborted approaches to and withdrawal from, the lever. When the signalled period is no longer in operation, the animal again responds avidly to earn food.

The effect of treatment with the benzodiazepine drug, chlordiazepoxide (Librium), is also shown in Figure 8.8. Note that the animal continues to respond at high rates during the rewarded periods which indicates that the drug is not exerting a sedative effect at this dose. The striking aspect of the drug's action is that it automatically increases the punished responding of the conflict period. This action probably represents an anxiolytic effect because drugs from other classes, such as the stimulant drug amphetamine or the opiate analgesic drug morphine, do not produce this release of punished responding. Therefore, the release is unlikely to result from a simple action of the benzodiazepine to reduce the pain of the shock and

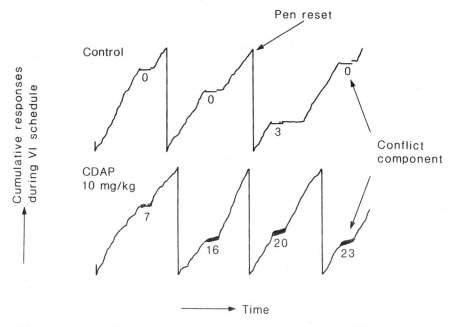

Fig. 8.8 Effects of chlordiazepoxide (CDAP or Librium) on 'conflict' behaviour in the rat. The record shows cumulative (instrumental) lever pressing (x axis) by hungry rats under an intermittent schedule of food presentation during which a recording pen moves up the page every time there is a response, resetting after a certain number have been made. There is, generally, a steady rate of responding until a CS is turned on associated with punishment for each lever press (conflict component), when hardly any responding occurs. Under control conditions, responding is suppressed during these 'conflict' periods. CDAP produces an increase in these punished responses, shown by the numbers of responses displayed beneath each conflict period.

more probably results from a reduction of fear shown to the signal for the conflict period. Other control experiments can be used to rule out the possible effects of chlordiazepoxide to enhance hunger or affect the animal's sensory discrimination. Perhaps the most convincing evidence that this release of punished responding is relevant to human anxiety comes from a rank-ordering of the clinical potency of various anxiolytic drugs in terms of their capacity to release punished responding in the Geller–Seifter conflict test. There is a striking correlation between the two actions of the drugs, which suggests that the Geller–Seifter test may be of value in the screening of potential anxiolytic drugs. Other drugs effective in treating anxiety, the barbiturates and (in non-clinical contexts) alcohol, also increase punished responding in the conflict procedure (see Iversen and Iversen, 1981, for more information). Evidently, the anticonflict effects have not only good face (i.e. common sense) validity, but also good predictive validity. However, it should be cautioned that the results do not mean that human anxiety always entails a conflict or that the anticonflict effect in animals is necessarily the basis of the anxiolytic effect in man.

Instrumental or operant conditioning

The major difference between Pavlovian and instrumental conditioning is that the latter allows the animal a degree of control over its environment through its own actions. In Pavlovian conditioning, of course, the animal has no control over the delivery of the CS or US, and its conditioned and unconditioned responses are elicited by these events. Generally, instrumental conditioning requires an association to be formed between an action and a particular consequence. This consequence could be an appetitive event such as a morsel of food, or a pleasant picture, or an aversive event, such as an electric shock or an unpleasant social encounter. When the frequency or vigour of behaviour followed by a particular stimulus is increased, the stimulus is said to be a **positive reinforcer** (the less technical term, reward, is often used instead). When similar increases in behaviour are correlated with the omission or termination of a stimulus, it is said to be a **negative reinforcer**. It is important to distinguish negative reinforcement from punishment, even though the same type of stimulus could, in different circumstances, serve both as a punisher and as a negative reinforcer. Whereas negative reinforcement results in an increase in behaviour, (such as the avoidance of situations that are associated with phobic stimuli), punishment results instead in a suppression of a particular response (as seen in Fig. 8.8).

Biofeedback

Although instrumental conditioning generally occurs for voluntary actions, mediated by the skeletal musculature, there is some evidence that the involuntary responses of the ANS can sometimes be controlled by instrumental contingencies. Miller and his colleagues were the first to suggest this possibility from the results of animal experiments involving prepara-tions immobilized with curare. These experiments have been difficult to replicate. Nevertheless, it has become apparent that it is possible for human subjects to exert some degree of voluntary control over bodily responses if they receive feedback from the peripheral responses that are being continuously monitored, and this has possible important applications in medicine (see Grings and Dawson, 1978 and Chapter 11). Figure 8.9 shows the average changes in systolic blood pressure in people receiving reinforc-ing feedback for either increasing or reducing their blood pressure over the course of a single test session. Knowledge of results and encourage-ment was a sufficient reinforcer for these individuals to drive their heart rates either up or down. This apparent conditioning of involuntary responses is impressive but it is distinctly likely that the subjects are actually effecting the changes by directives to the skeletal muscles of the chest, the movements of which can produce changes in heart rate. The provision of feedback, which augments the normally weak signals from the ANS thus allows the subject to capitalize upon instrumental contingencies inherent in the situation and bring what is normally an involuntary response under a degree of voluntary control. Examples of the clinical applications of biofeedback are given in Chapter 11.

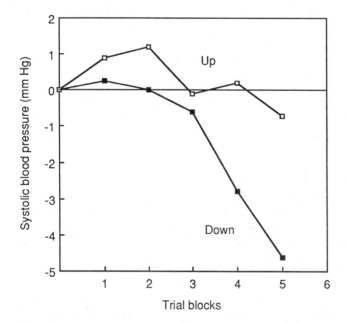

Fig. 8.9 Average systolic blood pressure change in persons reinforced for increas-ing (up) and decreasing (down) blood pressure. (Redrawn from Shapiro, D., Tursky, G., Gershon, E. and Stern, M. (1969). Reproduced by permission of *Science* and The American Association for the Advancement of Science.)

Appetitive instrumental conditioning

Some of the most effective natural stimuli acting as positive reinforcers are food, water, the opportunity to copulate, novel stimuli to explore, social contact and knowledge of results. As mentioned earlier, not all of these stimuli function to restore deficits, produced for example by food or water deprivation. Indeed, some of the stimuli seem to act as reinforcers because of sensory properties, for example, as palatable tastes or interesting visual designs which have hedonic or attractive properties.

One of the most potent positive reinforcers for rats is the opportunity to self-administer small amounts of electric current to particular brain regions. Olds and Milner showed that rats with electrodes implanted in the region of the lateral hypothalamus, or in certain portions of the limbic system will press a lever at high rates if brain stimulation is contingent upon responding. These rats may continue to self-stimulate for long periods of the day, and their response rate is lawfully related to the amount of current administered. Intracranial self-stimulation is perhaps one of the most vivid examples of behaviour that is not directed towards alleviating any obvious deficit state: the self-stimulating rat responds as though it is receiving a highly palatable food which has no caloric value. The positive reinforcing effects of brain stimulation have also been demonstrated in human subjects during the course, for example, of treatment for intractable pain or epilepsy. From the vantage of Schachter's two-factor theory of the emotions it is interesting that subjective accounts of the effects of stimulation vary quite widely; and often these accounts arise from effects of the stimulation which give rise to peripheral sensations (see Valenstein, 1973). There is some evidence that some of the reinforcing effects of brain stimulation in rats may similarly depend in part upon the perception of autonomic feedback (see LeDoux, 1986). However, it is possible that such stimulation is acting to 'short circuit' some of the central pathways which normally carry this information.

Drug abuse as a problem of instrumental conditioning

The opportunity to take certain drugs is also a potent reinforcer in animals, including of course humans where the effects are often socially disastrous. Drug abuse can be understood from the perspective of conditioning, although the problem is compounded by the well-known problems of **tolerance** (the need to increase the dose to avoid a progressive reduction of the drug effect) and **withdrawal** (the effects of stopping or omitting drug administration).

Drug self-administration has been studied in several infrahuman species by allowing the animal to respond to produce an intravenous infusion of the drug via an implanted jugular catheter. This technique has become increasingly important in screening new compounds for abuse potential. As can be seen from Table 8.3, several drugs and drug classes (notably stimulants and opiate narcotics) have been shown to have positive reinforc-

Table 8.3 Reinforcing effects of drugs in animals

Positive	Negative	Neutral
Amphetamine Cocaine Caffeine Nicotine (stimulants)	LSD (hallucinogen) haloperidol (antipsychotic)	Fenfluramine (weight-reducing drug)
Morphine Heroin (opiates)	nalorphine in morphine-dependent animals (opiate antagonist)	Imipramine (antidepressant)
Barbiturates Benzodiazephines (minor tranquillizers)		Scopolamine (anticholinergic)
Tetrahydrocannibol (THC) (cannabis)		

The table shows the reinforcing properties in animals of the main psychoactive drugs within their pharmacological class, as assessed by self-administration procedures. LSD is a hallucinogenic drug, haloperidol is a representative of the antipsychotic compounds which also include chlorpromazine and pimozide. Scopolamine antagonizes muscarinic receptors and causes amnesic and cognitive deficits. For further details see the text or Seiden and Dykstra, 1977.

ing properties, some negatively reinforcing properties (e.g. the antipsychotic or major tranquillizing drugs), and some have neutral effects. By comparison with human drug abuse, the only anomaly is that of LSD, which other animals find aversive.

It is problematic to establish that a drug definitely has positive reinforcing properties, as opposed to some non-specific action which, for example, would increase the instrumental response merely by enhancing general activity. Figure 8.10 shows an example of an experiment designed to answer this question. A rat with an intravenous catheter was provided access to two levers, one of which provided infusions of small doses of d-amphetamine. The rat's pattern of responding on the lever providing the drug is shown in Figure 8.10(a). After 100 minutes, the contingency was changed so that the lever became inactive but the rat continued to receive doses of amphetamine from the automatic, preprogrammed operation of the infusion pump over which it therefore had no control. As can be seen from the last 100 minutes of recording in Figure 8.10(a), the rat ceased to lever press, showing that increases in general activity produced by the drug could not have generated the pattern of responding seen initially. In Figure 8.10(b), the effects of substituting saline for the drug are seen in an extinction test. The rat initially responds faster than usual, perhaps because of the frustrating effects of the omission of reward, but then ceases to respond altogether. A similar effect is seen in Figure 8.10(c), where the rat continues to receive the same stimuli that usually accompany the drug

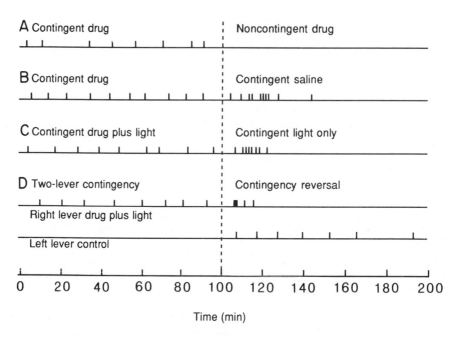

Fig. 8.10 Instrumental responding maintained by intravenous infusions of d-amphetamine in the rat. The ticks on the event record indicate responses (lever presses) during the course of the test session. In record **A**, for the first 100 minutes, the drug is contingent upon lever pressing, that is, a lever press is required for one infusion. After 100 minutes, the experimental animal receives automatic infusions of the drug independent of its own behaviour. Note how the lever-pressing ceases when the drug is no longer contingent upon it. **B**. The effects of extinction, when saline control infusions are substituted for the drug. Note the initial burst of responding that has been termed 'frustrative', then the rapid decrease in instrumental behaviour. **C**. Similar results of extinction occur when there is a conditioned reinforcer of a light associated with each drug infusion. **D**. Effects of reversing the contingency to a second, previously inactive, lever. Note how the rat 'tracks' this contingency and switches to respond from the previously active lever to the presently active one. These experiments demonstrate positive reinforcing properties of amphetamine infusions by showing the contingent relationship that exists in this case between responding and drug infusion. (Redrawn from Pickens, R. and Thompson, T. (1968). Reproduced by permission of the author, American Society for Pharmacology and Experimental Therapeutics and Williams and Wilkins, Baltimore.)

infusion, but not the drug itself. In Figure 8.10(d), the contingency is reversed, so that pressing the previously inactive lever is now reinforced, but pressing the previously active lever is no longer reinforced. As shown in Figure 8.10(d), the rat tracks this change by switching to respond on the second lever. These experiments together convincingly show that the maintenance of lever-pressing is due to the positive reinforcing actions of d-amphetamine.

Schedules of reinforcement and conditioned reinforcement

Another problem in assessing the reinforcing properties of drugs comes from the state of drug intoxication resulting from high rates of continuously reinforced responding which interferes with further instrumental behaviour and impedes behavioural analysis. This makes it difficult to collect important pharmacological data, such as dose-response curves. An addict is also seldom able to self-administer large quantities of drugs without interpolated periods of drug-seeking behaviour. Reinforcement by drugs (and by other rewards) in real life is very much more intermittent than shown for example in Figure 8.10, where every response by the rat results in a drug infusion. To overcome these problems, **schedules of reinforcement** are used, which programme reinforcers intermittently, according to the passage of time or the number of responses made. A **fixed interval** schedule, for example arranges that reinforcement will be delivered contingent upon the first response after a fixed amount of time since the last reinforcer was delivered, for example, 30 s or 15 min. By contrast, a **fixed ratio** schedule arranges reinforcement to occur after x responses. Other schedules arrange reinforcement to occur after **variable intervals** or **variable ratios** (see Davey, 1981).

Schedules of reinforcement generate different patterns of instrumental responding. The rather steady rate of responding in variable interval schedules is shown in the non-conflict portions of the cumulative record of lever-pressing shown in Figure 8.8. An example of a fixed interval schedule (60 min) is shown in Figure 8.11. Here a squirrel monkey received cocaine for the first response made after 1 hour had elapsed. Note how this schedule generates a gradually increasing rate of responding throughout the interval. As soon as the reinforcing dose of cocaine had been given, the session terminated for the day, so that the monkey had worked for as long as an hour in the undrugged state to earn a single infusion. How is it possible to maintain responding over such long periods? In fact, the schedule shown in Figure 8.11 was more complex than a simple fixed interval: the first response made after each 6 min during the hour led to the presentation of the yellow light that was paired with the cocaine infusion at the end of the session. This embedding of one schedule within another is termed a **second order schedule**.

The yellow light of Figure 8.11 is clearly a reinforcer in its own right, which helps to maintain responding by virtue of its association with the

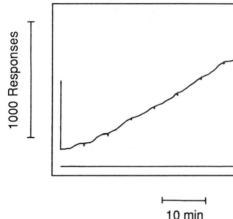

10 min

Fig. 8.11 Second order schedules of reinforcement. The record shows the cumulative responding of a monkey for a single dose of cocaine delivered after 1 hour (bottom record), in the presence of a brief yellow light. Responses within the hour did not produce the drug and responding was maintained by the presentation of the brief yellow light which was turned on contingent upon the first press occurring after each 6 minute segment of the 1-hour period (downwards ticks). Thus, the schedule consists of a fixed interval 60 min component with cocaine as the reinforcer, but embedded within this period are ten fixed interval 6 min components where behaviour is maintained by the presentation of the yellow light as a conditioned reinforcer. (Based on results of Goldberg, S.R.)

cocaine infusion. If the yellow light is omitted, then responding within the one hour period is not maintained. The yellow light is termed a **conditioned reinforcer**. It gains its conditioned reinforcing properties from its Pavlovian association with cocaine, which acts as the US as well as the primary reinforcer. Conditioned reinforcers are important in mediating emotional effects and their association with rewarding bodily sensations may help to bridge the delay that Cannon referred to as problematic for the James–Lange theory. Certain human addicts, (called 'needle-freaks') experience a euphoric rush when they inject themselves, even if the syringe contains saline rather than drug (O'Brien *et al.*, 1986). The syringe, as well as the ritual act of injection can have a special emotional significance for the addict, presumably because of the conditioned associations they have with the drug experience.

Conditioned reinforcers are easily identifiable in everyday life, the most obvious example being money. Some forms of behaviour therapy used for the mentally retarded, or schizophrenic subjects, use the principle of conditioned reinforcement for training socially useful and responsible behaviour. Specified behaviour earns tokens which can be accumulated and exchanged for more tangible rewards.

Withdrawal and opponent motivational processes

The euphoric effects of drugs in human heroin addicts are well-known to become weaker upon repeated administration, and thus show tolerance (see O'Brien *et al.*, 1986). Almost coincidentally, the initially mildly aversive effects of the drug that occur as its positive effects subside begin to grow in intensity and are only alleviated if more drug is administered. Heroin withdrawal effects include severe autonomic symptoms, including lacrimation, diarrhoea, rhinorrhoea, stomach cramps, tremor and piloerection ('cold turkey'). There are also dysphoric subjective effects. This sequence of changes and apparent opponent (or conflicting) motivational effects may be a general property of appetitive and aversive motivational systems and has wider generality than the effects of drugs (see Solomon (1980) for a fuller account).

The occurrence of withdrawal begs the question of how drug-taking behaviour is ultimately maintained. Is it due to the hedonic effects of the drugs, or to avoiding or escaping withdrawal, or to some complex mixture of these positive and negative reinforcing effects? Autonomic withdrawal symptoms do not seem to be a *necessary* condition for continued drug-taking: monkeys will continue over long periods to self-administer small doses of morphine that are insufficient in themselves to produce physiological signs of dependence and some drugs, such as cocaine, are not associated with very severe physical withdrawal symptoms like those of the opiates. Thus, in some circumstances at least, positive reinforcement may continue to be crucial in the maintenance of drug-taking, although avoidance or escape from dysphoric states could also play an important role.

Wikler's theory of conditioned withdrawal and relapse

Wikler proposed a conditioning theory of relapse, following his own clinical observations of how addicts who had been rehabilitated suffered relapse into drug-taking after they were restored to their social environment (see O'Brien *et al.*, 1986). This theory has two stages:

1. Pavlovian conditioning of withdrawal symptoms (UR) to environmental cues and situations (CS).

2. Previous experience of negative reinforcing effects of drug-taking to alleviate withdrawal symptoms.

Thus, when the rehabilitated addict returns to his or her original social setting, withdrawal is elicited and this leads to a resumption of drug-taking.

Animal experiments have provided evidence in support of Wikler's theory. These experiments made use of the fact that it is possible to elicit withdrawal in morphine-dependent animals by injections of opiate antagonist drugs, such as naloxone or nalorphine. Monkeys were made dependent on morphine by injections of the drug in their home cage. They were then trained to respond for food according to a fixed ratio schedule of reinforcement. This provided a baseline for observing how badly their normally efficient behaviour was disrupted in the state of morphine withdrawal. When responding for food was stable, the animals received a control infusion of saline preceded by an auditory tone CS. This had little effect, but the tone was then paired with an injection of nalorphine, to elicit withdrawal. The nalorphine produced signs of withdrawal such as brady-cardia, emesis and salivation, and completely disrupted responding for food. However, of particular significance for the first stage of Wikler's theory, these signs of withdrawal became conditioned to the tone CS, so that its presentation by itself elicited these responses even if it was no longer followed by nalorphine. The conditioned withdrawal was quite long-lasting and did not disappear for several weeks (Goldberg and Schuster, 1967).

Evidence for the second stage of Wikler's theory is provided by another laboratory experiment in which monkeys had been trained to self-administer morphine, so that a low rate of about 5 infusions was received per session. Figure 8.12 shows that presession control injections of saline had no effect on the frequency of self-administration, but an injection of nalorphine produced a four-fold increase so that the animals were self-administering more morphine to counteract the withdrawal produced by nalorphine. Self-administration returned to the baseline on day 15 when no presession injections were made. However, when saline injections were made over days 16–20, there was an initial increase in morphine self-administration, showing once more that withdrawal can become con-ditioned. As Figure 8.12 indicates, although the conditioned withdrawal extinguished over successive sessions it was possible to reinstate it with further injections of nalorphine.

In summary, these laboratory experiments have shown that drug abuse, withdrawal and relapse are all affected by conditioning, either of a Pavlovian or instrumental type. The implications for rehabilitation are that not only must one eliminate the pharmacological effects of the drug reinforcer, but also the stimuli that have become associated with the drug itself or with the symptoms elicited by its withdrawal. Wikler's theory may explain some puzzling observations of the relatively low incidence of relapse to heroin abuse of veterans of Vietnam upon their return to the United States. These GIs had been both addicted and detoxified in Vietnam and so their return home ensured that they would no longer be exposed to the conditioned reinforcers and withdrawal-related stimuli to which they may have become conditioned (see O'Brien *et al.*, 1986).

Stress

Prediction, control, and coping

There is little doubt that psychological stress can produce organic as well as psychological deficits. Selye described three stages in the response to

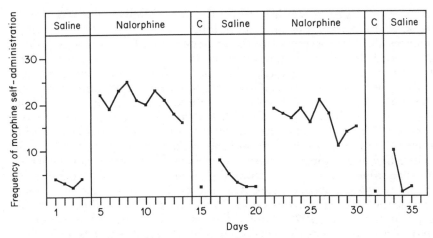

Fig. 8.12 Experimental demonstration of Wikler's theory in morphine-dependent monkeys. Morphine self-administration is increased above normal values when withdrawal is elicited by pre-session injections of nalorphine, an opiate antagonist. On sessions 16 and 32 the similar stimuli or rituals associated with saline injections were sufficient to produce a small conditioned increase in self-administration, by comparison with control (C) days, when no injections were administered. (Redrawn from Goldberg, S.R., Woods, J.H. and Schuster, C.R. (1969). Reproduced by permission of *Science* and The American Association for the Advancement of Science.)

chronic stress, as part of the **general adaptation syndrome**. He referred to these stages as **alarm, resistance** and **exhaustion**. According to Selye, Cannon's emergency reaction is only the initial response to stress. During the resistance stage, there is increased activity in the pituitary–adrenal axis so that there are elevated levels of plasma corticosteroids as well as plasma catecholamines. If the chronic stress continues, in experimental animals, there is long-term elevation of blood pressure, gastric ulceration and a breakdown in immune responses, which constitutes Selye's exhaustion stage (see Axelrod and Reisine, 1984). These effects may be paralleled by psychosomatic aspects of hypertension, gastrointestinal disease and cancer in man (see Chapter 10).

The response to stress is crucially dependent upon psychological factors, such as the predictability of the stressful events, and perhaps more importantly, the degree of control the animal has over their occurrence. This can be illustrated by one experiment in which rats were stressed by the repeated presentation of shocks to the tail. The rats were divided into three main groups, according to a so-called 'triadic design'. In this design, the control group received no shocks at all. The two important groups were the Master (avoidance-escape) group which could turn a wheel to avoid or escape from the electric shock (which thus acted as a negative reinforcer), and the Yoked group which received the same number and intensity of shocks as the Master group, but without effective avoidance or escape responses. After the experiment the presence of gastric pathology (ulcers) was assessed. Figure 8.13 shows that the length of the gastric lesions was different in the three groups with the control group unsurprisingly showing the smallest ulcers. However, the important comparison was between the Master and Yoked groups. Although both groups received the same degree of physical stress, the Master group showed significantly less ulceration. Thus, the capacity to control the shock in this condition reduced the effects of the stress and the avoidance-escape response could be described as a coping response which alleviates the effects of the stress. The ulceration arises partly from the action of excess corticosteroids secreted from the adrenal cortex. The effects of the availability of a coping response on plasma corticosteroid levels are similar to those seen for ulceration (see Weiss, 1977). Similar factors can even affect the concentration of central neurotransmitters, such as noradrenaline (see below).

The predictability of the stress is also an important factor that modulates its impact. In the experiment described above there was an additional feature of the design in which the shocks were either signalled by a CS or not signalled. Figure 8.13 shows that the incidence of gastric pathology was significantly higher in the no signal condition and this factor appeared to add to the effects of uncontrollability. Presumably, the ability to predict stress also aids in the learning of effective coping responses which serve to reduce the deleterious effects of stress, even when the occurrence of the stressor cannot be controlled. Other coping responses can be recruited in response to stress. If rats are subjected to the stress of shock in pairs they may fight but, despite the presumably increased stress of fighting, they actually develop less severe gastric lesions than rats shocked alone (Weiss, 1977). Earlier in this chapter, the overeating by obese subjects in stressful circumstances was also considered as a possible coping response, but in this case, it should be emphasized that no endocrine measures were taken that might have substantiated the coping hypothesis. It remains unclear exactly how coping responses can reduce stress: at a psychological level a type of attentional mechanism may be involved that somehow 'gates' the sensory input in a way analogous to that described for pain (see Chapter 2).

Learned helplessness and models of depression

Animals exposed to uncontrollable stress also exhibit psychological deficits. Seligman (1971) and his colleagues originally showed that dogs subjected to inescapable shocks were deficient in learning the simple avoidance response of moving to the other side of a two-compartment chamber, even if they were physically dragged over to the safe side. Similar effects can be seen in a Y-maze avoidance task in the rat. Animals previously receiving inescapable shock eliminate errors more slowly in learning to choose the safe arm of the maze. To explain these results, Seligman suggested that the

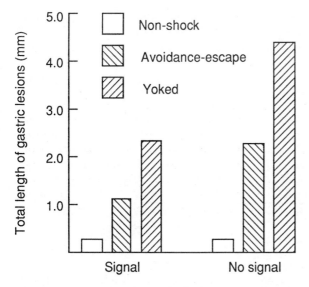

Fig. 8.13 Length of gastric lesions as a function of the predictability and controllability of stress in rats. The yoked groups received the same amount of shock as the master (avoidance/escape) group, but had no effective avoidance or escape response available. Controls received no shocks. Predictability of the shock was increased by the provision of a CS signalling its occurrence (left panel). (Redrawn from Weiss, J. (1977). Reproduced by permission of the author, editors and W.H. Freeman and Co., San Francisco.)

pre-exposure to uncontrollable stress leads to a state of **learned helplessness** in which there is:

1. Perception of a lack of contingency between actions and outcomes (i.e. the ineffectiveness of one's actions)

2. An expectancy that future actions will be ineffective.

Learned helplessness was linked by Seligman (1971) to the feelings of hopelessness and helplessness that occur in human depression. Further attempts to extrapolate the theory experimentally to man and to clinical depression are covered in Chapter 9. Models of depression such as learned helplessness are important in at least two ways: first, in trying to specify causes of depression and the types of psychological mechanism that are affected; and second in the development of improved treatments for depression, including antidepressant drugs. Although learned helplessness constitutes a viable animal model of depression, it might be argued that it is too artificial to capture even some of the complexity of human depression, especially in its social aspects.

A more naturalistic model of depression is provided by the effects of

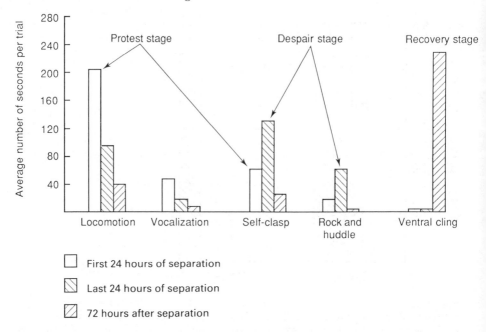

Fig. 8.14   Effects of brief periods of social separation on different behavioural responses in adult rhesus monkeys separated from their peers. (Redrawn from Suomi, S. and Harlow, H.F. (1977). Reproduced by permission of the authors and the American Psychological Association.)

social separation in monkeys, which can also, perhaps, be regarded as a form of uncontrollable stress. Harlow and his colleagues (1977) raised infant rhesus monkeys with their mothers in a playpen apparatus that allowed the infants to interact with their own mothers and other adult mothers and their offspring. At 6 months of age, each infant was separated from its mother for a period of 3 weeks, during which time it could see and hear, but not physically contact her, and could also interact with its peers. After 3 weeks, each mother and infant were reunited. The results showed, on initial separation, increases in vocalization and random, disorganized locomotor responses ('protest stage'), followed by behavioural signs of inactivity and drastic reductions in social interaction, such as play with peers ('despair stage'). Stereotyped rocking and self-clasping also sometimes occurred in the despair stage. These phases are strongly reminiscent of those described by Bowlby in depression occurring in human infants separated from their mothers from between 6 months and 6 years of age (see Chapter 4). When the infant monkeys were reunited with their mothers, their behaviour generally returned to normal, as it generally does also in childhood depression (Suomi and Harlow, 1977).

One possible criticism of the social separation model of depression is that it is confined to infants, and therefore irrelevant to adult depression. However, an extension of Harlow's work has shown that milder, but qualitatively similar effects occur in rhesus monkeys if peers are separated later in development and that the effects are replicable with repeated separations. Figure 8.14 shows some results for the effects of an initial 4-day separation. All of the subjects exhibited protest behaviour such as vocalization and locomotion, and then responses characteristic of the despair stage, such as huddling, self-clasping and rocking. After the animals were reunited, there was a great increase in social contact, as indicated by the ventral clinging response, in which the previously separated animal grasps onto the back of one of his or her peers.

In evaluating the utility of this model for human depression, it should be pointed out that there are wide species variations in the effects of separation among the primates that appear to depend on the characteristic social structure of the colony. There are also changes in certain psychological indices that are consistent with some of the changes seen in depression. For example, there are changes in the sleep pattern, with reduced levels of REM sleep. There are also elevations in plasma corticosteroids, as also can occur in depression (see Akiskal and McKinney, 1973).

Table 8.4 shows a comparison of some of the main features of human unipolar depression, according to the Diagnostic and Statistical Manual (DSM) of the American Psychiatric Association, and the effects produced in animals by social separation and learned helplessness. As can be seen, there is a rough correspondence between the symptoms seen in the animal models of social separation and learned helplessness. Both of these conditions have also been reported to be ameliorated by treatment with antidepressant drugs. A parsimonius account would suggest that the similar effects of social separation and learned helplessness are mediated

Table 8.4 Validity of animal models of depression

Human depression	Learned helplessness	Social separation
Poor appetite and weight loss	Yes	Yes
Psychomotor alterations (reductions in activity)	Yes	Yes
Loss of energy or fatigue	Yes	Yes
Sleep changes (particularly reductions in REM sleep)	Yes	Yes
Decreased ability to think or decide	Impaired learning	Not tested
Feelings of worthlessness	?	?
Recurrent thoughts of suicide	No	No

by actions on those systems concerned with the adaptation to stress; there are probably some important differences between the two which future research will uncover. Although there is a rough correlation between the behavioural and physiological symptoms of the animal models and clinical depression, the inadequacies of the animal models become clear when considering cognitive signs of depression, such as feelings of guilt or worthlessness. It is also clear that there is no corresponding animal model of the cyclic changes in mood that occur in bipolar depression.

Brain mechanisms of emotion and motivation

A good deal of William James' theorizing was based on the assumption that there were no specialized brain regions for the emotions, but anatomical and physiological discoveries in this century have shown this assumption to be false. There is now little doubt that three major anatomical divisions of the central nervous system control aspects of motivation and emotion: the ascending reticular activating system, the hypothalamus, and the limbic system. However, the precise mechanisms by which this control is achieved are still a matter of controversy.

No function as complex as a particular form of motivation or emotional response is likely to depend only upon one structure in the CNS. From an early stage it was clear that emotional responses in animals were controlled by a hierarchy of mechanisms, so that, for example, a cat with its brain transected at the level of the pons in the hindbrain was still able to exhibit signs of rage, though in a disorganized and indiscriminate manner. More modern concepts of how the brain functions, such as parallel distributed processing (see Chapter 1) also dictate that the various forms of emotional responding are likely to be controlled by somewhat independent brain mechanisms. This mode of thinking argues against there being specific neural centres for particular forms of motivated behaviour, although there is clearly a degree of specialization and localization of function.

Hypothalamic mechanisms

Mainly on the basis of experiments involving experimental destruction of parts of the hypothalamus or electrical stimulation of that structure through implanted electrodes, Stellar and others argued for the existence of discrete hypothalamic 'centres' in control of hunger, thirst, sex and other specific motivational states. These areas would also support positive reinforcing effects of brain stimulation, and it used to be thought that the stimulation mimicked the effects of natural reinforcers such as food. However, much of the experimental evidence has now been reinterpreted and some authorities now believe that these effects are far less specific than was formerly thought (see Valenstein, 1973). For example, electrolytic lesions of the lateral hypothalamus were shown to produce aphagia and adipsia (lack of eating and drinking) in animals, but such lesions are now, crucially, known to destroy fibres of the ascending dopaminergic system that arise in the midbrain and innervate the basal ganglia (Fig. 8.15), and, in man, have been implicated in the motor symptoms of Parkinson's disease. At least part of the aphagia was due to the interruption of this system, although more recent work has established that some of the homeostatic responses to glucoprivation and hypovolaemia may be mediated by hypothalamic mechanisms (see Robbins, 1986 for a review). Sexual behaviour in male rats depends upon the steroid testosterone and an intact

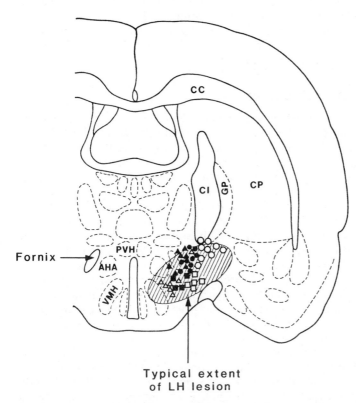

Typical extent
of LH lesion

Fig. 8.15 Coronal section through the hypothalamus to show some of the specific neurotransmitter systems coursing through the area via the medial forebrain bundle. Abbreviations: CC corpus callosum; CP caudate-putamen; CI internal capsule; GP globus pallidus; PVH paraventricular hypothalamus; AHA anterior hypothalamic area; LH lateral hypothalamus; VMH ventromedial hypothalamus; LH lateral hypothalamus.
○ mesostriatal dopaminergic projection; ● mesolimbic dopamine projection; ▲ dorsal noradrenergic bundle; △ ventral noradrenergic projection; ■ medial serotoninergic projection; □ lateral serotoninergic projection. (Reproduced from Robbins, T.W. (1986). Reproduced by permission of the author and Blackwell Scientific Publications, Oxford.)

preoptic area, where the hormone exerts its effects. However, it is clear that lesions of this region do not reduce sexual motivation, but instead cause impairments in the ability to copulate (see Johnson and Everitt, 1988).

The hypothalamus appears to participate in the organization of simple reflexes that form the basis of the consummatory responses, such as defensive or predatory aggression, eating and copulation, that are generated by specific stimuli in the presence of the appropriate motivational state. These simple responses are mainly organized at the level of the midbrain and expressed via spinal motor mechanisms. The hypothalamus also controls the secretory activity of the pituitary gland, with which it has an intimate anatomical relationship. (For a synopsis of hypothalamic–pituitary interactions and the functioning of the pituitary–adrenal axis, see Gray (1988) or Kandel and Schwartz (1985).)

Ascending reticular activating system

The ascending reticular activating system (ARAS), or reticular formation, was originally considered to be the neural substrate for the hypothetical process of **arousal**, which was implicated in the control of the sleep-waking cycle and, during waking hours, in the maintenance of the efficiency of neuronal functions within the cerebral cortex. Understood in this way, the process of arousal is somewhat distinct from that of emotion or motivation. However, some blurring of these concepts derives from the fact that arousal is often associated, like motivation, with the energization of behaviour and, like emotion, with relatively non-specific feedback from the periphery. Certainly, a unitary concept of arousal is now inadequate, partly for reasons described in Chapter 3.

The term 'reticular formation' refers to a diffuse network of neurons with widely ramifying collaterals that originates from cell groups in the hindbrain and midbrain to innervate widespread portions of the forebrain including the cerebral cortex. Some of the collaterals of the neospinothalamic tracts that convey spatiotemporal information about somatosensory inputs, have collaterals to nuclei considered to form part of the reticular formation which may be responsible for providing the affective components of nociception that result in escape responses (Melzack and Wall, 1982). It is also likely that visceral afferents which impinge upon hindbrain structures such as the nucleus tractus solitarius also reach the nuclei of the reticular formation (see Kandel and Schwartz, 1985). In terms of Schachter's two-factor theory of the emotions, the reticular formation could, potentially, be the neural source of the non-specific arousal that provides intensity to the emotions, and which is interpreted by higher centres according to the environmental context, as different types of emotion, but this remains hypothetical.

The central monoaminergic neurotransmitters

Neuroanatomical discoveries have shown that the reticular formation is, in fact, a much more highly differentiated structure than was formerly supposed and several distinct components may now be defined on the basis of their chemical neurotransmitters. Thus, Figure 8.16 shows the origin, course and termination of the ascending noradrenergic systems from cell groups in the locus coeruleus and medulla oblongata, of the ascending serotoninergic systems from the mesencephalic raphé nuclei, and of the ascending dopaminergic projections from the ventral tegmental region and substantia nigra, pars compacta, of the midbrain.

Functions of the monoamine transmitters in arousal, stress and reward

The monoaminergic systems all seem to participate in processes related to stress and arousal (see Anisman *et al.*, 1981). For example, Figure 8.17 illustrates the effects of uncontrollable stress on central noradrenaline levels in the hypothalamus and cortex. The Master group exhibited a mild reduction in levels which is in fact consistent with an elevation in turnover or activity of the system. However, the Yoked group showed a considerable depletion, perhaps because the synthesis of noradrenaline failed to keep up with the demand caused by the massive release of the neurotransmitter in this condition. This pattern of results is, of course, reminiscent of Selye's exhaustion stage of the general adaptation syndrome, and it seems possible that the reductions in central noradrenaline are, in part, responsible for the cognitive dysfunction that occurs in the state of learned helplessness, and possibly in less severe circumstances, where elevated stress causes a breakdown in the executive control of performance (Chapter 3).

There are several lines of evidence implicating the central catecholamines, noradrenaline and, more particularly, dopamine in the mediation of reward. First, 'positive' sites for rewarding effects of brain stimulation correspond very well to the anatomical distribution of the catecholamine pathways. Second, drugs which alter catecholaminergic function affect the rate of responding for brain stimulation reward. For example, drugs such as amphetamine and cocaine, which are indirect catecholamine agonists, increase rates of responding and appear to reduce the threshold of the rewarding current, whereas drugs which antagonize catecholamine activity such as reserpine, and dopamine-receptor blockers, such as haloperidol, have the opposite action. Third, several of the main drugs of abuse, such as amphetamine or cocaine, facilitate central catecholaminergic activity. Rats will self-administer d-amphetamine directly into the nucleus accumbens which receives major mesencephalic dopaminergic projections and has been described as an interface between the basal ganglia and the limbic system. Wise (1981) has proposed an ambitious hypothesis that the dopaminergic system is part of the final common pathway for the mediation of all forms of reward, including not only drugs such as amphetamine and cocaine, but also morphine, and natural rewards such as food.

(a)

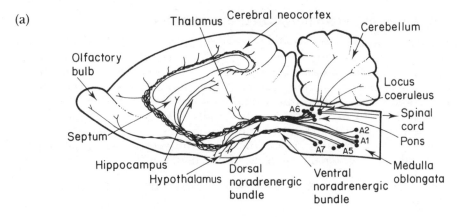

(b)

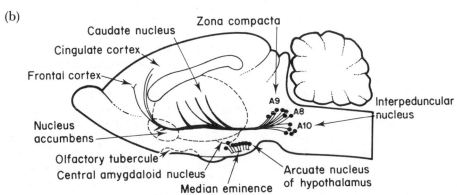

(c)

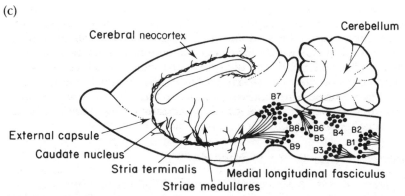

Fig. 8.16 Sagittal sections through the rat brain to show the origin and anatomical distribution of the central monoaminergic neurotransmitter pathways. (The distribution of these systems is essentially similar in man.) A noradrenergic pathways; B dopaminergic pathways; C serotoninergic (5-HT) pathways. The designations A9 or B7 etc, refer to defined monoaminergic cell groups.

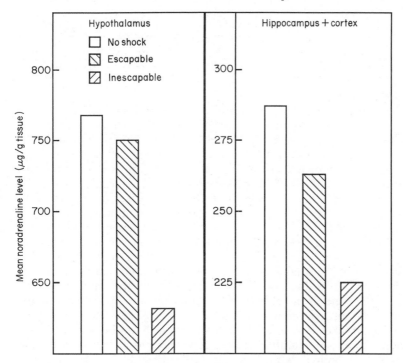

Fig. 8.17 Effects of controllable and uncontrollable stress on central levels of noradrenaline (Redrawn from Anisman, H., Pizzino, A. and Sklar, L.S. (1980) by permission of Elsevier Science Publishers, Amsterdam.)

The major question still remains of how neurotransmitter systems such as the dopamine projections to the nucleus accumbens and prefrontal cortex (Figure 8.16) can mediate the effects of reward. It seems likely that these dopamine projections are providing the central correlate of what Schachter took to be the non-specific arousal which is interpreted according to cognitive context. Alternatively, activity in these systems may serve to intensify the impact of emotional stimuli in structures specialized for their cognitive evaluation.

Monoaminergic hypotheses of depression

Most of the physical treatments for depression, including electroconvulsive therapy and antidepressant drugs, appear to act by increasing the activity of the central monoamine systems, and the monoamine-depleting drug, reserpine, was associated with reports of depression when it was used to treat hypertension. However, recent neuropharmacological findings have suggested that the monoaminergic theory may be in need of revision. A particular problem has been that acute treatment with antidepressants is often ineffective in depression, even though the drugs are having their expected pharmacological effects to block the reuptake of monoamines (mainly noradrenaline and serotonin). By contrast, chronic treatment has somewhat different pharmacological effects, but is more effective in treating depression.

In clinical studies of depression, most of the emphasis has been on the noradrenergic and serotoninergic systems, and experimental evidence, such as that shown in Figure 8.17, certainly implicates these systems in the response to stress (see also Akiskal and McKinney, 1975; Green and Costain, 1981). Another monoaminergic theory of depression has focused on the 'anhedonia' or lack of pleasure shown by depressed people. This anhedonia has been linked with elevated thresholds for stimuli to produce rewarding effects, as stimuli typically have to be more intense than normal to elicit a pleasurable response. From the evidence described above, the postulated elevation in reward threshold might be linked to a less active dopaminergic system, for example, in the nucleus accumbens. This hypothesis is not mutually incompatible with that implicating the monoamines in stress because, as was seen from the animal models discussed earlier, one of the effects of stress can be an apparent reduction of interest in the environment and natural sources of reward. While there has been little direct evidence for the dopaminergic hypothesis in studies of human depression, some animal studies have suggested that antidepressant drugs can produce changes in reward threshold by affecting this system.

Figure 8.18 shows the effects of acute and chronic antidepressant treatment on rates of self-stimulation at varying levels of current in rats from electrodes in the vicinity of dopamine cell-bodies in the ventral tegmental region. Only chronic treatment was effective in reducing the threshold of the current level necessary to maintain instrumental lever-pressing, consistent with the clinical experience with these drugs. Part of the therapeutic action of antidepressants may be to reduce the threshold for environmental stimuli to become rewarding, and thus to improve mood.

The limbic system

William James' supposition that there was no specialized region for the emotions was challenged by discoveries that damage to certain interconnected nuclei in the forebrain produced changes in both emotional behaviour and experience. Many of these structures formed part of what came to be known as the limbic system, which is largely an anatomical concept applied to some of the primitive regions that border the cerebral cortex. Among the structures now included in the limbic system are the septum, hippocampus, amygdala, hypothalamus, and primitive regions of the cortex, including the entorhinal, cingulate, pyriform and insular cortex. The prefrontal cortex is also generally included as a limbic system

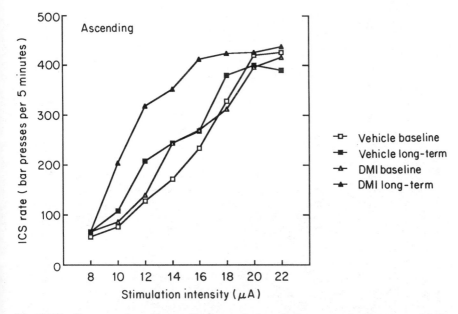

Fig. 8.18 Comparative effects of acute and chronic (long-term) treatment with an antidepressant drug on intracranial self-stimulation in the rat. The rate of responding is plotted as a function of different current intensities. The chronic treatment appears to reduce the 'reward threshold' and shift the function to the left. (Redrawn from Fibiger, H. and Philips, A.G. (1981) by permission of *Science* and the American Association for the Advancement of Science.)

structure (see Figure 8.19). These structures are heavily interconnected and this may justify their designation as a natural system. However, the main rationale for the concept of the limbic system derives from its hypothesized functions in emotion.

In the 1930s, Papez proposed a detailed neurological theory of the emotions involving limbic system structures which had two major components. Following the evaluation of an emotional stimulus by cortical mechanisms, this information was processed by one circuit to the hypothalamus to mediate the behavioural and visceral expression of emotion. The information was passed, hypothetically, from the cingulate cortex to the hippocampal formation, and relayed to the hypothalamus by way of the fornix and mammillary bodies. Information from the hypothalamus was postulated to be relayed back to the cingulate cortex by way of the mammillary bodies and the anterior thalamic nuclei, where it completed 'Papez's circuit' and contributed to conscious emotional experience. Papez thus conceived the cingulate cortex to be a 'receiving area' for emotional stimuli for the hypothalamus in the way that the striate cortex is a receiving area for visual input. The sensory inputs to the cingulate cortex from other regions of the

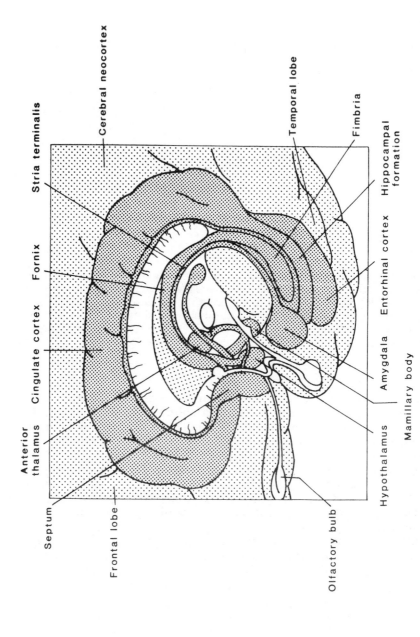

Fig. 8.19 Diagram to show the main structures of the limbic system, including elements of Papez circuit. The main components of the limbic system are darkly shaded.

cortex were thus given emotional intensity by its input from the hypothalamus. The importance of Papez's theory was that it provided an explanation of how sensory stimuli can reach the limbic system structures, after cortical processing, and generate both emotional responses and the substrates of subjective emotional experience (see LeDoux, 1986).

There has not been much evidence to support the detailed aspects of Papez's theory. Indeed, the hippocampus has more recently been implicated more in cognitive functions such as memory (see Chapter 7) rather than the emotions. Classical work by Kluver and Bucy showed that bilateral destruction of the temporal lobe, which damaged many underlying limbic structures, led to drastic changes in emotional behaviour in monkeys, including increased timidity, lack of fear to stimuli such as lit matches, abnormal sexual behaviour, and an apparent lack of discrimination in food objects which did not arise from a simple sensory deficit. Subsequent work showed that the damage to the amygdala was a major contributor to this syndrome. These effects of temporal lobe lesions in monkeys are complemented to some extent by findings that epileptic seizures in the temporal lobe in man are strongly associated with the induction of emotional experience and behaviour. Seizures in the amygdala have been associated with paranoid fears and with uncontrollable aggression leading to homicide (Trimble, 1985).

Converging evidence suggests that the amygdala mediates anxiety. For example, the cardiac deceleration that occurs in aversive conditioning in the rat is blocked by lesions of the amygdala. There is also evidence that the anxiolytic effects of the benzodiazepines may be mediated in part by the amygdala, as intra-amygdaloid infusions of benzodiazepines produce a similar increase in punished responding in conflict schedules to that seen after peripheral administration of the drug. This result is consistent with the evidence of mapping studies that benzodiazepine receptors are concentrated particularly in the limbic system (Iversen, 1985). The presence of specific receptors for anxiolytic drugs suggests the possibility that there may be an endogenous anxiety-inducing agent which normally binds to those receptors. However, no such compound has yet been isolated. Drugs which act as inverse agonists at the benzodiazepine receptor, such as the β-carboline derivative FG 7142, can, however, induce profound fear or anxiety in human volunteers. The reliability of these effects, even in subjects fully aware of what they are taking, perhaps questions the view that emotions always arise from attributions of unexplained sources of arousal.

Damage to limbic structures, including the septum and hippocampus, similarly produces in animals a disinhibition of behaviour which may include punished responding. Disinhibition is also a characteristic of behaviour following damage to the frontal lobe. In the last century, the railway worker Phineas Gage became impulsive and socially irresponsible following a severe accidental injury to the frontal lobes from a tamping iron, losing his job as a result. This impulsivity and social irresponsibility is now known to result from damage to orbitofrontal regions of the frontal lobe, and has been called a 'pseudopsychopathic' syndrome. By contrast, damage to more dorsolateral regions results in a behavioural apathy that has been termed 'pseudodepression' (Stuss and Benson, 1983). Damage to the frontal or cingulate cortex can also lead to a peculiar apathy towards pain, which the subject can still feel, but no longer cares about.

There has been a great deal of research directed towards the precise role of limbic mechanisms in the emotions which is beyond the scope of this chapter. A gross simplification would be that the limbic system is intimately concerned in evaluating the emotional significance of stimuli, whether positive or negative, by virtue of their previous associations with peripheral feedback. For example, choosing one stimulus may previously have led to reward, whereas choosing another led to punishment, and both of which may have been associated with specific visceral effects. This information is important in both formulating actions that are made in response to stimuli and producing visceral responses. The limbic system is anatomically well placed to effect actions, via such structures as the nucleus accumbens and the prefrontal cortex, and co-ordinated visceral (including ANS) responses, via the hypothalamus and pituitary gland. The limbic system may also provide the context that enables the labelling of states of non-specific arousal that leads to conscious emotional experience.

Some of the clinical applications of research into limbic system function are in assessing the utility and effects of psychosurgery. Ablation of the frontal lobe (frontal lobotomy) or of structures such as the amygdala, and the severing of fibre connections between the frontal cortex and the rest of the brain (leucotomy) have been used quite widely in the treatment of psychiatric disorder. Whereas such surgery is often unavoidable in the case of removing tumours or in preventing the spread of intractable epilepsy, its use in treating aggressive, or obsessive-compulsive or psychotic patients must be viewed especially critically, as so little, still, is known of the functions of these regions (see Valenstein, 1973 or Stuss and Benson, 1983, for a history and critical account of psychosurgery).

The problem of conscious emotional experience revisited

The fundamental problem in understanding the neural basis of the emotions remains that of specifying which structure or structures participate in conscious emotional experiences. This specification in turn depends upon understanding at which point in the processing of emotional stimuli subjective experience arises. One view has been that emotional experience does not depend primarily upon cognition (Zajonc, 1980). A number of alternative views have been advanced which implicate cognitive processes in a variety of ways (see Fig. 8.3). For example, the cognitive evaluation of an emotional event has been considered to be part and parcel of the emotional experience. On the other hand, Schachter (1966) has argued that the experience depends more upon the cognitive interpretation of bodily responses. Either or both of these cognitive operations may depend upon the capacity for language, and the search for neural substates of emotion would then, perhaps, focus on those critical regions where linguistic and visceral processing converge. One problem with this account is that it seems to deny animals other than ourselves the capacity for emotional experience. Another problem is that damage to the right hemisphere, which is less specialized than the left for linguistic function, may lead to greater deficits in emotional response than damage to the left (see Buck, 1986).

Results of studies by Sperry and his colleagues on patients that have received a sectioning of the corpus callosum as a treatment for the spread of epilepsy can be used to support the view that language is not a prime requirement for emotional experience but contributes simply to its expression. As a result of this surgery, communication between the cerebral hemispheres of these patients is largely prevented. In addition, stimuli presented in one sensory field are conveyed largely exclusively to the contralateral hemisphere. An emotional stimulus, such as a slide of a nude, will evoke emotional responses and experiences (e.g. pleasant/unpleasant) if presented to the right hemisphere, but the subject is unable to verbalize his feelings (see Buck, 1986). This result is reminiscent of ones described in Chapter 1 in normal subjects, in supporting Zajonc's view that emotions do not have to depend upon cognitive processes such as language or cognitive analysis.

However, there is no reason why emotional experience has to involve just one of the mechanisms described above. They could all contribute to it in different circumstances. In general, as a result of conditioning a cognitive evaluation system could enable the organism to anticipate, perhaps verbally label, and even modulate behavioural or physiological emotional responses in many different situations, but need not be *necessary* for those responses to occur. Similarly, cognitive factors may affect the evaluation of bodily feedback, and the latter may be especially important for determining the intensity rather than the type of experienced emotion. If the brain does function in part like a series of parallel distributed processors, then there may be occasions when the independent activation of a particular physiological system has led to ambiguous feedback, which requires cognitive evaluation to produce a more co-ordinated response. Study of the neural basis of emotion is now likely to concentrate on identifying the separate systems which are engaged during the response to an emotional event, and then upon the ways in which these systems normally function to provide us with the illusion of being a unified system (or 'self').

Suggested reading

Citations in this chapter have, of necessity often been restricted to review articles in which the relevant evidence is described in greater depth.
The following are recommended for their consideration of particular areas noted in the text:

On the psychology and physiology of emotions and motivation:
Buck, R. (1986). The psychology of emotion. In *Mind and Brain*, pp. 275–300. Edited by LeDoux, J.E. and Hirst, W. Cambridge University Press, Cambridge.
A good, integrated account.

Carlson, N.R. (1986). *Physiology of Behaviour*, 3rd edition. Allyn and Bacon, Boston.
A useful textbook of physiological psychology which may be useful for its treatment of motivation.

Davey, G. (1981). *Animal Learning and Conditioning*. Macmillan, London.
Elementary consideration of conditioning mechanisms.

Gray, J. (1988). *The Psychology of Fear and Stress*. 2nd edition. Cambridge University Press, Cambridge.
A successful attempt at integrating conditioning principles with the physiology of emotion.

Grings, W.W. and Dawson, M.E. (1978). *Emotions and Bodily Responses*. Academic Press, New York.
Particularly useful for information on the physiological indices of emotion.

Kandel, E. and Schwartz, J.S. (1985). *The Principles of Neural Science*. 2nd edition. Elsevier, Amsterdam.
A high-powered neuroscientific background text, particularly for aspects of neuroanatomy and neuropharmacology.

LeDoux, J.E. (1986). The neurobiology of emotion. In *Mind and Brain*, pp. 301–54. Edited by LeDoux, J.E. and Hirst, W. Cambridge University Press, Cambridge.

Mackintosh, N.J. (1983). *Conditioning and Associative Learning*. The Clarendon Press, Oxford.
Advanced consideration given to conditioning mechanisms.

Valenstein, E.S. (1973). *Brain Control*. John Wiley, New York.
A readable historical account of physiological psychology.

On psychopharmacology:
Green, R. and Costain, D.W. (1981). *The Pharmacology and Biochemistry of Psychiatric Disorders*. J. Wiley and Sons, Chichester.

Iversen, S.D. and Iversen, L.L. (1981). *Behavioural Pharmacology*. 2nd edition. Oxford University Press, Oxford.

O'Brien, C.P., Ehrman, R.N. and Ternes, J. (1986). Classical conditioning in human opioid dependence. In *Behavioral Mechanisms of Drug Dependence*, pp. 329–56. Edited by Goldberg, S.R. and Stolerman, L.P. Academic Press, Orlando.

On psychopathology:
Maser, J. and Seligman, M. (1977). *Psychopathology: Experimental Models*. W.H. Freeman and Co., San Francisco.
Contains several relevant chapters on animal models of psychopathology.

References

Akiskal, H. and McKinney, W. (1973). Depressive disorder: towards a unified hypothesis. *Science* **182**, 20.

Anisman, H., Kokkindis, L. and Sklar, L.S. (1981). Contribution of neurochemical change to stress-induced behavioural deficits. In *Theory in Psychopharmacology* pp. 65–102. Edited by Cooper, S.J. Academic Press, London.

Anisman, H., Pizzino, A. and Sklar, L.S. (1980). Coping with stress, norepinephrine depletion and escape performance. *Brain Research* **191**, 583.

Axelrod, J. and Reisine, T.D. (1984). Stress hormones: their interaction and regulation. *Science* **224**, 452.

Bruch, H. (1973). *Eating Disorders*. Basic Books, New York.

Buck, R. (1986). The psychology of emotion. In *Mind and Brain*, pp. 275–300. Edited by LeDoux, J.E. and Hirst, W. Cambridge University Press, Cambridge.

Carlson, N.R. (1986). *Physiology of Behavior*, 3rd edition. Allyn and Bacon, Boston.

Davey, G. (1981). *Animal Learning and Conditioning*. Macmillan, London.

Ekman, P., Sorenson, E.R. and Friesen, W.V. (1983). Autonomic nervous system activity distinguishes among emotions. *Science* **221**, 1208.

Fibiger, H. and Phillips, A.G. (1981). Increased intracranial self-stimulation in rats after long term administration of desipramine. *Science* **214**, 683.

Goldberg, S.R. and Schuster, C.R. (1967). Conditioned suppression by a stimulus associated with nalorphine in morphine-dependent monkeys. *Journal of the Experimental Analysis of Behavior* **10**, 235.

Goldberg, S.R., Woods, J.H. and Schuster, C.R. (1969). Morphine: conditioned increases in self-administration in rhesus monkeys. *Science* **166**, 1306–1307.

Gray, J. (1988). *The Psychology of Fear and Stress*, 2nd edition. Cambridge University Press, Cambridge.

Green, R. and Costain, D.W. (1981). *The Pharmacology and Biochemistry of Psychiatric Disorder*. J. Wiley and Sons, Chichester.

Grings, W.W. and Dawson, M.E. (1978). *Emotions and Bodily Responses*. Academic Press, New York.

Iversen, S.D. (1985). Where in the central nervous system do the benzodiazepines act? In *Recent Advances in Psychopharmacology*, pp. 75–88. Edited by Iversen, S.D. Oxford University Press, Oxford.

Iversen, S.D. and Iversen L.L. (1981). *Behavioral Pharmacology*. 2nd edition. Oxford University Press, Oxford.

Johnson, M. and Everitt, B.J. (1988). *Essential Reproduction*. Blackwell Scientific Publications, Oxford.

Kandel E. and Schwartz, J.S. (1985). *The Principles of Neural Science*. 2nd edition. Elsevier, Amsterdam.

Lazarus, R.S., Speisman, J.C., Morakoff, A.M. and Davison, L.A. (1962). A laboratory study of physiological stress produced by a motion picture film. *Psychological Monographs* **76**, 1.

LeDoux, J.E. (1986). The neurobiology of emotion. In *Mind and Brain*, pp. 301–54. Edited by LeDoux, J.E. and Hirst, W. Cambridge University Press, Cambridge.

Mackintosh, N.J. (1983). *Conditioning and Associative Learning*. The Clarendon Press, Oxford.

Maser, J. and Seligman, M.E.P. (1977). *Psychopathology: Experimental Models*. W.H. Freeman and Co., San Francisco.

Melzack, R. and Wall, P. (1982). *The Challenge of Pain*. Penguin, Harmondsworth, Middlesex.

Minecka, S. (1987). A primate model of phobic fears. In *Theoretical Foundations of Behaviour Therapy*, pp. 81–111. Edited by Eysenck, H. and Martin, I. Plenum Press, New York.

O'Brien, C.P., Ehrman, R.N. and Ternes, J. (1986). Classical conditioning in human opioid dependence. In *Behavioral Mechanisms of Drug Dependence*, pp. 329–56.

Edited by Goldberg, S.R. and Stolerman, I.P. Academic Press, Orlando.

Ohman, A., Dimberg, U. and Ost, L-G. (1985). Animal and social phobia: biological constraints on learned fear responses. In *Theoretical Issues in Behavior Therapy*, pp. 123–75. Edited by Reiss, S. and Bootzin, R.R. Academic Press, Orlando.

Pickens, R. and Thompson, T. (1968). Cocaine-reinforced behavior in rats: effects of reinforcement magnitude and fixed ratio size. *Journal of Pharmacology Experimental Therapeutics* **161**, 122.

Rachman, S. (1983). The modification of agoraphobic avoidance behaviour: some fresh possibilities. *Behavior Research and Therapy* **21**, 567.

Reisenzein, R. (1983). The Schachter theory of emotion: two decades later. *Psychological Bulletin* **94**, 239.

Robbins, T.W. (1986). Hunger. In *Neuroendocrinology*, pp. 252–303. Edited by Lightman, S.J. and Everitt, B.J. Blackwell Scientific Publications, Oxford.

Schachter, S. and Singer, J. (1962). Cognitive, social and physiological determinants of emotional states. *Psychological Review* **69**, 378.

Schachter, S. (1966). The interaction of cognitive and physiological determinants of emotional states. In *Anxiety and Behavior*, pp. 193–224. Edited by Spielberger, S. Academic Press, Orlando.

Seiden, L.S. and Dykstra, L.A. (1977). *Psychopharmacology*. van Nostrand Reinhold Company, New York.

Seligman, M.E.P. (1971). *Helplessness: On depression, development and death*. W.H. Freeman and Co., San Francisco.

Shapiro, D., Tursky, G., Gershon, E. and Stern, M. (1969). Effects of feedback and reinforcement on the control of systolic blood pressure. *Science* **163**, 588.

Slochower, J. (1977). Emotional labelling and overeating in obese and normal weight individuals. *Psychosomatic Medicine* **38**, 131.

Solomon, R.L. (1980). An opponent theory of acquired motivation: the costs of pleasure and the benefits of pain. *American Psychologist* **35**, 691.

Stuss, D.T. and Benson, D.F. (1983). Emotional concomitants of psychosurgery. In *Neuropsychology of Human Emotion*, pp. 111–40. Edited by Heilman, K. and Satz, P. The Guilford Press, New York.

Suomi, S. and Harlow, H.F. (1977). Production and alleviation of depressive behavior in monkeys. In *Psychopathology: Experimental Models*, pp. 131–73. Edited by Maser, J.D. and Seligman, M.E.P. W.H. Freeman and Co., San Francisco.

Suomi, S., Harlow, H. and Domek, C.J. (1970). Effects of repetitive infant–infant separation of young monkeys. *Journal of Abnormal Psychology* **76**, 161–72.

Trimble, M.R. (1985). Limbic system disorders in man. In *Psychopharmacology of the Limbic System*, pp. 110–24. Edited by Zarafian, E. Oxford University Press, London.

Tyrer, P.J. (1976). *The Role of Bodily Feelings in Anxiety*. Maudsley Monographs. No. 23. Oxford University Press, London.

Valenstein, E.S. (1973). *Brain Control*. J. Wiley, New York.

Weiss, J. (1971). Effects of coping behavior in different warning signal conditions on stress pathology in rats. *Journal of Comparative Physiological Psychology* **77**, 1.

Weiss, J. (1977). Psychosomatic disorders. In *Psychopathology: Experimental Models*, pp. 232–69. Edited by Maser, J. and Seligman, M.E.P. W.H. Freeman and Co., San Francisco.

Wise, R. (1981). Brain dopamine and reward. In *Theory in Psychopharmacology* **1**, pp. 103–22. Edited by Cooper, S.J. Academic Press, London.

Zajonc, R.B. (1980). Feeling and thinking: preferences need no inferences. *American Psychologist* **35**, 151.

9

Psychological Models of Psychopathology

JMG Williams

Anxiety, phobic disorders and depression have been discussed so far from the perspective of animal and human laboratory studies. This chapter will examine the same psychological phenomena from a clinical perspective: What are the signs and symptoms of these disorders? How can they be understood by adopting psychological frameworks?

Two points need to be made at the outset. First, as suggested in Chapter 8, it is important to distinguish between three indices of an individual's symptoms: their subjective experience about which they tell us; their manifest behaviour; and their somatic symptoms. Patients with depression may experience guilt and low self-esteem, those with anxiety may experience feelings of dread; but these are only detectable on the basis of self-report of the patient. In contrast, the behaviour of the patient is observable. The depressed patient may be retarded or agitated and the anxious person may be seen actively to avoid certain feared situations. Patients may also show some somatic symptoms: in depression there may be weight loss and in anxiety there may be increased heart rate and muscle tension. The distinction between the experiential, behavioural and somatic aspects of these disorders is helpful in several ways: first, it is a way of dividing the complex symptomatology of these disorders into manageable subparts; second, the distinction is useful in treatment. Anxious patients sometimes show 'asynchrony' in the sense of exhibiting one or two but not the third of the symptom cluster. Some studies have shown that if the type of treatment is matched to the particular pattern of symptoms shown by the patient, the outcome tends to be more favourable than if general therapy strategies are applied for all patients.

The second important point to be made before providing a psychological account of psychopathology is that, in some patients suffering from these disorders (especially severe depression), some biochemical disturbance is likely to be involved in the cause of the disorder. However, psychological descriptions of these disorders remain important because even where biological factors are involved in the cause of a disorder, effective treatments may depend on a full assessment of what psychological functioning is impaired.

This chapter will concentrate on **anxiety** and **depression** since these are the most common forms of psychopathology. In each case clinical signs (observations by clinicians) and symptoms (reports by the patient) will be considered first, followed by a discussion of their psychological basis.

Anxiety

Recognizing the symptoms

Anxiety is a normal part of everyday life which serves to warn us of impending dangers. However, many people have fears and anxieties which they realize are out of proportion to the situation. These vary in their intensity and it is only when people find their anxieties are impeding their normal functioning that they come for treatment. Table 9.1 shows the prevalence of some common fears and phobias in the general population compared with (a) fears that people rate as being very intense, (b) fears of people who could be diagnosed as having a clinical phobia but who have not sought psychiatric treatment, and (c) fears in a series of patients with phobias. The 'common fears' are dominated by fears of snakes, heights and storms, and two of these are represented also in the most 'intense' fears. However, of the fears of phobic proportions that exist in the population, illness and injury are most common. In a series of patients with phobia, agoraphobia is the most common, followed by fear of injury and illness, with other fears being relatively uncommon.

Table 9.2 shows main symptoms that occur in anxiety. In a general anxiety state these symptoms would arise in a number of different situations. Although there are several different ways in which anxiety can present in the clinic, there exists a common theme of impending threat and danger. People realize that these thoughts are irrational but nevertheless perceive these dangers and threats as very real.

In chapter 8 the **fear conditioning model** of anxiety was outlined and found to account for the origin and maintenance of some pathological fears. The fear conditioning model has been influential in the development of treatments for anxiety and phobic disorders. Including the range of experiential, behavioural and somatic phenomena helps to elaborate further the way in which fear conditioning affects current functioning.

'Worry' *v* somatic anxiety

Although both the experiential and the somatic components of anxiety affect behaviour, it is sometimes the worry component and sometimes the somatic component that plays the predominant role. For example, in social phobia, if patients go to a social gathering, they will experience recurring

Table 9.1 Prevalence of common fears, intense fears, and phobia: comparison of clinical series of phobic patients

Commons fears/% population		Intense fears/% population		Phobia/% population		Clinical Phobic Series (% of series, n = 50)	
Snakes	39.0	Snakes	25.3	Illness	4.2	Agoraphobia	50
Heights	30.7	Heights	12.0	Injury	1.8	Injury	
Storms	21.1	Flying	10.9	Storms	1.4	Illness	34
Flying	19.8	Enclosures	5.0	Animal	0.8	Death	
Dentist	19.8	Illness	3.3	Agoraphobia	0.7	Crowds	8
Injury	18.2	Death	3.3	Death	0.5	Animal	4
Illness	16.5	Storms	3.1	Crowds	0.5	Heights	2
Death	16.1	Dentists	2.4	Heights		Darkness	2
Enclosures	12.2	Injury	2.3				
Journeys alone	7.4	Journeys alone	1.6				
Being alone	4.4	Being alone	1.0				

(From Agras *et al.* 1969)

Table 9.2 Common symptoms and diagnostic categories of anxiety

---

Symptoms of anxiety
Experiential
1. Mood (anxious, nervous, jittery, tense, restless, 'up tight')
2. Persistent worrying about future events

Behavioural
1. Difficulty falling asleep
2. Fidgeting or inability to sit still

Somatic
1. Sweating, blushing, dizziness, palpitations, shortness of breath
2. Muscular tension or tremor

Phobic disorder
Persistent and recurring irrational fears of a specific object, activity or situation which the subject tends to avoid usually 'unreasonably'. The symptoms are sufficient to lead to impaired functioning.

Agoraphobia	*Social phobia*	*Simple phobia*
Fear of leaving familiar home/setting	Fears of situations involving other people not associated with leaving home	Fear of a single object, e.g. animals— especially reptiles, insects, rodents, birds
Fear of travelling, crowds, closed spaces, stores, heights	Fears of public speaking, blushing, eating in public, writing in front of others, using public lavatories	
Progressive restriction of activities		
Episodes of panic		

(From Spitzer *et al.* 1978)

thoughts of how they will not enjoy themselves, that people will think he is odd, that he is bound to feel embarrassed and have to leave, etc. This 'self talk' itself leads to the symptoms that the person is anticipating and a self-fulfilling prophecy ensues which makes it less likely that the person will decide to accept an invitation next time. A vicious circle operates and the patient becomes more and more isolated.

Chapter 8 provided evidence from laboratory models that phobic fear is irrational. Clinical evidence confirms that it is not sufficient to tell the patient that the situations are not all dangerous and that they have nothing to worry about. Part of the reason for this is that some of these 'danger signals' may not be under conscious control.

Recently psychologists have become more aware of the way in which people can perceive threatening stimuli without actually being consciously aware of those stimuli. This research has used experimental paradigms such as dichotic listening described in Chapter 3. If a person is wearing headphones through which two messages are played, (one in each ear), then instructing the subject to shadow one of the messages (repeating it out loud as soon as they are able) makes them only barely aware of the content of the other message. They can report some general characteristics of the other message (such as whether it was a male or female voice), but it appears that people ignore the content of the non-shadowed message. Despite this, it appears that the brain processes this non-shadowed information to quite a high level.

In an early experiment (Corteen and Wood, 1972) to demonstrate this unconscious awareness of threatening stimuli, subjects in a fear conditioning experiment were presented with one of two lists of 12 nouns, some of which were names of cities. After the presentation of each city name, they received a 1 s mild electric shock. In the test phase of the experiment, subjects were given a dichotic listening task in which they were required to shadow a 600-word passage from a novel in one ear, and ignore a list of words being presented to the other ear (at the rate of 1.6/s). At intervals in the non-shadowed message, 12 critical words were presented: 3 city names which had been paired with shock; 3 new city names which had not been paired with shock; 3 nouns which had appeared in the same list as the shocked city names; and 3 new nouns. Galvanic skin response (i.e. skin conductance) to each of these words was measured. An autonomic response was considered to have occurred if there was a change of at least 1 K ohm within 3 s of the presentation of the word in the non-shadowed message. Figure 9.1 gives the overall percentage of occasions on which such a response was detected for each of the four categories of nouns. It also shows the response levels of control subjects who had undergone no

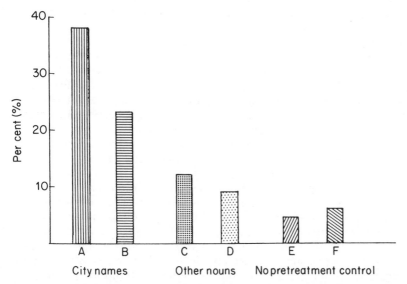

Fig. 9.1 Percentage of occasions on which autonomic responses were detected following presentation of stimuli in unattended channel: City names: (A) Associated with shock; (B) not associated with shock; Other nouns: (C) presented in same list as shocked city names; (D) presented in list with unshocked city names; No pretreatment controls: (E) city names; (F) other nouns.

pretreatment. These controls were included to ensure that subjects did not normally show more autonomic response to city names than other nouns. The results show that, although the subjects were unable to report the occurrence of the city names, they nevertheless showed evidence of autonomic arousal. They also showed autonomic arousal to new names of cities that had not been paired with shock but not to other nouns which had been in the same list as the shocked city names in the fear conditioning phase of the experiment. The investigators concluded that, although the person was not becoming consciously aware of the non-shadowed message, its meaning, rather than just the sound of the message was being analysed.

A similar experiment has been performed with anxious patients (Mathews and MacLeod, 1986). In this case it was not necessary to provide fear conditioning trials prior to the dichotic listening experiment, because there were already sufficient noxious stimuli that could be used in the non-shadowed message (e.g. words like 'embarrassment', 'failure', 'blood', 'cancer'). The study involved assessing performance on a secondary reaction-time task (speed with which a button was pressed when a visual signal occurred) when such threat words were played in the non-shadowed message outside the patient's conscious awareness. It was found that the patients could not report afterwards what the threatening words had been in the non-shadowed message, or even whether the words that had occurred had been threatening. As a further check on whether the patients were consciously aware of the content of the non-shadowed message, they interrupted the message and asked people to report what they had heard in the non-shadowed message. They were unable to do so. Finally, they put the words that people had received in the non-shadowed message together with new words into a recognition task immediately after the dichotic listening experiments. People were unable to recognize the words they had heard in the non-shadowed message above chance level. Nevertheless, when these words were played, the ability of anxious patients to react to a visual stimulus by pressing a button was impaired compared with occasions when neutral words were being played in a non-shadowed message (see Fig. 9.2). In this experiment, then, they found evidence that threatening stimuli could disrupt performance, even though the patients were not consciously aware of the threatening stimuli.

The Mathews and MacLeod study shows that stimuli which through conditioning, acquire fear-eliciting properties can be very subtle indeed. It is not surprising, therefore, that telling patients to exert voluntary control over their emotional responses is ineffectual. However, it may be possible to teach subjects to be more vigilant for thoughts and images that are normally barely conscious but which nevertheless have an anxiety-producing effect. Indeed, this is the basis of some contemporary therapies for anxiety which combine the notions of relaxation and desensitization with teaching the patients to practise becoming aware of their anxious thoughts and making them explicit. This is not easy for patients to do and sometimes considerable practice is needed. Nevertheless it appears to be beneficial because even the act of making these thoughts and images

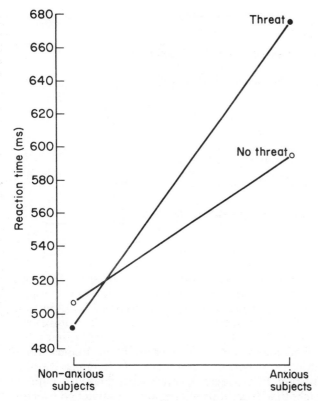

Fig. 9.2 Probe reaction time (ms) for anxious and non-anxious subjects showing effect of threat versus non-threat words in the unattended channel for anxious subjects (Reproduced from Mathews, A. and MacLeod, C. (1986) by permission of The American Psychological Association.)

explicit can sometimes distance the patient from them and make the negative stimuli seem less real and threatening.

Somatic factors: panic attacks

Although the experiential component sometimes predominates over the somatic component, recent research has emphasized how the somatic component may also contribute to the onset of symptoms. This is most clearly seen in the aetiology and treatment of **panic attacks**.

Panic has always been recognized as a feature of some anxiety syndromes, for example, agoraphobia, but more recently some authorities have come to regard it as a diagnostic category in its own right. As can be seen from Table 9.3, there are a number of symptoms which are regularly

Table 9.3   Characteristics of symptoms of panic

Symptoms experienced during a panic attack

1   Shortness of breath (dyspnoea) or smothering sensation
2   Dizziness, unsteady, feelings or faintness
3   Palpitations or accelerated heart rate (tachycardia)
4   Trembling or shaking
5   Sweating
6   Choking
7   Nausea or abdominal distress
8   Depersonalization or derealization
9   Numbness or tingling sensation (paraesthesia)
10   Flushes (hot flushes) or chills
11   Chest pain or discomfort
12   Fear of dying
13   Fear of going crazy or of doing something uncontrolled

(From DSM III-R, 1987)

shown by those who have panic attacks, and one of the most disabling aspects of panic is the general nervousness that people show between attacks. Because when the next panic attack is going to occur is not known, their ability to function effectively at home or work or socially is impaired.

Over the past ten years evidence has accumulated to suggest that many of these symptoms of panic may result from **stress-induced hyperventilation** (defined as breathing in excess of metabolic requirements). Studies have found that the resting PCO_2 level is consistently lower in patients experiencing panic attacks than in groups of age- and sex-matched controls (Salkovskis *et al.*, 1986). Further evidence has suggested that treatment of panic results in the rapid restoration of a patient's PCO_2 to normal levels. As shown in Table 9.3, many of the sensations accompanying panic are the same as those sensations accompanying hyperventilation which are mediated by increased plasma pH. Salkovskis *et al.* (1986) have shown how symptoms of panic are related to hyperventilation. They indicate that although chronic hyperventilation does not in itself produce symptoms, the adaptation of the blood buffering system to chronic hyperventilation results in increased sensitivity to changes in P_aCO_2 such as those produced by stressors and exercise. This means that decreases in P_aCO_2 will result in relatively larger changes in pH and hence more rapid onset of greater intensity of the bodily sensations of hyperventilation. Although many of these symptoms can be related to hyperventilation, it is evident that the patients rarely make this connection. Rather, patients tend to produce 'catastrophic' interpretations of their symptoms. They believe they are about to die or lose control. This vicious circle is illustrated in Figure 9.3.

Explanation to the patient that his symptoms may be due to over-breathing is not sufficient to produce an improvement in symptoms. It is necessary to allow him to demonstrate it to himself. Treatment therefore involves instructing the patients to overbreathe for 1 or 2 minutes until he

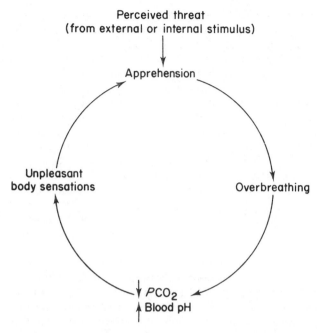

Fig. 9.3 A model of the development of a panic attack. (Reproduced from Clark, D.M., Salkovskis, P.M. and Chalkey, A.J. (1985) by permission of Pergamon Press, Oxford.)

reproduces the symptoms. This demonstration is used as the basis of a reinterpretation of his symptoms in terms of hyperventilation rather than in terms of threatening causes. Patients are taught how to avoid hyperventilation, for example, by using a form of breathing which is relatively slow and shallow and incompatible with hyperventilation. The therapist will also teach patients how to become more aware of their catastrophic thoughts so that they may be examined.

Salkovskis *et al.* (1986) described successful treatment of panic attacks in a renal dialysis patient who was having such attacks towards the end of the period of dialysis. He had begun to experience a number of frightening sensations during the last hour of the dialysis. To him these indicated that some disaster was imminent, that he was close to death. Reassurance had been tried but actually made him worse. Minor tranquillizers had had no effect. The therapist hypothesized that the symptoms which occurred at predictable times might be due to hyperventilation. The patient complained of 'tight feelings' in his head and chest associated with tachycardia, palpitations and paraesthesia. He described difficulty in breathing and was clearly observed to be hyperventilating during these episodes. Analysis of blood gases during this last hour of dialysis as the panic symptoms reached the maximum are shown in Figure 9.4. This was consistent with the hypothesis that the symptoms were due to hyperventilation since the P_aCO_2 levels were dropping markedly during the end of dialysis.

Treatment started with 2 minutes of voluntary hyperventilation away from the dialysis machine. This hyperventilation produced identical symptoms and became the basis of a discussion in which the patient was encouraged to reinterpret his bodily sensations as due to the hyperventilation induced by the stress. He was taught the use of slow, shallow breathing in a pattern which would be incompatible with hyperventilation. He was also taught to become more aware of his catastrophic thoughts, to label them as catastrophic and thereby to allow them gradually to be replaced by more realistic thinking about the causes of his symptoms. The result was a markedly reduced panic frequency. This was difficult to explain on any other basis than the treatment intervention since many other physical and psychological interventions had failed. Figure 9.4 shows that the level of PCO_2 at the end of dialysis following treatment had returned to normal levels.

Finally, it is often useful to make patients' overvigilance towards their bodily state an explicit focus of treatment. Once again, it is insufficient simply to point out to patients that part of their problem is that they are noticing their bodily state to too great an extent. It has to be demonstrated in a similar way as the hyperventilation described above. For example,

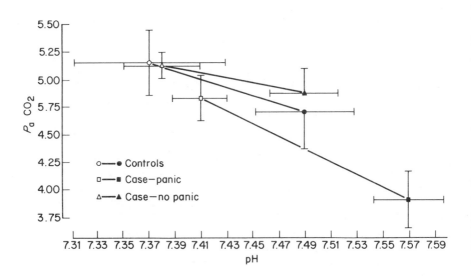

Fig. 9.4 P_aCO_2 (KP_a) and pH at start of a dialysis (open symbols) and end of dialysis (closed symbols). (Reproduced from Salkoviskis, P.M., Warwick H.M.C., Clark, D.M. and Wessels, D.J. (1986) by permission of Pergamon Press, Oxford.)

patients asked to rate their symptoms (e.g. palpitations, dizziness etc.) and then to concentrate on his bodily state for 3 or 4 minutes and re-rate his symptoms for intensity. Generally speaking, symptoms will have increased during this time. There may follow an equivalent period in which he is asked to focus their attention outwards towards the features of the room, describing aloud the colours and shapes and figures in pictures that can be seen. After this, it is often found either that patients' symptoms have subsided or that, while doing the distraction task, they were not so aware of their bodily sensations. In this way, the power of attentional focus can be demonstrated. Clearly, just one demonstration is insufficient and there may have to be several over some days or weeks to reduce the panic symptoms. Nevertheless, this work has shown the way in which both somatic and experiential symptoms can combine to create a very disruptive and threatening syndrome and how, by taking both aspects into account in treatment, the prognosis can be improved (see Clark, 1986).

Depression

Recognizing the symptoms

The central symptom of depression is low mood. Patients may describe this in a variety of ways as depression, sadness, feeling low, hopeless, down in the dumps, not caring any more, or even, irritability. Table 9.4 shows the diagnostic criteria for Major Depression stipulated in the latest Diagnostic and Statistical Manual of the American Psychiatric Association (DSM-III-R, 1987), and it is apparent that a number of symptoms comprise the diagnostic concept. These symptoms constitute sufficient grounds for a diagnosis of Major Depression, provided the criteria for schizophrenia (see Table 9.5) and related disorders have not been fulfilled. Once again, the symptoms specified in DSM-III-R criteria for Major Depression can be divided into experiential, behavioural and somatic types. For example, the definitions of agitation and retardation are made on the basis of what can be observed about the patient rather than what the patient says. Retardation is diagnosed if the patient has slowed speech, pauses excessively before answering, has a low, monotonous rate of speech and has slow bodily movements. Agitation is diagnosed if the person paces, wrings hands, is unable to sit still, or pulls or rubs hair, skin or clothing.

Most clinicians now make the distinction between **bipolar depression** (which alternates with episodes of mania) and **unipolar depression**. But within unipolar depression there has been some controversy over whether there are different subtypes. Some clinicians distinguish between **endogenous** and **reactive** depression. It used to be thought that the endogenous form was caused by a biochemical disturbance, whereas the reactive depression was due to environmental stress. It now appears, however, that the incidence of psychological stressors in the six months prior to the onset of depression is similar in both subtypes (Paykel, 1985); and both subtypes

Table 9.4   Summary of the DSM III-R criteria for major depression*

At least five of the following must be present for a diagnosis of major depression:

1   Depressed mood (or irritable mood in children and adolescents) most of the day, nearly every day, as indicated either by subjective account or observation by others
2   Markedly diminished interest or pleasure in all, or almost all, activities most of the day, nearly every day (as indicated either by subjective account or observation by others of apathy most of the time)
3   Significant weight loss, when not dieting, or weight gain (e.g. more than 5 per cent of body weight in a month), or decrease or increase in appetite nearly every day (in children, consider failure to make expected weight gains)
4   Insomnia or hypersomnia nearly every day
5   Psychomotor agitation or retardation nearly every day (observable by others, not merely subjective feelings of restlessness or being slowed down)
6   Fatigue or loss of energy nearly every day
7   Feelings of worthlessness or excessive or inappropriate guilt (which may be delusional) nearly every day (not merely self-reproach or guilt about being sick)
8   Diminished ability to think or concentrate, or indecisiveness, nearly every day (either by subjective account or as observed by others)
9   Recurrent thoughts of death (not just fear of dying) recurrent suicidal ideation without a specific plan, or a suicide attempt or a specific plan for committing suicide.

* Depressed mood or loss of interest are necessary features; and certain exclusion criteria are stipulated (see DSM III-R, 1987).

Table 9.5   Summary of the DSM III-R criteria for schizophrenia*

Presence of characteristic psychotic symptoms in the active phase either 1, 2 or 3 for at least one week[†] is necessary for a diagnosis of schizophrenia.

1   Two of the following:
   • Delusions
   • Prominent hallucinations
   • Incoherence or marked loosening of associations
   • Catatonic behaviour
   • Flat or grossly inappropriate affect
2   Bizzare delusions (e.g. thought broadcasting, being controlled by a dead person)
3   Prominent hallucinations of a voice with content having no apparent relation to depression or elation, or a voice keeping up a running commentary on the person's behaviour or thoughts, or two or more voices conversing with each other.

* Five types of schizophrenia are distinguished: catatonic, disorganized, paranoid, undifferentiated and residual.
† See DSM III-R (1987) for qualifying criteria.

appear, from family history studies, to have a biological basis. Thus, all depressions are 'endogenous', in the sense of there being biological contributions to aetiology; and all are 'reactive' in the sense of social factors contributing to onset. The 'endogenous symptoms' (see Table 9.4) are associated with more severe depressions. These classificatory issues are discussed in detail by Kendell (1976).

Chapter 8 referred to two psychological models of depression. The **'reduced reward' hypothesis** appeared compatible with what is known of the biogenic amine disruptions in depression, whereas the **'learned helplessness' hypothesis** claimed that it was not simply reduced reward that explained the symptoms of helplessness and depression, but that the perception and expectation of lack of control over the environment was an important mediating factor.

Reduced reward–deficits in social skills in depression

Most clinical interest in the reduced reward hypothesis has focused on whether depressed patients have deficient social skills, and are thereby unable to elicit rewards from others. The observations of Lewinsohn and colleagues (Lewinsohn *et al.*, 1970) showed that depressed patients differed from non-depressed patients in at least five areas: the total amount of verbal behaviour, the number of times the individual initiated behaviour (i.e. was not just reacting to another person), the degree to which the person distributed his or her behaviour equally towards a group of others, the time taken to respond to the behaviour of another, and the rate of positively reinforcing behaviour. However, subsequent research has revealed a paradox. Depressed patients rate themselves (and are rated by others) as being socially deficient. Nevertheless, when attempts are made to quantify precisely what this deficiency might be, the evidence for it is weak. Given that there is only weak evidence of specific skills deficits, the question arises how it is that patients and observers agree that there is something wrong with their social behaviour.

The question has been partly answered in a series of studies on the effect that a depressed person's behaviour has on other people. In one such study (Coyne, 1976), psychologists recorded conversations between an undergraduate and a depressed patient on the telephone. This was compared with conversations between other undergraduates and non-depressed patients. They did not find any difference in the elements of social behaviour exhibited by the depressed patients compared to non-depressed patients (total amount of speech, number of approval responses, number of approval statements, etc.). However, when the undergraduate subjects were asked to rate their own feelings after the telephone conversations, it was found that they felt more depressed, anxious and hostile following the conversations with depressed patients than after the conversations with non-depressed patients. They were also more likely to say that they did not want any future contact with the depressed individuals. When the authors analysed the *content* of the depressed persons' conversation, it was found that the depressed patients spent more time giving personal information about themselves than the non-depressed person; they talked freely of deaths, marital infidelities, hysterectomies, family strife, and so on. In another similar study (Hammen and Peters, 1978), it has been found that, even when the content of a conversation is controlled, the presence of self-blameful statements in the conversation of the depressed patient has an alienating effect on the person to whom they are talking. It appears that the combination of disclosure of personal problems with blame attributed to the self elicits negative reactions from the listener.

This shows that the social skills deficits which act to reduce rewards in depression do not consist of impairments in the elements of social behaviour such as voice volume and gaze. Instead, it appears to be due to the content of the conversation of depressed patients. The depressed patients may therefore be accurate when they say that few people are interested in speaking to them any more, but a modification of the sort of things they are saying to people in conversation is likely to be required in order to increase the probability that the patients will receive rewards from their environment.

Learned helplessness

The original learned helplessness hypothesis (see Chapter 8) was useful in demonstrating clearly that exposure to physical stressors was not sufficient to explain why an organism becomes helpless or depressed; but it soon became clear that even uncontrollable stress was not sufficient to account for human depression. In humans, for stress to induce depression it must be personally significant. Yet one can find many uncontrollable stressors which, although they lead to great sadness (e.g. bereavement), do not lead to the symptoms of long-term depression.

One important element could be that some people are more likely than others to react to the same stress with depression. Since the original learned helplessness model was proposed, it has been reformulated (Abramson *et al.*, 1978) in terms of the predisposition of some people to view stressful events as being caused by certain factors. When a stress occurs, some people appear to attribute the cause to themselves (internal) rather than to other people or circumstances (external); to explain the cause of the stress in terms of factors which are unlikely to change (stable), rather than to changeable factors (unstable). Finally, people may attribute the cause of the stress to factors which affect a great many areas of their lives (global) rather than to factors which have only a restricted relevance (specific). For example, if depressed people fail an examination, they would tend to say that it was because they did not have the necessary ability (an internal, stable attribution) rather than that this particular examination was very difficult (external, unstable). Note that not all internal attributions need be stable. For example, 'lack of effort' is internal but unstable: it can be changed. Furthermore, depressed people might say that it is not just this particular subject at which they are poor, but that they are unsuccessful in exams in general. In this case, he has made a global rather than a specific attribution, and is more likely to conclude that all his attempts to take examinations for the rest of his course will be hopeless. It is not difficult to see that somebody who makes an attribution to internal, stable, and global causes will tend to give up, will become more depressed, and might feel that it is not worth continuing with his education. If he comes to see this particular failure as just one example of the fact that he is a failure as a person, this will further increase his sense of despair and hopelessness about the future (see Peterson and Seligman, 1984 for a review of evidence on attribution style as a vulnerability factor in depression).

Depression and memory bias

Depressive attributional style has been argued to contribute to depression by making a person vulnerable to depressive breakdown. The question arises: What psychological factors are important in maintaining depressions once they occur (even if arising out of biochemical imbalances)? The effect that endogenous changes in mood can have on cognitive performance has recently been investigated more fully: specifically, the possibility that depression, however caused, may reverse the normal tendency to forget unpleasant aspects of the past.

Lloyd and Lishman (1975) studied this reversal in 37 depressed patients who were under 60 years of age and none of whom had received electroconvulsive therapy during the six months before testing. Their technique consisted of measuring, for each patient, the time taken to recall a series of 'real-life personal experiences', some with pleasant, others with unpleasant affective connotations. Memories were elicited in response to a predetermined list of 24 cue words (e.g. table, house, wall, fast) to which patients were instructed to recall either pleasant or unpleasant memories. The ratio of time taken to recall unpleasant memories to the time taken to recall pleasant memories (U/P) was calculated for each patient. Figure 9.5 shows this ratio in relation to the patient's level of depression assessed by a standard self-report questionnaire (the Beck Depression Inventory). The results clearly showed that the more severe the depression the quicker the patient received an unpleasant memory relative to a pleasant memory ($r = -0.67$, df $= 37$).

There are two problems in interpreting these results. First, the more depressed patients may have had more negative experiences in their life and so may have found it relatively easy to retrieve any one of them. Second, the more severely depressed patients may be evaluating their neutral or ambiguous experiences more negatively, thus inflating the number of memories from which to choose. Both of these have been taken account of in two separate research strategies employed by Teasdale and co-workers at Oxford (Teasdale, 1983).

The first strategy involved the use of non-depressed volunteers whose mood had been experimentally manipulated by instructing the subjects to read through depressing or mood elevating self-statements (e.g. "I feel

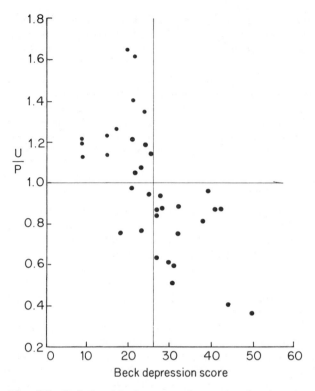

Fig. 9.5 Relationship between depression level and relative speed to retrieve unpleasant (U) and pleasant (P) memories. (Reproduced from Lloyd, G.G. and Lishman, W.A. (1975) by permission of the authors and Cambridge University Press, Cambridge.)

downhearted and miserable"; "I feel so good I almost feel like laughing"). In this case, where normal subjects are randomly allocated to 'elation' or 'depression' conditions, the amount of actual depressive experiences can be assumed to be equal prior to mood induction. The results showed that latencies remember positive or negative personal events were different under the two conditions, though most of this difference was due to differences in recall of positive material between depressed and elated mood rather than speeded recall of negative material (see Fig. 9.6a).

The second strategy employed by Teasdale and colleagues involved the use of clinically depressed individuals selected for the presence of diurnal variation of mood. Patients were given words as cues and asked to respond with the first personal memory which came to mind. The results showed that happy memories were less probable and depressing memories more probable when patients were more depressed. When the same patients were at the less depressed point in their diurnal cycle, this picture was reversed (see Fig. 9.6b). These within-subject results clearly cannot be explained with reference to different frequencies of actual depressive experiences. They have important clinical implications for they indicate how the change in the contents of conscious thoughts which result from mood shifts, however caused, may act to maintain the depression.

The evidence reviewed above has indicated that distortions in thinking which occur in emotionally disturbed patients cannot be changed simply by telling them that they are wrong. New methods of treatment, called

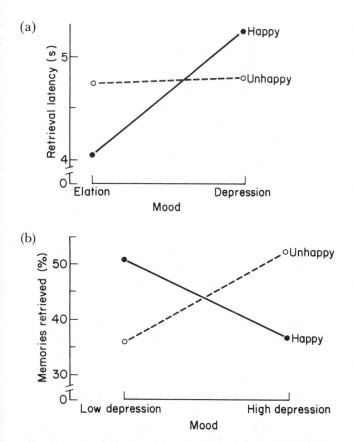

Fig. 9.6 (a) Mean retrieval latencies of pleasant and unpleasant memories in experimentally induced elated and depressed mood. (b) Percentage of memories retrieved that were of positive and negative incidents depending on whether retrieval occurred in the more depressed or less depressed phase of the diurnal cycle. (Reproduced from Teasdale, J.D. (1983) by permission of the author and *Philosophical Transactions of the Royal Society of London*.)

collectively **'cognitive behaviour therapy'**, provide certain procedures for dealing with the negative thoughts, memories and beliefs which play a role in maintaining current depression and rendering the person vulnerable to future episodes. Cognitive techniques aim first at making patients reconceptualize their thoughts and memories as simply thoughts and simply memories (which may have been susceptible to distortion) rather than as reflecting reality. It does this in three ways: 1. by eliciting the patient's thoughts, 'self-talk', and interpretations of events; 2. gathering, with the patient, evidence for or against the interpretation; and 3. setting up 'experiments' (homework) to test out the validity of the interpretations and gather more data for discussion. The major techniques used in cognitive therapy are listed in Table 9.6, together with a brief description of their purpose.

Table 9.6   Five core techniques of cognitive therapy

Technique	Purpose
Thought catching	To teach the patient to become aware of depressing thoughts as they occur
Task assignment	To encourage activities which the patient has been avoiding
Reality testing	To prescribe tasks which involve testing out the veracity of fixed negative thoughts or beliefs
Cognitive rehearsal	To get the patient to recount to the therapist all the stages involved in an activity they have been avoiding, together with the accompanying thoughts and feelings
Alternative therapy	To instruct the patient to imagine an upsetting situation and get them to generate strategies for coping.

Several studies evaluating the effectiveness of cognitive behaviour therapy techniques with depressed patients have now been published (e.g. Teasdale *et al.*, 1984; Murphy *et al.*, 1984). These show that the techniques appear to work as rapidly and as effectively as tricyclic antidepressant medication in both patients with an 'endogenous' symptom pattern as well as those with less severe symptoms (Williams, 1984). They are more costly than drugs because each patient takes an average of 15 hours of therapist time, but it is suitable for those patients who cannot take medication (for example, because of heart problems). Furthermore, there are indications from a number of follow-up studies (e.g. Simons *et al.*, 1986) that the relapse rate following cognitive therapy is significantly lower than that following antidepressant medication. This therapy is thus a good example of how a psychological model of psychopathology can generate effective treatments. Research has not yet established whether there are some techniques which are particularly appropriate for some subtypes of patient and other techniques which are ineffective for some patients. Such research may need to wait until there are good psychological models to characterize subtype differences in depression which will generate differential predictions for remedial work with different aspects of the psychopathology.

The generalization of psychological models of psychopathology

This chapter has concentrated on anxiety and depression, but it is important to realize that a similar psychological approach may be applied to other areas of psychopathology with similar therapeutic implications. For example, 'cognitive rehearsal' can be used in a number of situations in which people find that they cannot easily imagine themselves going into a certain situation or performing a certain activity. Following bereavement, for example, some patients find that even months afterwards when they would like to be able to deal with the person's belongings, they cannot do so. It is possible to remediate this with the approach of guided imagery within therapy. The person first imagines himself going into that situation. Second, the person generates ways of coping with the possible difficulties that might arise. Third, he is instructed to imagine clearly the possible benefits.

The attributional distortions that occur in depression have also been found in those school children who tend persistently to fail at reading or mathematics despite the fact that their level of intelligence should enable them to succeed. Close observation of what these children say to themselves when they find such tasks difficult suggests that they attribute their failure to internal, stable and global factors, for example, that they are 'stupid and incapable'. Attempts to deal with their tendency to give up in the face of difficulty, by giving these children experience of success or increasing their self-esteem, appears not to work. Dweck (1975), has hypothesized that this might be because it did not teach the children how to deal with failure. They suggested that the children be allowed to fail as part of their remedial training so that their maladaptive attributions become explicit and can be changed. They attempted to change children's attributions concerning their experiences of failure: rather than seeing them as evidence for incompetence, they were taught to interpret them as arising from lack of appropriate effort. The results showed that when the children met difficulty again in the real classroom they persisted for longer and were more likely to succeed. This was consistent with their notion that the children had learnt to cope with failure and showed how an attributional account of the children's problems enabled specific, testable predictions about remedial strategies to be made.

Conclusion

At the outset of this chapter the three factors of experiential, behavioural and somatic symptoms were distinguished. This has remained a useful distinction in discussing the problems associated with anxiety and depression. Each factor deserves separate assessment for the management of patients to be matched to the particular pattern of symptoms he shows. Psychological factors are important in determining the onset and course of psychopathology in three ways. First, habitual tendencies to interpret situations in a negative or threatening way can render the person **vulnerable** to stressors, such as a threatening life-event or a physical illness. Second, the psychological factors can act as **precipitants** which augment the level of stress experienced when a negative event occurs. Third, psychological factors appear to contribute to the **maintenance** of emotional disturbance whatever the cause of the initial disturbance. Psychological treatments based on knowledge of underlying psychological processes have contributed much to the alleviation of these conditions.

Suggested reading

Last, C. and Hersen, M. (Eds) (1987). *Handbook of Anxiety Disorders*. Pergamon Press, New York.
This provides an up-to-date account of current psychological approaches to anxiety. See especially the chapter, *Cognitive Approaches* by D.M. Clark and A.T. Beck.

Williams, J.M.G. (1984). *The Psychological Treatment of Depression: A Guide to the Theory and Practice of Cognitive Behaviour Therapy*. Croom Helm, Beckenham, Kent and Free Press, New York.
This book gives more details about models of depression which have been described in this chapter and the range of techniques which have been derived from them.

References

Abramson, L.Y., Seligman, M.E.P. and Teasdale, J.D. (1978). Learned helplessness in humans: critique and reformulation. *Journal of Abnormal Psychology* **87**, 49.

Agras, S., Sylvester, D. and Oliveau, D. (1969). The epidemiology of common fears and phobia. *Comprehensive Psychiatry* **10**, 151.

Clark, D.M. (1986). A cognitive approach to panic. *Behaviour Research and Therapy* **24**, 461.

Clark, D.M., Salkovskis, P.M. and Chalkley, A.J. (1985). Respiratory control as a treatment for panic attacks. *Journal of Behaviour Therapy and Experimental Psychiatry* **16**, 23.

Clark, D.M. and Teasdale, J.D. (1982). Diurnal variation in clinical depression and accessibility of positive and negative experiences. *Journal of Abnormal Psychology* **91**, 87.

Corteen, R.S. and Wood, B. (1972). Autonomic responses to shock-associated words in an unattended channel. *Journal of Experimental Psychology* **94**, 308.

Coyne, J.C. (1976). Depression and the response of others. *Journal of Abnormal Psychology* **85**, 186.

Dweck, C.S. (1975). The roles of expectations and attributions in the alleviation of learned helplessness. *Journal of Personality and Social Psychology* **31**, 678.

Hammen, C.L. and Peters, S.D. (1978). Interpersonal consequences of depression: responses to men and women enacting a depressed patient. *Journal of Abnormal Psychology* **87**, 323.

Kendell, R.E. (1976). The classification of depressions: a review of contemporary confusion. *British Journal of Psychiatry* **139**, 265.

Lewinsohn, P.M., Munoz, R.S., Youngren, M.A. and Zeiss, A.M. (1978). *Control Your Depression*. Prentice Hall, New York.

Lloyd, G.G. and Lishman, W.A. (1975). Effect of depression on the speed of recall of pleasant and unpleasant experiences. *Psychological Medicine* **5**, 173.

Mathews, A. and MacLeod, C. (1986). Discrimination of threat cues without awareness in anxiety states. *Journal of Abnormal Psychology* **95**, 131.

Murphy, G.E., Simons, A.D., Wetzel, R.D. and Lustman, P.J. (1984). Cognitive therapy and pharmacotherapy. *Archives of General Psychiatry* **41**, 33.

Paykel, E.S. (1985). Life-events, social support and psychiatric disorder. In *Social Support: Theory, Research and Applications*, pp. 321–347. Edited by Sarason, I.G. and Sarason, B.R. Martinus Nijhoff, The Hague.

Peterson, C. and Seligman, M.E. (1984). Causal explanation as a risk factor for depression: Theory and evidence. *Psychological Review* **91**, 347.

Salkovskis, P.M., Warwick, H.M.C., Clark, D.M. and Wessels, D.J. (1986). A demonstration of acute hyperventilation during naturally occurring panic attacks. *Behaviour Research and Therapy* **24**, 91.

Simons, A.D., Murphy, G.E., Levine, J.L. and Wetzel, R.D. (1986). Cognitive therapy and pharmacotherapy for depression. *Archives of General Psychiatry* **43**, 43.

Spitzer, R.C., Endicott, J. and Robins, E. (1978). *Research Diagnosis Criteria (RDC) for a Selected Group of Functional Disorders*, 3rd Edition, New York State Psychiatric Institute, Biometrics Research, New York.

Teasdale, J.D. (1983). Affect and accessibility. *Philosophical Transactions of the Royal Society of London* **302**, 403.

Teasdale, J.D., Fennell, M.J.V., Hibbert, G.A. and Amies, P.L. (1984). Cognitive therapy for major depressive disorder in primary care. *British Journal of Psychiatry* **144**, 400.

10

Psychological Antecedents and Consequences of Physical Illness

PJ Cooper

Current thinking about the role of psychological factors in physical illness has been strongly influenced by a body of theory and practice known as **psychosomatic medicine**. This field was developed largely by clinicians with a psychoanalytic orientation, notably Flanders Dunbar who founded the American Psychosomatic Society, and Franz Alexander. The central theme of the traditional psychosomatic position is that psychological factors, in particular emotional conflicts, play an important role in causing the onset of certain physical illnesses, and that once such illnesses are present, psychological factors contribute to their persistence or to relapse. Alexander proposed that there were only seven psychosomatic diseases: bronchial asthma, rheumatoid arthritis, ulcerative colitis, essential hypertension, neurodermatitis, thyrotoxicosis, and peptic ulcer.

Certain central tenets can be distilled from psychosomatic theory. These have been summarized as follows (Gelder *et al.*, 1985):

- A particular emotional disturbance or conflict can evoke a particular form of physical pathology

- A characteristic personality type is associated with a particular form of physical pathology

- Certain physical disorders are commonly preceded by stressful events

- Physical improvement occurs in response to psychological improvement in psychosomatic disorders

- Particular organs or systems in a particular individual are especially vulnerable and liable to manifest disturbance in response to stress.

Although the ideas of psychosomatic medicine were taken up enthusiastically by some—especially in North America—there were many problems with their application to clinical practice. For example, despite considerable research endeavour it proved difficult to establish an association between personality type and disease. Thus, the postulated association between an egocentric, impulsive and affection-seeking personality and bronchial asthma proved problematic to demonstrate. Also, psychosomatic illnesses did not appear to be associated with a specific stress or emotional upheaval to any greater extent than illnesses not considered psychosomatic. Furthermore, although there were numerous reports of patients' illnesses improving or resolving in response to psychological treatment, it could not be demonstrated that recovery was as a result of the psychological intervention.

There are a several reasons why the research arising from the ideas of the traditional psychosomatic position has been so inconclusive. First, the emphasis on particular kinds of unconscious mental processes, for which there are no reliable measures, has rendered much of the theory untestable. For example, Engel, a prolific writer in this field, argued that the symptoms of ulcerative colitis become manifest when a patient attempts to defend himself against feelings of hopelessness and helplessness 'as a result of real, threatened or fancied loss'. However, since there are no generally accepted ways of establishing the presence of these defence mechanisms the postulate that they are present in a given situation is essentially untestable. The second major problem concerns the inadequacy of the research methods used. These weaknesses relate to inadequate sampling procedures, lack of appropriate controls, unstandardized and subjective methods of assessment and, above all, an almost total reliance upon retrospective research designs. Thus, in 1955 Engel reported a study in which he reviewed over 700 patients with ulcerative colitis concluding from clinical observation that their illness was associated with particular deficits in personality, notably 'dependent and restricted relationships with other people' and 'a failure to achieve full heterosexual adjustment'. However, no attempt was made to define operationally the meaning of these terms, no effort was made to determine whether a similar level of disturbance might not be present to an equivalent extent in patients with other similarly debilitating disorders, and the possibility that certain characteristics like dependency might be a consequence of a severely handicapping illness was not given serious consideration. The psychosomatic literature is replete with largely uninterpretable studies of this kind.

There is another objection to the traditional psychosomatic approach which is of a more general nature. The idea that psychological factors are of particular aetiological relevance to only a limited subset of physical illnesses has been questioned. Instead, it has come to be accepted that psychological factors are important in a wide range of disorders. Also, whilst the traditional psychosomatic approach concentrated on the aetiological role of psychological factors, it has become clear that such factors are also of relevance to other aspects of illness, such as to the presentation of symptoms, the course of illnesses, patients' responses and reactions to disease and to treatment, and so on. Two of these points of contact between psychological factors and physical illness will be considered in the remainder of this chapter: namely, psychological antecedents of physical illness and psychological consequences of physical illness.

Psychological antecedents of physical illness

Personality

The notion of **personality** refers to individuals' predisposition to behave in certain characteristic ways; and the idea that particular personality types are vulnerable to certain illnesses is central to the traditional psychosomatic view. Despite the disquiet with this general view, the idea that personality may be an aetiological factor in illness has received more serious consideration in recent years because of its apparent role in cardiovascular disease. The search for aetiological factors in coronary heart disease has been particularly intense because it is such a major cause of death amongst middle-aged men and the causative factors which have been established are collectively of somewhat limited predictive value.

In order to appreciate what one might expect of a psychological aetiological agent, it is worth examining briefly the influence that other factors are known to have. In 1978, data were published from the Pooling Project: the combined results from five longitudinal studies of coronary heart disease in middle-aged men. Over 8 000 men were followed up for an average of 8.6 years, and 650 originally disease-free men suffered myocardial infarction or sudden cardiac death. The role of the three classic risk factors of blood pressure, serum cholesterol and smoking are shown in Table 10.1. Their influence is expressed in terms of **relative risk**, that is,

Table 10.1 Relative risk of coronary heart disease for the three classic risk factors (highest versus lowest quintile)

	Relative risk
Systolic blood pressure	2.10
Serum cholesterol	2.19
Smoking	3.39

(From the Pooling Project, 1978)

the extent to which the presence of the factor raises the chances of having the disease (Table 10.2). It can be seen that the independent effect of these factors is to raise the chances of coronary heart disease considerably. If the population is divided into quintiles of combined risk for blood pressure, serum cholesterol and smoking, those in the highest quintile were more than six times more likely than those in the lowest quintile to suffer coronary heart disease. These essential findings have been found to be highly reliable.

Nearly 30 years ago Friedman and Rosenman (1959) described a behaviour pattern, **Type A behaviour**, which, they argued, increased

Table 10.2   The calculation of relative risk

$$\text{Relative risk} = \frac{\text{number with disease with factor} \times \text{number without disease without factor}}{\text{number with disease without factor} \times \text{number without disease with factor}}$$

i.e.

	Disease	No disease
Factor	a	b
No factor	c	d

$$\text{Relative risk} = \frac{a \times d}{b \times c}$$

= 1 if there is no association between the disease and the factor

vulnerability to coronary heart disease. They maintained that the core components of this pattern are extreme competitiveness, a striving for achievement and a sense of time pressure, together with aggressiveness and hostility. There have now been numerous retrospective and some prospective studies investigating the possible role of Type A behaviour in the aetiology of coronary heart disease. The most compelling evidence for an association comes from a prospective study carried out in California, the so-called Western Collaborative Group Study (Rosenman *et al.*, 1975). The presence of Type A behaviour was assessed by means of a reliable standardized interview conducted on over 3 000 employed middle-aged men who were followed-up for eight and a half years. During this time, 257 developed coronary heart disease. The data were analysed separately for a younger (39–49 years) and older (50–59 years) group. For both groups, the rate of coronary heart disease was roughly twice as high amongst Type A as the remainder, independent of the other three classic risk factors. Figure 10.1 illustrates how Type A behaviour added to the other factors in raising the risk of disease. It is apparent that Type A behaviour adds considerably to the risk of coronary heart disease; and it appears that, at least in older men, this increment is greater the higher the risk in terms of the other classic factors.

Several studies have broadly confirmed the findings of the Western Collaborative Group, notably two separate prospective studies conducted in Framingham, USA (Haynes *et al.*, 1980) and in Europe (French–Belgian Collaborative Group, 1982), although there are difficulties comparing results because of differing methods of assessing Type A behaviour. The characteristic constellation of such forms of behaviour appears to be a Western phenomenon, fostered by the material and social rewards of occupational success, and therefore is not as universal as the standard risk factors (Marmot, 1987). Nevertheless, it appears to make a significant

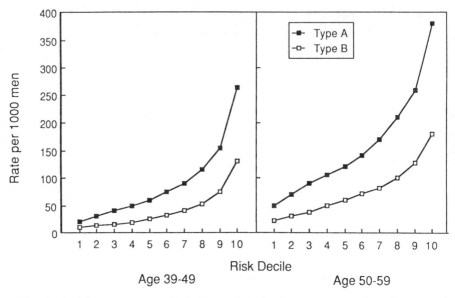

Fig. 10.1 The extent to which Type A behaviour pattern raises the risk of coronary heart disease. (Reproduced from Brand *et al.* (1976) by permission of American Heart Association, Dallas.)

contribution to the rate of morbidity from coronary heart disease in western countries.

Preliminary evidence suggests that modifying Type A behaviour in people at risk for coronary heart disease has a significant impact on the rate of morbidity and mortality. The strongest evidence for this comes from a major study conducted in California (Friedman *et al.*, 1982; Thoreson *et al.*, 1982). A large group of patients, all of whom had had at least one myocardial infarction, were assigned to one of two groups. One group received standard cardiological care including group counselling sessions in which patients were advised about diet, exercise and medication. The other group, in addition to standard cardiological care, received a treatment designed to develop an awareness of the effects of Type A behaviour on their lives and to assist the patients in altering relevant behaviour. The therapeutic techniques used were essentially 'cognitive-behavioural' in nature of the sort developed for the treatment of depression (see Chapter 9). The main techniques used are listed in Table 10.3. Differences in clinical outcome between the two treatment groups were apparent after a year; and after three years, the reinfarction rate was twice as high in the group who received standard care compared with the group who received the Type A treatment (i.e. 14.6 per cent compared with 7.9 per cent). The latter group also showed significant changes in Type A behaviour.

The concept of Type A behaviour refers to a complex amalgam of

Table 10.3 Main treatment techniques used in modifying Type A behaviour

Self-monitoring	Keeping detailed records of relevant behaviour
Self-reinforcement	Arranging definite rewards for specific changes in behaviour
Behavioural rehearsal	Demonstrating appropriate behaviour
Behavioural contracting	Making a commitment to perform certain tasks
Environmental restructuring	Re-arranging aspects of the physical environment to maximize the probability of effecting change
Cognitive restructuring	Altering dysfunctional styles of thinking

responses to situations, and it is therefore unclear which particular features of this behaviour pattern are pathogenic. It is also unclear how Type A behaviour is translated into coronary pathology. Although Type A scores have been found to be correlated with a degree of stenosis (Zyzanski *et al.*, 1976), there have been several negative angiographic studies and there are no compelling data linking Type A status to any long-term pathogenic process, such as the development of coronary atherosclerosis. Blood pressure reactivity is the most promising candidate for the mechanism whereby Type A behaviour is translated into cardiac pathology. A number of studies on healthy adults reviewed by Steptoe (1981) have found that, compared with non-Type A men, Type A men respond with greater increases in systolic blood pressure under conditions of competitiveness. Although Type A and essential hypertension are unrelated and hence independent risk factors for coronary heart disease, it is possible, as Steptoe notes, that similar physiological processes are implicated in the development of essential hypertension and in the occurrence of coronary heart disease in people displaying Type A behaviour.

A recent review (Booth-Hewley and Friedman, 1987) of the research into the relationship between psychological factors and coronary heart disease, in which the results from a number of studies were combined, has somewhat broadened this question. In addition to anger and hostility which contribute to the Type A behaviour pattern, other emotions, particularly depression, appear also to be predictive of heart disease. This raises some doubt about the specificity of a coronary-prone personality on the one hand but adds to the general view that personality and illness are related.

The literature documenting an association between particular personality characteristics and the development of **cancer** (Greer, 1983) is in some respects similar to that on Type A behaviour and coronary heart disease. The constellation of personality features which have been reported as significant are an affective style involving suppression of affect, especially aggression, and avoidance of conflict. This affective style has been related to a variety of tumours including breast (Wirsching *et al.*, 1982), gynaecological (Mastrovito *et al.*, 1979) and lung tumours (Grossarth-Maticek *et al.*, 1985). Unfortunately, most of the research has been methodologically weak, and the absence of a reliable standardized procedure for assessing the key personality variables is particularly problematic. Nevertheless, as Dorian and Garfinkel (1987) note, the consistency of the findings across investigations is striking. The most impressive results came from the Yugoslav Prospective Study (Grossarth-Maticek *et al.*, 1985). They selected for inclusion in the study the oldest disease-free inhabitant of every second house of an industrial town, Crvenka, comprising some 14 000 inhabitants. Subjects were interviewed using a 109-item psychosocial questionnaire and certain physical measurements made. A ten-year follow-up of this sample was conducted and deaths from different causes, including various cancers, were related to the initial psychosocial measures. As can be seen from Figure 10.2, there was a reliable association between the personality construct of 'rational and anti-emotional behaviour' and the incidence of cancer. Similar findings have emerged from a number of other studies (see Greer, 1983).

There is some evidence that psychological factors also influence the course of cancer. In one carefully conducted study (Greer *et al.*, 1979) patients' psychological response to their breast cancer was assessed three months after mastectomy. The patients were assigned to four broad categories: 'stoic acceptance' where patients acknowledged the diagnosis without seeking further information; 'denial' which involved an active

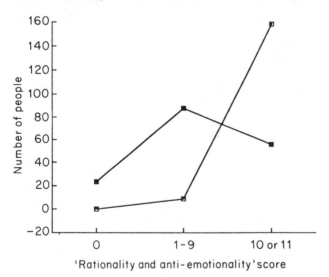

Fig. 10.2 A comparison between the expected rate of cancer (closed symbol) if there were no association with 'rationality and anti-emotionality' and the observed rate (open symbols). (From Grossarth-Maticek *et al.*, 1985.)

rejection of any evidence concerning the seriousness of the diagnosis; 'fighting spirit' where patients adopted a highly positive and optimistic attitude; and 'helplessness/hopelessness' where patients demonstrated extreme emotional distress about their illness and a total preoccupation with their diagnosis. It was found that the outcome after five years was significantly related to these categories. Survival without recurrence of the malignancy was reliably associated with an attitude of denial or having a fighting spirit: 75 per cent of those in these two groups had a favourable outcome as compared with 35 per cent of those in the other two groups. Similar findings have been reported by other researchers (e.g. Derogatis *et al.*, 1979).

Environmental stress

Although animal research has demonstrated a clear association between stress and illness (see Chapter 8), the question of whether environmental stress is pathogenic in humans has proved difficult to investigate. There is, however, good evidence that major traumatic events and circumstances are associated with increased morbidity. An example of such an association was provided in a classic epidemiological study reported by Reid (1948) on so-called 'flying stress' amongst World War II pilots. 'Flying stress' was a condition characterized by attacks of extreme anxiety, thought to be caused by a combination of exposure to cold and anoxia resulting from long periods of flying. However, by comparing the rate of flying stress amongst different combat units it became apparent that these factors were not relevant. There was no association, for example, between the rate of illness and the number of flying hours or the length of time on combat duty. Instead, there was a strong relationship between the incidence of disorder and both the intensity of the air war and the mortality rate. Flying stress was thus a psychological reaction to a situation of extreme environmental stress and personal danger.

The example of flying stress is an instance of stress being causally related to the onset of psychological rather than physical disorder. There is now a considerable body of sophisticated research on this association between stress and psychiatric disorder, particularly in relation to depression (see Paykel, 1985 for a review of this work). For example, the rate of adverse life-events before the onset of the depression in hospital patients has been found to be seven times greater amongst the cases than amongst controls (Brown and Harris, 1978); and amongst a sample of cases identified in the community, the rate is ten times greater than amongst controls (Brown and Prudo, 1981).

An association between adverse social events or circumstances and physical disorder has been less easy to demonstrate. In an early study, Rahe *et al.* (1970) conducted one of the few prospective investigations in this area and did demonstrate a small but significant effect of stress on the development of illness. They devised a self-report questionnaire, the **Social Readjustment Scale** (Holmes and Rahe, 1967), which comprised 43 occurrences of events each of which would require 'some adaptive or coping behaviour'. Each event was given a weighted score representing the degree of social readjustment it would require. These weighted scores were derived by consensus: a large group of randomly selected people were asked to score each event in terms of an arbitrary score given to one event. Table 10.4 lists some of these events together with their weighted scores. The researchers administered this questionnaire to 2 500 American naval personnel before they departed on a six month cruise. On their return, their health records were reviewed and the number of illness episodes was recorded. Figure 10.3 shows the relationship between the number of illness episodes and the score on the questionnaire divided into 10 segments. It is apparent that the greater the score on the Social Readjustment Scale the greater the number of illnesses. However, the actual correlation between these two variables, whilst statistically significant, was rather small ($r = 0.12$), which is a consistent finding in similar studies.

Table 10.4   Weighted scores of selected items from the social readjustment scale

Rank	Life-event	Mean value
1	Death of spouse	100
2	Divorce	73
3	Marital separation	65
4	Gaol term	63
.		
7	Marriage	50
.		
12	Pregnancy	40
.		
23	Child leaving home	29
.		
27	Begin or end school	26
.		
43	Minor violation of the law	11

Clearly, an examination of the relationship between an undifferentiated stress index and undifferentiated illness is most unlikely to reveal anything other than a modest positive correlation. To understand what such an association might mean it is necessary to consider the various ways in which stress and disease might be related. Craig and Brown (1984) described various ways in which such an association might operate. As noted earlier, somatic symptoms, such as muscle tension, can arise as a symptom of an affective disorder. The term 'masked depression' is sometimes used for affective disorder which is presented as a physical problem. In so far as the onset of the affective disorder is likely to be associated with adverse events

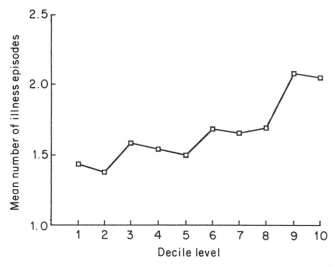

Fig. 10.3 Mean number of illness episodes for 10 groups stratified by their score on the Social Readjustment Scale. (From Rahe *et al.*, 1970.)

or circumstances, the somatic symptoms can be regarded as caused by environmental stress.

Evidence for a relationship between affective disorder and physical symptoms of no known organic basis (functional disorder) has been provided by Creed (1981) in an elegant study of stress in patients presenting with acute appendicitis. One hundred and nineteen patients admitted for emergency appendicectomy were interviewed a few days after surgery and the occurrence of stressful life-events and difficulties in the preceding year as recorded. These events were rated by independent assessors who were blind to the histological report on a four-point scale of 'contextual threat'.

On the basis of histological examination patients were classified as those with definite inflammation of the appendix or those with minimal or no inflammation.

As can be seen from Figure 10.4, in the 38 weeks before the onset of pain, 25 per cent of those with definite inflammation had experienced a severely threatening life-event which is similar to the rate of the normal control group. By contrast, amongst the group whose appendix was not acutely inflamed, 59 per cent had experienced a severely threatening event. Furthermore, the rate of psychiatric symptoms in this latter group was twice as high as in the inflamed appendix group. Creed concluded that the abdominal symptoms in the non-inflamed group may have been preceded by depression which led to the complaint of pain. A similar process may operate for other functional conditions such as some cases of reported menorrhagia.

Social adversity might also lead directly to physical illness. There is little

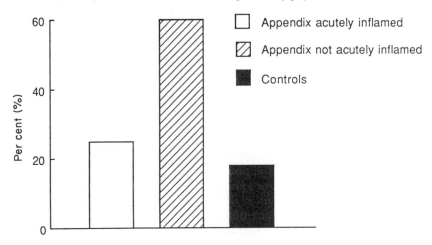

Fig. 10.4　The rate of severely threatening life-events amongst patients receiving appendicectomy. (Reproduced from Creed, F. (1981) by permission of the author and *The Lancet*.)

firm evidence to support such a direct link between environmental stress and organic disease, but a few studies do suggest such an association. In a classic early investigation, Meyer and Haggerty (1962) studied streptococcal throat infection over the course of a year in 16 families comprising 100 people. Throat cultures were made on all family members every three weeks and at times of illness; and the parents kept a diary of events occurring during the course of the study. It was found that streptococcol acquisition and illness were four times more likely to have been preceded by a period of acute stress than to be followed by one. Indeed, the relative risk of infection following a family upset or tension was raised by a factor of 12.6. Craig and Brown note that this demonstration of onset of illness following emotional upheaval within a matter of a week or two parallels the findings with the onset of florid symptoms in patients with schizophrenia. There is some indication that this relationship also obtains for myocardial infarction. Connolly (1976) found that, compared with controls, more of these patients reported experiencing a life-event in the few weeks prior to infarct.

Psychiatric illness

Psychiatric patients have an increased mortality rate compared with the rest of the population. Sims (1978) reviewed a number of studies and concluded that there was a two-fold increase in mortality for psychiatric outpatients and a two to three-fold increase for psychiatric inpatients. In some studies (e.g. Eastwood *et al.*, 1982) this effect was entirely accounted for by suicide and accidental death. However, other studies have found the raised rate of deaths to be due to specific illnesses, such as diseases of the circulatory and nervous systems in men and cancer in women (Rorsman, 1974). Sims and Prior (1978) found the increased mortality among psychiatric patients attributable to respiratory, cardiovascular and neurological disease.

Much of the association between psychiatric illness and morbidity and mortality is likely to be explained by such variables as smoking, alcohol, obesity and the poor utilization of social and medical resources. A clear example of such a mediation effect has been found in patients with advanced liver disease. In one study such patients were found to have a significantly higher rate of psychiatric disorder than those with other hepatic pathology, and in nearly half the patients the psychiatric disorder had preceded the onset of heavy drinking. Such mediating factors do not appear to explain all the association between psychiatric disorder and physical morbidity, and it has been suggested that one possible explanation for this finding is that positive mental health may act to retard the inevitable physical decline that comes with age (Vaillant, 1979). As noted above, in so far as social adversity is implicated in the onset of psychiatric disorders, the raised morbidity amongst psychiatric patients suggests an indirect causal link between stress and physical illness.

In addition to psychiatric disorder acting as an antecedent to physical illness, these two types of disorder are also associated in another way. There are a number of instances in which frank psychiatric disorder presents with a complaint of a physical symptom. Depression in the elderly, for example, frequently presents with complaints about a new physical symptom or about the exacerbation of pre-existing minor physical problems. A similar presentation sometimes arises after a bereavement. A more striking example of psychiatric disorder presenting as a physical symptom is in so-called **'monosymptomatic hypochondriacal psychosis'** (Munro, 1980). Patients suffering from this disorder believe with delusional conviction that they are suffering from an illness. A typical example is a patient who presents complaining of a particular part of their body being infested by insects. These patients are not reassured by the negative findings of clinical investigations. Table 10.5 shows a summary of the conditions which can be considered part of this complex of disorders. They are grouped under two headings: **coenaesthopathia**, where there is an exaggeration or distortion of real proprioceptive, kinaesthetic or haptic sensation; and those involving a **disturbance of body image** of some form. The frequency of monosymptomatic hypochondriacal psychosis is unknown. Psychiatrists do not see many cases; but these patients are a familiar group to dermatologists, venerealogists and plastic surgeons. They are also well known to pest control agencies. In terms of psychiatric nosology, the condition is usually regarded as a variant of schizophrenia of the paranoid kind; and it responds to treatment with neuroleptic drugs.

There are a number of physical symptoms which suggest the presence of an underlying psychological disorder. A patient complaining of tiredness, sleep disturbance and anergia could well be suffering from a depressive illness. Similarly, patients reporting palpitations, dyspnoea, and diarrhoea

Table 10.5 Main modes of presentation of monosymptomatic hypochon-driacal psychosis

Coenaesthopathia
1   Delusions of skin infection
2   Delusions of internal parasitosis
3   Delusions that there are lumps or small seed-like objects under the skin
Body Image Distortion
4   Dysmorphophobic delusions
5   Olfactory delusions
6   'Phantom Bite'
7   Delusional body-image disturbance in anorexia nervosa
8   Hypochondriacal delusional quality in chronic pain

(From Munro, 1980)

might have an anxiety disorder. There are also some less obvious examples. Patients with the eating disorders anorexia nervosa and bulimia nervosa frequently present to their general practitioner with physical complications of their disturbed behaviour without explicitly declaring their eating disorder. For example, amenorrhoea could be a result of self-induced weight loss or disturbed carbohydrate intake; tetany and dizziness could be due to hypokalaemia from frequent vomiting or laxative abuse; and parotid gland swelling could be caused by episodes of bulimia. It is only by being aware of the secondary physical complications of psychiatric disorders that a clinician can arrive at the appropriate diagnosis and treatment.

The special case of hysteria

Despite persistent disquiet about its reference, the term **hysteria** has survived its critics. It is a term which has been used rather widely for a number of rather loosely related clinical phenomena. Thus, the outbreak of hyperventilation among Lancashire school girls described by Moss and McEvedy (1966) and frequently cited as an example of 'mass hysteria', is more properly considered as a state in which suggestibility and shared apprehension play a key role in producing anxiety. Similarly, the pattern of responses often termed **'hysterical personality'** is more properly described as histrionic; and, although the constellation of characteristics to which it refers (attention seeking, demanding behaviour with theatrical or dramatic self-presentation) is common among those who develop hysterical symptoms, the majority of those with these characteristics never develop such symptoms (Kendell, 1983).

The essence of hysteria is that symptoms and signs of organic disease arise in the absence of physical pathology, and that these symptoms result, in some sense, from the workings of a system of unconscious desires and intentions. Two main varieties of hysteria can be distinguished: **dissociative reactions** and **conversion hysteria**. Dissociative reactions, first described by Pierre Janet towards the end of the nineteenth century, involve a disturbed sense of personal identity or a restriction of conscious awareness of disturbing events or circumstances—including fugue and trance states, hysterical amnesia and multiple personality. Conversion hysteria was first conceived of as a purely psychological disorder by Breuer and Freud in their classic *Studies on Hysteria* (1896). The term conversion hysteria is applied to disturbances of motor or sensory functioning in the absence of a demonstrable neurological lesion. The motor symptoms include a paralysis of voluntary muscles, tremor, tics, disorders of gait and aphonia. Sensory symptoms include disturbances of cutaneous sensation and pain as well as blindness and, occasionally deafness. As noted by Kendell (1983), the disabilities tend to correspond to lay concepts of dysfunction rather than to anatomical and physiological reality: in hysterical aphonia, the otherwise mute patient may be able to enunciate perfectly in a whisper; and limb anaesthesia has a 'glove and stocking' distribution, selectively affecting the extremities.

The concept of hysteria rests on the *exclusion* of physical pathology and this leads to problems with its reliability. These were highlighted in a classic study by Slater and Glithero (1965) who conducted a nine-year follow-up of 85 patients intensively investigated in a neurological hospital and diagnosed as suffering from hysteria. Many had died, probably from disorders the symptoms of which were originally regarded as hysterical; in most, the 'hysterical' symptoms had come to be recognized as symptoms of an organic illness; and only 33 of the patients remained with no significant organic disease. With further exclusions (i.e. those who developed other psychiatric disorders or committed suicide), only a quarter retained their original diagnosis of hysteria. Unsurprisingly, Slater (1965) has argued strongly for the abandonment of the concept of hysteria. Whilst many disagree with him, it is now widely accepted that if such a diagnosis is made it has to be regarded as provisional.

Kendell (1983) has provided a framework for understanding hysterical symptoms in terms of the 'sick role' these people adopt and the illness behaviour they exhibit (Fig. 10.5). According to this view, hysterical symptoms confer on the individual particular social advantages. Being ill exempts one from many social responsibilities and earns one a multitude of privileges. People who exhibit symptoms when life becomes too demanding for them should not be regarded as malingering, but rather as having learnt that having the symptoms provides an escape from particular demands and pressures as well as certain rewards the sick role confers. This view is consistent with both the common finding that many of these patients appear unconcerned about the serious nature of their symptoms ('belle indifference'), and the observation that there is a meaningful connection between the particular symptom and particular stressors. It follows from this account that recovery is dictated by a shift in the balance between the advantages of having the symptoms and the disadvantages of being sufficiently well to have to cope with the world. Kendell's account provides a conceptual framework for understanding hysterical symptoms which has the merit of not resorting to a 'Systems Unconscious' whilst

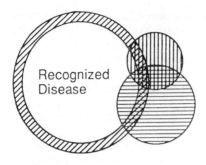

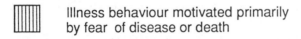

Illness behaviour motivated primarily
by fear of disease or death

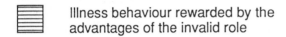

Illness behaviour rewarded by the
advantages of the invalid role

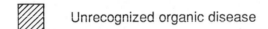

Unrecognized organic disease

Fig. 10.5 A classificatory scheme for illness behaviour. (Reproduced from Kendell, R.E. (1983) by permission of Cambridge University Press, Cambridge.)

providing a coherent and humane approach to the management of the condition. It must be added that the account accommodates dissociative phenomena rather less easily than conversion symptoms.

Psychological consequences of physical illness

Physical illness can be regarded as a special class of adverse life event with a greater or lesser degree of threat or negative impact. As such, it is hardly surprising that it can lead to significant psychological problems. All illnesses demand some adjustment and, although most people manage this process perfectly adequately in most cases, there are circumstances where the necessary adjustment is not managed well. The term often used to describe the strategies that people adopt in the face of stress is **coping.** Coping responses have been divided into four main types: denial, vigilance, avoidance and tackling. The way in which illness is perceived and dealt with is related to aspects of the patient's personality and in particular to their style of coping with stress, to the nature of the illness itself, and to the social context in which the illness has occurred.

One way in which some individuals attempt to deal with the threatening implications of physical illness is, as noted above, by **denial.** This refers to a range of strategies which involve attempts to minimize the severity of the illness or the implications of the disease. While it is clear that some degree of denial may protect patients from being overwhelmed by depression or anxiety, it may also be maladaptive if it either prevents people from making a realistic assessment of their symptoms and seeking medical help, or leads them to disregard medical advice. For example, Greer (1974) found that in women who delayed seeking treatment for breast disease, denial was a habitual coping strategy. On the other hand, a number of studies have provided support for the notion that denial can also be a highly adaptive strategy: these studies have demonstrated that, compared with others, those judged to be 'deniers' had a better adjustment to their illness and long-term outcome. The study discussed earlier of breast cancer patients (Greer *et al.*, 1979) clearly demonstrated this effect. Essentially similar findings have been reported in relation to survivors of myocardial infarction (Stern *et al.*, 1976).

Organic causes of psychological symptoms

Many physical illnesses directly induce psychological symptoms; and many drugs used to treat physical illnesses have adverse psychological sequelae. Table 10.6 (from Gelder *et al.*, 1985) contains a list of some common psychological symptoms together with some of the physical disorders which can produce them. All these psychological symptoms also commonly occur in patients presenting with primary psychiatric disorder in the absence of physical illness. Thus, just as it is essential for the practitioner of physical medicine to be aware of the possibility that physical symptoms might suggest the presence of a psychological disorder, the practitioner of psychological medicine must be equally vigilant about the possibility of psychological symptoms suggesting the presence of physical illness.

Affective disorders

It is common for patients to react to physical illness by becoming depressed or anxious. Thus, in a study of patients who had suffered an acute myocardial infarction a week earlier, Lloyd and Cawley (1983) found that a fifth had developed significant psychological symptoms. The nature of these symptoms was closely related to the illness and the implications it would have for their future. Such emotional reactions, classed in psychiatric terms as 'adjustment disorders' (DSM III-R, 1987), tend to consist of mild transitory symptoms. Thus, in the study by Lloyd and Cawley, the great majority of those with emotional problems in the week after infarct were not found to be suffering from a psychiatric disorder when reassessed four months later.

Affective symptoms which are more severe than those found in adjustment disorders and which persist for longer satisfy criteria for a diagnosis

Table 10.6   Some organic causes of common psychiatric symptoms

Depression	Drug side-effects, carcinoma, infections, neurological disorders including dementias, diabetes, thyroid disorders, Addison's disease, SLE
Anxiety	Hyperthyroidism, hyperventilation, phaeochromocytoma, hypoglycaemia, neurological disorders, drug withdrawal
Fatigue	Anaemia, drug side-effects, sleep disorders, chronic infection, diabetes, hypothyroidism, Addison's disease, carcinoma, Cushing's syndrome, radiotherapy
Weakness	Myasthenia gravis, McArdle's disease and primary muscle disorders, peripheral neuropathy, other neurological disorders
Episodes of disturbed behaviour	Epilepsy, hypoglycaemia, phaeochromocytoma, porphyria, early dementia, toxic states, transient global amnesia
Headache	Migraine, giant cell arteritis, space-occupying lesion
Loss of weight	Carcinoma, diabetes, tuberculosis, hyperthyroidism, malabsorption

(From Gelder *et al.* (1985). *Oxford Textbook of Psychiatry.* Reproduced by permission of the publisher, Oxford University Press, Oxford.)

of depression. Moffic and Paykel (1975) studied 150 medical inpatients using a standard self-report measure of depression and found that a quarter of these patients were significantly depressed. Such depression was more common in those with a more severe illness, those who had additional concomitant social stress, and those who had had a previous history of affective disorders. A finding of particular practical importance in this study was that in 86 per cent of those who were significantly depressed, the affective symptoms were undetected by the medical and nursing staff. A careful examination of the nature of the depressive symptoms of these patients revealed that they were sufficiently standard not to present any particular diagnostic difficulty, and the failure to recognize depression was simply a reflection of the fact that it was not being considered as a possibility. Given the high prevalence of affective disorder on medical wards, its assessment should be routine.

Psychotic reaction

Physical illness may occasionally be followed by a *psychotic reaction* which is usually characterized by paranoid behaviour. Thus, patients develop paranoid delusional systems which often concern the medical and nursing staff treating their physical illness. These reactions are usually brief but can lead to highly disturbed behaviour which can be seriously detrimental to the treatment of the underlying illness. For example, a patient may fiercely resist the nurses' attempts to administer medication because he believes them to be part of a plot to poison him. These reactions often last for only a few days but treatment with major tranquillizers is likely to be necessary to alleviate the psychotic symptoms until the patient is discharged from hospital into a familiar home environment when they tend to recover.

In addition to these brief psychotic reactions to illness, it has also been observed that chronic paranoid psychoses are sometimes associated with physical illness; and, in particular, that deafness may play a role in paranoid or affective psychoses of late onset. There is some supportive evidence for the existence of such an association (Cooper *et al.*, 1974).

Conclusion

In the introduction to this chapter it was argued that psychological factors were relevant to physical illnesses in a number of different respects. Some of these are dealt with in Chapter 11. The present chapter has only been concerned with psychological antecedents and consequences of illness. It is apparent that research in this area is at an early stage. For example, although the evidence relating environmental stress to the onset of psychiatric, and to a lesser extent, physical illness is now moderately strong, the mechanisms by which this process operates are not at all understood. Similarly, although certain aspects of personality have been found to be related to the incidence of particular diseases, the physiological bases of these relationships are still obscure. Progress in these areas depends on further refinement of the measures of the crucial psychological dimensions of interest, as well as on developing the appropriate means of relating psychological concepts to pathological physiological processes.

Suggested reading

Christie, M.J. and Mellett, P.G. (Eds). *The Psychosomatic Approach: Contemporary Practice of Whole-Person Care.* John Wiley and Sons, Chichester.
A collection of useful reviews of some of the areas covered in this chapter, including contributions on the concept of psychosomatics, cardiovascular disorders and cancer.

Lambert, V.A. and Lambert, C.E. (1979). *The Impact of Physical Illness.* Prentice-Hall, New York.
A sympathetic account of the psychological impact of illness, trauma and medical and surgical interventions.

Ray, C. and Baum, M. (1985). *Psychological Aspects of Early Breast Cancer*. Springer, New York.
A comprehensive treatment of the psychological factors involved in the aetiology, management and outcome of this disease.

Steptoe, A. (1981). *Psychological Factors in Cardiovascular Disorders*. Academic Press. London.
An excellent exposition of the psychological factors relevant to aetiology, treatment and outcome of this class of disorder.

Steptoe, A. and Mathews, A. (1984). *Health Care and Human Behaviour*. Academic Press, London.
A collection of stimulating reviews relevent to this chapter and to Chapter 11. Of particular note are those contributions concerning life stress and illness and psychophysiological process in disease.

Totman, R. (1979). *Social Causes of Illness*. Chaucer Press, Suffolk.
A general readable account of ways in which social and psychological factors operate in the presentation and amelioration of physical symptoms.

References

American Psychiatric Association (1987). *DSM III-R Diagnostic and Statistic Manual of Mental Disorders*. American Psychiatric Association, Washington DC.

Booth-Kewley, S. and Friedman, H.S. (1987). Psychological predictors of heart disease: a quantitative review. *Psychological Bulletin* **101**, 343.

Brand, R.J., Rosenman, R.H., Sholtz, R.I. and Friedman, M. (1976). Multivariate prediction of coronary heart disease in the Western Collaborative Group Study compared to the findings of the Framingham Study. *Circulation* **53**, 348.

Brown, G.W. and Harris, T. (1978). The Social Origins of Depression. Tavistock Press, London.

Brown, G.W. and Prudo, R. (1981). Psychiatric disorder in a rural and urban population: aetiology of depression. *Psychological Medicine* **11**, 581.

Connolly, J. (1976). Life events before myocardial infarction. *Journal of Human Stress* **2**, 3.

Cooper, A.F., Kay, D.W.K., Garside, R.F. and Roth, M. (1974). Hearing loss in the paranoid and affective psychoses of the elderly. *Lancet* **ii**, 851.

Craig, T.K.J. and Brown, G.W. (1984). Life-events, meaning and physical illness: a review. In *Health Care and Human Behaviour*. Edited by Steptoe, A. and Mathews, A. Academic Press, London.

Creed, F. (1981). Life events and appendicectomy. *Lancet* **i**, 1381.

Derogatis, L.R., Abeloff, M.D., and Melisaratos, M. (1979). Psychological coping mechanisms and survival time in metastatic breast cancer. *Journal of the American Medical Association* **242**, 1504.

Dorian, B. and Garfinkel, P.E. (1987). Stress, immunity and illness: a review. *Psychological Medicine* **17**, 393.

Eastwood, M.R., Stiasny, S., Meier, H.M.R. and Woogh, C.M. (1982). Mental illness and mortality. *Comprehensive Psychiatry* **23**, 377.

French–Belgian Collaborative Group (1982). Ischaemic heart disease and psychological patterns: prevalence and incidence studies in Belgium and France. *Advances in Cardiology* **29**, 25.

Friedman, M. and Rosenman, R.H. (1959). Association of specific overt behaviour pattern with blood and cardiovascular findings. *Journal of the American Medical Association* **169**, 1085.

Friedman, M., Thoreson, C.E.; Gill, J.J. (1982). Feasibility of altering Type A behaviour pattern after myocardial infarction. *Circulation* **66**, 83.

Gelder, M.G., Gath, D. and Mayou, R. (1985). *The Oxford Textbook of Psychiatry*. Oxford University Press, Oxford.

Greer, S. (1974). Psychological aspects: delay in the treatment of breast cancer. *Proceedings of the Royal Society of Medicine* **67**, 470.

Greer, S. (1983). Cancer and the mind. *British Journal of Psychiatry* **143**, 535.

Greer, S., Morris, T. and Pettingale, K.W. (1979). Psychological response to breast cancer: effect on outcome. *Lancet* **ii**, 785.

Grossarth-Maticek, R., Bastiaans, J. and Kanazin, D.T. (1985). Psychosocial factors as strong predictors of mortality from cancer, ischaemic heart disease and stress: the Yugoslav Prospective Study. *Journal of Psychosomatic Research* **29**, 167.

Haynes, S.G., Feinleib, M. and Kannel, W.B. (1980). The relationship of psycho-social factors to coronary heart disease in the Framingham study. *American Journal of Epidemiology* **111**, 37.

Holmes, T.H. and Rahe, R.H. (1967). The Social Readjustment Rating Scale. *Journal of Psychosomatic Research* **11**, 213.

Kendell, R.E. (1983). Hysteria. In *Handbook of Psychiatry IV: The Neuroses and Personality Disorders*, pp. 232–46. Edited by Russell, G.F.M. and Hersov, L. Cambridge University Press, Cambridge.

Lloyd, G.G. and Cawley, R.H. (1983). Distress or illness? A study of psychological symptoms after myocardial infarction. *British Journal of Psychiatry* **142**, 120.

Marmot, M.G. (1987). Stress and cardiovascular disease. *Health Trends* **19**, 21.

Mastrovito, R.C., Deguire, K.S., Clarkin, J., Thaler, T., Lewis, J.L. and Cooper, E. (1979). Personality characteristics of women with gynaecological cancer. *Cancer Detection and Prevention* **2**, 281.

Meyer, R.J. and Haggerty, R.J. (1962). Streptococcal infection in families: factors altering individual susceptibility. *Pediatrics* **29**, 539.

Moffic, H.S. and Paykel, E.S. (1975). Depression in medical inpatients. *British Journal of Psychiatry* **126**, 346.

Moss, P.D. and McEvedy, C.P. (1966). An epidemic of overbreathing among schoolgirls. *British Medical Journal* **ii**, 1295.

Munro, A. (1980). Monosymptomatic hypochondriacal psychosis. *British Journal of Hospital Medicine* **24**, 34.

Paykel, E.S. (1985). Life-events, social support and psychiatric disorder. In *Social Support: Theory, Research and Applications*, pp. 321–41. Edited by Sarason, I.G. and Sarason, B.R. Martinus Nijhoff, The Hague.

Rahe, R.H., Mahan, J.L. and Arthur, R.J. (1970). Prediction of near-future health change from subjects' preceding life changes. *Journal of Psychosomatic Research* **14**, 401.

Rosenman, R.H., Brand, R.J., Jenkins, C.D., Friedman, M., Straus, R. and Warm, M. (1975). Coronary heart disease in the Western Collaborative Group Study: final follow-up experience of $8\frac{1}{2}$ years. *Journal of American Medical Association* **233**, 872.

Rorsman, B. (1974). Mortality among psychiatric patients. *Acta Psychiatrica Scandinavica* **50**, 354.

Sims, A.C.P. (1978). Hypotheses linking neuroses with premature mortality. *Psychological Medicine* **8**, 255.

Sims, A.C.P. and Prior, M.P. (1978). The pattern of mortality in severe neuroses. *British Journal of Psychiatry* **133**, 299.

Slater, E.T.O. (1965). Diagnosis of hysteria. *British Medical Journal* i, 1395.

Slater, E.T.O. and Glithero, E. (1965). A follow-up of patients diagnosed as suffering from 'hysteria'. *Journal of Psychosomatic Research* **9**, 9.

Steptoe, A. (1981). *Psychological Factors in Cardiovascular Disorders*. Academic Press, London.

Stern, M.J., Pascale, L. and McLoone, J.B. (1976). Psychosocial adaptation following an acute myocardial infarction. *Journal of Chronic Diseases* **29**, 513.

Thoreson, C.E., Friedman, M., Gill, J.K. and Ulmer, D.K. (1982). The Recurrent Coronary Prevention Project: some preliminary findings. *Acta Medica Scandinavica Supplement* **660**, 172.

Vaillant, G.E. (1979). Natural history of male psychologic health: effects of mental health on physical health. *New England Journal of Medicine* **301**, 1249.

Wirsching, M., Stierlin, H., Hoffman, F., Weber, G. and Wirsching, B. (1982). Psychosocial identification of breast cancer patients before biopsy. *Journal of Psychosomatic Research* **26**, 1.

Zyzanski, S.J., Jenkins, D., Ryan, T.J., Flessas, A. and Everist, M. (1976). Psychological correlates of coronary angiographic findings. *Archives of Internal Medicine* **136**,1234.

11

Psychological Contributions to the Treatment of Medical Patients

FN Watts

Psychological treatments of medical disorders

There are two main ways in which psychological principles are relevant in the treatment of medical patients. First, psychological methods can be used in the direct treatment of at least a proportion of medical patients. Second, because established medical and surgical procedures often require the understanding and co-operation of patients for their success, the interaction between patients and clinician is of considerable importance. These two broad contributions of psychology to medical practice will be considered in the ensuing chapter.

Hypertension

When new treatments for medical conditions are developed, opinion tends to polarize into those who are uncritically enthusiastic and those who are highly sceptical. Only careful evaluations of treatment efficacy can overcome this. This section will begin by evaluating the evidence for the psychological treatment of hypertension as this is the most carefully evaluated psychological treatment in the medical field (Johnston, 1982). Some of the most impressive results have come from using a variety of related psychological treatments in combination. Thus, Patel (1985) has described a treatment which combines relaxation exercises, meditation, yogic breathing exercises, biofeedback assisted reduction of skin resistance, and training in stress management. Evaluations of treatment of hypertension using one or more of these components have been encouraging:

1. The reduction in blood pressure is substantial enough to be clinically useful. In a series of about 150 patients treated by Patel, systolic blood pressure (SBp) reduced from 160 to 140 mmHg (i.e. by approximately one standard deviation). This would be expected to reduce the

incidence of coronary heart disease by a quarter. Thus, although the level to which blood pressure was reduced was still higher than the optimal, the magnitude of reduction was clinically significant.

2. In a controlled study carried out by Patel, the reduction of SBp in the treated group was 2.5 times that obtained in the untreated control group. It is always necessary to show that a treatment has better results than a 'control' condition, as even control groups given no treatment often show some improvement.

3. The results generalize outside the clinic. There have now been studies using semiambulatory monitoring of blood pressure that have obtained significant results of treatment (Southam *et al.*, 1982).

4. Long-term benefits sustained over 4 years, have been demonstrated in a follow-up study of treatment effects (Patel *et al.*, 1985).

5. Comparable results have been obtained in a variety of different clinics. The efficacy of the psychological treatment of hypertension is thus a well replicated finding.

There remains the question of what the effective mechanisms in the psychological treatment of hypertension are, which will be addressed in the context of a wider consideration of treatment mechanisms. The point here is that there is at least one well-evaluated psychological treatment of a medical condition.

A conceptual framework for psychological treatments in medicine

There are various points at which it is possible, in principle, to administer psychological treatments to medical patients. In this section a conceptual framework will be set out which illustrates the range of ways in which psychological interventions can influence the target medical symptom (Fig. 11.1). The psychological treatment of asthma will be selected to illustrate this, because the interventions that have been attempted with this particular condition are unusually diverse (see Knapp and Wells, 1978).

Asthma

An initial distinction must be made between the kind of treatment which results in asthmatic patients ceasing to be asthmatic, and interventions that have the more modest aim of reducing the frequency and severity of asthmatic symptoms. At present, it would be true to say that no treatment, medical or physiological, completely eliminates vulnerability to asthmatic attacks. The tendency to respond to stress with bronchoconstriction rather than the normal bronchodilation is one of the factors that underlies this vulnerability. There is no evidence that any current psychological treatments can alter this; rather, treatment is aimed at reducing the symptoms.

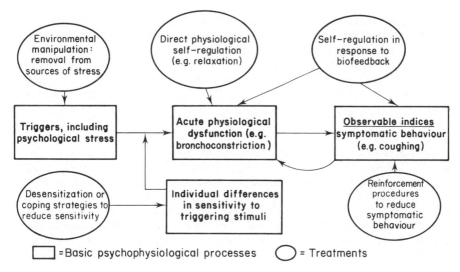

Fig. 11.1 Points at which psychological treatments can affect the asthmatic process.

Asthma is an episodic disorder, and there are clear and well-known triggers for asthmatic attacks. These include allergens and the medical treatment of asthma includes desensitizing patients. The triggering factors also include psychological stress, and the psychological treatment of asthma similarly includes desensitization to psychological triggers. Such triggers fall into two classes, some general and some specific to asthma. General social stressors (having arguments, speaking in public) have different psychological effects in different people. In 'normal' subjects, there is often 'response specificity'; that is, a tendency for one response system (heart-rate, blood-pressure, etc.) to be particularly responsive to stress. In patients with a systemic disease, the particular physiological system concerned will show the effects of stress. For example, whereas in diabetic patients stress will destabilize their metabolic control, in asthmatic patients it will result in breathlessness and bronchoconstriction.

Other triggering stressors are more specific to asthma. As is the case with many medical conditions in which psychological factors are involved, there is a vicious circle involving somatic symptoms and anxiety. In the case of asthma, breathlessness can lead to anxiety, especially if the patient is alone, and it would be difficult to obtain help if a bad attack developed. The physiological effects of the resulting anxiety can include the exacerbation of what was initially quite mild breathlessness. The operation of this vicious circle can result in very mild symptoms of anxiety developing into a serious asthma attack.

The technique of **systematic desensitization** developed by Joseph Wolpe as a treatment for phobias (see Chapter 8) has been used with asthmatic patients. Desensitization is one of a family of treatments for specific anxiety-arousing stimuli. To ensure that anxiety during treatment is minimized, anxiety cues are presented in ascending hierarchical order, often by requiring the patient to imagine them, against a background of relaxation. Imaginal desensitization has been shown to be a highly effective treatment for specific phobias. In asthma, it is used to reduce patient sensitivity to psychological triggers. Both general and asthma-specific sources of stress and anxiety can be so treated. Obviously, the treatment is appropriate only to those asthmatics for whom psychological triggers are important.

Yorkston and his colleagues (1974) have reported a randomized controlled trial comparing imaginal desensitization with relaxation in asthmatics. The study used multiple outcome measures and showed improved physiological function, reduced drug usage and greater clinically-rated improveprovement in the desensitized group (see Table 11.1). The results of the study are impressive because all three measures showed significantly greater improvement in the desensitization group than the relaxation control group.

Table 11.1   Changes in functioning as a result of psychological desensitization of asthmatics

	FEV*	Drug usage	Rated improvement
Desensitization treatment	+20%	−2.67	+3.00
Control (relaxation)	−5%	+1.00	+1.25

*Forced expiratory volume as % of prediction from age and height.

Reproduced from Yorkston, N.J., McHugh, R.B., Brady, R., Serber, M. and Sergeant, H.G. (1974).

Another approach to the social stressors which may trigger asthmatic attacks is to remove the patient from the environment where these occur. For a number of asthmatics, the family home is the main locus of relevant stressors. Purcell and Weiss (1970) have reported a series of studies which demonstrated how, in selected asthmatic children, separation from their families led to a marked improvement in their symptoms. They began by observing that certain children showed rapid remission on admission to the clinic without the use of steroid medication. Interviews with these children showed that they were more likely than other asthmatics to report emotional triggering of asthma attacks; while interviews with their parents revealed them to be more authoritarian and punitive. Of course, the remission of symptoms in hospital could also be explained in terms of changes in the physical environment. To separate these factors, Purcell and Weiss compared the children's asthmatic condition while living at home with their families with their condition while living in a home cared for by a substitute mother. Over half the children showed a marked improvement while being cared for by a substitute mother; and it was possible to predict with a high degree of accuracy which children were likely to improve in these circumstances.

Family contact can also influence the asthmatic symptoms of adults. This is illustrated by a single-case study by Metcalfe (1956) of a hospitalized female asthmatic patient. Metcalfe examined the association between asthma attacks and the patient meeting her mother. The study extended over an 85-day period and showed that the patient was much more likely to be free of symptoms when she had not seen her mother for a 24-hour period (see Table 11.2). Meetings with the mother at home were particularly likely to be followed by an attack.

Table 11.2   Relationships between asthma attacks and meetings with mother

	Days with asthma	Days without asthma
	15	70
Within 24 hours of being with mother	9(60%)	14(20%)
Not in contact with mother for preceding 24 hours	6(40%)	56(80%)
chi^2 = 10(p<0.01)		

Reproduced from Metcalfe, M. (1956) by permission of the author and the British Psychological Society, Leicester.

The vicious circle involving breathlessness and anxiety that may lead to an asthmatic attack has already been noted. Another point of intervention, therefore, is to teach patients self-regulation skills that they can use to intervene and prevent an asthmatic attack before it is fully developed. For example, a patient with asthma was trained to use muscle relaxation, breathing exercises, and induction of calmness at the early signs of an attack (Rathus, 1973). The frequency of the attacks fell from between 4 and 7 per week before treatment to just 2 attacks in the three months following treatment. Where methods such as relaxation are used, the results are likely to be enhanced by explicitly training patients in their use outside the treatment sessions. There are several possible ways of inducing patients to use these methods. An alternative to training patients to detect the early signs of an attack, which some may find difficult, is to initiate relaxation at frequent, randomly selected points in the day. Another successful case study using relaxation in the treatment of asthma required the patient to carry a portable timer that sounded at random intervals. Each time the signal sounded she was required to relax. An objective index of her improvement was that her previously excessively frequent use of a portable inhaler was reduced to zero after two weeks.

Although there is clear evidence for the value of treatments focusing on anxiety and stress factors in some asthmatics, there is a need for caution in extrapolating from these findings. First, it is still not known what proportion of asthmatics is helped by these treatments. Second, the role of anxiety in triggering specific episodes of asthma should not be taken to imply that psychological factors were responsible for the original onset of the condition. Third, the fact that anxiety-focused treatments can be effective for some patients does not imply that they should be applied universally or be used to the exclusion of other approaches.

Another possible self-regulation approach is to train patients directly in bronchodilation using **biofeedback** (see Chapter 8). Such feedback can be provided in a number of ways. Some methods have involved a light signalling when respiratory functioning has reached a prescribed criterion. Others have involved the use of a tone. Sometimes 'informational' feedback has been augmented by verbal praise or other rewards. A series of case studies has indicated that patients *can* use biofeedback to improve respiratory functioning, but it is doubtful whether the changes produced are of a clinically significant magnitude. There are a number of recurrent limitations in the results obtained from such investigations. The amount of physiological change produced is often quite small. Even when statistically significant change occurs, it is not clear that the improvement is any greater than can be achieved by other methods. As with many clinical applications of biofeedback, in the case of asthma, relaxation training without such feedback produces comparable results (e.g. Alexander, 1981). Finally, most of the evidence that has been reported has been concerned with the immediate effects of biofeedback and there is, of course, little clinical value in biofeedback if the effects do not extend outside the clinic. As yet there has been no clear demonstration that any beneficial effects of biofeedback are enduring. Furthermore, biofeedback techniques generally seem more successful at bringing about a deterioration than an improvement in physiological functioning; that is, it is easier to achieve bronchoconstriction than bronchodilation, just as it is easier to raise blood pressure rather than to lower it. It is worth adding that patients with a particular disorder often have most difficulty in regulating the physiological function concerned in that particular illness. Thus, asthmatic patients are likely to be less able to bring about bronchodilation than non-asthmatics.

Another group of treatments for asthma has focused on behaviours such as coughing which can exacerbate symptoms. A vicious circle can operate similar to that involving anxiety: coughing leads to bronchoconstriction, which in turn leads to more coughing. In cases where coughing is excessive, operant procedures can be used (see Chapter 8).

Of the available methods, direct **punishment** is least predictable in its effects. Punishment procedures can often have paradoxical effects leading to an increase in the punished behaviour. This has been termed by Neil Miller the 'fear-pain paradox': the pain of punishment can lead to an enhanced state of fear or anxiety which, for ill-understood reasons, results in an increase in the undesirable behaviour. There are three more satisfactory alternative procedures available. One is to reinforce a behaviour incompatible with the undesirable behaviour. Another is to reinforce abstinence from the undesirable behaviour. Finally, if the behaviour is being maintained by an identifiable source of reinforcement, it may be sufficient to remove this. So, if the excessive coughing of an asthmatic child at night time is being maintained by the attention that it elicits from his parents, they would be advised not to respond to his coughing once he was in bed. The coughing should then reduce and the asthma improve.

Asthmatic symptoms may be maintained by the reinforcement gained from the positive aspects of the hospital environments, such as the social contact it provides and its recreational facilities. In such cases, operant techniques can be used, though they are probably more appropriate for children than for adults. For example, the behaviour for asthmatic children who appeared to be seeking excessively frequent admissions to the US National Asthma Centre was modified by instituting a procedure ('time out' from positive reinforcement) in which they were given individual rooms without a television, comics or games: this was shown to reduce subsequent admissions. However, the effects were specific to hospitalization and no other measures of clinical state were affected. This treatment should therefore be considered as a contribution to the social management of asthmatic patients rather than as a treatment technique operating directly on symptoms.

Epilepsy

The range of psychological approaches to the treatment of asthma has parallels in a variety of other conditions, as is illustrated by the case of epilepsy (Mostofsky and Balaschak, 1977). As with asthma, psychological stressors and anxieties can trigger seizures in patients with epilepsy, and desensitizing patients to these can result in a decrease in the frequency of seizures. However, a vicious circle in which early symptoms provoke anxiety which in turn increases the risk of seizures is found less often than in patients with asthma. While some treatments have focused on decreasing worries about having seizures, such an approach may therefore have limited use. Thus, reports of desensitization with epilepsy have generally focused on social stressors. Self-regulation procedures, such as the scheduling of relaxation (e.g. by a 'bleeper') have also been claimed to reduce the frequency of seizures.

Social stressors are not the only relevant external source of stress. In a proportion of epileptics, sensory stimuli provoke seizures and psychological treatments have been used in such cases. For example, it has been reported that in patients in whom stroboscopic lights induce seizures, desensitization to these through controlled, graded exposure reduced their sensitivity. Visual sensitivity can also be controlled directly by providing patients with dark glasses to wear in high-risk places. The more precisely the triggering visual stimuli are specified, the more readily remedial procedures can be developed. For example, in a patient for whom the parallel horizontal lines of a page of print were a relevant triggering stimulus, providing a reading aid which left only three lines of print exposed was found to be helpful (Wilkins and Lindsay, 1985).

Since the report by Kamiya (1968) that normal subjects could use biofeedback to control voluntarily EEG rhythms, such techniques have been used extensively in the treatment of epilepsy. Various EEG rhythms have been used as the target response to be modified, although the 'sensorimotor' rhythm has been used most commonly. Research is still largely at the level of case reports rather than controlled trials. However, the data have indicated that stable reductions in the frequency of seizures have been achieved in many patients. Biofeedback in the treatment of epilepsy thus promises to be more effective than in the treatment of asthma in bringing about clinically significant improvements. However, there remains some doubt about the mechanism of the effect (Carroll, 1982). Various different EEG rhythms have been used as the target response, and it is not clear that any one is more effective than the others. Also, there is sometimes little correlation between the amount of control achieved over EEG rhythms and the extent to which seizures are reduced. These issues will be returned to in the context of the use of biofeedback in treating tension headaches.

Modification of reinforcement contingencies has also been used to reduce seizures that are self-induced. For example, in some patients, voluntary overbreathing can induce seizures, and using operant techniques to reduce overbreathing has been claimed to reduce seizures. Similarly, where the tendency to exhibit seizures is increased by social attention, modifying family interactions has been found to reduce the frequency of the seizures.

Treatment mechanisms

Even where psychological treatments have been shown to be effective, the question remains of how they work.

Pain

Relaxation, cognitive therapy, biofeedback, hypnosis and reinforcement procedures all have a place in the treatment of chronic pain (Gibson, 1982). None has been shown to be conspicuously more successful than the other, although the use of two or more methods in combination is often found more effective than individual methods used alone. The failure of any one method to be superior to others raises the possibility that all may achieve their effects in similar, non-specific ways. It has become clear from the outcome of research on psychological treatments in other fields that, even where psychological treatments are shown to be effective, a significant proportion of their effectiveness is attributable to non-specific effects such as having contact with a therapist and expecting treatment benefit. When the relevant research is done, it is often found that psychological treatments, though effective, work in ways that differ from those originally supposed.

Biofeedback treatment for headache pains assumes a very specific psychological process: that pain is reduced by lowering the level of tension in the frontalis muscles of the forehead. This raises general issues about the relationship between physiological and psychological aspects of pain. It is well established that there is often very little correlation between the extent of tissue damage and the amount of subjective pain reported: the experience of pain in the natural environment seems to be heavily influenced by psychological and sociocultural factors. Expectations, anxiety levels, and the interpretation of the potentially painful experience all have marked effects (see Chapter 2). Further, it has been possible to distinguish sensory and affective aspects of the experience of pain. The words used to describe pain can be separated out into relatively specific sensory terms, (e.g. 'sharp'), and more affective terms (e.g. 'burning'). These two facets of pain experience can be assessed separately and have different determinants.

One implication of this potential separation between sensory and affective aspects is that reducing the stress caused by pain does not depend on distracting people from the sensory features of the experience. Indeed, one of the more intriguing findings in the field of pain management is that attention to the sensory aspects of pain can be a *more* effective strategy than distraction (Ahles *et al.*, 1983). It is particularly impressive that the advantage of sensory attention is, if anything, more effective in the post-training period than during training (see Fig. 11.2). So far, this somewhat counterintuitive finding has been demonstrated only for laboratory pain caused by the 'cold-pressor' test. Its clinical applicability remains to be explored.

A relevant test of the physiological hypothesis about how biofeedback achieves its effects is whether it is superior to other relatively non-specific procedures such as relaxation. Early work seemed to indicate that this was the case. In a classic study (Budzyuski *et al.*, 1973) subjects with tension headache were divided into three groups. One group learned to relax the frontalis muscles with the aid of EMG feedback, another was given a control treatment in which information was provided about the EMG levels of the treated subjects rather than themselves. The second group was not asked to use this information to control muscle tension, but simply to use it as a focus of attention while they were relaxing. A third group received no treatment. The results were that only the first group showed reductions in frontalis muscle EMG levels, and also in a measure of headaches based on a daily diary. This difference persisted for the three month follow-up period during which regular measures were taken. In the treated group, clinical improvements continued 18 months after treatment.

More recent research has made it increasingly doubtful whether biofeedback treatment for tension headaches achieves its clinical results by operating directly on tension in the frontalis muscles in the forehead. Several subsequent studies (see Carroll, 1982), though confirming that biofeedback is a useful treatment procedure, indicate that is no better than

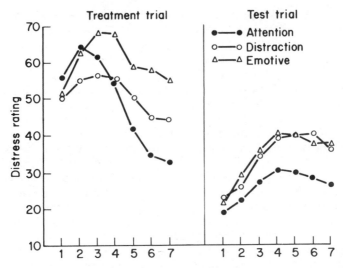

Fig. 11.2   Mean distress ratings for each group over rating times divided by trials. (Reproduced from Ahles, T.A., Blanchard, E.B. and Leventhal, H. (1983) by permission from the author and Plenum Publishing Corporation, New York.)

simpler procedures such as relaxation training. There are also several unexpected findings that point to a dissociation between EMG tension levels and the experience of headaches. EMG levels of patients with headaches are not notably higher than those of control subjects. Also, when headaches are reported by patients their EMG levels are not consistently higher than at other times. Further, although feedback can effectively reduce headaches, this beneficial clinical test is not always accompanied by corresponding reductions in EMG levels. Finally, increasing EMG levels of biofeedback does not reliably result in greater reports of headaches. Indeed, it has been shown that using biofeedback to maintain a *high* EMG level can also reduce headaches! It is thus, at present, unclear how biofeedback in the treatment of tension headaches achieves its effects. Conceivably, it achieves part of its impact through relatively non-specific factors such as inducing in patients the belief that they are in control of their symptoms. Whether biofeedback and relaxation differ in their effectiveness in any particular study may depend on their relative effects on such non-specific factors.

However, there are clear instances in which psychological treatments in medicine achieve their results solely because of specific factors. One such instance is EMG biofeedback to help stroke patients to regain muscle control (Marcer, 1986). Such treatment is particularly valuable to patients who are not receiving natural feedback from the actual limb movements. This application of biofeedback differs from others in that its effects cannot be simulated by simpler procedures such as relaxation training. Also, the patients receiving such treatment have generally shown little response to conventional procedures.

Psychological aspects of medical and surgical treatments

There are a number of psychological factors that are relevant to the presentation of illness (see Chapter 10). These can operate at any of a number of stages. Whether a person develops symptoms will, in part, reflect their personality and lifestyle. People also differ in their sensitivity to somatic experiences, some being excessively conscious of minor fluctuations and others tending to ignore relatively serious physical disturbances. When people do identify symptoms in themselves, they have to decide whether it represents a serious illness. At this stage, patients have to be their own diagnostician, not always an easy task. For example, distinguishing the early symptoms of a coronary thrombosis from fatigue and indigestion is quite difficult, and made more so by the fact that many patients have no previous experience of such episodes when they are required to make this discrimination. The conclusion that symptoms represent nothing serious tends to be rejected if they are qualitatively different from anything experienced before, if they are unusually painful and disabling, and if they are prolonged (Cowie, 1976). Anxiety about illness is also relevant and increases the probability of judging that there is something seriously amiss.

Having decided that one is ill, the next decision is whether to consult a doctor. The seriousness of the symptoms, the availability of a sympathetic doctor, and the inconvenience of consultation in particular circumstances, are all relevant. There are also stable individual differences in attitude to medical consultations. For example, people who self-prescribe medicine tend not to follow their doctor's advice about medications; whereas those who do follow such advice tend not to prescribe drugs for themselves (Dunnell and Cartwright, 1972). Anxiety about possible illness is likely to increase the probability of consulting a doctor, except when such anxiety concerns the possibility of a serious disease such as cancer when it may actually delay consultation (Rosenstock and Kirscht, 1979).

Surveys of reasons for consultation reveal that the majority of patients want to be told if there is something seriously wrong with them. Indeed, it is a consistent complaint of patients that they are not told enough by their doctor. Doctors are often reluctant to tell patients what is wrong, and will more often tell relatives than patients themselves (McIntosh, 1974). Although doctors argue that the decision about providing patients with diagnostic information needs to be made in the light of how an individual patient would react, individual doctors tend to be consistent in how much information they provide patients; and individual patient factors account for less variance than might be expected. It is a reflection of patients' interest in knowing what is wrong with them that they are twice as likely to remember diagnostic information as doctor's advice (Ley, 1982).

The effectiveness of medical and surgical treatments depends on patients' cooperation with the treatment process. In this context the preparation of patients for surgery will be considered, and the related issue of gaining patients' cooperation in rehabilitation from traumatic illness.

Preparation for surgery

There is now abundant evidence that taking particular care over psychological preparation for surgery improves postoperative recovery on a wide range of criteria. Such preparation reduces length of hospitalization and therefore is cost-effective; and it also reduces patients' postoperative distress. One of the clearest demonstrations of the value of preparation for surgery was reported by Egbert *et al.* (1964). Patients admitted for abdominal operations were allocated to one of two groups. One group received general 'procedural' information about when the operation would take place; and the other group received more specific information about the sensations they would experience together with practical advice about how to cope with them. Those receiving the practical advice were found to differ from the remainder on a wide range of postoperative outcome criteria: they experienced less anger, resentment and discomfort; they were rated by the staff as making a faster recovery; they required significantly less postoperative medication; and they were discharged on average three days sooner. In addition to these benefits other studies have shown preparation for surgery to improve aspects of postoperative behaviour such as ambulation, to reduce postoperative pain, and to have beneficial effects on physiological indices of recovery such as blood pressure and medical complications such as respiratory infection.

In Egbert's study it was not possible to unravel the possible effects of providing information about sensations and practical instructions about how to manage the recovery process. However, the picture that emerges from a number of subsequent studies is that providing sensory information alone is less effective than providing instructions about how to deal with the recovery process (Kendall and Watson, 1981). Providing sensory information alone is also generally less effective (except in actually increasing knowledge) than a cognitive treatment designed to train patients to confront their worries and anxieties about surgery and think about ways of coping with them (Table 11.3). The most effective procedure for reducing patients' anxiety about surgery appears to be an adaptation of the techniques of cognitive therapy.

There have been indications that response to preparation for surgery depends on personality characteristics, with some people benefiting more than others. There are important individual differences in how people cope with stress (Mathews and Ridgeway, 1981), although researchers have not always agreed on how best to conceptualize or measure them. One common distinction is between those who cope with stress by 'monitoring'

Table 11.3 Comparison of average post-treatment levels on five different criterion variables

	Sensory information	Coping advice	No-treatment control
Any worries?	40%	20%	53%
Know timetables?	85%	75%	53%
Actual items known	4.0	2.6	1.8
Oral analgesics	23.8	16.3	24.1
Days of pain	9.9	5.9	12.0

Reproduced from Ridgeway, V. and Mathews, A. (1982) by permission of the author and the British Psychological Society, Leicester.

what is happening to them, and those who adopt a 'blunting' strategy of distracting themselves from what is happening as much as possible. Only the 'monitoring' group have been found to benefit from being given sensory information. Similarly, patients who have an internal 'locus of control' (i.e. who perceive events as being influenced by themselves) benefit most from preparatory information. There may also be a class of patients for whom full surgical preparation impairs postoperative recovery, although it is unclear whether there are alternative procedures that would be helpful to such patients (Mathews and Ridgeway, 1981).

Some researchers have investigated the benefits of showing patients a film providing information about the procedures followed in hospital and the nature of the operation. Melamed (1977) has demonstrated that showing such films to children before they enter hospital has impressive results. Positive effects of intervention were found by Melamed on a wide range of behavioural, physiological and self-report measures, and were shown to last for a month after discharge from hospital. These benefits occurred despite the fact that the film produced an immediate increase in anxiety. Stressful events may be less distressing when they occur if people have done their worrying in advance. The short-term increase in anxiety, but long-term advantage found in Melamed's research is consistent with this idea.

Related issues arise in the management and rehabilitation of patients who have suffered a 'traumatic' illness such as a heart attack, though in this case patients' cooperation has to be enlisted after the illness. The trauma will have exposed patients to unfamiliar and painful experiences, and having these described clearly and explained may be helpful. They also need clear behavioural instructions about what to do to help themselves in the future. Finally, they are likely to be anxious about their condition and this problem can be tackled by behavioural and cognitive techniques.

Research into the management of patients with heart attacks has been less extensive than on preparation for surgery, but some preliminary conclusions can be drawn (Cromwell and Levenkron, 1984). Psychological variables are important in predicting whether a patient will have another

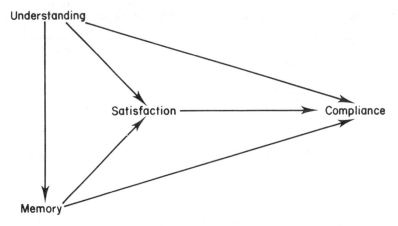

Fig. 11.3   The cognitive hypothesis. (Reproduced from Ley, P. (1982) by permission of the author and The British Psychological Society, Leicester.)

attack (see Chapter 10). Length of stay in hospital is dependent on how much patients are told and how effectively they are involved in their treatment. Soliciting patients' participation in their treatment is especially important in shortening the duration of their hospitalization. Individual differences in personality may predict the most appropriate treatment regime: patients with an internal perceived 'locus of control' respond well to being allowed discretion in aspects of their management; whereas patients with 'external' locus of control may respond better to clearly specified instructions (Watts, 1982).

Psychological variables are also important in **rehabilitation**. How much pain patients with angina will experience and how long they will be absent from work are both predictable from their level of anxiety and depression about their illness. There is encouraging evidence that providing patients with help in adjusting to their illness improves their prospects for rehabilitation.

Treatment compliance

A high proportion of medical patients are prescribed medication, but the effects obviously depend on whether the patients actually take the medication prescribed. Many patients are also given advice about how to prevent illness or to promote recovery; and again, for such advice to be effective, patients have to comply.

There is now abundant evidence that the level of patients' **compliance** with treatment instructions is very poor. For example, only about 50 per cent of patients take medication in the way prescribed (Ley, 1982). The assessment of treatment compliance is, of course, not straightforward.

Most studies have used the patient as an informant which is likely, if anything, to overestimate compliance. However, if patients are interviewed in a non-threatening way by someone other than their own doctor, valid indices of compliance can be obtained which correlate well with other more objective measures such as pill counts or physiological indices of the effects of medication. A good deal is not known about the factors affecting treatment compliance. It is obviously essential that patients should remember the doctor's instructions. Patients' general medical knowledge is not especially pertinent, no correlation often being found between patients' knowledge about their condition and treatment compliance. For example, there have been extensive attempts to improve diabetic patients' knowledge of their condition; and although these have been successful in terms of increasing their knowledge, they have often failed to make an impact on treatment compliance (Watts, 1980).

Satisfaction with the medical consultation has been found to be an important determinant of compliance. A model of the role of cognitive variables and of satisfaction in determining compliance has been put forward by Ley (1982) (Fig. 11.3). The importance of satisfaction was illustrated in a classic study carried out by Korsch and Negrete (1972). They studied a series of 800 mothers attending the acute emergency clinic of a paediatric hospital. The advice given was carried out in full by 49 per cent; it was carried out in part by 38 per cent; and 13 per cent did not follow any of the advice at all. There was a clear relationship between the level of compliance and the reported satisfaction with the medical consultation. Four factors were found to be particularly associated with such satisfaction. These were the doctors who 1. showing that they were aware of the mothers' worries; 2. giving the mother a clear statement about the nature of the child's problem; 3. showing their approval of the mother's own efforts to deal with the problem; and 4. being friendly in their manner. The length of the consultation was unrelated to satisfaction.

Inpatients show the highest level of compliance, followed by day patients, with outpatients showing poorest compliance. The implication is that if supervision could be increased, treatment compliance would improve. There are indications that various methods of increasing supervision are helpful. The patient's family can be involved in providing medication; patients can be visited at home by a community nurse; and mechanical devices can be used as a substitute for supervision. An example of the latter strategy is reported by Azrin and Powell (1969) using a cupboard for medicine which sounded an alarm at the times when the patient is supposed to take medication. Finally, the interaction between the doctor and the patient can be restructured so as to provide better supervision. One effective method is to draw up a 'therapeutic contract' which clarifies the goals agreed between the clinician and patient and the relative responsibilities of each of them in achieving it.

Compliance is also affected by the nature of the regime. Treatment which is complex, prolonged, expensive, inconvenient, or disruptive of the patient's normal life style is least likely to be followed (Sackett and Haynes,

1976). There is considerable scope for restructuring treatment regimes to minimize these features. For example, where several different items of medication have been prescribed, care needs to be taken to integrate their scheduling. Larger and less frequent doses lead to better compliance. It is also helpful to integrate the times when medication has to be taken into the patient's daily routine.

Such considerations are particularly important in the treatment of serious, chronic conditions. Doctors generally believe that treatment compliance is better in more serious conditions, but in fact the opposite is the case. Presumably this is because the treatment regimes for serious, chronic conditions are likely to be complex and inconvenient, and it is here that particular care needs to be taken to keep the treatment regime as simple as possible. Patients tend to comply poorly with advice which involves changing their lifestyle. For example, in a study of cardiac patients given three items of behavioural advice, it was found that most patients followed one or two items but very few followed all three (Davis, 1967). Advice about exercise was the most popular, and advice about smoking and drinking the least popular. If a particular piece of advice is especially important, compliance may be better if it is given on its own.

Diabetes

Diabetes is an example of a condition that imposes a complex regime of self-treatment on patients. An extensive and carefully conducted series of studies on treatment compliance in diabetes (reviewed by Watts, 1980) illustrates the scale of the problem. The results were disturbing: 80 per cent of patients administered the wrong dosage of insulin; 77 per cent tested the sugar levels in their urine incorrectly and misinterpreted the results; 75 per cent were also eating the proscribed foods; and 75 per cent were not eating with satisfactory regularity.

Improvements in diabetic self-care depend on good monitoring of sugar levels. Techniques have recently been developed which enable patients to monitor their own blood glucose levels for themselves. Such blood glucose measures are more reliable than the measures of urine glucose levels that diabetics have traditionally used. Unfortunately, patients tend to take measures too infrequently and to interpret them poorly. However, recent studies of training patients in methods of metabolic self-regulation have demonstrated encouraging results (Wing *et al.*, 1986).

An approach that reduces the need for external metabolic measures is to train patients to recognize high blood sugar levels directly, which recent work has shown to be possible (Pennebaker *et al.*, 1981). The symptoms that provide the best index of glucose levels vary from one patient to another, so each patient needs to be investigated individually to determine the best indices to use. Some patients can improve their ability to monitor blood sugar levels by titrating them against symptoms. Additionally, it is important for patients to learn to anticipate the effects of variations in stress, exercise and food-intake on blood sugar levels. This means that corrective action can be taken earlier. There are also marked effects of emotional stress on metabolism in diabetes, and good control cannot be achieved without taking this into account.

Patients' beliefs about health also affect their compliance (Becker and Rosenstock, 1984). If they are to take advice they need to believe that the disease is potentially serious, that they are personally at risk, and that the treatment would be effective. These issues are particularly relevant to conditions such as hypertension where medication plays a vital preventative role, but where the symptoms do not cause immediate distress. Perceiving the risk to *oneself* as being high is important. The widespread tendency of people to misconstrue statistical data, particularly as far as it applies to themselves (see Chapter 6) interferes with estimates of risk.

The findings of research on treatment compliance may seem obvious, but at some points they do run counter to popular medical opinion. Doctors, especially senior ones, underestimate the scale of non-compliance although it has now been abundantly documented. They also regard non-compliance as a trait of particular kinds of patients. In fact, research has shown that patient variables such as personality, gender, age, social class, intelligence and education are generally unrelated to treatment compliance (Sackett and Haynes, 1976). How the treatment is presented and structured has much more effect.

Conclusion

This chapter has considered a few of the best-researched ways in which psychological factors can enhance the effectiveness of medical and surgical treatments. They are merely examples of a much wider class of psychological contributions to medical treatment which are being developed and investigated. Direct physiological treatments of the kind reviewed in the first half of the chapter have some promising applications, although the magnitude and durability of the effects is sometimes disappointing and the range of patients with whom they can be used may be limited. However, psychological procedures designed to increase patients' cooperation with medical and surgical treatments, thereby potentiating their effectiveness, are almost universally applicable and have paid significant dividends.

Suggested reading

Cohen, S.J. (Ed) (1980). *New Directions in Patient Compliance*. Gower Press, London. An edited volume including good discussion of the main issues in research on compliance with treatments.

Gatchel, R.J. and Baum, A. (1983). *An Introduction to Health Psychology*. Random House, New York.
A another useful general introduction to health psychology, written at undergraduate level.

Marcer, D. (1986). *Biofeedback and Related Therapies in Clinical Practice*. Croom Helm, London.
A well-presented text on the principles of biofeedback and its range of applications.

Mathews, A. and Steptoe, A. (Eds) (1982). *Behavioural Medicine*. British Psychological Society, Leicester.
A reprint of a special issue of the British Journal of Clinical Psychology including some very useful invited review papers of topics in health psychology.

Pinkerton, S.S. (1982). *Behavioural Medicine: Clinical Applications*. John Wiley, Chichester.
A comprehensive text on psychological treatments organized by clinical conditions.

Prokop, C.K. and Bradley, L.A. (1981). *Medical Psychology: Contributions to Behavioural Medicine*. Academic Press, London.
A comprehensive edited volume, organized by clinical conditions.

Rachman, S.J. and Philip, C. (1975). *Psychology and Medicine*. M.T. Smith, London.
A clear and readable exposition of the general role of psychology in medicine. No longer an up-to-date summary of research findings, but still a valuable introduction.

Steptoe, A. and Mathews, A. (Eds) (1984). *Health Care and Human Behaviour*. Academic Press, London.
An excellent collection of review of chapters, focusing mostly on psychological aspects of medical and surgical treatments.

References

Ahles, T.A., Blanchard, E.B., and Leventhal, H. (1983). Cognitive control of pain: Attention to the sensory aspects of the cold-pressor stimulus. *Cognitive Therapy and Research* **7**, 159.

Alexander, B.A. (1981). Psychological aspects in the understanding and treatment of bronchial asthma. In *Comprehensive Handbook of Behavioural Medicine*, pp. 3–45. Edited by Ferguson, J.M. and Taylor, C.B. M.T.P. Press, Lancaster.

Azrin, N.H. and Powell, J. (1969). Behavioural engineering: the use of response priming to improve prescribed self-medication. *Journal of Applied Behavioural Analysis* **2**, 39.

Becker, M.H. and Rosenstock, J.M. (1984). Compliance with medical advice. In *Health Care and Human Behaviour*, pp. 175–208. Edited by Steptoe, A. and Mathews, A. Academic Press, London.

Budzynski, T.H., Stoyva, J.M., Adler, C.S. and Mullaney, D.J. (1973). EMG biofeedback and tension headache: a controlled outcome study. *Psychosomatic Medicine* **35**, 484.

Carroll, D. (1982). *Biofeedback in practice*. Longman, London.

Cowie, B. (1976). The cardiac patient's perception of his heart attack. *Social Science and Medicine* **10**, 87.

Cromwell, R.K. and Levenkron, J.C. (1984). Psychological care of acute coronary patients. In *Health Care and Human Behaviour*, pp. 209–29. Edited by Steptoe, A. and Mathews, A. Academic Press, London.

Davis, M.S. (1967). Predicting non-compliant behaviour. *Journal of Health and Social Behaviour* **8**, 265.

Dunnell, K. and Cartwright, A. (1972). *Medicine Takers, Prescribers and Hoarders*. Routledge and Kegan Paul, London.

Egbert, L.D., Battit, G.W., Welch, C.E. and Bartlock, N.K. (1964). Reduction of postoperative pain by encouragement and instruction of patients. *New England Journal of Medicine* **270**, 825.

Gibson, H.B. (1982). *Pain and its conquest*. Peter Owen, London.

Johnston, D.W. (1982). Behavioural treatment in the reduction of coronary risk factors: type A behaviour and blood pressure. *British Journal of Clinical Psychology* **21**, 281.

Kamiya, J. (1968). Conscious control of brain waves. *Psychology Today* **1**, 56.

Kendall, P.C. and Watson, D.C. (1981). Psychological preparation for stressful medical procedures. In *Medical Psychology: Contributions to Behavioural Medicine*, pp. 198–221. Edited by Prokop, C. and Bradley, L. Academic Press, London.

Knapp, T.J. and Wells, L.A. (1978). Behaviour therapy for asthma: a review. *Behaviour Research and Therapy* **16**, 103.

Korsch, B.M. and Negrete, U.F. (1972). Doctor patient communication. *Scientific American* **227**, 66.

Ley, P. (1982). Satisfaction, compliance and communications. *British Journal of Clinical Psychology* **21**, 241.

McIntosh, J. (1974). Process of communication, information seeking and control associated with cancer. *Social Science and Medicine* **8**, 167.

Mathews, A. and Ridgeway, V. (1981). Personality and surgical recovery: a review. *British Journal of Clinical Psychology* **20**, 243.

Melamed, B.G. (1977). Psychological preparation for hospitalization. In *Contributions to Medical Psychology Volume 1*, pp. 43–74. Edited by Rachman, S.J. Pergamon Press, Oxford.

Metcalfe, M. (1956). Demonstration of a psychosomatic relationship. *British Journal of Medical Psychology* **29**, 63.

Mostofsky, D.I. and Balaschak, B.A. (1977). *Psychological Bulletin* **84**, 723.

Patel, C., Marmot, M.G., Terry, D.J., Carruthers, M., Hunt, B. and Patel, M. (1985). Trial of relaxation in reducing coronary risk: four year follow-up. *British Medical Journal* **290**, 1103.

Pennebaker, J.W., Cox, D.J., Gonder-Frederick, L., Wunsch, M.G., Evans, W.S. and Pohl, S. (1981). Physical symptoms related to blood glucose in insulin-dependent diabetics. *Psychosomatic Medicine* **43**, 489.

Purcell, K. and Weiss, J. (1970). Asthma. In *Symptoms of Psychopathology*, pp. 597–623. Edited by Costello, C.G. John Wiley, New York.

Rathus, S.A. (1973). Motoric, automatic and cognitive reciprocal inhibition in a case of hysterical bronchial asthma. *Adolescence* **8**, 29.

Ridgeway, V. and Mathews, A. (1982). Psychological preparation for surgery: a comparison of methods. *British Journal of Clinical Psychology* **21**, 271.

Rosenstock, I.M. and Kirscht, J.P. (1979). Why people seek health care. In *Health Psychology: A Handbook*, pp. 161–88. Edited by Stone, G.C., Cohen, F. and Adler, N.B. Jossey-Bass, San Francisco.

Sackett, D.L. and Haynes, R.B. (1976). *Compliance with Therapeutic Regimens*. Johns Hopkins University Press, Baltimore.

Southam, M.A., Agras, W.S., Taylor, C.B. and Kraemer, M.C. (1982). Relaxation training: blood pressure during the working day. *Archives of General Psychiatry* **39**, 715.

Watts, F.N. (1980). Behavioural aspects of the management of diabetes mellitus: education, self-care and metabolic control. *Behavioral Research and Therapy* **18**, 171.

Watts, F.N. (1982). Attributional aspects of medicine. In *Attributions and Psychological Change*, pp. 135–55. Edited by Antaki, C. and Brewin, C. Academic Press, London.

Wilkins, A. and Lindsay, J. (1985). Common forms of reflex epilepsy: physiological mechanisms and techniques for treatment. In *Recent Advances in Epilepsy, No. Two*, pp. 239–71. Edited by Pedley, T.A. and Meldrum, B.S. Churchill Livingstone, Edinburgh.

Wing, R.R., Epstein, C.H., Nowalk, M.P. and Lamparski, D.M. (1986). Behavioral self-regulation in the treatment of patients with diabetes mellitus. *Psychological Bulletin* **99**, 78.

Yorkston, N.J., McHugh, R.B., Brady, R., Serber, M. and Sergeant, H.G. (1974). Verbal desensitization in bronchial asthma. *Journal of Psychosomatic Research* **18**, 371.

Index